365 Impressive Soup Recipes

(365 Impressive Soup Recipes - Volume 1)

Karen Hurd

Content

365 Awesome Soup Recipes

***

1.   Lentil Curry Stew

Serving: Serves 2 | Prep: | Cook: |Ready in:

Ingredients

- 1   garlic clove
- 1/2   onion
- 1/2 cup   ground beef (or Quorn mince)
- 1   carrot, minced
- 1 cup   red lentil
- 1/2 cup   edamame
- chicken broth (or vegetable broth)
- 1 tablespoon   apple cider vinegar
- 1 pinch   curry powder
- Dash   salt and pepper to taste
- Splash   coconut milk
- 1 handful   small banana
- Handful   dried coconut (unsweetened)

Direction

- Cook garlic, onion, carrot, and Quorn mince together in a large pot or skillet, until fragrant and the vegetables are kind of soft.
- Throw in the red lentils and edamame with the broth.
- Flavor and season with vinegar, s&p, curry powder, cumin powder, garam marsala, cayenne pepper. Remember to TASTE and TEST!
- Add more broth as necessary. Bring to a boil and simmer until the lentils are all cooked through.

- Stir in coconut milk, and banana. Mix until smooth and thick. Serve with coconut sprinkled on top.

2.   Red Lentil Pasta Sauce

Serving: Makes about 2 quarts | Prep: 0hours0mins | Cook: 0hours0mins |Ready in:

Ingredients

- 1/2 cup   coarsely chopped celery
- 1/2 cup   coarsely chopped carrot
- 1/2 cup   chopped green bell pepper
- 1 cup   chopped onion
- 4 to 5 cloves garlic
- 3 tablespoons   olive oil
- 1/2 teaspoon   crushed red pepper flakes (optional)
- 1 teaspoon   dried basil
- 1 teaspoon   dried oregano
- 1/2 teaspoon   fennel seed
- 1 cup   red lentils
- 28 ounce can of good quality tomatoes, crushed
- 1 teaspoon   salt
- 1 teaspoon   black pepper
- 3 to 4 cups water
- 1/2 cup   chopped parsley
- 5 or 6 leaves sliced fresh basil
- Cooked pasta
- Extra virgin olive oil for drizzling over each serving (optional)

Direction

- Place the celery, carrot, onion, bell pepper and garlic in the bowl of a food processor and pulse until the mixture is pretty finely ground (like a sofrito).
- In a 4 to 5-quart pot heat the olive oil, add the processed mixture with the crushed red

pepper, basil, oregano and fennel seed and sauté for a few minutes until soft and fragrant.

- Add the tomatoes and lentils and stir.
- Add the salt and pepper and 3 cups of the water, bring up to the boil and then simmer for about 30 minutes, stirring occasionally.
- If after the 30 minutes the sauce seems too thick, add another cup of water and continue to simmer another 10 to 15 minutes.
- If you like, blend the mixture a little with an immersion blender, just enough to thicken the sauce.
- Stir in the parsley and fresh basil just before serving over cooked pasta.
- NOTE: Blend until smooth for a smooth marinara sauce or add broth and veggies for an easy gazpacho or soup.

3. "Soupe Du Jour Du Jour" (aka Grandma Jacobs' Potato Soup)

Serving: Makes 6 generous servings | Prep: | Cook: | Ready in:

Ingredients

- A large pot of cold water (a 5-quart dutch oven)
- 4 large Idaho (russet) potatoes
- 2 ribs celery, coarsely chopped
- 2 carrots, coarsely chopped
- 1 small onion, chopped
- 1 medium-large onion, peeled, stuck with 2 cloves and poked through with a knife
- Sea salt and freshly ground white pepper
- 1 dried (green) bay leaf
- 1/2 cup unbleached flour (2 ounces)
- 1 stick unsalted butter (4 ounces)

Direction

- Cube the potatoes and add them to the pot of water along with all the other vegetables. Bring the mixture to the boil, and allow to simmer merrily for 30 minutes.

- In a medium sized skillet, melt the butter and add the flour to make a roux. Stir constantly to remove any potential lumps and make a smooth paste. Continue stirring constantly until the roux turns VERY dark brown. BE CAREFUL NOT TO BURN THE ROUX or you have to start all over again.
- Remove the pot from the heat and add the roux, stirring constantly. When the foaming subsides, taste, and correct the seasoning. Remove the bay leaf and the whole onion before serving.
- Serve with (Jewish style) rye bread and good butter, and a tossed green salad.
- Teacher's Tip: I've been known to gussy this soup up by adding a pound of bay scallops or Maine shrimp about 2 minutes before serving; or slice some garlicky sausage into the soup and allow to heat through – or BOTH. Then, of course, this soup won't be "dirt cheap!"

4. "Spicy" Bean Mix Soup

Serving: Serves 4-6 | Prep: | Cook: | Ready in:

Ingredients

- Homemade Chili Paste
- 50 grams Indian Dry Red Chillies
- 1 cup Water
- 3 tablespoons Olive oil
- 13 Bean-Mix Soup
- 1 cup 13 Bean Soup-mix
- 1 tablespoon Olive Oil
- 4 Garlic Cloves, minced
- 1 Onion, chopped
- 2 Jalapeños
- 2 cups Water
- 2 cups Vegetable Broth
- 1 teaspoon Cumin powder
- 1 teaspoon Chilli Paste (as prepared above)
- 1.5 tablespoons Tomato Paste
- 8 Small tomatoes, Campari type
- 1/8 cup Chopped Cilantro

- 4 teaspoons Lime Juice
- Salt to taste

Direction

- Homemade Chili Paste
- Heat 1 cup of water and bring it to a rolling boil. Soak dry red chilies in hot water for about an hour.
- Drain chilies out of the water and grind into a fine paste. Use 1/8 cup of water at a time as needed.
- Heat olive oil in a pan, add chili paste and sauté for 10-15 mins on medium heat.
- 13 Bean-Mix Soup
- Wash and soak bean-mix overnight (or) 6-8 hrs. in cold water. After 6-8 hrs. of soaking, rinse the beans 2-3 times and drain. Pressure cook in 2 cups of water for 2 whistles.
- Roast jalapeños directly over flame until blackened. Roll it loosely in a kitchen towel and set it aside for 5 mins. After 5 mins, the outer layer should come off easily. Peel & chop jalapeños finely.
- In a sauce pan, heat olive oil. When hot, add minced garlic, chopped jalapeños and sauté briefly. To this, add chopped onion and sauté until translucent.
- Next, add cumin powder, tomato paste, chili paste and give a brief stir. Add chopped tomatoes and wait for it to soften. To this, add 2 cups of veg broth and let it come to a boil.
- Add cooked beans (along with cooked water), salt and let it simmer on low-medium heat for 10-15 mins. Mix chopped cilantro, lime juice and serve hot.

5. "UNCORK YOUR BEST" SALMON BOUILLABAISSE

Serving: Serves 6 | Prep: | Cook: | Ready in:

Ingredients

- 3 pounds of salmon, preferably wild, filleted and sliced into approximate half-pound salmon steaks, skin left on
- 1 bony skeletal frame of a large salmon
- 1 head of a large salmon
- 2 leeks
- 1 large red onion, peeled and diced
- 3 carrots, preferably organic
- 1 celery stalk, preferably organic
- 7 sprigs of mint leaves
- 750 milliliters Chardonnay, of good drinking quality
- 3 tablespoons freshly ground black pepper, "fine" setting
- 11 bay leaves
- 5 lemons, preferably Meyer
- 6 tablespoons kosher or sea salt

Direction

- Immerse the bay leaves in cold filtered water, add 2 tablespoon of kosher or sea salt, and let stand for a half hour. Rinse with cold filtered water, removing any impurities. Do the same for the sprigs of mint leaves. Remove the rough green ends of the leeks and discard them. Then separate the individual leaves of the leeks, and cut into rectangular pieces about 2 inches long. Immerse them in cold filtered water, add 2 tablespoons of kosher or sea salt, and let stand for a half hour. Rinse with cold filtered water, removing any impurities.
- Add the diced red onion to the other ingredients, chop the leeks, and add them as well. Mince the mint leaves and add to the pot.
- Sprinkle the fish steaks and the fish head with some of the freshly ground black pepper. Add the rest of the black pepper to the pot.
- Add the fish skeleton, the fish head, and the fish steaks to the pot. Halve and squeeze the lemons, filtering out any seeds. Add the lemon juice to the fish. Make incisions in the fish steaks, and insert the bay leaves into these incisions.
- Uncork the bottle of Chardonnay and add to the pot. Add cold filtered water as necessary to just cover all of the ingredients. Cover the

pot, turn the heat up to moderate until the liquid is boiling, at which point the flame should be lowered. After twenty minutes, a fork should be used to test the doneness of the fish steaks. If the fish is completely tender, turn off the flame and remove the pot from the stove.

- Remove the bay leaves from the fish steaks, insuring that they are all removed since the bay leaves are inedible. Remove the fish skeleton from the stew. The broth may be served hot with the fish steaks, or the fish steaks may be removed and served separately. Alternatively, the fish soup as well as the salmon steaks may be served chilled, after being refrigerated.

6. 'rajma' Or Kidney Beans Curry

Serving: Serves 4-5 | Prep: | Cook: | Ready in:

Ingredients

- 1 cup Rajma or kidney beans
- 1   medium onion, chopped
- 1   large tomato, chopped
- 2-3   garlic cloves, finely chopped
- 1"   piece of ginger, finely chopped
- 1   green chilli, or to taste
- 2 teaspoons cumin seeds
- 1 teaspoon red chilli powder, or to taste
- 1/2 teaspoon turmeric powder
- 2 teaspoons coriander powder
- 1 teaspoon garam masala (optional)
- 2 tablespoons canola oil
- Salt, to taste
- Cilantro, for garnishing

Direction

- Wash and soak the beans in water overnight.
- Drain the water used for soaking and pressure cook them in 3-4 times the water till tender. It should take around 15-20 minutes.

- Turn off the heat and once the pressure is gone, transfer the contents of the cooker into a separate bowl.
- Rinse the cooker and put it back on the flame.
- Add 2 tablespoons of oil and once the oil is hot, add the cumin seeds.
- Let the seeds crackle, then add onions, ginger, garlic and green chili.
- Sauté till the onions turn brown, then add the tomatoes.
- Sauté for 2-3 minutes and add the dry spices. Cook them for 10 seconds.
- Then add the boiled rajma back into the cooker and pressure cook again for 20 minutes or so. Although the rajma was already boiled, the second round of pressure cooking ensures that the spices, onions etc. are fully integrated and not merely floating around. The exact time needed will depend on the quantity of beans and the make of your pressure cooker. Basically, cook it till everything is properly combined. Another trick to amalgamate the mixture is to take out a few spoonfuls of boiled rajma, mash them and then add back to the cooker before cooking them for the second time.
- Garnish with cilantro and eat with white basmati rice!

7. 10 12 12 12 (Sprouted) Lentil Soup

Serving: Serves a lot (about 4 qts) | Prep: | Cook: | Ready in:

Ingredients

- 10 ounces sprouted green lentils (or regular dried green lentils)
- 2 quarts chicken stock or vegetable broth (for you vegetarians)
- 12 ounces carrots, diced (about 2 medium-sized ones)
- 12 ounces celery, diced (about 5 stalks)

- 12 ounces onions, diced (about 2 medium)
- 5 cloves garlic, smashed and minced
- 1 can tomato paste (unsalted)
- 1/4 cup oil of your choice
- sea salt and fresh ground pepper

Direction

- In an 8-quart pot, bring 1 quart of stock/broth to boil. Add lentils and boil for 5 minutes. Bring to simmer for 10 minutes (prepare the vegetables).
- Heat up a large, heavy skillet on medium-high heat. Add oil. About half a minute later, add all the chopped vegetables and garlic. Sauté for about 15 minutes, until onions are lightly browned. (Liquid will start collecting in the bottom of the pan. Don't let this evaporate!)
- Add the second quart of stock to the lentils and return to a simmer. Add the sautéed vegetables, its liquid and the tomato paste. Simmer for about 40 minutes, or until lentils have a soft, palatable bite.
- Turn off heat from soup. Puree directly in pot with a stick blender, just enough to keep a little chunky consistency. Or let cool and blend about half in a blender and return to pot. You may want to add a cup or so of water if it's too thick. Add salt and pepper to taste.
- Save in individual portions and freeze for lunch.

8. 3 Bean Chili

Serving: Serves 6-8 | Prep: | Cook: |Ready in:

Ingredients

- 1 splash olive oil, enough to coat the pan/pot
- 1 cup dried black beans, soaked overnight and cooked approx 2 hours, until al dente
- 1 cup dried chickpeas/garbanzo beans, soaked overnight, cooked in crockpot on high for appox 2-3 hours, until al dente

- 1 cup dried navy beans, soaked overnight, cooked appox 2-3 hours, until al dente
- 1 large ripe tomato, rough chopped, a can of whole tomatoes is fine
- 3 carrots, peeled and diced
- 3 stalks celery, diced
- 1 medium onoin, diced
- 3 red bell peppers, diced
- 2 bay leaves
- 3 cloves garlic, minced
- 1 jalapeno, deseeded and diced
- 2 teaspoons heaping, unsweetened cocoa powder
- 2 tablespoons italian seasoning
- 2 teaspoons cumin
- 1 teaspoon more or less, smoked paprika
- 1 teaspoon chili powder
- 3 cups strong black coffee
- 1-2 cups leftover cooked bean liquid (or water or stock is fine)
- salt/pepper to taste

Direction

- One of the things that I've learned from watching cooking shows and competitions: season well! For every layer of vegetables that I add to the pot, I sprinkle in salt & pepper.
- In a big pot, heat olive oil at medium high heat. Add in the diced onion and sauté until translucent. Next add in the other vegetables, being sure to season between layers and allowing each veg proper sauté time. You're building flavors, don't skimp.
- Add in the dry seasonings and mix thoroughly.
- Pour in liquids, coffee and bean liquid (or water), bring to a boil. Lower temp to gentle simmer and cook until beans are soft, up to 45 min – an hour.
- *If using canned beans, don't add the beans until the final 30 minutes. But do allow the other vegetables to simmer in the liquids.*
- This is even better the next days when all the spices mingled and got merry.

- Serve with toast, sometimes I added diced avocado if I was feeling fancy, other times, I ate it simply.

9. 3 In 1 Soup (Mushroom Barley Soup With Flanken)

Serving: Serves 6 | Prep: | Cook: | Ready in:

Ingredients

- 1 teaspoon canola oil
- 6 pieces flanken (short ribs)
- 8 cups water
- 1 6 oz. cellophane "tube" Lima Bean and Barley Soup Mix
- 2 medium potatoes, peeled and quartered
- salt to taste, if necessary

Direction

- In a large pot, heat oil over medium-high heat. When hot, add flanken and brown on all sides (about 2-3 minutes per side). You can omit this step, but the searing adds flavor.
- Carefully add water and the contents of the tube of Lima Bean and Barley Soup mix (reserve small seasoning packet). Bring to a boil, then reduce heat to low and simmer for 2 hours, stirring occasionally.
- Add contents of small packet from soup mix along with potatoes. Continue to simmer for another 10 minutes.
- Remove from heat. If you are not serving immediately, let stand for 1 hour to cool down, then refrigerate for 8 hours or overnight.
- The next day, peel off and discard layer of fat. Reheat over medium heat, almost to a boil. Then remove flanken and potatoes to a covered dish; set aside and keep warm.
- Taste and add salt, if necessary. Ladle soup into bowls and serve. Serve flanken and potatoes as the entree.

10. Abuela's Sopa De Avena Con Pollo (Grandma's Chicken And Oat Soup)

Serving: Serves 4 to 6 | Prep: | Cook: | Ready in:

Ingredients

- Chicken and Vegetable Stock
- 1 medium yellow onion
- 1 clove garlic
- 1 whole stalk of celery
- 2 organic whole chicken legs
- 4 carrots
- 4 cups water
- 2 tablespoons olive oil
- The Hearty Goodness
- 1 1/2 cups whole oat groats
- 6 roma tomatoes
- 1 cup green (string) beans
- 2 cups water
- 2 bay leaves
- 1/2 teaspoon dried oregano
- 2 cinnamon sticks
- 1 teaspoon white pepper
- 3/4 cup arbequina olives (stone-in)
- 1 teaspoon whole cumin seeds
- 1 teaspoon ground cumin
- 2 teaspoons salt (or to taste)

Direction

- Place 2 tablespoons of olive oil into a deep cooking pot.
- Coarsely chop the onion, garlic, and celery. Add them to the pot and sauté over a medium flame until the vegetables have softened. Stir frequently.
- Cut the chicken legs in half at the knee joint and add to the pot. Sauté until lightly browned, stirring frequently.
- Coarsely chop the carrots and add to the pot. Add the 4 cups of water and let simmer over a medium flame. When it comes to a boil, turn down the flame and allow to simmer until the

chicken has cooked through and the meat is falling off the bone, about 1 hour.

- Remove the bones and cut any remaining meat from them. Add the meat back to the broth and discard the bones.
- Chop the tomatoes into eighths. Snip off the ends of the beans and cut them into 1-inch pieces. Add both to the soup.
- Rinse the groats in cold water 3 times, or until the water drains away clear. Drain and then add them to the soup base along with 2 more cups of water.
- Add the spices and the olives.
- Cook, covered and over a low flame, for an hour before adding the salt.
- Add salt to suit your taste. Feel free to modify the vegetables and spices as well. I happen to like more cumin, and sometimes I add mushrooms at the very end. This is sort of an anything goes recipe. ;)
- Enjoy.

11. Alton Brown's Shrimp Gumbo

Serving: Serves 6 | Prep: 0hours45mins | Cook: 3hours15mins | Ready in:

Ingredients

- 4 fluid ounces vegetable oil
- 4 ounces all-purpose flour (or about 1 cup less 4 teaspoons, if measuring by volume)
- 1 1/2 pounds raw, whole, head-on, medium-sized (31-50 count) shrimp
- 2 quarts water
- 1 cup diced onion
- 1/2 cup diced celery
- 1/2 cup diced green peppers
- 2 tablespoons minced garlic
- 1/2 cup peeled, seeded, and chopped tomato (fresh or canned)
- 1 tablespoon kosher salt
- 1/2 teaspoon finely ground black pepper
- 1 teaspoon fresh thyme, chopped

- 1/4 teaspoon cayenne pepper
- 2 bay leaves
- 1/2 pound andouille sausage, cut into 1/4-inch slices and browned in a little oil
- 1 tablespoon filé powder
- Rice for serving

Direction

- Heat the oven to 350° F.
- Place the vegetable oil and flour into a 5- to 6-quart cast iron Dutch oven and whisk together to combine. Place on the middle shelf of the oven, uncovered, and bake for 1 1/2 hours, whisking 2 to 3 times throughout the cooking process.
- While the roux is baking, de-head, peel, and devein the shrimp. Place the shrimp in a bowl and set in the refrigerator. Place the heads and shells in a 4-quart saucepan along with the 2 quarts of water, set over high heat and bring to a boil. Decrease the heat to low and simmer for 1 hour or until the liquid has reduced to 1 quart. Remove from the heat and strain the liquid into a container, discarding the solids.
- Once the roux is done, carefully remove it from the oven and set over medium-high heat. Gently add the onions, celery, green peppers, and garlic and cook, moving constantly, for 7 to 8 minutes or until the onions begin to turn translucent. Add the tomatoes, salt, black pepper, thyme, cayenne pepper, and bay leaves and stir to combine. Gradually add the shrimp broth while whisking continually. Decrease the heat to low, cover, and cook for 35 minutes. Turn off the heat, add the shrimp and sausage, and stir to combine. Add the filé powder while stirring constantly. Cover and allow to sit for 10 minutes prior to serving. Serve over rice.

12. ArtiChicken Stock

Serving: Serves 4-6 | Prep: | Cook: | Ready in:

Ingredients

- 1-2 artichokes
- 1 roast chicken carcass
- 1 large onion- quartered
- 2-3 lemon slices
- 3-4 cloves garlic-unpeeled and smashed
- 1 rosemary sprig
- 2-3 teaspoons sea salt
- 2-3 teaspoons black peppercorns

Direction

- On Sunday, Roast a chicken for dinner. Eat it... it's delicious. Save the bones!
- On Monday, eat an artichoke (or 2) for dinner- preferably dipped in melted butter. To cook - cover artichoke with water in large stock pot, boil until tender. Keep the artichoke water on the stove!
- To boiling artichoke water, add remain ingredients, and a few more cups water (until you have desired amount- about a gallon). Bring back to a steady boil for 5-10 minutes, then reduce heat and simmer for 2-3 hours.
- Strain to remove large chunks. Continue straining if you want it clear, but I like some of the tasty little bits in there!
- Divide into small containers and refrigerate.
- On Tuesday, make soup for dinner! Delicious with basil, tomatoes, noodles, beans, and veggies!

13. Asian Corn And Chicken Soup

Serving: Serves 4 | Prep: | Cook: | Ready in:

Ingredients

- 2 boneless, skinless chicken breasts
- 2 tablespoons rice wine or dry sherry
- 1 1/2 teaspoons Asian dark sesame oil
- 3 tablespoons cornstarch
- 2-3 cloves of garlic, peeled and chopped

- 2 tablespoons fresh ginger root, peeled and finely minced
- 6 cups best quality chicken stock
- 1 carton of silky tofu
- 1 1/2 cups frozen corn
- 1 teaspoon low-sodium soy sauce
- 1 egg, beaten
- 1/2 cup chopped scallions
- 1 dash hot sauce or chili oil (optional)

Direction

- Chop the chicken into spoon-sized pieces. Mix with the sherry or rice wine, 1/2 t. sesame oil, 1 T. cornstarch. Set aside.
- Heat 1/2 t. sesame oil and briefly cook the garlic and ginger. Add the chicken, cook 2-3 minutes, then add the stock and bring to a boil.
- Cut the tofu into 1/2 inch cubes. Add to stock mixture. Add corn as well. Cook ten minutes.
- Blend 2 T. cornstarch with the soy sauce and 1/4 c. water and whisk until smooth. Add to soup and stir for a minute or two.
- Beat the egg and pour slowly into the soup, stirring the soup with a fork so as to shred the egg in the soup. Add final 1/2 t. sesame oil to float on top of the soup. Garnish with chopped scallions. Add a dash of hot sauce or chili oil, if desired.

14. Asparagus & Green Garlic Soup W/ Parmesan Croutons

Serving: Serves 2 | Prep: | Cook: | Ready in:

Ingredients

- For the Asparagus Green Garlic Soup
- 1 bunch asparagus (about 28 spears)
- 3 stems green garlic (w/ bulbs about ¾ inch round)
- sea salt
- 9 sprigs fresh thyme (plus more for garnish)
- Parmesan Croutons (see recipe below)

- olive oil (for cooking)
- your very best olive oil (for drizzling)
- 1 cup chicken stock (homemade or I like Wolfgang Puck's organic)
- ¼ cup white wine
- For Parmesan Croutons:
- 1 round rustic bread (about 5" in diameter)
- 1 tablespoon extra virgin olive oil
- 1 tablespoon unsalted butter
- 3 tablespoons fresh grated parmesan
- salt
- fresh ground pepper

Direction

- For the Asparagus Green Garlic Soup
- Wash, dry and cut off thick bottom stems of asparagus. Drizzle with olive oil, sprinkle with sea salt and black pepper, distribute oil evenly and thoroughly throughout spears using either your hands or tongs and roast in 425 degree oven for about 9 minutes (until bright green and tender).
- Thinly slice whites of garlic and chop greens.
- Sauté whites and greens of garlic (reserving a few greens for garnish) with a sprinkling of sea salt in a little olive oil until whites are tender and almost translucent.
- Sauté roasted asparagus in a little olive oil to heat through and soften further (but make sure still bright green). (Note: You do this because the roasting of the asparagus adds an extra layer of flavor, but if you leave them in the oven long enough to soften them up, then ends become dark and the color dims -- you want a bright green beautiful soup...)
- In a blender add asparagus, garlic and oils from both pans and chicken stock. Blend on high until thick and somewhat smooth.
- Pour into saucepan over low to med-low heat (make sure it just gently warms through and does not boil so that you do not lose color).
- Chop thyme and add to soup along with the white wine. Stir and let slowly warm through (about 10-12 mins.). Adjust salt and pepper as necessary.
- Meanwhile make croutons (below)

- Ladle into bowls, garnish with a little chopped green garlic, a sprig of thyme, a drizzle of your very best (fruity) olive oil and a few parmesan croutons. Enjoy!
- Note: Healthy Version: Omit croutons...
- For Parmesan Croutons:
- Cut bread in half lengthwise and then cut into about 1 inch squares.
- Melt olive oil and butter in medium saucepan over medium heat.
- Turn heat up to medium high, add bread squares, generously sprinkle with salt and pepper (you want them to be a little more salty than usual to counter the mild subtle earthy flavor of the soup) and brown over medium high until lightly browned.
- Turn heat down to medium sprinkle have the cheese over the croutons, let brown, turn over, sprinkle with the rest of the cheese; let brown and then immediately remove to a plate to cool. (Cheese tends to cook quickly and burn so make sure you take them off right away after they are toasty-brown).

15. Asparagus Potato And Fennel Soup

Serving: Serves 4 | Prep: | Cook: |Ready in:

Ingredients

- 1 pound asparagus
- 1/2 pound red 'c' potatoes
- 1/2 fennel bulb, plus the greens
- 1 cup chopped sweet onion
- 3 cups low salt chicken broth
- 1/2 cup half n half
- zest from 1 lemon
- salt and pepper
- minced chives
- crispy proscuitto - chopped **

Direction

- Bring a pot of salty water to a rolling boil. Grab each asparagus stalk at both ends and gently bend - it will break naturally at the tender to tough transition point. I think I learned that from Alton Brown. When the water is boiling, add the asparagus and blanch for about a minute, then plunge it into a big bowl of ice water. When it is completely chilled remove and pat dry.
- Cut the potatoes in 8ths, chop the white part of the fennel and add the potatoes, fennel and onion to a pot with the broth. Add a couple grinds of pepper and a pinch of salt. Bring to a simmer and continue to simmer until they are all quite tender. Meanwhile cut just the tips off the asparagus and chop the stalks.
- Once the potatoes and friends are tender add in the asparagus stalks and the half n half. Simmer a few more minutes, then add a handful of chopped fennel greens and turn off the heat. Use an immersion blender (or move the soup to a blender) and blend it until it's uniform but still has a bit of texture and flecks of red and green. Taste and adjust the seasoning. Return to the heat and stir in the asparagus tips and the lemon zest and leave it just long enough for them to get warm. Serve topped with chives and crisp prosciutto.
- ** for the prosciutto, you can just lay thin slices between paper towels and put them on a paper plate, and microwave them on and off until they are crispy. Easy peasy!

16. Avocado Dumplings In Curry Tomato Broth

Serving: Serves 4 | Prep: | Cook: | Ready in:

Ingredients

- Broth
- 2 tablespoons olive oil
- 1 medium onion, chopped
- 1 celery stalk, chopped
- 3 cloves of garlic, minced
- 5 cups chicken stock (preferably homemade)
- 1/2 cup canned crushed tomato (I prefer San Marzano brand)
- 1/2 teaspoon tomato paste
- 1 teaspoon chili powder
- 2 tablespoons yellow curry powder
- 1/4 teaspoon freshly ground black pepper
- 1/2 teaspoon kosher salt
- 1/4 teaspoon coriander
- 1/4 cup chopped cilantro for garnish
- 1/4 cup queso fresco, for garnish
- Dumplings
- 2 cups all-purpose flour
- 4 teaspoons baking powder
- 3 tablespoons unsalted butter, cut into chunks
- 2 teaspoons kosher salt
- 1/4 teaspoon black pepper
- 1/4 teaspoon lime zest
- 2 cloves of garlic, minced
- 1/4 cup chopped cilantro
- 1 1/2 avocados, cut into chunks
- 3/4 cup whole milk

Direction

- Begin with the broth. Heat the oil in a deep-sided sauté pan with a lid.
- Add the onion and celery and cook over medium heat until the onions are semi-translucent, about 3 minutes.
- Add the minced garlic and cook a minute more.
- Add the chicken stock, canned tomato, tomato paste, chili powder, curry powder, salt, pepper, and coriander.
- Bring to a boil, then reduce to a simmer while you prepare the dumplings.
- Dumplings: In a medium bowl, combine the flour, baking powder, butter, salt, and pepper.
- Combine with your hands until small chunks of butter remain.
- Stir in the avocado, lime zest, chili powder, minced garlic, and cilantro.
- Pour the milk on top and stir with a fork until just combined.

- Add the dumplings by the spoonful to the simmering broth.
- Cover the pot and cook for 15 to 20 minutes. Dumplings will be slightly puffed.
- Serve in shallow bowls, and top with chopped cilantro and crumbled queso fresca.

17. Bacon Onion Puree

Serving: Serves 4 as a hearty appetizer | Prep: | Cook: | Ready in:

Ingredients

- Puree
- 10 small yellow onions, plus 1 more for garnish
- 1 grannysmith apple
- 4 pieces thick-cut bacon, cut small like confetti
- 2 carrots, roughly chopped
- 1 celery rib, roughly chopped
- 3 sprigs thyme
- 1 cinnamon stick
- 1 bay leaf
- 4 cloves
- 2 pinches whole fennel seeds
- 4 tablespoons butter
- olive oil or bacon drippings
- salt, pepper, and sugar
- For Garnish
- 2 pieces thick-cut bacon, cut into lardon
- 10 small shitake mushrooms, cleaned and halved
- 2 sprigs thyme, leaves only, for sprinkling

Direction

- Preheat oven to 350F. Peel the 10 onions and cut them into eighths, taking car to leave a piece of the root end on every wedge so that they don't fall apart. Cut the apple into similarly sized wedges. Toss the onions and apple in olive oil or bacon drippings, and arrange them in a single layer on a wire rack set in a sheet pan. Sprinkle with salt and then with sugar. Roast in the oven, turning the onion and apple wedges over once, until lightly browned and tender — about an hour or an hour and a half. Once cool enough to handle, cut the inedible root ends off the onions.
- Meanwhile, make bacon broth, as follows: In a heavy-bottomed pot, cook the confetti-cut bacon over medium low heat, stirring often until most or all of the fat is rendered out. Quarter and add the remaining onion to the pot, along with the carrot and celery. Cook, stirring for minute. Then turn the heat to high and add the thyme sprigs, cinnamon, bay, cloves, fennel seeds, and 6 cups of cold water. Scrape the yummy stuff off the bottom of the pot, bring to a boil, and simmer for an hour or so, while the onions roast.
- When the onions are almost done, strain the broth into a sauce pan, and boil hard until the liquid has reduced by half. While the broth reduces, cut the inedible root ends off of the onions wedges. Once the broth has reduced, add the roasted onions and apple to the broth and boil for another 15 minutes, or until the ratio of solid to liquid looks about right to make a thick puree. (You want relatively little liquid since there is a good amount of residual water in the roasted onions and apple.)
- Puree the mixture in a blender, along with the butter. Season. Put the puree back into the saucepan (after rinsing it out), and place it over low heat until ready to serve. (Don't wait too long.)
- For the garnish, render the lardon in a small skillet, and then remove the crispy bacon pieces to a paper towel. Get the residual bacon fat very hot, and then quickly sear the shitakes until they are well-browned and tender, seasoning near the end. Serve the soup in a warm bowl garnished with the bacon lardon, the mushrooms, and a few fresh thyme leaves. Don't forget some crusty bread action!

18. Bean Soup (zuppa Di Fagioli) Toscana, Primo (First Course)

Serving: Serves 6 | Prep: | Cook: | Ready in:

Ingredients

- 300 grams dried cannellini beans
- 60 milliliters extra-virgin olive oil, plus extra for drizzling
- 1 onion, peeled and finely chopped
- 3 garlic cloves, 2 finely chopped and one bruised
- 2 carrots, rinsed, peeled, ends removed and finely chopped
- 2 celery ribs, rinsed, ends removed and finely chopped
- 4 sage leaves
- 10 grams grams ham or prosciutto fat or lardo, finely chopped (can substitute 20 mls olive oil)
- 1.5 liters vegetable stock or water
- 100 milliliters tomato sauce or 2 medium tomatoes rinsed, seeds removed and coarsely chopped
- 20 grams flat leaf parsley, rinsed and finely chopped
- 1 branch of rosemary, rinsed, leaves removed and finely chopped
- 300 grams cavolo nero, rinsed and sliced
- 30 grams Parmigiano-Reggiano cheese, finely grated
- 1 spring onion, rinsed, end removed and finely sliced
- sea salt
- freshly ground black pepper
- 6 slices grilled bread

Direction

- Soak the beans in cold water to cover by 5 cm overnight (minimum
- Drain the beans and place in a stockpot covered with fresh cold water by 5 cm. Add 10 grams of salt to the beans. Heat the pot over medium heat until it begins to simmer and then reduce the heat to low and cover. Let the

beans cook for 1.5 to 2 hours until tender but not falling apart. Remove from the heat and let cool.

- Pour 30 mls of the olive oil into another stock pot and heat over medium heat. Add the onion, carrot, 2 cloves of minced garlic, celery, ham fat and sage and cook for 10-15 minutes, stirring occasionally until the vegetables have softened and begin to sweat.
- Add the water or stock to the pot. Remove a quarter of the whole beans with a slotted spoon and set aside. Place the rest of the beans and 300 mls of the cooking liquid in a food processor and blend until the beans have been pureed.
- Add the bean puree to the vegetables and then add the tomato sauce, rosemary, parsley, 5 grams of salt and black pepper to taste. Bring the mixture to a boil and reduce to a simmer. Let it cook for 3 hours, stirring occasionally. During the last 20 minutes of cooking, add the whole beans and taste the soup to adjust the salt and pepper if needed.
- In a frying pan, heat the remaining 30 mls of olive oil over medium heat.
- When the oil is hot add the cavolo nero with its washing water still attached. If there is not enough water, add 30 mls of water to the pan and cover.
- Cook for 10-15 minutes and taste to see if it is done.
- Ladle the soup into the serving bowls, top with the cavolo nero, a sprinkle of spring onions, 5 grams of the grated Parmigiano-Reggiano cheese, and drizzle olive oil over the top. Serve the soup with the grilled bread.
- Note: Eliminate the meat to make the dish Vegetarian.

19. Bean, Barley, And Hamhock Stew

Serving: Serves 10 | Prep: | Cook: | Ready in:

Ingredients

- 1 hamhock, smoked
- 1 pound dry beans (I use a medley of pink beans, Lima, and habichuela, but any 2-3 medium-large sized bean mix you like will do)
- 3 tablespoons oil (vegtable, olive, or whatever you like)
- 1 large carrot, or 2 small, diced small
- 5 celery stalks, diced small
- 2 yellow onions
- 2 cups canned italiam plum tomatoes, roughly diced
- 3 bay leaves
- 1 tablespoon whole peppercorns
- 1 cup pearl barley or farro, dry and uncooked
- 2 cups frozen spinach, rinsed and drained (could also use fresh and chop it up, but frozen is so easy)

Direction

- Soak the beans for at least 6 hours, or overnight.
- Heat the oil on medium-high heat in a Dutch oven or big pot. Add the onions, celery, carrots, and sauté for about 5 minutes. Add the barley/farro, stir to coat with oil, and sauté a few more minutes until vegetables are limp and barley is toasted.
- Add the whole ham hock, the tomatoes with some juice from the can, the bay leaves, peppercorns, and the soaked beans. Add enough water to fill the pot up to the height of the ham hock -- you can leave an inch sticking out if that's how things work out. Bring to a simmer and then reduce heat and cover to keep a light simmer going. Add water when the level decreases.
- After 2 hours simmering, remove the ham hock and let cool for about 10 minutes or until it's easy to handle. Meanwhile, keep the pot at a light simmer. Slice meat from the ham hock, leaving the fat on (this is the most delicious part). Slice into thin slices, about 1/4 inch thick, then slice the other direction to end up with 1/4 thick matchsticks of ham, fat on. Toss

the meat and bone back in the soup, cook until beans are tender or even soft.
- When the beans are at their desired texture, add the spinach and simmer a few minutes more. Add salt to taste. Serve with smoked paprika and freshly ground black pepper.

---

20. Beans And Greens Soup

Serving: Makes 4 to 6 | Prep: 0hours10mins | Cook: 0hours30mins | Ready in:

Ingredients

- 1/4 cup extra-virgin olive oil
- 1 red onion or leek, sliced into thin half-moons
- 1 clove garlic, peeled and smashed
- 5 cups rich chicken stock or vegetable stock
- 2 tablespoons good wine vinegar (sherry or Champagne is great)
- 1 cup cooked beans, chickpeas, or lentils
- 2 cups cleaned and roughly chopped cooking greens (kale, spinach, chard, bok choy, napa cabbage, watercress, amaranth, broccoli raab or mix of any)
- 1 dried chile, optional
- Salt and pepper
- 2 tablespoons really good extra-virgin olive oil
- Grilled bread, for serving

Direction

- In a large heavy-bottomed pan, warm the olive oil over medium heat. Add the onions or leeks and garlic clove and gently brown.
- When lightly colored, add stock and vinegar. Bring to a light simmer and add cooked legumes. Bring back to a simmer and add greens and chile, if using.
- Depending on what greens you use, you will cook the soup a little more or less. Spinach and watercress would cook in a minute or two, while kale and broccoli rabe would take more

like 3 to 4 minutes (or as many as 5 to 8). You want to simmer long enough to wilt and cook the greens but not to overcook them.

- Taste and adjust salt. Serve by itself or over grilled bread with a drizzle of olive oil on top

21. Beans And Greens Soup (With A Little Italian Sausage)

Serving: Makes 3 to 4 quarts | Prep: | Cook: | Ready in:

Ingredients

- 1 pound dried northern white beans, soaked overnight in water to cover
- 1 pound Sweet Italian sausage baked at 350F for 30 minutes
- 1 cup sliced leeks
- 2 cloves minced garlic
- 1/4 to 1/2 teaspoon crushed red pepper flakes
- 2 tablespoons olive oil
- 8 cups chicken broth
- 8 cups chopped greens (kale, spinach,collards -your choice)
- 3 medium potatoes,peeled and diced in 3/4 inch cubes
- salt and black pepper to taste

Direction

- Cook the soaked beans in water for 40 to 50 minutes until tender, reserving one cup of the cooking liquid. Set aside.
- In a large soup pot sauté the leeks, crushed red pepper and garlic in the olive oil until soft.
- Slice the baked Italian sausage in 1/2 inch rounds and add to the pot. Sauté for about 3 minutes.
- Add the chicken broth, the reserved bean broth and the potatoes. Bring to a boil and then simmer for 15 to 20 minutes.
- Add the greens and the cooked beans, bring back to the boil and simmer until the greens have wilted.
- Season to taste with salt and pepper.

22. Beer French Onion Gratinee With Garlic Thyme Croutons

Serving: Serves 4-6 | Prep: | Cook: | Ready in:

Ingredients

- Soup
- 1 large tomato
- 2 tablespoons unsalted butter
- 2 tablespoons olive oil
- 2 pounds yellow onions, thinly sliced lengthwise
- 1 teaspoon sugar
- 3 garlic cloves, minced
- 1 tablespoon flour
- 2/3 cup beer
- 4 cups vegetable stock (chicken or beef stock can be used also for a more robust flavor)
- 1 tablespoon dijon mustard
- 1 1/2 teaspoons salt
- 1/2 teaspoon black pepper
- 1 teaspoon fresh thyme
- 1 teaspoon balsalmic vinegar
- 3 tablespoons parmesan cheese, grated
- 8 ounces Gruyere cheese, grated
- Garlic Thyme Croutons (recipe below)
- Garlic Thyme Croutons
- 1 small loaf of french bread
- 6 garlic cloves, minced (or more if you want more garlicky taste)
- 1/2 teaspoon fresh thyme, minced
- 2 tablespoons olive oil (enough to moisten bread pieces)

Direction

- Soup
- Preheat the oven to 275F. Slice the tomato into 1/4" slices. Lay them on a cookie sheet, lightly sprinkle with olive oil, and roast for at least 1 hour until they are no longer loose and moist.

They should have a rich tomato paste aroma, but not be completely dried out. Set aside.

- Melt the butter and oil together in a saute pan over medium heat. Add the onions. When the onions become soft, sprinkle the sugar over them and continue to slowly cook until they caramelize and are a deep golden brown, about 45 minutes. Add the garlic and continue to cook for another minute. Add the flour and cook until the flour is a golden brown, about 3-4 minutes.
- Stir in the beer and cook most of the moisture is gone. Stir in the stock.
- Mash the roasted tomato into a paste with a mortar and pestle and add to the soup. Add the mustard, salt, pepper and thyme. Simmer for 30 minutes while you make the Garlic Thyme Croutons. Finish the soup with the balsamic vinegar in the last 5 minutes of simmering.
- Turn on the broiler. Ladle the soup into the soup bowls. Top with the Garlic Thyme Croutons. Sprinkle the parmesan cheese on top followed by a generous pile of Gruyere cheese. Place the soup bowls on a thick cookie sheet and place under the broiler until the cheese is golden and bubbling.
- Serve and enjoy!!
- Garlic Thyme Croutons
- Preheat the oven to 400F. Remove the crusts from the bread loaf. Tear the bread into bite sized pieces and place in a bowl with the olive oil, garlic and thyme. Toss with your hands until the bread pieces are coated with the oil, garlic and thyme. Lay out on a baking sheet and bake until lightly crisp (about 15 minutes).

23. Bell Pepper Gazpacho With Mint

Serving: Serves 4 | Prep: | Cook: |Ready in:

Ingredients

- 1   yellow onion, minced
- 4   ed bell peppers, seeded and diced
- 3 tablespoons olive oil
- 1 teaspoon sugar
- 1   garlic clove, minced
- zest of 1/2 Lemon
- 1 teaspoon Espelette pepper or other mild pepper powder
- 500 milliliters vegetable stock
- Mint leaves
- Salt and pepper

Direction

- In a saucepan, sauté the onion with 1 tbsp. of olive oil. Add the garlic and 2/3 of the bell peppers. Cook for 5 minutes then add the pepper powder, sugar, salt and pepper to taste.
- Add the vegetable stock and bring to boil. Then reduce the heat and let simmer for 15 minutes. Mix the soup until smooth and let it cool first on the counter then in the fridge.
- When the soup is cold, add the lemon zest and the rest of the bell peppers. Drizzle with the rest of the olive oil and serve!

24. Black Eyed Pea Soup

Serving: Serves 6 - 8 | Prep: | Cook: |Ready in:

Ingredients

- 2 tablespoons Olive oil
- 6 Strips Thick-sliced bacon, cut into 1/2 inch pieces
- 1 Medium Onion
- 5 Garlic Cloves, sliced
- 1 teaspoon Salt
- 1/2 teaspoon Black Pepper
- 1/2 teaspoon Cayenne Pepper
- 1 teaspoon Garlic Powder
- 4 cups Chicken Stock
- 4 cups Beef Stock
- 2 cups Water

- 3   Bay Leaves
- 3 cups Black-Eyed Peas (fresh or canned)
- 1 tablespoon Apple Cider Vinegar
- 3 sprigs Fresh Thyme

Direction

- Heat the oil in a large pot over medium-high heat.
- Add the bacon, onion, and garlic to the pot and cook until the onion and garlic are lightly browned, about 6 - 8 minutes.
- Add the salt, black pepper, cayenne and garlic powder. Cook until the entire mixture is coated with the spices, about 2 minutes.
- Pour in the stock and water, and add the bay leaves. Bring the mixture to a boil, then reduce heat and simmer, covered, for about 15 minutes.
- Add the prepared peas to the pot and simmer until tender, about 1 hour.
- Add vinegar, discard the bay leaves, and ladle the soup into bowls.
- Serve over white rice, and garnish with fresh thyme.
- Enjoy!

25. Boston Baked Beef

Serving: Serves 4-6 | Prep: 0hours15mins | Cook: 1hours0mins | Ready in:

Ingredients

- 12   slices bacon, cut into bits
- 1   large sweet onion
- 1 pound 80/20 ground beef
- 1 teaspoon black pepper
- 6 ounces tomato paste
- 1/3 cup grainy mustard
- 2 tablespoons honey
- 1/3 cup molasses
- 1/3 cup apple cider vinegar
- 1 teaspoon salt

Direction

- In a heavy-bottomed pot over medium high, brown the bacon. Set aside, leaving all drippings in the pan.
- Add the onions and sauté until translucent.
- Add the ground beef and brown.
- Reduce heat to medium-low, then add the molasses, tomato paste, mustard, honey, salt, and pepper. Reduce heat to medium. Stir vigorously to break up chunks and prevent sticking, using a whisk if you need to. Add the bacon.
- Allow mixture to come to a boil, then reduce heat to low. Cover and simmer for 1 hour or more (the longer, the better!).

26. Braised Leek And Bacon Bisque

Serving: Serves 4 | Prep: | Cook: | Ready in:

Ingredients

- For the Bisque
- 1/4 pound bacon, diced (about 4 slices)
- 3   large leeks
- 3 cups chicken stock, homemade if available
- 1   garlic clove, smashed and peeled
- 1 tablespoon lemon thyme (or regular thyme)
- kosher salt and freshly ground black pepper
- 1/3 cup heavy cream
- 1 tablespoon lemon juice
- For the Fried Leek Garnish
- leek trimmings, leftover from making the bisque
- 2-4 tablespoons all purpose flour
- 1/4 cup olive oil

Direction

- For the Bisque
- Preheat the oven to 325 degrees.
- Prepare the leeks. Trim the root and dark green ends and set the trimmings aside- you'll use them for the garnish. Cut the leeks in half

lengthwise, but do not cut all the way through the root end- the leek halves should still be connected at the base. Rinse the leeks under running water, fanning out the layers to rinse away any dirt that might be trapped there. Set the leeks aside.

- Fry the diced bacon in a small Dutch oven (3-4 quart) over medium-low heat, until crispy. Remove the bacon with a slotted spoon and drain on paper towels.
- Transfer 1-2 teaspoons of the rendered bacon fat to a 9x9 inch baking or gratin dish and use a pastry brush to grease the pan with the hot bacon fat. Save the remaining bacon fat for another day.
- Add one cup of chicken stock to the empty Dutch oven and turn the heat up to high. Bring to a boil and scrape up the good crusty bits from the bottom of the pot with a wooden spoon. Turn off the heat. Stir in the smashed garlic clove and chopped lemon thyme.
- Place the cleaned leeks in the greased baking dish. Sprinkle with kosher salt, pepper, and the crispy bacon. Pour the chicken stock mixture over the leeks. Cover the baking dish with foil, and place in the oven to braise for 30 minutes.
- After the first 30 minutes, use tongs to flip the leeks over to the other side and recover with foil. Braise for an additional 30 minutes, or until the leeks are very tender.
- Meanwhile, make the fried leek garnish (recipe below).
- Remove the baking dish from the oven and let cool briefly. During the cooling time, add the remaining two cups of stock to the Dutch oven you used earlier and bring to a simmer over low heat.
- Puree the leeks and braising liquid in a blender along with a ladleful of the stock from the Dutch oven. (You stand with the dish trembling in your hands, your face aghast: "surely she doesn't expect me to puree the bacon too?!". Yes. Yes, I do. And friend, it will be delicious. Your bisque will be flecked with dancing particles of bacon-y goodness.) Transfer the puree to the Dutch oven with the

rest of the simmering stock. Bring the soup to a simmer, and then remove from heat. Stir in the heavy cream and lemon juice, and add salt and pepper to taste. Garnish with fried leeks.

- For the Fried Leek Garnish
- While the leeks are braising, prepare the fried leek garnish.
- From the tops of the leeks that you trimmed earlier, remove the outer layers until you get to the lighter green, more tender center. Slice these tender bits thinly, lengthwise, so that you're left with little strips of leek. These should be about 2 inches in length, so cut them in half if need be. Rinse these to get rid of any sand, then pat dry.
- Heat the oil in a small skillet over medium-high heat until shimmery. Toss the leeks and the flour in a small bowl. Shake off any excess flour and drop the leeks into the hot oil. Fry until the leeks just begin to turn golden- they should still be mostly green. Remove from the skillet and drain on paper towels, and sprinkle immediately with salt.

27. Broccoli Potato Soup

Serving: Serves 4 | Prep: | Cook: |Ready in:

Ingredients

- 1/4 cup red onion and shallots
- 1/4 cup bell pepper
- 1/4 cup cup tomatoes, diced
- 2 tablespoons Earth Balance margarine (non-dairy)
- 3 tablespoons cornstarch
- 2 cups potatoes, peeled, diced
- 1 1/4 cups broccoli, chopped, steamed
- 1 1/2 cups vegetable broth
- 1 cup cheese, shredded
- 1 cup unsweetened soy milk
- 1/8 teaspoon black pepper
- 1/8 teaspoon paprika
- Fresh parsley, garnish

Direction

- In a large saucepan, sauté onion, shallots and bell pepper in margarine over medium heat until tender.
- Add cornstarch, pepper, and paprika. Stir until smooth.
- Add broth, milk, and potatoes, stirring constantly until it boils and thickens.
- Reduce heat; cover and simmer for 10-15 minutes or until potatoes are tender.
- Stir in cheese, tomatoes, and cooked broccoli. Cook over low heat until cheese is melted and soup is heated thoroughly.
- Sprinkle individual servings with parsley.

28. Broccoli Soup

Serving: Serves 4 | Prep: | Cook: | Ready in:

Ingredients

- 2 tablespoons olive oil
- 1 medium onion, chopped
- 1 bunch broccoli (a couple of heads), coarsely chopped
- 2 quarts water
- 1/2 teaspoon celtic sea salt

Direction

- Heat oil in a large pot and sauté onion over medium to low heat until soft, about 15 minutes
- Add broccoli and sauté for 5-10 minutes
- Add water and cook until broccoli is soft about 15 minutes
- Puree hot soup in tiny batches in a Vitamix until smooth and creamy
- Reheat soup and serve

29. Brothy Tomato And Bean Soup

Serving: Serves 4 to 6 | Prep: | Cook: | Ready in:

Ingredients

- For the tomato sauce
- 1 14.5 ounce can plum tomatoes, crushed
- 3 tablespoons butter
- 1/2 cup roughly chopped onion
- 1 garlic clove, halved
- 1 cup water
- 1/4 teaspoon salt
- For the soup
- 1/2 pound Great Northern beans which have been soaked overnight and then cooked for about 45 minutes until done.
- 1 cup of the bean broth, reserved from the cooked beans
- 4 1/2 cups chicken broth
- The tomato sauce
- 1 large sprig fresh thyme
- Salt and pepper to taste

Direction

- For the tomato sauce
- Place all ingredients in a medium sauce pan and simmer for 20 to 30 minutes until thick. Set aside.
- For the soup
- Place the chicken broth and thyme sprig in a medium soup pot and simmer for about 8 minutes.
- Meanwhile place the tomato sauce (including the onion and garlic), 1/2 cup bean broth and 1/2 cup of cooked beans in a bowl or blender and blend until smooth. If using a bowl, blend with an immersion blender.
- Remove the thyme sprig from the broth, add the tomato mixture, the remaining bean broth and the beans. Simmer for another few minutes and season to taste with salt and pepper.

30. Brown Lentil Soup With Sausage And Spinach

Serving: Serves 6 | Prep: | Cook: |Ready in:

Ingredients

- 2 tablespoons oil
- 1 pound sweet or spicy Italian sausage, casings removed (I found Italian sausage with the casings already removed at the grocery store)
- 1 medium onion diced
- 2 celery stalks, sliced or diced
- 2 medium carrots peeled and sliced into half moons or diced
- 2 garlic cloves sliced
- sea salt and freshly ground black pepper
- a pinch of crushed red pepper flakes- optional and might not need if using spicy sausage.
- 1 cup brown lentils, rinsed(use green, yellow or red lentils if that's what you have on hand)
- 2 bay leaves
- 1-28 ounces can of diced tomatoes with juices
- 6 cups water
- add a little agave syrup or sugar to cut the tang of the tomatoes if necessary
- 1 cup frozen chopped spinach, thawed with excess juices squeezed out- 4 cups of fresh spinach, swiss chard or kale would also work
- Grated parmesan cheese and julienned fresh basil for garnish

Direction

- Heat oil in a large pot on medium heat. When hot, add the sausage, breaking it up with a wooden spoon until it starts to brown, about five minutes. I like to leave the sausage kind of chunky when I break it up. I also like to drain off some of the excess fat from the cooking sausage before I add the vegetables. Add the onion, celery, carrots and two sliced garlic cloves, a pinch of salt, and if you like your soup spicy, a pinch of red pepper flakes. Cook with the sausage until the vegetables soften a bit, another 5 minutes. Add the lentils, bay leaves, tomatoes, water, more salt and black pepper to taste. Bring to a simmer and allow to cook until the lentils are tender, about 40 minutes. (It might be necessary to add more water if the soup gets too thick, that's up to you.)
- When the lentils are cooked, add the spinach. Discard the bay leaves. Add agave syrup and salt and pepper to taste.
- To serve, top with freshly grated parmesan and julienned fresh basil. Leftovers will keep for several days in the refrigerator.

31. Brunswick Beef Stew

Serving: Serves four to six | Prep: | Cook: |Ready in:

Ingredients

- 1 Lb. Ground beef
- 1 Yellow onion, finely chopped
- 4 Cloves garlic, minced
- 1 1/2 c. Matchstick or shredded carrots
- 1 Yellow pepper, seeded and chopped
- 1 c. Chopped tomatoes with juices
- 1 1/2 c. Cooked lima beans
- 1 T. Worcestershire sauce
- 1 T. Dijon
- 2 T. Red wine vinegar
- 3 T. Butter
- 3 T. Flour
- 2 oz. (4 T) Cream cheese, room temperature
- 4 T. Parsley, chopped
- Olive oil
- Kosher salt & pepper
- 3 c. Beef stock
- 3 T. Ketchup

Direction

- Brown the ground beef in a large Dutch oven over medium high heat. Once the beef has browned, add the onions, garlic, carrots, chopped yellow peppers, and tomatoes.

- Next, add the beef stock, Worcestershire sauce, Dijon, red wine vinegar, ketchup, and cooked lima beans. Give the stew a quick stir to ensure everything has been properly mixed together.
- Then, stir in the butter, cream cheese, and the flour. Add the flour one tablespoon at a time to ensure that the flour has been properly absorbed by the soup.
- Simmer the soup for about 20 minutes, stirring occasionally. Serve immediately, sprinkling a little parsley or crushed red pepper over the top and dunking a few biscuits in the stew, as well.

32. Buckwheat And Red Lentils Soup

Serving: Serves 2 | Prep: | Cook: | Ready in:

Ingredients

- 1 cup Buckwheat
- 3/4 cup Red lentils
- 1/4 cup onion, minced
- 1 carrot, cut into small pieces
- 1/2 stack of celery, cut into small pieces
- 3 cups hot water
- 1 tablespoon tomato paste
- 2 tablespoons extravirgin olive oil
- salt
- spices of choice

Direction

- Place red lentils in a pot and rinse very well until the water runs clear. Finely chop onion, carrots and celery and sauté in a pot with extra virgin olive oil. Add buckwheat, stir and add water and tomato paste. Cook for 5 minutes. Add red lentils and cook, stirring occasionally, for 15 minutes. Season with salt and spices of your choice, to taste.
- Serve immediately, garnished with fresh parsley and a few drops of extra virgin olive oil.

33. Buffalo Chicken Soup

Serving: Serves 3-4 | Prep: | Cook: | Ready in:

Ingredients

- 2 large chicken breasts, cut into chunks
- 1/4 cup whole wheat flour
- salt and pepper to taste
- 2 tablespoons unsalted butter, divided
- 1 onion, diced
- 2 carrots, peeled and sliced
- 2 stalks of celery, sliced
- 4 cups chicken broth
- 1/4 to 1 cups Frank's Red Hot Sauce
- 1 cup shell pasta
- blue cheese, for topping

Direction

- In a medium bowl, add flour, salt, and pepper. Dredge the chicken chunks and set aside.
- In a Dutch oven over medium heat, melt 1 tablespoon of butter. Add the chicken and cook until browned on all sides. Remove the chicken and set aside again.
- Add remaining tablespoon of butter to pot and add vegetables. Cook until soft and translucent, about 10 to 15 minutes, stirring occasionally.
- Add back in the chicken, chicken stock, hot sauce, and shells. Cook until noodles becomes soft. The longer you let it sit, the spicier it will get!
- Top with blue cheese and dig on in!

34. Build Your Own Tortilla Soup

Serving: Serves many | Prep: | Cook: | Ready in:

Ingredients

- 1 pasilla chile, dried
- 1 guajillo chile, dried
- 1 chipotle chile, dried
- 2 arbol chiles, dried (optional)
- 1 tablespoon coriander seeds
- 3 garlic cloves
- 4 medium onions, quartered
- 8 roma tomatoes or 1 qt canned, crushed tomatoes
- 6 quarts rich chicken or turkey stock
- 2 bottles dark beer (I use Negra Modelo)
- 1 tablespoon Mexican oregano
- 3-4 cups pinto beans (I use Rancho Gordo pinquitos), cooked
- 2 cups whole corn kernels
- 2 cups hominy, soaked and cooked
- 3-4 cups shredded or chopped cooked chicken or turkey meat
- 1 cup chopped cilantro
- 3 tablespoons fresh epazote (optional)
- 6 avocados, cubed (garnish)
- 2 cups chopped cilantro (garnish)
- 2 cups Queso fresco, crumbled (garnish)
- 2 cups chopped scallion (garnish)
- 12 corn tortillas cut in strips and fried (garnish)
- 4 ancho chiles, toasted and cut in strips (garnish)
- Various hot sauces (garnish)

Direction

- On a hot, dry comal, griddle or cast iron skillet, briefly toast the chiles. Be cautious - they can burn very easily. You just want to warm them until they are pliable. Split the chiles open and remove the seeds and stem. Add to your blender.
- Toast the coriander seeds until fragrant, add to the blender.
- Toast and slightly blacken the tomatoes, onions and garlic cloves, then add those to the blender. If using canned tomatoes, add those to the blender directly.
- Whiz up all these ingredients to make a slurry. Heat the oil in the bottom of a large stock pot. Add the blender ingredients and cook for 5-10

minutes, until reduced slightly and starting to smell extra wonderful.
- Add the stock, beer and oregano and simmer for an hour, until the flavors have melded.
- Add the beans, corn and hominy and cook for about half an hour. Taste and correct the seasoning.
- Add the chicken, cilantro and epazote and warm through. Serve hot from a crock pot or a pot simmering on the stove. Have all the garnishes nearby. Watch your guests swoon.

35. Buttercup Squash Soup

Serving: Serves 8 | Prep: | Cook: | Ready in:

Ingredients

- 1/4 cup unsalted butter
- 1 large onion, finely chopped
- 4 large garlic cloves, chopped
- 3 14.5 ounce cans of low-salt chicken broth (about 6 cups) or homemade chicken broth
- 8 cups 1-inch pieces of peeled buttercup squash
- 1 1/4 teaspoons minced fresh thyme
- 1 14/ teaspoons minced fresh sage

Direction

- Melt butter in large pot over medium heat. Add onion and garlic and sauté until tender, about 10 minutes. Add broth, all squash and herbs; bring to boil. Reduce heat, cover and simmer until squash is very tender, about 20 minutes.
- Working in batches, puree soup in blender or with an immersion blender. Return soup to same pot and bring to a simmer. Season with salt and pepper. The soup can be made 1 day ahead. Chill. Rewarm over medium heat before serving.
- This could easily be converted into a vegetarian recipe by using vegetable broth instead of chicken broth.

36. Butternut Sqaush Tomato Soup

Serving: Serves 3 | Prep: | Cook: |Ready in:

Ingredients

- 2 pounds Butternut Squash, peeled and chopped
- 8 ounces Whole Peeled Tomatoes
- 1 Onion, chopped
- 2 teaspoons Cumin
- 1 teaspoon Paprika
- 1 teaspoon Salt
- 1 cup Water

Direction

- Sweat onions in a large pot with some olive oil for 3 minutes.
- Add the tomatoes, squash, and water to the pot. Stir and add in the spices. Cook this for a half hour.
- Once the squash is fork tender put in blender or use immersion circulator to make smooth.
- Taste soup for seasoning. I like to serve this with the seeds from the squash that I roast in the oven like pumpkin seeds.

37. Butternut Squash Coconut Soup With Basil Pesto

Serving: Serves 4-6 | Prep: | Cook: |Ready in:

Ingredients

- 800 grams butternut squash
- 1 onion
- 1 garlic clove
- 2 tablespoons olive oil
- 1 teaspoon ginger paste
- 1 teaspoon lemongrass paste
- 1/2 teaspoon cinnamon
- 1 teaspoon dried chilli flakes
- 400 milliliters coconut milk
- 700 milliliters vegetable stock
- 4-6 teaspoons good quality basil pesto
- salt and pepper

Direction

- Get started by peeling and deseeding your butternut squash. Cut it into cubes, roughly 2 cm each. Chop the onion and finely chop the garlic.
- Pour 2 tablespoons of olive oil into a heavy saucepan. Fry the onion until it becomes translucent. Add the garlic, ginger and lemongrass paste and fry for another minute. Add the butternut squash, the cinnamon and the chili flakes and fry for another 5 minutes until the butternut squash has heated up and is releasing some of its juices.
- Add the coconut milk and stock and bring to boil. Once boiling, turn down the heat and let it simmer for about 15 minutes until the butternut squash is soft.
- Let the mix cool down a bit and pour into a blender (you might have to do this is batches – don't overfill the blender unless you want your kitchen exploding with soup). Blend into a smooth soup. Taste the soup and season with salt and pepper.
- Serve each portion of soup with a generous tablespoon of good quality pesto.

38. Butternut Squash Pumpkin Soup

Serving: Makes 6 | Prep: | Cook: |Ready in:

Ingredients

- 15 ounces pumpkin puree
- 15 ounces cooked buttnerut squash
- 4.5 ounces sweet potato
- 1/2 cup light coconut milk
- 1.5 cups vegetable stock

- 1/8 teaspoon nutmeg
- 1/8 teaspoon all spice
- 1/2 teaspoon salt
- 1 teaspoon cinnamon
- 1.5 tablespoons honey

Direction

- Combine all ingredients in a high powered blender and blend on high for 6-7 minutes, should be steaming when done. OR Combine all ingredients in a blender or food processor and puree. Once pureed transfer to a large pot and heat on medium till bubbling/boiling. Stir ever 1-2 minutes while heating.
- SERVE immediately while hot, garnish with pumpkin seeds and parsley. Bacon would be lovely to if you are a meat eater.

39. Butternut Squash Soup

Serving: Serves 6 | Prep: | Cook: | Ready in:

Ingredients

- 2 onions
- 4 cloves of garlic
- 1 2 inch piece of ginger
- 2 carrots
- 2 celery stalks
- 1 yam
- 1 butternut squash
- 2 tablespoons olive oil
- 3/4 tbsp tablespoons salt, adjust to your own taste
- 1 tablespoon lemon juice or apple cider vinegar
- 2 tablespoons maple syrup
- 1/2 teaspoon allspice
- 1/4 teaspoon nutmeg
- 1/4 teaspoon cloves
- 1/4 teaspoon cumin
- 1/4 teaspoon coriander
- 1/4 teaspoon smoked paprika
- 1/4 teaspoon cinnamon

- 1/4 teaspoon chili flakes

Direction

- Cut the onions, garlic and ginger and put into a bowl.
- Peel the carrots, apple, yam and squash and cut into rough equal pieces. Chop two stalks of celery.
- Brown the onions, garlic and ginger with the olive oil in a pan over medium heat. Stir in the salt and spices. Add the remaining vegetables and pour water until everything is JUST covered.
- Bring to a boil, then simmer until all vegetables are fork or knife tender (you can cut through them easily). This means they are ready to be blended.
- Blend in batches. Add back to the pot and adjust seasoning with salt and spices to your preference. Also, this is where you add the vinegar or lemon juice, and maple syrup.
- I garnished with celery leaves, pepper flakes and olive oil but you can use whatever you have in your pantry. Yoghurt, herb oils, toasted nuts, parsley or julienned apple would be nice garnishes as well.
- Bon appetit from The Simmering Pot

40. Butternut Squash And Black Bean Chili

Serving: Serves 8 | Prep: | Cook: | Ready in:

Ingredients

- 1 tablespoon olive oil
- 2 medium onions, chopped
- 4 cloves garlic, minced
- 4 poblano peppers, cut in 1/4 inch dice
- 2 jalepeno peppers, seeded and minced
- 3 tablespoons ancho chili powder
- 1 tablespoon ground cumin
- 1 teaspoon cayenne
- 1 teaspoon oregano

- 1 teaspoon salt
- 1 14.5 ounce can diced tomatoes
- 1 14.5 ounce can tomato sauce
- 1 bottle of wheaty beer
- 3 cups butternut squash cut into 1/2 inch dice
- 2 cans of black beans, rinsed and drained
- grated manchego cheese for serving

Direction

- Heat the oil in a heavy pot over medium high heat. Add onions and garlic and sauté for about 5 minutes, stirring occasionally, until softened and just starting to brown.
- Add peppers and cook for 5 minutes, then add spices and cook for 2 minutes.
- Add the tomatoes, beer and butternut squash and cook over medium heat for 25 minutes, until squash is softened. Add black beans and simmer for 15 minutes. Serve with a bit of grated manchego on top.

41. Butternut Squash, Red Lentil, And Eggplant Sambhar

Serving: Serves 4 | Prep: | Cook: | Ready in:

Ingredients

- 1 cup red lentils
- 4 tablespoons canola oil, divided
- 1/2 teaspoon fenugreek seeds
- 2 teaspoons coriander seeds
- 1 1/2 teaspoons cumin seeds
- 3/4 teaspoon black mustard seeds
- 12 fresh curry leaves
- 4 shallots, finely sliced
- 8 ounces butternut squash, cut into 1-inch cubes
- 1 small eggplant (10 1/2 ounces), cut into 1-inch cubes
- 4 medium, ripe tomatoes, chopped
- 1 1/2 teaspoons sugar
- 2 teaspoons tamarind paste

- 1 1/2 teaspoons nice red chili powder
- 7 ounces green beans, trimmed

Direction

- Wash the lentils with cold water until the water runs clear, then put into a deep saucepan, cover with three times the amount of water, and bring to the boil. Simmer for 25 minutes, or until soft, scooping off any foam.
- Meanwhile, put 1 tablespoon of oil into a wide, lidded frying pan and add the fenugreek, coriander, and cumin seeds. Stir-fry for a minute, then take off the heat and grind to a coarse paste with a pestle and mortar.
- Put the remaining oil into the frying pan over a medium-high heat. When hot, add the mustard seeds and curry leaves, followed closely by the shallots, and cook for around 10 minutes, until the shallots are golden. Then add the diced squash and a couple of tablespoons of water, cover with the lid, and cook for 5 minutes.
- Add the eggplant and another couple of tablespoons of water, cover and cook for another 5 minutes, then add the tomatoes, along with the spices you ground earlier, the salt, sugar, tamarind paste, and chilli powder. Cover again and leave to cook for a further 5 minutes, until the tomatoes have broken down and the squash is tender. Add the lentils to the vegetables (or the other way around, depending on which pan is bigger), then add the green beans and enough water to make a thick, soupy texture, and cook for a final 5 minutes. Taste and adjust the salt, sugar, and tamarind as you wish.

42. CHILLED AVOCADO SOUP + CILANTRO OIL

Serving: Serves 4 | Prep: | Cook: | Ready in:

Ingredients

- CILANTRO OIL
- 1 cup coarsely chopped fresh cilantro leaves
- 1/4 cup organic extra-virgin olive oil
- 1/2 teaspoon kosher salt
- CHILLED AVOCADO SOUP
- 1 ear corn, husks removed
- 4 cups organic low-sodium vegetable broth
- 1 garlic clove, smashed
- 1-1/2 teaspoons kosher salt
- 2 firm but ripe avocados, peeled and pitted
- 3 tablespoons fresh lime juice
- 1/4 cup sour cream

Direction

- CILANTRO OIL
- In a blender or food processor, puree the cilantro, oil, and salt. Pour the mixture into a fine-mesh sieve set over a bowl and let it drain for 15 minutes. Store the oil in an airtight container at room temperature for up to 5 days. I used a plastic squirt bottle to store the oil in. It works great for adding swirls into the soup.
- CHILLED AVOCADO SOUP
- Heat a dry skillet over medium-high heat and roast the whole corn, turning occasionally, until charred in spots. Transfer the corn to a cutting board and cut the kernels from the cob. Cut the cob into thirds.
- Bring the kernels, cob pieces, broth, garlic, onion and 1½ teaspoons salt to a boil in a large saucepan and boil until the liquid is reduced to about 3 cups, about 20 minutes. Remove from the heat and cool, uncovered. Discard the cob pieces.
- In a blender, puree the corn mixture. Add 1 of the avocados and 2 tablespoons of the lime juice to the blender; puree until smooth. Season to taste with salt. Transfer to a covered container and chill the soup for at least 1 hour, until very cold.
- To serve, dice the remaining avocado into small cubes and gently mix with the remaining tablespoon of lime juice. Ladle the soup into bowls, dividing the avocado among the bowls, then drizzle each with a little sour cream

(thinned with water) and a swirl of cilantro oil. Use plastic squirt bottles for the sour cream and cilantro oil. Makes it a lot easier to add swirls into the soup. Use a butter knife to spread out the swirls into a decorative pattern.

43. CHORIZO CORN SOUP

Serving: Serves 4 servings | Prep: | Cook: |Ready in:

Ingredients

- 1 pound Spanish Chorizo, chopped
- 2 tablespoons Extra Virgin Olive Oil
- 1 Baking Potato, peeled and diced
- 6 Ears of Corn, kernels removed or 3 to 4 cups frozen corn
- 1 Red Bell Pepper, chopped
- 1 medium Onion, chopped
- 3 large Garlic Cloves, chopped
- 4 - 5 sprigs Sprigs Thyme, leaves removed and chopped
- 1 Dry Bay Leaf
- 1 28-oz can Fire-roasted Tomatoes
- 1 quart Chicken Stock
- 1 Large Bunch Kale, thick stems removed, leaves roughly chopped (about 4 cups)
- Bread, for dipping

Direction

- Place a large pot over medium-high heat with 2 turns of the pan of olive oil, about 2 tablespoons. Add the chorizo and cook stirring every now and then for 2-3 minutes. Add the potatoes and corn, and brown that up a little bit, then add bell pepper, onions, garlic, thyme, bay leaf, salt and pepper, and cook for 5 minutes. Pour in the tomatoes and chicken stock, and bring up to a bubble. Simmer for 5 minutes. Add the kale and simmer for 5 more minutes. Garnish soup with parsley or cilantro and lime juice and serve with lots of bread for dipping alongside.

44. CREAMY CARROT SOUP WITH COCONUT MILK AND PEANUT BUTTER

Serving: Serves 4 | Prep: | Cook: | Ready in:

Ingredients

- 7-8 bigger carrots
- 1 onion
- 2 cloves of garlic
- 1 cup creamy coconut milk
- 2 cups vegetable stock
- 2 tablespoons peanut butter
- 1 teaspoon coconut oil
- small pieces ginger
- Pinch salt
- Pinch pepper

Direction

- Heat the coconut oil in a sauce pan, add the finely chopped onions and cook for about 3 minutes. Add the thinly sliced carrots and garlic and cook them on for 3-5 more minutes.
- Add the spices with the veggie stock to the carrots and cook for about 15-20 minutes or until the carrots get soft.
- Add the soup, coconut milk and peanut butter to a blender and blend everything well together. You can add less or more vegetable stock depending on how thick you like your soup. Pour the soup into bowls and sprinkle with roasted almond.

45. CREAMY ROASTED VEGGIE SOUP

Serving: Serves 2 | Prep: | Cook: | Ready in:

Ingredients

- 3 cups broccoli
- 2 cups butternut squash
- 14 ounces light coconut milk
- 1/2 cup steamed edamame beans
- 2 tablespoons nutritional yeast
- 1 teaspoon salt
- 3 pieces garlic clove
- 1/4 teaspoon crushed red pepper flakes
- 3 sprigs thyme

Direction

- Heat the oven to 400 degrees. If you're using frozen broccoli and squash, let them thaw for 10-20 minutes (or zap hem in the microwave for a few minutes). Toss the broccoli and squash in olive oil and roast for about 20 minutes.
- Add all of the soup ingredients to a high speed blender for about 5 minutes. (If using a vitamix, put it on the 'soup' setting)
- Pour into 2 bowls and top with anything you'd like really! I used bacon pieces, edamame beans, pepitas, pine nuts, flax seeds, barley, and fresh thyme (or anything else you have in your pantry!)

46. Cabbage And Kielbasa Soup

Serving: Makes 4 to 5 quarts | Prep: | Cook: | Ready in:

Ingredients

- 2 tablespoons olive oil
- 1 large onion, chopped
- 2 large carrots, cut into rounds
- 2 stalks celery, sliced
- 2 cloves garlic, minced
- 1 pound kielbasa (or up to a half pound more), sliced into thin rounds
- 4 to 5 medium potatoes, peeled and chopped
- 10 cups chicken broth
- 5 cups rough chopped cabbage
- 1/2 cup chopped parsley
- 2 teaspoons black pepper
- 1/4 cup red wine vinegar (or more to taste)

- Salt to taste

Direction

- In a large soup pot, sauté the onion, celery, carrot and garlic until soft and fragrant.
- Add the sliced sausage and sauté 5 minutes more.
- Stir in the potatoes and broth, bring to a boil and simmer for 15 minutes until the potatoes are tender.
- Add the chopped cabbage, parsley and pepper and continue to simmer until the cabbage wilts.
- Season with salt and the vinegar after taking off the heat.

47. California Gazpacho

Serving: Serves 6 to 8 | Prep: | Cook: |Ready in:

Ingredients

- 6 tomatoes (preferably heirlooms)
- 3 to 4   small kirby cucumbers (preferably organic)
- 1 medium sweet onion
- 1 green pepper
- 2 cloves   garlic, minced
- 1/3 cup good olive oil
- 1/4 cup good red wine vinegar
- 1 1/2 cups tomato passata
- your favorite hot pepper sauce
- sea salt
- freshly cracked black pepper
- sour cream

Direction

- Place the minced garlic into a dish and pour the olive oil and vinegar over. Let it sit while you chop the vegetables.
- Slice tomatoes into 1/2-inch thick disks, stack them on top of one another, and chop them into 1/2-thick dice. When you empty them

into a serving bowl, be sure to include all their juices.
- Slice Kirby's in half lengthwise, then into 1/4-inch thick layers. Stack and slice them into 1/4-inch wide rows, and then chop the lot into fine dice. I love the juicy crunch of cucumbers as an accent, so I chop them a little smaller than the tomatoes, who are the (unofficial) star in this recipe. Add the cucumbers to the tomatoes.
- Finely chop the green pepper. It should be just-shy of a mince, as its bright and crunchy presence can easily compete with the other two, and we don't want that. Add the peppers into the bowl.
- Mince the sweet onion. Add it in with the rest, and give it a gentle stir to combine.
- Pour in the passata and the garlic mixture, and add a few pinches of sea salt. Add some freshly cracked pepper and a teaspoon or two of hot sauce. Stir everything together and taste. Feel free to add more hot sauce, sea salt, or cracked pepper, to your taste. The end experience should feel refreshing and a bit spicy, so that the addition of that sour cream dollop makes its soothing pleasure felt.
- Cover and refrigerate overnight. Serve chilled in shallow bowls topped with sour cream - gazpacho!

48. Carrot Potato Soup With Tiny Buffalo Meatballs

Serving: Serves about 4-6 | Prep: | Cook: |Ready in:

Ingredients

- Creamy Carrot Potato Soup
- 2 tablespoons extra virgin olive oil
- 1 pound carrots, peeled and diced
- 1 large onion, chopped
- 1 medium potato, scrubbed and chopped
- 3 garlic cloves, smashed
- 1 tablespoon tomato paste

- 1/2-1 teaspoons salt
- few grindings of black pepper
- 5 cups not too salty stock (vegetable, beef, chicken, duck...it's up to you)
- Tiny Buffalo Meatballs
- 1 pound ground buffalo meat
- 2 handfuls breadcrumbs (I use ground up seasoned whole wheat matzoh)
- 1 egg
- 1/2 cup grated Parmigiano-Reggiano cheese
- 3/4 teaspoon salt
- pinch of red pepper flakes

Direction

- Creamy Carrot Potato Soup
- In a large stockpot, heat the olive oil over medium high heat. Add the carrots, onions, potato, and garlic. Add the salt and pepper. Sauté for a few minutes and add the tomato paste and stir to coat. Add the stock of your choice, bring to a boil, lower heat to low, cover, and simmer for about 35 minutes. In two batches, blitz the soup until smooth and creamy (don't fill the blender up completely and blend with a towel placed over the hole in the cover to keep from spattering all over your kitchen). Return to stockpot and adjust for salt and pepper.
- Tiny Buffalo Meatballs
- Preheat oven to 350F. Mix the buffalo mixture together and form into little meatballs. Bake for 8-10 minutes. Put into the soup and serve.
- I also chopped up some kalamata olives and stirred them into the soup as I was serving it. They deepened to color of the soup and gave a welcome tang to it.

49. Carrot Soup With Mango And Coconut

Serving: Serves 4-6 | Prep: | Cook: | Ready in:

Ingredients

- 750 g carrots
- 40 g fresh ginger
- 1 onion
- 3 tablespoons canola oil
- 500 milliliters vegetable broth
- 1 can of coconut milk
- 2 Mangos
- 1 teaspoon chili flakes
- salt and pepper

Direction

- Peel the carrot, fresh ginger and onion. Cut into small dices.
- Peel the mango, remove the seed and puree
- Heat the canola oil in a large pan, add the carrots, onion and ginger. Cover with vegetable broth and cook for about 15 minutes until tender. Puree with an electric mixer.
- Add coconut milk and chili flakes. Finally, add the mango puree and season to taste
- The soup can be served warm or cold. Top with coconut flakes and coriander.

50. Cashew Cream Of Broccoli Soup

Serving: Serves 2-3 | Prep: | Cook: | Ready in:

Ingredients

- 1 cup raw (ie, not roasted or salted) cashews
- 2 cups vegetable stock, plus more to taste
- 4 cups broccoli, cut up (florets and stems - peel off any woody skin)
- 4 sprigs thyme leaves, off the stem

Direction

- Cover the cashews with water and set aside to soak for at least an hour (ideally overnight).
- Heat the vegetable stock in a large pot over high heat until boiling, and drop in the broccoli. Let it simmer until very tender, about

5-7 minutes. Add the thyme leaves and turn off the heat.

- Carefully transfer the broccoli to a blender and liquefy until completely smooth. Drain the cashews and add to the blender: liquefy again. Add more stock if the soup is too thick, and blend even further - I like mine viscous to the point of porridge, but you may not. Taste and adjust for seasoning. Serve warm.

51. Cauliflower Corn Chowder

Serving: Serves 0 | Prep: | Cook: | Ready in:

Ingredients

- 0 0

Direction

- Suggested Toppings: A few grinds of Ground Black Pepper, A bit of fresh Parsley (roughly chopped), Homemade Croutons, Grated Parmesan Cheese (for non-vegans)
- In a large pot, heat oil on a medium flame. Add in onions, potatoes, and carrots. Sauté them for about 5 - 10 minutes or until the potatoes have soften a bit. Then add in cauliflower and Cajun seasoning and sauté for an additional 5 - 10 more minutes and then stir in flour and let that brown a little, about 5 minutes or so. Then add in vegetable broth, corn, bay leaf and be sure to use your spoon to stir in all the browned bits on the bottom of your pot, if you have any. Bring the broth to a boil and then turn the heat down low, add in milk and let simmer for 10 minutes. Remove bay leaf, taste your chowder and add in sea salt to taste.
- **I used the flour to aide in thickening the chowder, but if your chowder is too thick, then add in a little more vegetable broth, but it should be fine. I found that, some people like their soup thick, and some like it a little more

soupy...so I always try to find a balance. But you adjust the liquids to your liking. **
- Now get yourself a big bowl, serve up a little soup, put your toppings on, and enjoy! Xoxo

52. Cauliflower Miso Soup

Serving: Serves 4-6 | Prep: | Cook: | Ready in:

Ingredients

- olive oil
- 8 garlic cloves, smashed
- 4 large shallots, peeled and quartered
- a few sprigs of sage
- 1/4 cup sherry vinegar, plus more for garnish
- 1 head cauliflower
- 3 carrots, roughly chopped
- a few dashes ground coriander
- a few dashes paprika
- 3 tablespoons white miso
- grapeseed oil
- scallions

Direction

- In a large stock pot add enough olive oil to coat the bottom of it. Warm it over medium heat and then add your smashed garlic cloves, quartered shallots and a sprig of sage. Sprinkle with a few pinches of salt. Allow to heat for 10-15 minutes, until everything is tender and browning. Remove the sprig of sage.
- Break up the head of cauliflower into small flowerettes and add to the pot with the carrots. Turn the heat up to high and add a few dashes of the coriander and paprika; stir. Once everything is sizzling, add 1/4 cup of the sherry vinegar, give it another few stirs and then add 6 cups cold water.
- Bring the pot to a boil and then turn it down a bit to let everything simmer for 30-45 minutes, or until the cauliflower is very tender.
- Turn off the heat and let cool a few minutes. Using an immersion blender (or working in

small batches carefully with a standing blender), blend the soup continuously until very smooth and creamy. Add in three heaping tablespoons of white miso and blend well into the soup. It may take several minutes to reach the smoothest consistency. Heat the soup back up while you make the garnish.

- In a separate, small/shallow pan, add a 1/4" layer of grapeseed (or other high heat) oil and heat up. Add a sprig of sage and slivered scallions. Fry briefly until golden. Drain on a paper towel.
- Put soup in bowl, top with crispy sage and scallions, and drizzle with olive oil and a few drops sherry vinegar.

53. Cauliflower Potato Soup

Serving: Serves 10 | Prep: | Cook: | Ready in:

Ingredients

- 2 tbsp (+ 2 additional teaspoons) olive oil
- 1 small (1 lb) cauliflower, cored, cut into small florets
- 1 small fennel bulb (reserve leaves for garnish) bulb cored and chopped
- 1 lb russet potatoes, peeled, cut into 1 inch chunks
- 1 large yellow onion, chopped
- 2 cans (14.5 oz each) chicken stock, plus 2 cans of water
- 2 tbsp kosher salt
- 1 bay leaf
- 1 tsp cumin
- ¼ tsp saffron threads, crumbled
- Freshly ground pepper to taste

Direction

- Heat 2 tbsp. of the oil in a large Dutch oven over medium heat; add cauliflower, fennel, potatoes, cumin, and onion and cook, stirring constantly, 4 minutes.

- Cover pot; reduce heat to low and sweat mixture 10 minutes, stirring once.
- Add chicken stock, water, salt, bay leaf, and saffron; bring to a boil, reduce heat to low, cover pot, and simmer 25 minutes, stirring several times, or until vegetables are very tender.
- Uncover; remove from heat and puree soup directly in the pot using and immersion blender or in a blender in 3 batches.
- Top with crumbled goat cheese or reserved fennel leaves.

54. Cauliflower Soup Drizzled With White Truffle Oil

Serving: Serves 4 | Prep: | Cook: | Ready in:

Ingredients

- 2 tablespoons unsalted organic butter
- 2 cloves garlic, chopped
- 1 large onion, finely chopped (about 1 cup)
- 1 pound cauliflower florets (about 5 cups)
- 1 teaspoon sea salt
- 3/4 teaspoon freshly ground pepper
- 6 cups low sodium chicken broth
- 1 teaspoon white truffle oil* or extra-virgin olive oil

Direction

- Melt butter in heavy large cast iron pot over medium heat. Add onion and sauté until tender, about 7 minutes. Add garlic and cauliflower and sauté 5 minutes. Add salt, pepper and chicken broth. Cover and simmer until cauliflower is tender, about 25 minutes.
- Working in batches, transfer soup to blender and purée until smooth. Return soup to pot. (Soup can be prepared 1 day ahead. Cool slightly. Cover and refrigerate.) Bring soup to simmer.
- Ladle soup into bowls. Drizzle truffle oil over and enjoy!

55. Cauliflower Soup With Coconut Milk & Chillies

Serving: Serves 4 | Prep: | Cook: | Ready in:

Ingredients

- 1 cauliflower
- 1 onion
- 2 garlic cloves
- 2 tablespoons olive oil
- 1 glass white wine
- 1 cup vegetable stock (water)
- 3 fresh chillies
- 2 teaspoons coriander seeds
- 1 teaspoon cumin
- 1 teaspoon nutmeg
- 2 teaspoons turmeric
- 1 teaspoon cinnamon
- 1 teaspoon fennel seeds
- 1-2 tablespoons fresh galangal(or 1 teaspoon dried)
- 1 fresh lemon grass
- 250 milliliters coconut milk
- salt&pepper
- fresh coriander leaves

Direction

- Clean and trim the cauliflower in small size florets. Cook them in a steamer basket until soft.
- In a dry heavy skillet, over medium heat toast the cumin, fennel and coriander seeds till they give off an aroma, stirring or shaking the pan often. Cool and grind in a seed grinder.
- In a large pot add olive oil, heat and add diced onions, mashed garlic, grated galangal, chopped lemongrass and the spices. Sauté for 2-3 minutes.
- Add the white wine. Reduce until half.
- Add the cooked cauliflower florets to the mix and pour the vegetable broth on top. Simmer for 10-15 minutes.

- Using a stick blender, blitz the soup until creamy and smooth, add a splash more water if it is too thick.
- Finally add the coconut milk and simmer for another 5 -10minutes. Serve with cilantro and chili slices.

56. Cauliflower Soup , Pickled Cauliflower And Roasted Almonds

Serving: Serves 6 | Prep: | Cook: | Ready in:

Ingredients

- Cauliflower soup
- 1 cauliflower into florets
- 4 cups vegetable broth
- 1 onion, finely chopped
- 1 tablespoon canola oil
- 1/4 teaspoon of salt
- The Garnish : Marinated Cauliflower
- half cauliflower, cut into florets
- 1 cup white vinegar or neutral
- 1 teaspoon turmeric
- 1/2 cup sugar
- 2 pinches of coarse salt

Direction

- Cauliflower soup
- In a saucepan over medium heat, cook an onion in oil until translucent. Add the cauliflower and vegetable broth, then bring to a boil. Cover and simmer about 10 minutes or until cauliflower is tender.
- In a blender, reduce all until smooth.
- Add salt and pepper to taste.
- For the garnishing: Add the marinated cauliflower florets, toasted slivered almonds and your best olive oil.
- The Garnish: Marinated Cauliflower

- In a sauce pan, bring vinegar, sugar, turmeric and salt to a boil. Remove from heat and let it cool to room temperature.
- Put the cauliflower florets in an airtight container (I use a Mason jar) and pour the pickling liquid. Refrigerate until needed.
- As long as the cauliflower is submerged, you can keep it in the refrigerator for a few weeks.

57. Charming Curried Lentil Soup

Serving: Serves 3 | Prep: | Cook: | Ready in:

Ingredients

- 3 tablespoons extra virgin olive oil
- 1 medium onion, chopped
- 2 large cloves garlic, minced and divided
- 1 medium carrot, chopped
- 3 tablespoons (or more) curry powder
- 1 cup french green lentils
- 4 1/2 cups water
- 1 1/2 cups cooked chickpeas
- 1 tablespoon lemon juice
- 2 tablespoons butter

Direction

- Heat 1 tablespoon olive oil in a large pot over medium heat. Add onion and carrot - sprinkle with salt and pepper. Cook onion until translucent, stirring occasionally - about 4 minutes add half chopped garlic, stir until everything is soft, but not brown. Add curry powder and stir another minute
- Add lentils and 4 cups of water. Sprinkle with salt and pepper. Increase heat to a boil, then reduce and let simmer until lentil are cooked - about 30 minutes
- Meanwhile, puree chickpeas, lemon juice, 1/4 cup water, the rest of the garlic, and 2 tablespoons olive oil in a food processor until smooth
- Add chickpea puree and butter to the lentil soup. Season to taste with salt, pepper, and

more curry powder if desired. Add water by the 1/4 if desired until your preference of consistency is reached. Divide soup among bowls, serve with toasted bread

58. Chayote Mousse With Mussels And Cime Di Rapa

Serving: Serves 4 | Prep: | Cook: | Ready in:

Ingredients

- Fish fumet
- 1 small fish to make the fumet: here I use gurnards
- 2 cups white wine
- 100 grams cherry tomatoes
- 1 onion
- 1 teaspoon tomato concentrate
- salt and pepper
- Chayote mousse
- 3 Chayotes
- 500 grams mussels
- 1 clove of garlic
- 10 Cime di Rapa node

Direction

- Fish fumet/Stock: Put the gurnards in a small roasting pan with salt and pepper.
- Add 1 cup of white wine and 4 cherry tomatoes cut into pieces.
- Put the fish in a hot oven at 180 C for 20 minutes.
- In the meantime, stir fry a small onion and 3 chopped cherry tomatoes in a large pan to make the fish stock.
- Once the gurnard is done transfer it in the stock pan and add 1 spoon of concentrated tomato sauce.
- To keep all the flavors of the roasting fish, pour some water in the roasting pan to deglaze it.
- Pour the water over the fish and add ½ cup of white wine.

- Let it simmer for 20 minutes.
- In the meantime peel the Chayotes and cut them in small cubes
- Boil the Chayotes with 1 tsp of salt for 20 minutes.
- Once the chayote is cooked, drain it and transfer it in a bowl to cool completely.
- Clean and boil the Cime di Rapa for 10 minutes in a separate pan with a tsp of salt.
- When done, drain them and put them in iced water to preserve their nice green color.
- If you cannot find the Cime di Rapayou can replace them with Cavolo Nero.
- Strain the fumet with a paper cloth and let it cool off completely.
- In a frying pan, stir fry 1 sliced clove of garlic.
- Put in the mussels and stir fry covered until they are all open.
- When they are ready, remove the mussel but keep the water.
- Strain the water through a paper cloth and let it rest so that any residual of sand will fall at the bottom.
- The water from the mussels is naturally salted and will be used instead of salt to season the Chayote mousse. As Le Bec Fin said, Chayote have no flavor!
- Clean the mussels and put them aside.
- Now mix the fish fumet, the water from the mussels and the Chayote to make the mousse. It is important to mix the right quantity to balance taste and consistency.
- To start add ½ cup of mussels water and 1/3 of fish fumet to the Chayote and blend.
- Taste and add more fish fumet or mussels water accordingly until you reach the desired taste and texture.
- Pour the mousse in the serving bowl and add 4 mussels and 4 Cime di Rapa per plate to garnish.
- When eating the sweetness of the mussel will be balance by the acidity of the Cime di Rapa, all softly bounded by the Chayote mousse.
- Best served at room temperature

59. Chestnut Wild Rice In Green Tea

Serving: Serves 2 | Prep: | Cook: |Ready in:

Ingredients

- 1 pound Chestnuts
- 1/2 pound Sugar Snap Peas
- 2 cups Whole Grain Rice
- 1 tablespoon Soy Sauce
- 2 teaspoons Brown Rice Syrup
- 1/4 cup Nori Seaweed (Shredded)
- 4 cups Brewed Japanese Green Tea
- Salt & White Pepper

Direction

- Roast the chestnuts (pre-heat oven to 375 F, make deep cross hatches on the humps of the chestnuts, place them on a baking sheet for about 20-25 minutes. Peel as soon as you're able to handle them).
- Meanwhile, cook the rice according to your package (or in a rice cooker).
- Chop up the sugar snap peas and chestnuts. Set aside.
- While your rice is finishing up its cooking process, brew some green tea.
- When your rice has cooked, add the chopped snap peas and chestnuts and mix well.
- Add to the rice soy sauce, brown rice syrup, and a little salt + white pepper.
- Prior to serving, add some shredded nori.
- Pour in the brewed green tea and serve immediately.

60. Chicken Orzo Soup

Serving: Serves 4 to 5 | Prep: | Cook: |Ready in:

Ingredients

- 4 tablespoons olive oil, divided, plus more as needed

- 1 pound boneless, skinless chicken breast, cut into small cubes
- Salt and pepper
- 1 yellow onion, diced
- 3 garlic cloves, minced
- 3 medium carrots, sliced into coins
- 3 celery ribs, trimmed and chopped
- 1 tablespoon tomato paste
- 1/4 cup dry white wine
- 4 cups homemade or low sodium broth (vegetable or chicken is fine)
- 4 cups water
- 1/2 cup loosely packed fresh cilantro
- 1 fresh or dried bay leaf
- 1/2 cup orzo
- 6 leaves Lacinato kale, stem removed and roughly chopped

Direction

- Start by cooking the chicken. In a sauté pan, heat 2 tablespoons olive oil over medium to medium-high heat. Add chicken breast to pan and season with salt and pepper to taste. Sauté until chicken is browned on all sides and mostly cooked through, about 8 minutes. Set aside.
- As chicken is cooking (yes, multi-task), heat the other 2 tablespoons of olive oil in a soup pot over medium heat. Add onion, garlic, carrots, and celery and season with salt and pepper to taste. Let cook until softened, about 10 minutes. Add tomato paste and white wine to deglaze the bottom of the pan. Let the wine simmer and thicken for 3 minutes. Add cooked chicken pieces to the pot.
- Stir in broth, water, cilantro, the bay leaf, and a good amount of salt and pepper. Cover and bring to a boil. Lower to a simmer and let cook for 10 minutes.
- Add orzo and kale. Re-cover the pot and let the orzo cook in the soup for 8 minutes.
- There you have it folks: Time to dish up a homemade bowl of chicken noodle soup for the kiddos. To store, place the soup in an airtight container in the refrigerator or freezer.

61. Chicken Soup For The Healthiest Soul

Serving: Serves 3 | Prep: 0hours0mins | Cook: 0hours0mins | Ready in:

Ingredients

- 1 cow femur
- 2 chicken breasts
- 8-10 basil leaves
- 4 shallots
- 2 cups chopped broccoli
- 4 garlic cloves
- 2 tablespoons ginger
- 4 carrots
- 3 cups chopped butternut squash
- 12-15 brussels sprouts
- 2 tablespoons raw honey

Direction

- Preheat oven to 350.
- Bring 6 cups of water to boil.
- Add the femur, turn down to medium and let sit.
- In a blender, combine ginger, basil, garlic, and shallots with 1/2 cup of water.
- Pour into your pot of water and let sit for 25 minutes.
- Meanwhile, wrap your chicken in parchment paper with 1 fresh squeezed lemon.
- Cook at 350 for 25 minutes.
- After the chicken is done, put your carrots, butternut squash and Brussels sprouts into your water after you take out the femur bone (be sure to get all of the marrow out into your soup!)
- Turn to high, to get a low boil, for 3-4 minutes.
- Then turn back down to medium and add broccoli and honey, and as much salt and as much pepper as you'd like
- Let warm for about 5 more minutes.
- Add the chicken just before you are ready to eat.

- Serve with a slice of delicious bread and enjoy!

62. Chicken Soup With Poblano, Parsnips & Leeks

Serving: Serves 4 | Prep: | Cook: | Ready in:

Ingredients

- 2 skin-on, boneless chicken breasts
- 6 cups water
- 1 poblano pepper
- 2 leeks, pale green and white parts only
- 3 cloves of garlic
- 1 14.5 oz can diced tomatoes
- 1 14.5 oz can chickpeas
- 3 parsnips
- 2 cups loosely packed Swiss chard
- 2 tablespoons olive oil

Direction

- Prep your ingredients: Season chicken breasts with salt and pepper. Thinly slice leeks cross-wise. Peel and slice parsnips on an angle. Mince garlic and set aside with the leeks. Drain and rinse chickpeas. Remove Swiss chard leaves from stems and tear the leaves into bite-size pieces.
- Place chicken in a two quart pot with 6 cups of water. Bring to a boil and then reduce heat and simmer the chicken for about 15 minutes, or until cooked through. Periodically skim the top of the water to remove any scum or excess fat. Reserve the leftover broth.
- While the chicken is cooking, roast the poblano (this will allow you to remove the thin skin). If you do not have a gas stove, place the poblanos on a sheet pan with a bit of olive oil and turn on the broiler. Allow them to roast, turning periodically until the skin is slightly charred and bubbly all over. If you do have a gas stove, slowly rotate the poblano above the open flame until skin is charred and bubbly all over (this made me feel so

dangerous, but it's not that dangerous, I swear). Once the poblano is charred, carefully remove the skin by rubbing it all over with a paper towel. Remove the stem and seeds and rinse the pepper off with water. Dice it up and set it aside.

- As the chicken continues to cook, heat two tablespoons of olive oil over medium heat. Add leeks and garlic and sauté for 4-5 minutes until the leeks have softened a bit.
- Add the tomatoes, diced poblano, parsnips, and chickpeas to the leeks and reduce heat to simmer. Let these ingredients do their thing for a few minutes as you prep the chicken.
- Remove chicken from the water and carefully remove the skin (be careful, it's hot!). Using two forks, shred the chicken breasts into bite-size chunks.
- Add the reserved stock to your pot. Increase heat to high and bring to a boil. Let the soup boil for 5-10 minutes or until the liquid has reduced slightly. Reduce heat to low and simmer the soup until the parsnips are tender. Right before serving, stir in the Swiss chard. Once the chard has wilted, the soup is ready to serve.
- Ladle soups into bowls and garnish with your choice of toppings! A few ideas: Crumbled cotija cheese, lime wedges, thinly sliced radishes, chopped cilantro, shredded cheddar cheese, sliced scallions, dollop of sour scream.

63. Chicken Tortilla Soup With Corn And Black Beans

Serving: Serves 2-4 | Prep: | Cook: | Ready in:

Ingredients

- 2 teaspoons olive oil
- 1 onion, chopped
- 2 cloves of garlic, sliced
- 1/2 jalapeno, seeds removed, chopped
- 2 chicken breasts

- 15 ounce can fire roasted tomatoes
- 32 ounce chicken broth
- 1 corn on the cob, kernels removed
- 2 cups cooked black beans (or use canned)
- cilantro, chopped
- avocado, diced
- tortillas, sliced and fried
- lime wedges
- sour cream

Direction

- Heat a heavy pot. Add oil. Add onions, garlic and jalapeno and sauté for about 10 minutes.
- Meanwhile, heat a cast iron skillet. Add a bit of oil and chicken breasts seasoned with salt and pepper. Cook uncovered for about 6 minutes on each side. Cover and cook for about 5 more minutes.
- Back to the onions, garlic and jalapenos: add fire roasted tomatoes and chicken broth. Simmer for 10-15 minutes. Using a stick blender puree the mixture. {Note: you can make it perfectly pureed, or leave some chunks of vegetables in the soup.}
- Add corn, beans and chopped chicken breasts. Simmer for 15 more minutes.
- Get all of your toppings ready.
- Ladle the soup and top with tortilla strips, chunks of avocado, cilantro leaves and a spoon-full of sour cream. Squirt with a lime wedge. Eat immediately!

64. Chicken Vermicelli Soup

Serving: Serves 4 | Prep: | Cook: | Ready in:

Ingredients

- 2 chicken breasts sliced into strips
- 2 tablespoons any flavourless vegetable oil such as canola or sunflower
- 1 large onion finely chopped
- 2 potatoes quartered
- 2 carrots cut into large quarters

- 4-5 cups chicken stock
- 1 1 inch piece of cinnamon
- 1 teaspoon chilli flakes
- 1 pinch saffron strands soaked in 2 teaspoons of warm water
- Juice of half lemon
- 1 tablespoon chopped, fresh parsely
- 150 grams thin, rice vermicelli
- flour for dusting the chicken
- salt
- 1/2 teaspoon freshly ground black pepper
- 2 eggs, separated

Direction

- Heat oil in a thick casserole dish and fry the onions till slightly soft. Add the chicken pieces dusted with flour and quickly brown (not too much or the onions will burn).
- Throw in the carrots and potatoes, cook for a couple of minutes and pour in the stock, cinnamon stick, chili flakes and salt. Bring to a boil, lower heat, cover and simmer till vegetables are tender but not mushy.
- In a small bowl, beat the egg yolks with the lemon juice and mix in the herbs and the soaked saffron with the water (cooled or else the eggs will be cooked).
- Add the vermicelli to the soup and cook for a further 7-8 minutes till they are done. Mix in the chicken followed by the egg mixture. It's important to keep the heat low or take the pan off the heat while stirring the eggs in. Once mixed, return to low heat, simmer for 2 minutes, add the pepper and serve piping hot.

65. Chicken And Green Chile Verde Soup

Serving: Serves 8 | Prep: | Cook: | Ready in:

Ingredients

- For The Soup:

- 4 boneless skinless chicken breasts (about 2 pounds), trimmed of fat & cut into 1-inch cubes
- 1 large yellow onion, chopped
- 4 carrots, finely sliced
- 4 garlic cloves, minced
- 4 cups chicken stock
- 2 cups green chile salsa - medium heat (or mild if preferred)
- 12 ounces canned diced green chiles
- 3 cans pinto beans
- 3 tablespoons cumin
- 1 teaspoon coriander
- 2 teaspoons salt
- 1 1/2 teaspoons pepper
- For The Garnish:
- fresh cilantro, chopped
- jalapeños, chopped or sliced
- sour cream

Direction

- Sauté onions, garlic and carrots in a large pot for 6 minutes.
- Season the veggies in the pot with 1 1/2 teaspoon salt, 1 teaspoon pepper, 2 tablespoons cumin, 1 teaspoon coriander, and cook 2 more minutes.
- Meanwhile, drain 1 can of pinto beans, rinse them, and smash with a fork into a paste in a small bowl. Add a little chicken stock to the beans when smashing and it will help with this step. Drain and rinse the other 2 cans of pinto beans and leave them whole. Set the beans aside.
- Add 3 small cans of diced green chiles and 2 cups of green chile salsa Verde (use a medium-spicy version or use mild if spice-averse) to the veggies and spices.
- Stir in 4 cups of homemade chicken stock, and bring the pot to a simmer.
- Add the whole and smashed pinto beans, let the soup come back up to a simmer.
- Next, season cubed chicken with 1 tablespoon cumin, ½ teaspoon salt and ½ teaspoon pepper then add to the soup.

- Cook for 10-15 more minutes, and temp chicken to be sure it has reached 165 degrees.
- Dish into soup bowls, and garnish with sour cream, cilantro, & jalapeños.

66. Chicken And Vegetable Soup With Butter Beans

Serving: Makes 3 1/2 quarts | Prep: | Cook: | Ready in:

Ingredients

- For the broth:
- 1 whole chicken
- 14 cups water
- 1 medium onion, root end left intact, peeled and quartered
- 5 large cloves garlic, peeled and smashed with the flat side of a knife
- 2 medium carrots, halved once lengthwise and once crosswise
- 3 celery stalks, cut into about 4" lengths
- 2 bay leaves
- 1 1/2 tablespoons kosher salt
- 1 tablespoon whole peppercorns, lightly crushed
- 1/2 teaspoon whole allspice, lightly crushed
- a few sprigs fresh herbs, whatever you have on hand. I used rosemary, thyme, and sage.
- For the soup:
- 2 tablespoons olive oil
- 2 cups chopped yellow or white onion
- 2 tablespoons minced garlic
- 3 celery stalks, trimmed and cut into about 1/4" sliced
- 4 medium carrots, peeled and cut diagonally into about 1/4" slices
- 2 bay leaves
- 1/4 teaspoon dried oregano
- 14 ounces whole tomatoes in juice
- 8 cups homemade broth
- 16 ounces frozen butter beans (lima beans)
- 3 medium Yukon Gold or other boiling potato, peeled and chopped into 1/2" pieces

- 15 ounces whole kernel corn
- 12 ounces shredded or diced chicken from the meat you reserved (about 4 cups)
- 1/2 teaspoon kosher salt
- freshly ground pepper

Direction

- For the broth:
- Rinse the chicken and remove the innards.
- Put everything in a large stockpot. I like to use a tea infuser ball instead of cheesecloth for the peppercorns and allspice. Bring to a boil, and then reduce heat to a bare simmer. Cook for about 2 hours, flipping the chicken once if it won't stay fully submerged.
- Remove the chicken from the pot, but keep the stock at a simmer. When the chicken is cool enough to handle, pick the meat off of it, but do not discard the skin and bones. Refrigerate or freeze the meat; you will use some of it in the soup.
- Put the chicken skin and bones back into the stockpot, partially cover the pot, and continue to simmer for another 3 hours or so. Strain the stock into a bowl or container, let it cool some, and then refrigerate it. The fat on top of the stock will congeal; remove as much or as little of it as you want. I ended up with about 8 cups of stock.
- For the soup:
- In a large stockpot, heat the olive oil over medium heat. Add the onion, garlic, celery, carrots, 1/4 tsp. of the kosher salt, and a few grinds of fresh pepper. Cook, stirring occasionally, under the onions are soft and translucent, about 10 minutes.
- Add the oregano, tomatoes, and the remaining 1/4 tsp. kosher salt. Break the tomatoes up with the back of a wooden spoon, then add the bay leaves and stock. Bring to a boil, and then reduce heat to a simmer. Cook for 10 minutes.
- Add the butter beans and simmer for 10 more minutes.
- Add the potatoes and simmer for 10 more minutes,

- Add the chicken and corn, and simmer until heated through, about 5 more minutes.
- Remove the bay leaves and adjust seasoning to taste before serving.

67. Chicken And Soba Noodle Soup

Serving: Serves 4 | Prep: | Cook: |Ready in:

Ingredients

- To serve:
- 400 grams Japanese soba noodles
- 250 grams mushrooms, chopped lengthways
- 2 stalks of spring onions (only the green parts), chopped
- For the chicken stock:
- 1 1/2 pounds chicken pieces, bone in
- 1 leek, chopped into 3" pieces
- 3 carrots, chopped into thick rounds
- 2 onions, quartered
- 1 whole head of garlic, halved crosswise
- 1 bunch coriander, roughly chopped (avoid the leaves)
- 15 black peppercorns, bruised
- 1 sprig thyme (optional)
- Salt, to taste

Direction

- Put all the ingredients listed for the chicken stock in a large pot and cover with 2½ liters of cold water. Turn on the heat; when it comes to a boil, reduce to a very gentle simmer and clamp on a lid. Leave on for 1½ hours. (Check on it once or twice in between and remove any impurities or white foam that may rise to the surface with a ladle).
- Once your chicken stock is done, scoop out the chicken pieces and shred them into pieces to use in your soup. Set aside. Send the vegetables and stock through a strainer, and press down to squeeze out most of the liquid from them.

- Cook the noodles as per the instructions on the packet until al dente. Add the mushrooms to the same pot as your noodles 2 minutes before its done, and strain them both out together.
- To serve, divide your noodles into bowls and top with mushrooms, shredded chicken, and boiled vegetables. Pour over your hot chicken soup and garnish with spring onions. Serve immediately.

68. Chicken, Bean & Kale Soup

Serving: Serves 8 to 10 | Prep: | Cook: | Ready in:

Ingredients

- 12 cups homemade or store-bought, low-sodium chicken broth
- 2-3 tablespoons olive oil
- 1 large onion, peeled and diced
- 3 medium carrots, washed, peeled and diced
- 3 large celery stalks, washed and diced
- 1 medium potato, washed, peeled and diced
- 2 cups kale, washed, chopped and loosely packed
- 1/2 cup Italian parsley, chopped
- 2-3 cloves garlic, minced
- 1 1/2 cups Royal Corona, cassoulet or cannellini beans, cooked or canned, drained
- 1 2- to 3-inch Parmigiano-Reggiano rind or 2-3 tablespoons grated Parmigiano-Reggiano
- 1 bay leaf
- 1/2 teaspoon dried basil (or 1 tablespoon fresh, chopped leaves)
- 1/2 cup white wine
- 1 1/2 cups cooked chicken, cubed or shredded
- salt and pepper to taste
- Parmigiano-Reggiano, shredded, for garnish

Direction

- If using dried beans, soak them overnight, drain, then cook until tender but not mushy.

Measure the requisite amount. If using canned, drain, then measure 1 1/2 cups.
- In a large skillet over a medium heat, add half the oil and fry chopped onions, celery, carrots and potatoes until softened and golden but not cooked through. Sprinkle with salt and pepper. Add to a stockpot, along with the chicken broth and bay leaf. Warm over a medium flame until simmering, then lower heat.
- Add the remaining oil to the skillet and cook kale until lightly wilted on medium heat. Add parsley and garlic, cooking for another minute or two. Add to the stockpot along with the cooked beans and Parmesan rind, if using. If using grated Parmesan, save it until later.
- Add extra salt and pepper to taste, plus thyme, basil, additional spices and wine. Cook for about 15 minutes or until the vegetables are soft and the flavors are well blended.
- Stir in cooked chicken and grated Parmesan, if using, right before serving.
- Ladle into bowls and top with additional Parmesan. Serve with a crusty bread (or crispy croutons), a green salad and vino!

69. Chilled Apricot Soup

Serving: Serves 4 | Prep: | Cook: | Ready in:

Ingredients

- 4 cups quartered apricots
- 3 cups water
- 1/4 cup agave nectar or 1/3 cup sugar
- 1 tablespoon freshly grated lemon zest
- Prosecco (if you happen to have an open bottle)

Direction

- In a heavy medium saucepan, simmer apricots, water and agave or sugar for 12-15 minutes, until apricots are very soft.
- Add lemon zest and stir.

- Puree with a stick blender until smooth and chill till very cold.
- Serve in small glass bowls or ramekins garnished with a bit of lemon zest or a tiny splash of Prosecco.

70. Chilled Cucumber Soup

Serving: Serves 4 | Prep: | Cook: | Ready in:

Ingredients

- 1 dash onion salt
- 1 piece garlic clove
- 1 tablespoon lemon juice
- 1 tablespoon Maggi seasoning
- 2 tablespoons Fresh dill
- 1/2 cup Sour cream
- 2 pieces English cucumbers, peeled, cored, chopped
- 1 quart Buttermilk to fill blender

Direction

- Process in blender 5 seconds
- Process until completely blended, Soup should somewhat chunky.

71. Chilled Fresh Pea Soup With Red Grapes And Chevre

Serving: Serves 6 | Prep: | Cook: | Ready in:

Ingredients

- 2 tablespoons Unsalted Butter
- 1 tablespoon EVOO, plus more for drizzling
- 2 shallots, chopped
- 3 cups low sodium vegetable broth
- 4 cups shelled fresh peas
- 1/4 cup fresh mint leaves

- 1/4 cup fresh flat leaf parsley, roughly chopped
- 1/2 teaspoon salt, plus more to taste
- 1/4 teaspoon black pepper, plus more to taste
- 1/2 cup chevre cheese, crumbled
- 2 dozen red grapes, halved

Direction

- Heat a large pot over medium heat and add the butter and EVOO. Once butter is melted, add the shallot and saute for 4-5 minutes until slightly golden and translucent. Season with salt and pepper. Pour in the broth and increase to medium high to bring to a boil. Once at a boil, add the peas and cook for 4-5 minutes until tender. Turn off the heat and add the mint, parsley, salt and pepper. With a slotted spoon, remove 1/2 cup of fresh peas from the broth and set aside.
- Puree the soup in multiple batches or with an immersion blender. When blending, fill the blender halfway with the pea mixture (keeping an even ratio of peas/herbs to liquid) to create a smooth puree. Pour the thick, pureed liquid into a large bowl and continue with the remaining soup. Stir in the lemon juice, reserved whole peas, and season to taste. Once cooled slightly, pour the soup into a tupperware container and place in the refrigerator to chill for at least 1 hour before serving.
- To serve, pour a couple of ladles of soup into each bowl. Sprinkle with about 1 T chevre (more or less depending on your cheese taste), sprinkle about 6-8 halved grapes on top and a drizzle of EVOO.

72. Chilled Mango Soup With Crema And Pepitas

Serving: Makes 3 cups | Prep: | Cook: | Ready in:

Ingredients

- 1 whole dried New Mexico red chile
- 3 ripe Champagne or Ataulfo mangoes, peeled and chopped for 3 cups of fruit
- 1 firm green mango, peeled and chopped for about a cup of fruit
- 1 cup peeled and sliced cucumber
- 1/4 cup chopped red onion
- 1 tablespoon rough chopped cilantro stems
- 1 1/2 teaspoons cumin seeds
- 1/2 teaspoon kosher salt (plus more to taste if necessary)
- 2 tablespoons extra virgin olive oil
- 1/4 cup water
- Crema Mexicana for serving (can substitute crème fraiche)
- Generous amounts of toasted pepitas for serving

Direction

- Using kitchen shears remove stem from chile and discard. Cut chile into small ½-inch squares and place in a bowl. Cover chile with hot water and let rehydrate for 15 minutes, stirring occasionally. Drain and discard the water (but not the seeds). Place soaked chile pieces (and seeds) in the bowl of a food processor.
- Add the next five ingredients (through cilantro stems) to the food processor.
- Toast cumin seeds in a dry pan over medium heat until fragrant, shaking pan to prevent burning. Crush seeds in a mortar and pestle. Add to soup mixture along with kosher salt.
- With the machine running, add olive oil and water in a stream through chute. Continue processing, stopping occasionally to scrape down sides with a spatula, until mixture is smooth and mango pieces are no longer visible.
- Transfer soup to a bowl or quart glass measure and cover with plastic wrap. Refrigerate for at least two hours and up to a day to allow flavors to meld. Before serving, stir and taste for salt, adding more if necessary.

- When serving, portion soup into small bowls, stir in crema (start with a teaspoon), and top with toasted pepitas. Enjoy.

73. Chorizo And Black Beans, "Meanwhile" Style

Serving: Makes nearly 3 quarts | Prep: | Cook: | Ready in:

Ingredients

- 1 pound / 453 grams black beans
- 12 ounces / 340 grams / 3 medium Spanish-style chorizo
- 1 large onion
- 6 cloves of garlic
- Small bunch - 15-20 sprigs - cilantro
- Olive oil (or any neutral oil)
- 2 teaspoon ground cumin
- 1 teaspoon ground coriander
- ½ teaspoon ground allspice
- 1 teaspoon smoked paprika
- 2 stalks of celery
- Salt
- Black pepper
- 1 large bay leaf - or 2 small ones
- 1 14-ounce can diced tomatoes (preferably fire roasted, with green chilis)
- 2 tablespoons tomato paste
- 1 16-ounce can of kidney beans
- Zest of one orange
- Chipotles in adobo, to taste
- Juice of 2 limes
- Optional items for serving:
- Cheddar, grated, for garnishing
- Lime crema - 1 tablespoon lime juice per ½ cup sour cream with a pinch of salt
- Brown rice
- Tortilla chips for eating with, instead of a fork or spoon (kids love that)

Direction

- Put 5 ½ cups of water on to boil in a kettle or covered pot. Turn the slow cooker onto its "High" setting. NB: you'll be turning it down before the long cooking period begins.
- Meanwhile, cut the chorizo lengthwise and then crosswise into 1" chunks. Put them into a medium microwavable bowl or Pyrex pitcher with ½ cup water; cover tightly and microwave on high for 3 minutes. (I use my 2 cup Pyrex measure for this, putting the water in first.) When the cooking time is done, remove and leave the container covered. You'll be putting them back in. We're cooking them like this to render as much fat as we can before they go into the slow cooker for the day.
- Meanwhile, coarsely chop the onions and garlic and put them into a medium microwavable bowl or Pyrex-style 4-cup measure. Microwave for 3 ½ minutes. Softening them first in the microwave results in a better texture later (this tip, and to warm the spices with the aromatics, courtesy of Cook's Illustrated).
- Meanwhile, use a mortar and pestle to crush the oregano with the cumin, coriander, allspice and 8 - 10 grinds of black pepper. Cut the cilantro stems below the leaves into ⅛" pieces.
- When the onions are done, remove the cover, make a small well in the middle of the onions, add the cilantro stems, the crushed herbs and spices, and the smoked paprika, as well as a good glug (a tablespoon or so, but don't bother measuring) of olive oil. Cover tightly and microwave for another 3 minutes.
- Meanwhile, chop the celery into ½" chunks. Pick over the black beans to remove any shriveled ones and any dirt or stones. Put the beans and celery into the slow cooker.
- When the onions are done, remove them from the microwave and put the chorizo back in for another 2 minutes on high. Meanwhile, put the aromatics and herbs into the slow cooker, give everything a good stir and pour in 5 cups of boiling water.
- When the chorizo is done, pour off the liquid and discard the liquid, and add the chorizo to the slow cooker, along with a bay leaf and a good pinch of salt. Give it all a good stir, cover, TURN THE HEAT DOWN TO LOW, and let it cook for 8 - 9 hours.
- No less than 30 minutes before you plan to serve the chili (or sooner if you like, but not until the beans are quite tender), turn the slow cooker up to High. Drain the juice from the tomatoes into a medium microwavable bowl or pitcher and cook on maximum power for 4 minutes.
- Meanwhile, remove a cup or so of broth from the beans and stir the tomato paste into it. Pour it back into the slow cooker.
- Open and drain the kidney beans, and coarsely chop the cilantro leaves.
- Put the heated tomatoes and the cilantro leaves into the slow cooker; add the orange zest and give everything a good stir to incorporate fully.
- Microwave the kidney beans for 3 minutes -- do it in the same bowl or pitcher you used for the tomatoes -- and then add them to the slow cooker. Meanwhile, remove the bay leaves from the slow cooker.
- Stir in the chipotles in adobo, if using. Test for salt and pepper and correct as necessary. Add more chipotles to taste. (We serve the sauce -- Frontera brand which is available at Whole Foods Market here -- on the side to allow people to add individually to taste.)
- Once the cooker has been on "High" for 30 minutes, feel free to turn it back down to "Low" or "Warm" until you're ready to serve. Stir in the lime juice right before serving.
- Serve with grated cheddar, lime juice-spiked sour cream, pickled red onions and good tortilla chips. (We use the chips instead of forks and spoons.)
- Make ahead tips: The night - or up to 2 days before - you can prep and microwave the chorizo. . . Prep and microwave the aromatics and herbs. . . Chop the celery (stir it into and store it with the onions, if you've cooked them) . . . and pick over the beans and put them right in the slow cooker with the bay leaf. Be sure to heat the cooked chorizo for

50

about two minutes, and the onions for about 2 minutes. Feel free to reheat them together for 5 minutes, if that's more convenient. If you're serving lime cream, that can also be made in advance. Give it a good stir and test for salt right before serving. If you're serving cheese, you can grate it up to 3 or 4 days in advance. If serving rice, you can make that up to 4 days beforehand, or take some out of the freezer and warm it up, if you've got some already made.

- If you are prepping the chorizo ahead of time (cutting and microwaving), you can reserve the cooking liquid, chill it, remove and discard the fat that rises to the top, and use the liquid to replace part of the water to be added to the slow cooker. Heat it in the microwave to near boiling before adding to the pot.

74. Choucroute Soup With Knoedels

Serving: Serves 4-6 | Prep: 0hours0mins | Cook: 0hours0mins | Ready in:

Ingredients

- For the Soup
- 3/4 pound sauerkraut
- 1/2 pound sweet Italian sausage
- 1   medium yellow onion, sliced into super thin ribs
- 2   garlic cloves, mashed
- 2   small bay leaves
- 1/4   teaspoon cumin seeds
- 4   juniper berries
- 8-9 cups beef broth
- Olive or vegetable oil
- Salt and freshly ground pepper
- For the Knoedels
- 2   egg whites
- 2 ounces Cream of Wheat (or farina)
- 2-3 cups beef broth (or water)
- A pinch of salt

Direction

- Rinse the sauerkraut well. Drain and set aside.
- Remove the sausage meat from the casing. Form tiny meatballs (about 1/2 to 3/4 inches in radius).
- Cover the bottom of a large skillet in oil. Add the sausage balls and sauté until nicely browned. Remove the sausage balls from the skillet and discard the fat.
- Cover the bottom of a large soup pot with oil. Add the onions and sauté until soft, for about three to four minutes. Add the garlic and cumin seeds and sauté for another minute or two, until very fragrant.
- Add the sauerkraut to the pot, cover with the broth and bring to a boil. Reduce the heat to medium low, add the sausage meatballs, bay leaves and juniper berries, and simmer partially covered for about an hour. When the soup is done, season with pepper (and if needed, with salt. I often find that both sauerkraut and sausage are seasoned well enough that no more salt is needed, but eventually it is up to you).
- While the soup is simmering, prepare the knoedels. In a small pot bring the broth (or water) to a gentle simmer.
- Beat the egg whites until firm. Slowly add the cream of wheat and continue to beat until fully incorporated. Season lightly with salt.
- Spoon about ¾ tablespoon of mixture per knoedel into the broth. Make sure that the broth maintains at simmer, otherwise the knoedels will fall apart. (You may want to make the knoedels in batches without overcrowding the pot, as the knoedels will expand slightly.) After three to four minutes, gently turn the knoedels and continue to simmer for another three to four minutes. Remove the knoedels from the broth.
- Pour the sauerkraut soup into the individual plates. Add the knoedels and then gently pour some more liquid from the soup. Serve immediately.

75. Chunky Butternut Squash And Potato Soup

Serving: Makes 8-10 servings | Prep: | Cook: | Ready in:

Ingredients

- 1 butternut squash (halved and seeds removed)
- 4 small/medium yukon gold potatoes (bite size cubes)
- 6 strips smoked bacon (cut into small pieces)
- 6 cups Zesty Herbed Chicken Broth (or regular low sodium chicken broth)
- 3 cups water
- 1/2 cup cream
- 1 tablespoon fresh thyme leaves
- olive oil
- salt and pepper

Direction

- Heat oven to 400 degrees. Coat halved butternut squash in olive oil, salt and pepper. Place on a baking sheet, cut side down, and bake for 40 minutes. Remove and let cool. When cool enough to work with, scoop out the soft squash and discard the skin. Cut into bite size cubes. Set aside.
- In a large soup pot, heat olive oil over medium heat. Add the bacon and cook until almost crisp. Drain about 1/2 the fat. Toss in onions, paprika, cayenne pepper, salt and pepper. Let soften for 10 minutes. Add garlic and cook for 3 minutes.
- Add the chicken broth, water and potatoes. Add a healthy amount of salt and pepper. Bring to a simmer. Using the homemade chicken broth really makes this dish. Let the potatoes cook for about 10 minutes, until soft. The starch from the potatoes will help thicken the broth.
- Add the butternut squash, cream and thyme. Let cook on medium low for 5 minutes, to make sure the squash is warmed through.
- At this point, you can serve chunky like it did, or run an immersion blender through the soup to make it creamy and smooth. Either way, delicious!

76. Chunky Mushroom And Asparagus Soup

Serving: Serves 8 | Prep: | Cook: | Ready in:

Ingredients

- .3 pounds Shiitake Mushrooms (sliced)
- .3 pounds Cremini Mushrooms (sliced)
- 3 medium size Portobello Mushrooms (roughly cube)
- Large bundle of Asparagus
- 1 large white onion (chopped)
- 2 large carrots (rough chop)
- 3 stalks celery plus leaved (rough chop)
- 2 tablespoons tomato paste
- 4 cloves garlic (minced)
- 4 cups Mushroom broth (homemade or store bought)
- 1/2 cup cream or half-and-half
- 3 sprigs fresh Thyme
- 1 teaspoon Crushed red pepper flakes
- 4 tablespoons unsalted butter
- Olive Oil
- Sea salt and freshly ground black pepper

Direction

- Preheat oven to 350 degrees. Put mushroom broth in a sauce pan over medium low heat with the sprigs of thyme.
- Clean and prep mushrooms. In 2 separate sauté pans, heat a little olive oil and 1 tbsp. butter in each pan over medium heat.
- In 1 of the sauté pans, add half the shitake and cremini mushrooms. Add some black pepper. Don't stir the mushrooms until after 5 minutes, and then flip and let them cook for 7 more minutes. Don't salt until last minute of cooking!
- Once the first half is done cooking, transfer to a plate, and add the other half of the

mushrooms, adding more oil and butter to the pan.

- In the other sauté pan, add the chopped up portobello mushrooms. Same rules apply. Don't move around, don't salt until the end.
- While the mushrooms are cooking, in a large soup pot, heat olive oil and 1 tbsp. of butter over medium heat. Add the onions, carrots, celery, tomato paste, garlic, crushed red pepper flakes and salt and pepper. Let this mixture cook for about 10 minutes, until all vegetables are nice and soft.
- While all vegetables are cooking on the stove top, trim the asparagus and put onto a baking sheet. Coat in olive oil and lots of salt and pepper. Put in the oven for 20 minutes.
- Once onion mixture has softened, add the mushroom broth to the pot, removing the thyme. Bring to a simmer.
- Carefully transfer the broth mixture to a large bowl.
- Remove the asparagus from the oven. All mushrooms should be on the plate cooling at this point. You're ready to start assembling the soup.
- Ladle 2 large scoops of the broth mixture and 1/4 of the asparagus to the food processor. Turn on and blend until smooth. (About 30 seconds) Return mixture to soup pot on stove over low heat. Repeat step until all broth and asparagus has run through the food processor.
- Add the 1/2 cup of cream to the soup and stir to combine.
- Put only the portobello mushrooms in the food processor. Hit the pulse button just once or twice. You want to get them into really small pieces, but large enough to give the soup texture. Add to the soup and combine.
- Finally, add the cremini and shiitake mushrooms to the soup. Add salt and pepper to taste.
- Let cook on very low heat for about 20 minutes to let flavors infuse. (It's actually best served the next day, reheated) Serve with a dollop of sour cream!

77. Cioppino (San Francisco Version Of Zuppa Di Pesce)

Serving: Serves 6 | Prep: | Cook: |Ready in:

Ingredients

- The Fish
- 24 small clams in shells
- 24 mussels
- 1 1/2 pounds halibut or other firm white fish
- 1 pound lge. shrimp in shells, split & deveined
- 3/4 pound Dungeness crabmeat or lobster meat
- The broth
- 1 medium yellow onion
- 6 sprigs Italian parsley
- 2-3 lge. garlic cloves
- 2 medium carrots
- 2 lge. stalks celery
- 1/4 cup good olive oil
- 28 ounces canned Italian plum tomatoes
- 14 ounces canned tomato puree
- 1 cup red Burgundy or other dry red wine
- 1 cup clam juice (or water)
- 2 tablespoons red wine vinegar
- 1 tablespoon crushed, mixed herbs (basil, rosemary, marjoram, oregano)
- 1 teaspoon red pepper flakes

Direction

- Place clams & mussels in a sink with cold water. Scrub the mussels to remove any grit and cut away the "beards" with a sharp knife.
- Chop the onion and parsley. Mince the garlic, carrots and celery.
- In a large pot with a tightly fitting lid, heat the olive oil and add the chopped/minced vegetables. Cook over low/medium heat until soft but not browned. (5-6 minutes stirring intermittently)
- Add the tomatoes, tomato puree, wine, clam juice, vinegar, herbs and red pepper flakes.

Bring to a boil, then lower heat and simmer uncovered for 30-40 minutes. Then place in another container. (This can be done ahead of time, cooled and refrigerated but be sure to bring back to a simmer before adding to the fish when finishing the soup.)

- While the soup is simmering, prepare the fish: Cut halibut into serving size pieces. Tear crabmeat or lobster into bite size pieces. Throw away any mussels or clams that float to the surface in the sink, drain in colander.
- Place the fish in the large pot, with the clams and mussels on the top. Pour over the soup that you've brought back to a simmer. Cover tightly and cook over low/medium heat for 20-25 minutes. Remove lid to see if all the clams and mussels have opened--if not, cook for another 5 minutes or until they open. It is unlikely that you'll need salt as the seawater released from the clams and mussels usually adds all the natural saltiness necessary.
- Serve in large heated bowls with a good crusty bread alongside and a simple salad. Red wine goes nicely with this but white is fine as well.

78. Clams In Spicy Lemon Bath

Serving: Makes a large pot | Prep: | Cook: |Ready in:

Ingredients

- 3 pounds Clams of your choice rinsed of sand
- 2 sprigs Large sprigs of lemon verbena
- 2 Stalks lemon grass sliced into half inch pieces
- 8 Cloves garlic peeled and sliced
- 2 Inch piece of chorizo diced
- 1 Onion sliced
- 1-3 Thai Chiles sliced in half.
- 1/2 Bottle of white wine, I use Sauvignon Blanc
- 1 Shallot sliced

Direction

- Place all ingredients in large pot except for the clams cover and bring to a boil. I like to do this to infuse a bit more flavor into the broth because the cooking time is so short.
- Add well washed clams and cook covered over medium to medium high heat for 5-10 minutes until clams open.
- Pour over pasta or eat with grilled bread.

79. Classic Virginia Brunswick Stew

Serving: Serves 6-8 | Prep: | Cook: |Ready in:

Ingredients

- 1.5 pounds boneless chicken breast or thighs (thighs are traditionally used)
- 1.5 ounces fatback, cut into 4 long slabs
- 4 cups cups of low sodium chicken stock (water is traditionally used)
- 1 pound Yukon Gold potatoes, peeled and chopped
- 1 yellow onion, chopped
- 1 teaspoon freshly ground black pepper
- 1/2 - 1 teaspoons cayenne pepper
- 1/2 teaspoon kosher salt, or to taste
- 3/4 - 1 tablespoons sugar
- 14 ounces canned, crushed, no-salt-added tomatoes plus their juices
- 14 ounces canned, drained butter beans (use fresh if in season)
- 14 ounces canned, drained white shoe peg corn, drained (use fresh if in season)
- 2 tablespoons unsalted butter, cut into small pieces
- Smoked paprika to taste

Direction

- Place the chicken and fatback in a large stockpot or Dutch oven. Cover with the chicken stock and bring to a boil over high heat. Reduce the heat to medium and cook, uncovered, for about 1 hour. Discard the fatback, and help the chicken shred (it will happen easily) in the pot with two forks.

- Next, add in the potatoes, onions, black pepper, cayenne pepper, salt and sugar. Increase the heat and bring the mixture to a boil. Then, reduce the heat to medium and cook, uncovered, until the potatoes are soft – roughly 30 minutes or so.
- After, stir in the tomatoes, their juices and the butter beans. Cook for another 15-20 minutes and then stir in the corn and butter pieces. Let the stew cook on low, uncovered, for an hour longer so it becomes nice and thick.
- Serve the stew hot and if you can't eat it all, store it in the freezer (after it cools) for another day!

80. Coconut Curry Noodle Soup

Serving: Serves 6-8 | Prep: | Cook: | Ready in:

Ingredients

- 1 pound firm tofu
- 8 ounces noodles of choice, I used brown rice pad thai noodles
- 1 tablespoon sesame oil
- 4 ounces carrot, thinly sliced
- 4 ounces snow peas
- 1 medium red bell pepper, thinly sliced
- 1 tablespoon sesame oil
- 1/2 cup onion, small dice
- 1 tablespoon garlic, minced
- 1 jalapeno, seeds intact or removed, minced
- 1 teaspoon ginger, minced or grated
- 1 - 3 teaspoons Thai red curry paste
- 1 teaspoon ground curry powder
- 1/2 teaspoon ground turmeric
- 1/4 teaspoon ground coriander
- 4 cups vegetable broth
- 15 ounces (1 can) coconut milk, regular or reduced fat
- 2 tablespoons tamari (or soy sauce)
- 2 tablespoons palm sugar (or white sugar)

Direction

- Bring a salted pot of water to a boil. Blanch tofu block for 1 minute (do not discard water). Slice horizontally in half and press between two plates lined with clean dish towels or paper towels. Allow tofu to press for 15 minutes, and slice into cubes.
- Return water to a boil, and boil noodles until al dente. Drain and toss noodles in 1 tablespoon sesame oil.
- Return the same pot to the stove, and heat an additional tablespoon of sesame oil over medium heat. Sauté the chopped onions, garlic, jalapeno, and ginger together, for several minutes until the onions are translucent. Add in the curry paste, ground curry powder, turmeric and coriander, and continue to sauté to heat the paste through.
- Whisk in the vegetable broth and coconut milk, bring to a boil. Season with tamari and palm sugar, and add in the vegetables {carrot, snow peas, and bell pepper}, and tofu, continuing to cook until vegetables are tender about 3 – 5 minutes.
- Place noodles in a bowl, and ladle hot soup over noodles, garnishing with sliced jalapenos, scallions, minced cilantro, roasted cashews, and lime wedges, if desired.

81. Coconut Noodle Soup With Crispy Fried Shallots

Serving: Serves 2 | Prep: | Cook: | Ready in:

Ingredients

- For the crispy shallots:
- 1 large shallot
- 1 tablespoon cornflour
- groundnut. sunflower or vegetable oil for deep frying
- For the soup:
- 1 tablespoon groundnut oil
- 2 tablespoons tom yum paste

- 1 thumb-sized piece of ginger, peeled and finely sliced
- 1 red chilli, finely chopped
- 100 milliliters coconut milk
- 1 large pak choi, chopped, green and white parts separated
- 1 green pepper, sliced
- 2 kaffir lime leaves
- 1-2 teaspoons fish sauce (to taste)
- 1 lime
- 1 handful sugar snap peas
- 5.5 ounces noodles
- 6 ounces raw king prawns
- 1 handful coriander, chopped
- 2 spring onions, finely sliced

Direction

- To make the shallots, peel and slice finely and toss in the corn flour. Heat the oil to 160C (if you have a thermometer, otherwise until a small chunk of bread sizzles and turns golden when you drop it in) and fry the shallots in batches until crisp and gold. Drain on kitchen paper.
- For the soup, heat the oil in a large saucepan and add the tom yum paste. Cook, stirring, until fragrant and add the ginger and chili, followed by the coconut milk.
- Once the noodles are a few minutes off being cooked, add the prawns, the green parts of the pak choi and a squeeze of lime. As soon as the prawns are pink and cooked through, add the coriander and check for seasoning adding more lime or fish sauce as desired.
- Ladle into bowls and top with spring onions and crispy shallots.

82. Coconut Pumpkin Soup

Serving: Serves 2 as a meal, 4 as a starter | Prep: | Cook: | Ready in:

Ingredients

- 1 teaspoon black mustard seeds
- 2 sprigs of curry leaves
- olive oil
- 1 small onion, chopped finely
- 1 teaspoon garlic, chopped finely
- 1 tablespoon ginger, chopped finely
- 1/2 tablespoon turmeric powder
- 1/2 teaspoon cayenne
- 1 1/2 cups pumpkin, mashed
- 1 can low-fat coconut milk
- salt and pepper to taste
- fresh coriander leaves for garnishing

Direction

- Heat up about a tablespoon of oil. Put in the mustard seeds and curry leaves and wait until the seeds to crackle.
- Then add the onion, garlic and ginger. Sauté until the onions caramelize slightly. Then add the turmeric and cayenne pepper powders and continue to cook for another minute or two.
- Add the pumpkin and cook on a gentle heat for about five minutes. Now add the coconut milk and stir gently until the pumpkin is well combined with it. Simmer gently for about ten minutes.
- Add seasonings and taste. Adjust accordingly. Serve garnished with some fresh coriander leaves along with crackers or toasted whole wheat bread.

83. Cold Red Pepper And Basil Soup

Serving: Makes 8-9 cups of soup | Prep: | Cook: | Ready in:

Ingredients

- Six large red peppers, roasted and peeled (If you are in a pinch, you can used jarred ones)
- 1 cup large basil leaves (Reserve the tops of the basil stalks for garnish)

- 2 Tablespoon basil infused olive oil (plus more for brushing the croutons)
- 1 ½ teaspoons chili oil
- 1 large sweet onion, chopped
- 4 garlic cloves, minced
- 1 Tablespoon tomato paste
- 2 cups good quality tomato juice
- 2 cups water
- 1 Tablespoon white sugar
- Sea salt
- Fresh ground black pepper
- Small loaf good French bread, cut on an angle for long croutons
- 3 Tablespoons of a good, aged cheddar, finely grated
- ½ cup of plain yogurt (if you can get goat yogurt, by all means, do!), thin this with a little milk so that it is about the same consistency as the chilled soup

Direction

- Puree the sweet peppers and basil in the food processor and set aside.
- Heat the oils in an ample heavy-bottomed saucepan. Sweat the onions until soft. Add minced garlic and cook for one more minute. Stir in the tomato paste and cook for 5 minutes more, stirring all the while.
- Stir in the processed peppers and basil, tomato juice and water. Add sugar and chili flakes. Bring to a gentle simmer and leave it there for 20 minutes to help incorporate the flavors.
- Remove from the heat and let the mixture cool for 10 minutes before seasoning with salt and pepper. Use an immersion blender to puree the soup completely. Cool completely.
- Just prior to serving, preheat the broiler. Cut the bread on an angle no thicker than ½-inch. Bush both sides of each elongated crouton with basil oil and place on a baking sheet under the broiler. Brown one side each of the croutons. Remove them from the oven, turn them over and sprinkle the cheddar cheese over them. Return them to the broiler so the cheese can melt and brown slightly.

- Portion the cold soup into bowls. Put 1-2 Tablespoons of thinned yogurt mixture in the center of each bowl of soup. Take a knife and make a swirl with the yogurt into the soup. Perch two croutons on top of the soup, garnish with the tops of the basil stalks and serve.

84. Corn And Coconut Chowder

Serving: Serves 2-4 | Prep: | Cook: | Ready in:

Ingredients

- Corn and Coconut Chowder
- 4 corn cobs, husks with silk removed
- 1 tablespoon coconut oil or olive oil
- 1 onion, chopped
- 2 garlic cloves, minced
- 1 red chile, seeded and chopped
- 1/4 lime, juiced
- 1/2 cup coconut milk
- 3/4 teaspoon sea salt
- sea salt and pepper
- basil oil, optional
- Basil Oil
- 1 cup basil leaves
- 1/2 cup extra-virgin olive oil
- sea salt, to taste

Direction

- Remove kernels from 4 corn cobs and set aside. Break corn cobs in half. I find this easiest to do with my hands.
- Make the corn stock. Heat oil in a medium pot over medium heat. Add onion and garlic and cook for 5-8 minutes or until softened. Add chile to onion mixture and cook 30 seconds. Add corn cobs and 2 cups of water, snuggling corn cobs under water as much as possible. Bring to boiling, then reduce heat to simmer. Allow to cook for 30 minutes.
- Remove corn cobs from stock and discard or compost. Reserve 1 cup corn kernels and set aside. Add remaining corn kernels and salt to

pot and cook for 5 minutes over medium heat. Allow mixture to cool briefly and then add to blender. Add lime juice coconut milk to blender and blend mixture until mostly smooth. Season to taste with salt and pepper.

- Meanwhile cook remaining corn kernels in now empty pot with a splash of water until just cooked, about 3-5 minutes. Sprinkle with sea salt.
- Ladle soup into bowls and spoon reserved cooked corn kernels over top. Drizzle with basil oil, if desired. Enjoy!
- To make the basil oil: Blanch basil oil for 10-20 seconds in boiling water. Cool immediately in ice bath. Drain and pat dry. Add to blender or food processor and add extra-virgin olive oil. Blitz until desired consistency is reached. Add a pinch or two of salt to taste. Can be stored in the refrigerator for up to 5 days. *You can skip the blanching step, knowing that the basil oil will not be quite as bright green due to oxidation. The flavor, however, will not be affected.

85. Cornish Hen Stew

Serving: Serves 4+ | Prep: | Cook: | Ready in:

Ingredients

- 2 Cornish Hens
- salt and black pepper to taste
- 2 tablespoons vegetable oil
- 8-10   dried red chiles
- 2 shallots, smashed and peeled
- 3 garlic cloves, smashed and peeled
- 1 inch piece of ginger, sliced thinly
- 2 stalks lemongrass, coarsely chopped
- 1 teaspoon ground tumeric
- 4 cups water
- 2 turnips, peeled and cubed
- 2 tablespoons fish sauce
- 2 scallions, sliced
- juice from 1 lime

Direction

- You want to start by breaking down both of the hens. Remove the wing tips and backbone. Separate the legs into drumsticks and thighs. Then remove the rib bones from the breasts.
- Season the hen pieces with salt and pepper. Heat the vegetable oil in a Dutch oven under medium high heat. Add the cornish hen pieces (I did 2 batches) and brown on both sides, about 4-6 minutes. Once browned, transfer the pieces to a plate.
- Add the dried chiles, shallots, garlic, ginger, lemongrass, and turmeric to the pot and stir until fragrant. This will be a whole lot of aromatics that will just smell AWESOME!
- Add in the water and turnips. Return the hen pieces to the pot and bring to a boil. Cover and lower heat to a simmer for about 15 minutes, until breasts are cooked through. Remove the breasts and cover with foil. Cook the remaining hen pieces for another 10 minutes.
- Return the breasts pieces and stir in fish sauce, scallions, and lime juice. Adjust seasoning to taste and then ladle into soup bowls!

86. Cozy Yellow Curry Vegetable Soup

Serving: Serves 3-4 | Prep: 0hours15mins | Cook: 0hours25mins | Ready in:

Ingredients

- 1 large onion, peeled and diced
- 3 stalks of celery, diced
- 2 small carrots, peeled and diced
- 2 garlic cloves, peeled and minced
- 1 to 2 tablespoons yellow curry paste (vegan or vegetarian, if required)
- 1 cup full-fat canned coconut milk (try to scoop out just the creamy part, keeping the watery stuff at the bottom to throw into some porridge or a smoothie)
- 4 cups veggie stock

- 1 tablespoon tamari
- 5 kaffir lime leaves
- 1 large sweet potato, scrubbed and cut into approximately 1" cubes
- 2 tablespoons coconut oil
- 1 cup frozen sweet peas
- sea salt, to taste
- 1/2 cup thinly sliced scallion greens
- 1/2 lime, plus more for garnish

Direction

- Preheat oven to 400 degrees Fahrenheit.
- Line a baking sheet with parchment paper. Toss sweet potatoes with 1 tablespoon of coconut oil and ½ teaspoon of salt, and roast on the baking sheet until golden and tender, about 20 minutes.
- Meanwhile, in a large soup pot set over medium-low heat, warm 1 tablespoon of coconut oil, then add the onion and sauté until lightly golden, about 5 minutes. Add the celery, carrot and garlic, and sauté for another five minutes or so.
- Add the yellow curry paste to the pot, and cook for 2 minutes, then add the coconut milk, tamari, lime leaves, and stock. Scrape the bottom of the pan with your spoon to ensure none of the veggie are sticking, then bring the mixture to a boil over high heat. Once mixture is boiling, reduce heat, and simmer for about 10 minutes, stirring occasionally. The broth should be slightly thickened at this point. If it isn't, simmer for a few minutes more.
- Once the mixture has been simmering for at least ten minutes and the sweet potatoes are cooked, add the sweet potatoes and peas to the pot, and cook for an additional two minutes. Add the juice of ½ lime, and season with salt (if required). Remove the lime leaves before serving.
- Serve, garnished with the scallion greens and a bit more lime juice, if desired.

87. Cream Of Asparagus Soup With Sorrel

Serving: Serves 6 as a first course | Prep: | Cook: | Ready in:

Ingredients

- 3 cups asparagus, chopped into 1" pieces
- 4 cups rich, homemade chicken stock
- 2 cups fresh sorrel leaves
- 1/2 cup minced chives
- 1/2 cup heavy cream

Direction

- Simmer the asparagus in the chicken stock for 10 minutes, or until tender.
- Ladle the stock and asparagus into the blender (careful, it's hot) and puree. Strain for smooth-like-velvet texture, or don't bother, for a more rustic texture.
- Slice the sorrel leaves into a chiffonade and mince the chives.
- Reheat the soup to a lazy simmer, stir in the sorrel and chives, then add the cream and bring the soup just short of a boil.
- Serve in small bowls with a few chives scattered over the top.
- Cream makes this soup extra rich and special. It's also nice just topped with a little dollop of Greek yogurt, for a lower calorie alternative.

88. Cream Of Carrot Soup With Fire Roasted Chiles, Toasted Pepitos And Crumbled Feta

Serving: Serves 4 as an appetizer | Prep: | Cook: | Ready in:

Ingredients

- 3 tablespoons olive oil
- 1/2 small yellow onion, diced

- 1 pound carrots, peeled and cut into 1/2-inch dice
- 2 cups chicken stock or water
- 1/2 cup raw pumpkin seeds (shelled)
- 1/4 teaspoon ground cumin
- 1/4 teaspoon chile powder
- 1 1/2 teaspoons kosher salt
- one 4-ounce can fire-roasted chiles
- 1 cup plain yogurt
- 1/4 cup crumbled feta cheese
- 1/4 cup loosely packed cilantro leaves
- 2 tablespoons pumpkin seed oil (optional)

Direction

- Heat 2 tablespoons of the olive oil over medium heat in a large saucepan. Add the onion and cook until soft, 4 to 5 minutes. Add the carrots and stock and bring to a boil. Cover and cook until tender, 15 to 20 minutes.
- While the carrots are cooking, heat the remaining 1 tablespoon olive oil in a small skillet over medium heat. Add the pumpkin seeds. Sprinkle the cumin and chile powder over the top and stir to coat evenly. When they begin to make popping sounds, stir frequently to prevent burning. Cook until slightly crisped, about 5 minutes. Sprinkle with 1/2 teaspoon salt. Set aside.
- Transfer the vegetables and liquid to a blender container and put on the top (You may need to do this in batches). Remove the center of the lid and cover with a clean towel to allow steam to escape. Puree until smooth. Add the chiles and yogurt, blend until completely smooth. Return to the pot, season with the remaining 1 teaspoon of salt and the pepper, and heat until warm. Ladle into bowls and sprinkle with each with toasted pumpkin seeds, crumbled feta and cilantro. Finish with a drizzle of pumpkin seed oil.

89. Cream Of Cauliflower Soup

Serving: Serves 6 (or 4 hungry people) | Prep: | Cook: | Ready in:

Ingredients

- 1 Large Cauliflower
- 4 cups Fresh Chicken Broth
- 5 tablespoons Unsalted Butter
- 1/3 cup White Flour
- 1 cup Half and Half
- Salt and White Pepper to Taste
- Pinch Ground Nutmeg

Direction

- Cut the cauliflower into rosettes, discarding the stem and leaves. Wash the rosettes and chop them into a pot. Add the stock and bring to a boil. Boil for about 10 minutes or until they are tender. Mash with a ricer. Melt butter for 30 seconds or until melted in the microwave. Add the flour and stir until it is combined well. Add some of the stock mixture to thin it, then add it into the stock pot stirring well, and continuing to stir until it is thickened. A whisk is great for this job. Add the half and half slowly. You may use milk or reduced fat milk to save calories, but the soup will not taste as rich. Add salt and white pepper to taste, and sprinkle with a hint of nutmeg. Heat just to a simmer and serve.

90. Creamed Pumpkin Soup

Serving: Serves 2 but can be scaled up | Prep: | Cook: | Ready in:

Ingredients

- 1 pumpkin weighing around 1lb (or 2 smaller pumpkins)
- 1/4 pint heavy cream
- 1 small garlic clove, flattened and peeled
- 2 ounces Gruyere cheese, grated

- salt and pepper

Direction

- Preheat the oven to 200C/Gas 6.
- Heat the cream with the garlic, salt and pepper until it barely simmers. Take off the heat and leave to infuse for 20 minutes.
- Slice off the top of the pumpkin a quarter of the way down to make a lid and keep to one side.
- Scoop out the seeds and stringy membrane.
- Strain the infused cream into the cavity and discard the garlic.
- Add the cheese. Top with the lid.
- Bake in a roasting tin in the oven for about 1 hour until the flesh of the pumpkin is tender when pierced with a fork. The skin should be lightly browned - turn the heat down slightly if it is becoming burnt.
- Lift off the lid and add the crisped sage leaves for decoration (if using) and serve with a crunchy salad.

91. Creamless Cream Of Mushroom Soup

Serving: Serves 4 | Prep: | Cook: |Ready in:

Ingredients

- 1/2 ounce Dried porcini mushroom
- 1 cup Boiling water
- 2 tablespoons Olive oil
- 4 Large shallots, sliced
- 4 ounces Baby portabella mushrooms, chopped
- 4 ounces White button mushrooms, chopped
- 3 Garlic cloves, peeled and minced
- 3 tablespoons Fresh chopped thyme
- 1/2 tablespoon Herbs de provence
- 1 Bay leaf
- 1/2 teaspoon Salt
- 1 teaspoon Fresh ground pepper
- 2 cups Low sodium chicken broth

- 1 cup 2% milk
- 3/4 cup Low fat Greek yogurt
- 1 1/2 tablespoons Cornstarch
- 3 tablespoons Fresh chopped parsley, plus more for garnish

Direction

- Place the porcini mushrooms in a small bowl and pour the boiling water over them. Set aside. Heat the olive oil in a large Dutch oven or stockpot over med-high heat. Add the shallots and sauté until translucent, about two minutes. Add the chopped portabella and button mushrooms continuing to cook until softened. Stir in the garlic, thyme, herbs de provence and bay leaf and cook for an additional 1 minute.
- Remove the porcini mushrooms from the water and roughly chop. Add the mushrooms and the mushroom infused water to the pot along with the salt and pepper stirring to combine. Add the broth to the mixture and bring to a boil.
- While the broth is coming to a boil, combine the milk, yogurt and cornstarch in the bowl of a mini food processor. Blend on low until thoroughly combined. You can also whisk in a small bowl by hand, just be sure the mixture is smooth and has no lumps.
- Add the milk/yogurt mixture to the pot and turn the heat down to med-low. Stir the soup constantly until the mixture begins to thicken. Approximately 4-5 minutes.
- Stir in the chopped parsley and serve immediately. You can top each serving with additional parsley or grated parmesan cheese.

92. Creamy Andalusian Gazpacho

Serving: Serves 4 | Prep: | Cook: |Ready in:

Ingredients

- 4 ripe, vine tomatoes

- 1 red capsicum
- 1/4 cucumber
- 2-3 slices of baguette or white bread
- 1/2 garlic clove, peeled and minced
- 3 tablespoons extra virgin olive oil
- 2 tablespoons white balsamic vinegar
- salt, cayenne pepper

Direction

- Core and dice the tomatoes, deseed the capsicum and cut the cucumber (lightly peel, if you prefer). Place all the ingredients, except seasoning, in a blender and whizz until smooth. Season with salt and cayenne pepper. Chill until you are ready to serve.

93. Creamy Broccoli Non Creamy Soup

Serving: Makes two quarts (maybe a little more) | Prep: | Cook: | Ready in:

Ingredients

- 2 tablespoons Extra Virgin Olive Oil
- 1 Large Vadilia Onion chopped bite size
- 1 Large Leek White part only chopped bite size
- 1 Medium size russet potato peeled and chopped bite size
- 2 boxes Low Sodium Fat Free Chicken Broth
- half cup Skim or low fat milk
- Salt and white pepper to taste
- small bunch broccoli tops

Direction

- Heat oil in large stock pot. Add chopped onion, and leek, cook for 5 minutes, add potato. Sweat veggies for about 5 minutes or until a little soft. Add chopped broccoli (cleaned stems and all) to pot. Cook another 5 minutes till broccoli starts to get a little soft.

- Add chicken broth salt and pepper to taste. Bring to slow boil and lower heat. Simmer till veggies are soft. About 20 minutes. Add milk. Use an immersion blender right in the pot but leave some broccoli pieces. The potato will make it "creamy". You can also use your regular blender in batches, but be careful, this is very hot. Serve with a crusty country bread. Any leftovers can be frozen, but I doubt there will be any.

94. Creamy Chilled Horseradish Soup With Tomato And Green Apple

Serving: Makes 3 cups | Prep: | Cook: | Ready in:

Ingredients

- For soup
- 30 ripe red cherry tomatoes
- 1 Granny Smith apple, peeled and cored, sliced and chopped
- 4 teaspoons prepared horseradish
- 1 garlic clove
- 3 tablespoons extra virgin olive oil
- 2 tablespoons apple cider vinegar
- Juice of 1/2 a lime
- 1/2 teaspoon sea salt plus more to taste if necessary
- For horseradish-dill-crème fraiche topping
- 2 tablespoons crème fraîche
- 1 teaspoon prepared horseradish
- 2 teaspoons fresh dill, snipped
- Squeeze or two of fresh lime wedges, to taste

Direction

- Halve cherry tomatoes. Place tomatoes and chopped apple into bowl of a food processor. Add remaining soup ingredients, and pulse until well combined. Taste for salt, adding more if necessary. Pulse again.

- Strain mixture through a sieve into a quart Pyrex measure or glass bowl. Press down on solids with a spatula to get the most out of the seeds and pulp. Continue to press on solids until quite dry and you have 3 cups of liquid. Discard solids. Cover strained soup with plastic wrap and chill for at least three hours, preferably overnight, to allow flavors to meld.
- When ready to serve, make your horseradish-dill-crème fraîche by combining ingredients in a small bowl, stirring until smooth. Remove soup from refrigerator, stir and taste, adjusting seasonings if necessary (salt, lime).
- Serve soup in small bowls and top with a dollop of the seasoned crème fraîche. Swirl in crème fraîche using a chopstick or spoon. Serve immediately. Enjoy!

95. Creamy Leek Soup

Serving: Serves 4 | Prep: | Cook: | Ready in:

Ingredients

- 2 - 3 leeks
- 8 ounces cream cheese (natural, if possible)
- 2 cups good chicken or vegetable stock
- 2 cloves roasted garlic (raw really won't do here)
- 1 small roasted onion, finely sliced.
- 1 tablespoon butter

Direction

- Slit the leeks in half. Slice the white and light green parts of the leeks into half-moons. Rinse under cold running water really well.
- Melt the butter over medium low heat until the foaming stops. Add the leeks, tossing them around a bit to make sure they're all coated with butter. Cover, and cook them until they're soft, but not browned.
- Add the roasted garlic and onion and mix in with the leeks. (The technical term I use is 'smush' the garlic and onions into the leeks.)

- Add the cream cheese in chunks, stirring it until it's melted. Stir in the chicken or vegetable stock, making sure there aren't any lumps of cream cheese floating around.
- Season with freshly ground pepper and sea salt to taste; heat until it barely simmers and serve. Some crispy crumbled bacon can be used as a final garnish. This reheats nicely if gentle heat is used on the stove or on low power in a microwave.

96. Creamy Mushroom Chestnut Soup

Serving: Serves 4 | Prep: | Cook: | Ready in:

Ingredients

- 3 tablespoons butter, divided
- 1 tablespoon olive oil
- 1/2 cup diced shallots
- 1 cup diced celery
- 2 1/2 cups peeled, diced red bliss potatoes (about 3)
- 8 cups mixed mushrooms, cremini and white button (about 2 1/2 pounds)
- 4 cups mushroom broth
- 8 ounces cooked chestnuts (about 20)
- 1/2 teaspoon ground cinnamon
- 1/4 teaspoon ground nutmeg
- 1 tablespoon fresh chopped rosemary
- 1 tablespoon fresh chopped sage
- 1/4 teaspoon sea salt
- 1/4 teaspoon freshly ground black pepper
- 1 1/2 cups cream
- fresh sage, rosemary, and chopped chestnuts for optional garnish

Direction

- Warm 2 tablespoons butter and olive oil in a large, deep pot over medium heat. Add shallots and celery, and sauté 3-5 minutes. Add potatoes and mushrooms, and cook for 8-10 minutes, or until mushrooms have released most of their liquid. Add broth, and bring to a boil. Reduce to low, and cook until potatoes are tender, about 10-12 minutes. Add chestnuts, cinnamon, nutmeg, rosemary, sage, salt, pepper, and cream. Turn off heat, and let cool for 10 minutes before pureeing.

- Working in batches, puree the soup in a blender until smooth; return to the pot over low heat. Stir occasionally until the soup is thoroughly heated, about 10 minutes. Just prior to serving, stir in remaining 1 tablespoon butter for added creaminess and depth of flavor. Season to taste with salt and black pepper.
- Garnish individual bowls with fresh herbs and chopped chestnuts, if desired.

97. Creamy Mushroom Soup

Serving: Serves 4 | Prep: | Cook: | Ready in:

Ingredients

- 3-4 cups mixed mushrooms of your choice (crimini, chanterelle, oyster, white button, etc.)
- 32 ounces veggie or beef stock
- 1/2 large yellow onion (sliced)
- 4 sprigs fresh thyme
- 2 tablespoons butter
- 2 tablespoons flour
- 2 tablespoons heavy cream
- 2 tablespoons sour cream
- 2 tablespoons olive oil
- 1/2 teaspoon chipotle chile pepper (more or less depending on your heat level preference)
- 1 teaspoon dried oregano
- 1 teaspoon truffle oil (optional)!

Direction

- In 2 quart pot, heat olive oil and add onions.
- Sauté the onions on medium heat and add the mushrooms.
- After the onions and mushrooms look golden, add thyme and stock.

- Bring the stock up to a simmer and cover. Cook covered on low heat for about 30 - minutes.
- Take off heat and let the soup cool. Start pureeing the soup in small batches, in a food processor or blender. Pour the blended mixture into a separate bowl.
- Using the same pot, melt butter and add flour on low heat while whisking constantly for a minute or two. You want the flour taste to cook off but make sure it does not burn or lump.
- While constantly whisking the roux (flour and butter mix), slowly pour the mushroom puree back into the pot. Keep stirring the mixture to prevent lumps until hot.
- Add sour cream and heavy cream.
- Crush the dried oregano in your palms and add to the soup, along with chipotle powder, salt and pepper to taste.
- Serve with some sourdough bread or a baguette.
- **If you are feeling crazy and would like to jazz this up with a touch of truffle oil, do this as the last step--either a tiny drizzle on each serving or about a teaspoon to the whole batch right before serving**

98. Creamy Pea Soup With Fresh Mint

Serving: Serves 4 | Prep: | Cook: | Ready in:

Ingredients

- 1 kg frozen peas
- 50 g bacon
- 1 onion, diced
- 1 tablespoon chopped garlic
- 1 tablespoon freshly chopped mint
- 4 tablespoons light cream to serve
- Salt and pepper to taste

Direction

- Super easy and quick! Heat up the pot, melt bacon. Sweat onions, add garlic.
- Mix in the peas. Add water just to cover the veggies.
- Boil for 15min. Season with salt and pepper. Blend till silky creamy.
- Drizzle with cream and sprinkle with mint. Enjoy!

99. Creamy Potato Soup With Bacon Vinaigrette

Serving: Serves 6 | Prep: | Cook: | Ready in:

Ingredients

- For the Soup
- 1 tablespoon butter
- 1 large onion diced
- 1 large carrot diced
- 1 rib celery diced
- 3 cloves garlic diced
- 1 sprig rosemary chopped
- 1 teaspoon salt
- 6 medium Russet potatoes (about 2 lbs.) peeled and diced into 1" cubes
- 7 cups chicken stock or water
- 1 cup low fat sour cream
- salt and pepper to taste
- For vinaigrette
- 4 pieces thick cut bacon
- 3 green onions finely sliced
- 3 tablespoons white wine vinegar
- 2 tablespoons olive oil
- pinch salt

Direction

- Add butter to large pot on medium high heat and melt
- Add carrot, onion, celery, garlic, rosemary and salt. Saute veggies until onions are soft, about 10 minutes.

- Add potatoes and stock. Cook on medium high until potatoes are very tender, about 20 minutes
- Turn off heat, add sour cream and puree in blender or with immersion blender
- To make vinaigrette, cook bacon until crispy on medium high heat. Drain fat onto paper town and chop into small pieces.
- To small bowl stir onions, bacon, vinegar, salt. Add oil and put 1 tbsp. of vinaigrette on top of each bowl of soup.

100. Creamy Red Lentil And Kale Soup

Serving: Serves 4 | Prep: | Cook: | Ready in:

Ingredients

- 1 1/2 cups organic red lentils (uncooked)
- 2 3/4 cups organic vegetable broth
- 1 organic full-fat coconut milk (13.5 oz can)
- 3 organic roma tomatoes (small/diced)
- 1/2 organic onions (large/diced)
- 1 cup organic kale (chopped)
- 2 tablespoons organic tomato sauce
- 1 1/2 teaspoons organic ground cumin powder
- 1 teaspoon pink himalayan salt
- 1 - 2 pinches organic ground cayenne pepper

Direction

- Prepare veggies: dice onions and tomatoes and chop kale into small pieces.
- Put all ingredients (EXCEPT: chopped kale and coconut milk) into a medium-sized pot, stir well and bring to a boil.
- Reduce heat to simmer (low/medium) and cover and cook for 30 - 40 minutes (or until the lentils are soft), stirring occasionally.
- Remove from heat, add the chopped kale and coconut milk, stir well.
- Add additional vegetable broth/pink himalayan salt/seasonings, if needed.

101.   Creamy Tomato Tortellini + Italian Meatball Soup

Serving: Makes 1 large pot of soup | Prep: | Cook: |Ready in:

Ingredients

- Base of soup
- 32 ounces chicken broth
- 10.5 ounces cream of chicken soup (1 can)
- 3 cans Hunts diced tomatoes (basil, garlic, oregano)
- 1 teaspoon minced garlic (jar)
- 1 tablespoon dry minced onion
- 1.5 tablespoons italian seasoning
- 1/4 teaspoon red pepper flakes
- 2 bay leaves
- 19 ounces Louisa cheese tortellini (any brand will work!)
- 2 cups heavy whipping cream
- 3 cups fresh chopped kale
- sea salt to taste
- black pepper to taste
- garnish with red pepper flakes and 4 Italian cheese
- Italian Meatballs
- 1/2 pound italian sausage
- 1/2 pound ground beef
- 1 tablespoon italian seasoning
- 1/2 cup bread crumbs (Italian)
- 1/4 cup 4 Italian shredded cheese
- 1 tablespoon dry minced onion
- 1/2 teaspoon minced garlic (jar)
- 1 egg
- sea salt to taste
- black pepper to taste
- olive oil to brown meatballs

Direction

- Base of soup

- Place chicken broth, cream of chicken, canned tomatoes (juice and all), garlic, minced onion, Italian seasoning, red pepper flakes, bay leaves, salt and pepper in a large pan on stove. We start to let this simmer when prepping other ingredients.
- Now go make the meatballs. Recipe below. After browning the meatballs on the skillet, add them to your soup. Right before serving cook, your tortellini per directions on package in a separate pan. Add tortellini, chopped kale, and heavy whipping cream. Stir and simmer until warm!
- Top your bowl with red pepper flakes and 4 Italian shredded cheese! Serve with warm buttered focaccia or French bread!
- Italian Meatballs
- Place all ingredients in a bowl and mix with hands until all ingredients are mixed. Roll into small balls (about a teaspoon worth of meat). We put olive oil in a skillet on medium and browned the outsides and let them finish cooking in the simmering soup!

102.   Creamy Vegan Parsnip Soup

Serving: Serves 1-2 | Prep: | Cook: |Ready in:

Ingredients

- 3 small parsnips, peeled and chopped
- 1/4 white onion
- 1 teaspoon olive oil
- 1 cup white beans
- 1 teaspoon caraway seeds
- 1 teaspoon mustard seeds
- 2 cups Stock (Vegetable if you want vegan, chicken if you'd like)

Direction

- Heat the oil on medium in a heavy bottom saucepan, add chopped onion, mustard seeds and caraway seeds. When the mustard seeds begin to pop and the onion begins to brown, add the stock. Once the stock gets warm add the beans and parsnips.

- When the parsnips are nice and soft, turn off the heat. Blend the soup either with an immersion blender in the pot, or carefully in a blender. Feel free to add more water or stock to achieve your desired thickness. Add salt and pepper to taste. This can easily be made in advance and re-heated on a low simmer before serving.

Serving: Makes 6 cups | Prep: | Cook: |Ready in:

Ingredients

- 1 tablespoon olive oil
- 1 tablespoon butter
- 1 onion, chopped
- 8 baby leeks, sliced
- 4 celery sticks (about 10cm) sliced
- 500 grams peeled and cubed butternut
- 2 medium potatoes, peeled and cubed
- large pinch of sea salt flakes
- ½ teaspoons turmeric
- ½ teaspoons ground ginger
- 1 teaspoon ground cinnamon
- 1 liter chicken or vegetable stock
- 150 milliliters cream
- 2 tablespoons sherry
- cream/parsley/black pepper/flaked almonds to garnish (optional)
- toasted ciabatta to serve (optional)

Direction

- Heat the olive oil and butter in a large pot over a low heat. Add the onion, leeks, celery, butternut and potatoes. Cover the pot and leave the vegetables to sweat for 10 minutes. Shake the pan regularly to prevent them from sticking to the bottom.

- Increase the heat to medium. Add the salt, turmeric, ginger and cinnamon and stir for a minute or two. Add the stock and stir well. Leave to simmer until the vegetables are tender, about 20-25 minutes.
- Set the pot aside to cool for a few minutes. Use a food processor or stick blender to puree the soup until smooth.
- Return the soup to the pot and stir in the cream and sherry. Heat through over a low heat. Check the seasoning and serve.

Serving: Serves 4 | Prep: | Cook: |Ready in:

Ingredients

- 1 green pepper
- 2 stalks celery
- 4" pieces greenhouse cucumber, or pickling cuke
- 1 large shallot
- 2 cloves garlic
- 1/4 -1/2 cups cilantro, packed
- 1 tablespoon olive oil
- 1 tablespoon balsamic vinegar
- 1 1/2 tablespoons lime juice with pulp
- 1/2 teaspoon cumin
- 1/8 teaspoon thyme
- 1 10 oz. can Ro-tel Chunky Diced Tomatoes & Green Chilies
- 1 avocado, ripe
- yogurt (regular, not Greek-style)

Direction

- Cut peppers, celery, cucumber, shallot, garlic in rough dice. Chop in the food processor. Cut cilantro roughly, pulse in the food processor with the other vegetables.
- Mix oil, vinegar, juice, spices in serving bowl, add chopped vegetables, contents of the Rotel

can. Cut the avocado in small dice and stir into the bowl.

- At serving, top with a good spoonful of yogurt. Mixed in or not, it adds another dimension to complete the flavor. If it is made a few hours ahead, the chile taste will infuse the dish. It is good the next day, but will be more liquid.

105. Crock Pot Chicken Soup To Come Home To On A Busy Evening

Serving: Serves 6 | Prep: | Cook: | Ready in:

Ingredients

- 1 whole chicken OR 3-6 chicken thighs
- 2 carrots, peeled and cut into strips with a vegi peeler
- 1 parsnip, peeled and cut into strips with a vegi peeler
- 1 onion, quartered and cut into thin slices
- 4-5 celery stalked, peeled and cut into thin strips with a vegi peeler
- 4-7 garlic cloves, crushed
- 1 T salt
- 2 T dried marjorum
- 15 grinds of black pepper - medium grind
- 1/2 to 3/4 bottle of cheap white wine
- 1 1/2 wine bottle of water
- spash of wine vinegar
- 6 thick slices of cheesy toast
- 6 eggs, fried in olive oil with soft yolks
- balsamic vinegar to taste
- harissa to taste

Direction

- Put veggies, herbs and spices into a crock pot/slow cooker, and mix together with hands. Nestle the chicken into the veggies. Put the wine and water into the crock pot, small splash of wine or champagne vinegar. Set the

counter top crock pot on LOW for 8-10 hours. Do this in the morning before you leave the house, and you will come home to yummy soup The chicken will fall off the bones (you May want to remove the bones before serving. One way to do this is to loosely wrap the chicken in cheese cloth before putting into the crock pot. When the chicken is cooked the cheese cloth package can be lifted out and the chicken can be boned... but I never do this. I should because it is a PIA to remove the bones!)

- Before serving you need to do two things. (1) Toast some thick bread with sliced cheese of your choice on top. Cheap Parmesan is particularly good here. (2) Quick fry some eggs sunny-side up in a hot olive-oiled skillet till whites are cooked but tender, and yolks are still soft.
- To serve: Ladle and some soup into a bowl till about 1/3 full. Add a thick slice of toasted cheesy toast, add more soup, but leave some room for the topping. Top the whole thing with a fried egg. Dress the egg with a drizzle of balsamic vinegar and a small blop of harrisa paste.
- Serve with a big but simple green salad

106. Crunchy Sweet Potato Fries Or "Croutons"

Serving: Serves 4 | Prep: | Cook: | Ready in:

Ingredients

- 2 sweet potatoes or yams
- 2 tablespoons olive oil
- sea salt

Direction

- Preheat oven to 450 degrees.
- Slice sweet potatoes into small, ½-inch cubes.

- Add sweet potatoes to a medium bowl with olive oil and a few sprinkles of sea salt. Stir until sweet potatoes are completely coated.
- Arrange sweet potatoes on a parchment-lined baking sheet (if they are too crowded, they'll come out mushy, so you might want to use two baking sheets to give your potatoes more "personal space".
- Pop them in the oven for 15-20 minutes and bake until lightly browned and crunchy at the corners
- Let cool then serve on top of salad, soup, or as a side dish.

107.   Cucumber Honeydew Soup

Serving: Serves 2 bowls | Prep: | Cook: |Ready in:

Ingredients

- 1 cup English cucumber - peeled and chopped
- 1 cup ripe honeydew melon, peeled seeded and chopped
- 1/2 cup coconut water (I used Zico)
- 2 tablespoons lemon yogurt
- 2 mint leaves
- paper thin slices of peeled cucumber and chopped mint for garnish

Direction

- Blend the cucumber, melon, yogurt and coconut water until smooth, then pour through a strainer to remove any lumps. Put in the fridge to chill.
- Chill 2 bowls. Stir the soup back together (it will separate a little) and pour into the bowls. Top each with thin slices of cucumber and mint and serve. That's all there is to it!!

108.   Curried Carrot Ginger Soup

Serving: Serves 6 | Prep: | Cook: |Ready in:

Ingredients

- 3-4 small potatoes, peeled and chopped
- 6 carrots, peeled and chopped
- 2 tablespoons canola oil
- 1 yellow onion, chopped
- 1 piece ginger (3 inches or more), peeled and chopped
- 1 cube vegetable bouillon (vegan-friendly preferred)
- 4-5 cloves boiled or roasted garlic, crushed into a paste
- 1 can coconut milk
- 1/2 teaspoon nutmeg
- 1 tablespoon curry powder, plus more (1/2 tsp.) at the end
- 1/4 teaspoon kosher salt (add only if needed; the bouillon should be enough)
- 1/2 teaspoon freshly grated black pepper
- 2-4 teaspoons chopped chives for garnish

Direction

- Boil the potatoes in 3-4 cups of water until tender, about 20 minutes. When the water comes to a boil, add the bouillon and stir to help it dissolve. Once the potatoes are tender. Turn the burner off and let them sit in the pot.
- In the meantime, pour the oil into a soup pot on medium heat. Add the onion, half the carrots, the ginger, nutmeg, curry powder, salt (if using additional salt), and pepper. Sauté for 6-8 minutes, stirring with a wooden spoon.
- Add the remaining carrots, the cooked potato, and the broth. Add 1 additional cup water, and stir. At this stage, you can also add the crushed garlic, which will resemble a paste.
- Bring to a boil, then reduce heat and simmer, covered, until the carrots are tender, about 25-30 minutes.
- In a blender or food processor, blend 3 ladlefuls of the soup.

- Return the blended soup to the pot with the remaining soup (if you prefer a fully pureed soup, puree it all; if, like most Americans, you like "stuff" in your soup, puree less for more texture).
- Then, stir in the coconut milk (make sure to shake the can of coconut milk before opening it; also, stir it before adding it to the soup to break it up).
- Add more curry powder, salt and/or pepper to taste. Ladle into bowls and garnish with the chopped chives. Enjoy!

109. Curried Corn And Zucchini Bisque With Crab

Serving: Serves 6-8 | Prep: | Cook: | Ready in:

Ingredients

- 1 tablespoon coconut or olive oil (or sub unsalted butter)
- 4 ears sweet corn, husked and de-silked
- 1 quart vegetable broth
- 1 bunch cilantro, well-washed and squeezed dry
- 1 small (or half of a bigger) red bell pepper, finely diced (1/2 cup, give or take)
- 2 jalapeno peppers, seeded and deribbed (or not, if you prefer more heat), minced, divided
- 2 green onions, thinly sliced
- 4 small-medium zucchini, chopped (3-4 cups; reserve 1/2 cup, finely diced, for the garnish)
- 4 ounces lump crab meat, picked over
- 2 tablespoons unsalted butter, or sub coconut oil
- 1 medium-large onion, chopped (2 cups)
- 1 pound yukon gold potatoes, peeled and cubed
- 2 tablespoons fresh ginger root, minced or grated
- 1 tablespoon curry powder, preferably hot (Julie Sahni's master recipe is a good one)
- 1 can coconut milk (13.5-15 oz)

- lime juice to taste (start with the juice of half a lime and adjust from there)
- salt and pepper, to taste
- 1/4 cup mint, finely chopped, plus extra for garnish

Direction

- Start by making a corn broth: Cut kernels from 4 ears of fresh corn. You should have about 3 cups, maybe a little more. Set aside one third for the garnish, and reserve the other two thirds for the soup. Put the corn for the soup in a bowl and, working over it, scrape the cobs with the back of your knife to extract the sweet corn "milk." Set the bowl aside. Break the scraped cobs up into pieces that will fit comfortably in a saucepan and pour the vegetable broth over. Pluck enough leaves and soft stems from the cilantro to make about 1/2 cup finely chopped. Set aside 2 tbsp. for the garnish, and the rest for the soup. Take a handful of the cilantro stems and toss them in with the corn cobs and vegetable broth. Simmer slowly, covered, on a back burner over low heat while you do the rest of your prep.
- Next, make the crab, corn, and pepper garnish: In a medium skillet (a 10-incher is good) over medium heat, warm 1 tbsp. coconut or olive oil (or butter). Add the 1/3 of the corn kernels you reserved for the garnish, along with the green onions, the bell pepper, half the minced jalapeno, and your reserved 1/2 cup of finely diced zucchini. Sauté 5 minutes or until lightly browned and the corn is tender, but not mushy. Remove from heat and season with salt. Let cool slightly, then gently fold in crab meat and cilantro. Adjust for seasoning and set aside until ready to serve.
- Now make the soup: Melt butter or coconut oil in a large soup pot or Dutch oven over medium heat. Add onions and sauté until tender and translucent and beginning to brown, 5-10 minutes. Add potatoes and cook for a minute or so. Add the remaining corn kernels (and accumulated corn milk), the

remaining jalapeno, zucchini, ginger, curry powder, and a good pinch of salt. Stir well and cook for another minute or so, then strain your corn-and-cilantro-infused vegetable broth into the pot. Bring to a boil. Reduce heat, cover, and simmer until potatoes are tender, 15 minutes or so. Stir in coconut milk, the juice of half a lime, the mint, and the remaining cilantro (retain a few pinches for additional garnish). Remove the pot from heat and let cool.

- Puree in batches in a blender or food processor, or directly in the pan using an immersion blender. Put pureed soup through a fine-mesh sieve to remove any stray solids (such as corn or zucchini skins) and ensure a velvety-smooth consistency. Add a little water or additional broth if soup is too thick. Adjust for lime juice and salt. Cool to room temperature, then chill in refrigerator several hours before serving, but preferably overnight, as this is definitely better the next day. (Taste again for salt once the soup is properly chilled--cold soups often need more salt than warm ones.) When ready to serve, ladle soup into shallow bowls and garnish each with a heaping spoonful of the crab, corn, and pepper mixture. Scatter additional cilantro and mint over and serve.

---

110. Curried Pumpkin Soup With Preserved Lemons

Serving: Serves 4-6 | Prep: | Cook: | Ready in:

Ingredients

- 1 pumpkin, cut into manageable pieces
- 4 tablespoons butter, melted
- sea salt
- 2 tablespoons walnut oil
- 1 medium onion, diced
- 4 teaspoons sweet curry powder (Penzey's is great)

- 4 cups chicken broth
- 2 cans coconut milk (full fat)
- 1 teaspoon fresh ginger, grated
- 1/4 teaspoon cayenne
- 1/4 preserved lemon, peel and pith only, diced fine
- salt and pepper as needed

Direction

- Preheat the oven to 365. Split the pumpkin manageable size pieces and remove the seeds. Brush with melted butter (or you can use some additional walnut oil) and sprinkle with sea salt. Roast for about an hour (it took me 85 minutes so translating to sea level will probably put it around the hour mark). When the pumpkin has cooled enough to handle, remove the skins and cut into smaller pieces
- In a heavy bottomed large pot, heat walnut oil until hot. Add the diced onion and cook until soft and translucent, about 7 minutes.
- When the onions are done, add the chicken broth and pumpkin and bring to a boil. Reduce heat and add the curry powder. Simmer for about an hour.
- When the vegetables are soft enough, remove from heat and puree using an immersion blender. Don't stress a few lumpy bits.
- Return to low heat. Add the coconut milk, grated ginger, cayenne and preserved lemons (don't forget to rinse the lemons well). Stir and let it sit around and ponder the mysteries of life until the ingredients have had a chance to get to know one another. Only then should you add salt if it needs any.

---

111. Curried Spinach And Cilantro Soup

Serving: Serves 4-6 | Prep: | Cook: | Ready in:

Ingredients

- 2 1/2 tablespoons butter (or ghee)

- 1 large yellow onion, chopped
- 2-3 garlic scapes, sliced
- 2 medium russet potatoes, peeled and diced
- 1 can light coconut milk
- 2 cups water or vegetable stock
- 1 1/2 tablespoons thai curry powder
- 5 cups tightly packed spinach leaves, stems removed
- 1 cup cilantro stems, leaves reserved for garnish
- juice of 2 limes
- salt and pepper, to taste

Direction

- Heat butter in a large pot over medium-high until melted. Lower heat, slightly, and add onions. Sauté until tender and lightly browned, about 8 minutes. Add garlic scapes and potatoes and cook until scapes are fragrant, about 1 minute. Add coconut milk, water, and curry powder and bring mixture to a boil. Reduce heat to low, cover, and simmer until potatoes are fork-tender, about 20 minutes.
- Once potatoes are cooked, add spinach leaves and cilantro stems and stir until spinach is wilted and soft, about 5 minutes. Using an immersion blender (or a food processor, in two batches) puree soup until smooth and creamy. Season with salt and pepper, stir well, and remove from heat. Add lime juice and stir to combine. Serve soup hot with a handful of cilantro leaves in each bowl, to garnish.

112. Curried Summer Squash Soup

Serving: Serves 4 | Prep: | Cook: | Ready in:

Ingredients

- 3-4 russet potatoes peeled and diced
- 4 zucchini or summer squash, peeled and cut into 1/2 inch pieces

- 1 yellow onion, diced
- 1 tablespoon minced garlic
- 1/3 teaspoon ground tumeric
- 1/3 teaspoon garam masala
- 1/3 teaspoon ground ginger
- 1/3 teaspoon ground coriander
- 1/3 teaspoon ground cumin
- 1/3 teaspoon chili powder (optional)
- large pinches dried fenugreek leaves, stems picked out
- large pinches dried parsley
- 3 cups chicken stock
- vegetable oil
- extra virgin olive oil
- apple cider vinegar
- salt, pepper, and tabasco to taste
- 3/4 cup milk

Direction

- In a heavy skillet, heat oil, bacon fat, butter, schmaltz, whatever tickles you're fancy. (I used chicken drippings and extra virgin olive oil)
- Add the onions and sauté over medium heat until golden, with a pinch of kosher salt and a few grinds of pepper.
- A few minutes into the cooking process, add the garlic. Stir frequently to assure nothing burns.
- In the stockpot, heat two tablespoons of vegetable oil on medium heat.
- Once the oil is bubbling, add the spice mix and let them bloom in the hot oil, stirring constantly so that they don't burn.
- After a minute, add the diced potatoes to the spice oil and sauté – try to get a nice browning on the potatoes if you can- it's okay if some pieces stick to the bottom of the pot.
- Once the onions are soft, add them to the potato spice mixture.
- Place the zucchini/squash slices in the skillet, stirring them around and scraping up any burned on goodness left by the onions and fat. If you need some extra liquid to accomplish this, a splash of chicken stock will help. Cook two minutes.

- Add the squash to the stock pot, stir well, and add enough chicken broth to cover the vegetables.
- Scrape the bottom of the stockpot with a spatula to free anything that burned on during the cooking process.
- Add the fenugreek leaves and parsley.
- Turn heat to medium low. Cover and cook until the potatoes are soft, about 20 minutes.
- When the potatoes break apart easily with your spoon, turn the heat to low. You can puree the soup with a hand blender or in a Cuisinart (please be careful!) or do what I did and just have at it with a potato masher.
- Drizzle in the milk and stir.
- Season to taste. Salt and Pepper for sure, plus a splash of cider vinegar and a few shakes of Tabasco to brighten flavors.

---

113.   Curried Sweet Potato Soup

Serving: Makes about 8 cups | Prep: | Cook: |Ready in:

Ingredients

- 1 1/2 tablespoons olive oil
- 1 2/3 cups coarsely chopped onion
- 1 large clove garlic, coarsely chopped
- 1 tablespoon coarsely grated ginger
- 1 teaspoon ground cumin
- 1/2 teaspoon ground coriander
- 1/4 teaspoon ground cardamom & tureric, each
- 1/8 teaspoon hot pepper flakes, optional
- 2 1/2 pounds sweetpotatoes, peeled and sliced 1/4 inch thick
- 6 cups no-salt-added chicken stock
- salt and freshly ground black pepper to taste
- 8 teaspoons fresh goat cheese

Direction

- Heat oil in a nonstick pot large enough to hold all the ingredients. Sauté onion until it begins

to brown, about 10 minutes. Add garlic, and sauté, stirring, for 30 seconds.
- To make the curry flavoring, add ginger, cumin, coriander, cardamom, turmeric and optional hot pepper flakes, and stir well. Add sweet potatoes and stock, and bring to a boil. Reduce heat, and simmer for about 20 minutes, until sweet potatoes are soft.
- Puree soup in batches in blender or food processor. Season to taste with salt and pepper. (Soup can be made ahead of time and refrigerated. Reheat slowly to serve.) If soup is too thick, add a little more stock. Ladle into mugs, top each serving with a teaspoon of cheese, and stir to melt a little – adds a wonderful tanginess!

---

114.   Curry Butternut Squash Soup

Serving: Serves 8-10 | Prep: | Cook: |Ready in:

Ingredients

- 2 medium butternut squashes
- 3 tablespoons olive oil
- 1 medium onion
- 3 carrots
- 2 tablespoons madras curry
- salt and peper to taste
- 1 can light coconut milk
- 1/2 cup chicken broth
- 3 tablespoons tomato paste

Direction

- Preheat the oven to 350
- Cut the squashes in have and remove seeds. Light brush with about 1 tablespoon of the olive oil. Bake until soft - about 45 minutes. Use a fork to test the neck of the squash.
- Meanwhile, heat the remaining 2 tablespoons of olive oil and sauté onions and carrots in a large pot until starting to soften. Add in curry

and salt and pepper and continue to cook until soft.

- When the squash is done, scoop out and add it into onions and carrots and mix together.
- Place squash mixture in a blender or food processor and mix until smooth.
- Put squash mixture back into pot and add in coconut milk and chicken broth (you may want to add more broth depending on how thick or thin you like your soup) and mix until well combined.
- Add in tomato paste and mix well.
- Simmer the soup until flavors have combined - about 15 - 20 minutes - and serve!

115. Curry Pho With Veal And Veggies

Serving: Serves 5-6 | Prep: | Cook: | Ready in:

Ingredients

- 1 tablespoon olive oil
- 1   medium onion, cut into quarters and then 1/4" slices
- 1 pound ground veal
- 2 tablespoons curry powder
- 10 cups vegetable broth or vegetable pho
- 5.5 ounces brown rice udon noodles
- 4   kale stalks- main artery removed, rolled and cut in chiffonade
- 1/3   of a bunch of beet greens, stalks separated from greens and greens sliced thin
- 3/4   of an orange pepper cut into 1/3" squares
- 1/4 cup chopped oil-cured black olives
- 1   tomatilla chopped
- 1 handful sorrel leaves, leaves sliced, stems chopped for garnish (or use sliced scallions)
- salt to taste

Direction

- Warm the olive oil with the onions in a large skillet. Cover and sweat the onions for 5 minutes on low heat. Add the ground veal and

brown partially, until just pink and broken up into small chunks. Add the curry powder and salt to taste. Stir well to combine.

- Meanwhile pour the broth into a large soup pot and bring to a boil. Add the udon and cook 2 minutes less than the package directions.
- Turn heat to low and add the meat and all the rest of the vegetables, except for the sorrel stems. Stir for a minute or two. Add the chopped olives at the very end.
- Serve immediately in bowls with chopsticks and LOVE. Garnish with the chopped sorrel stems, or you could use thinly sliced scallions. Enjoy!!

116. Curry Vegetable Soup

Serving: Serves 1 | Prep: | Cook: | Ready in:

Ingredients

- 3/4 cup Coconut milk, full fat
- 1/4 cup Water
- 1 tablespoon Green curry paste
- 1/4 cup Onions, chopped
- 1/2   Bell pepper, julienned
- 1 handful Mushrooms, chopped
- 2 cups Spinach
- 1/2   Zucchini (small), diced
- 3 dashes Curry powder
- 1 dash Basil (dried)
- 1 pinch Garlic powder
- 1 teaspoon Coconut sugar
- 2 ounces Soba noodles
- 1/3 cup Tofu, diced

Direction

- Sautéed vegetables (onions, bell pepper, mushrooms, zucchini) in a pot
- Add curry powder, dried basil, and garlic powder to the pot and let the vegetables tenderize
- Add spinach and wilt

- Pour in liquids and stir to distribute flavor
- Right before the soup boils, add tofu and coconut sugar
- Stir and let come to a boil
- Once a boil has been reached, add soba noodle and cook until tender
- Serve hot, with more dried basil, unsweetened coconut flakes, or crushed cashews on top (optional)

117.   Dal Saag

Serving: Serves 4-6 | Prep: | Cook: | Ready in:

Ingredients

- 4 tablespoons Canola Oil, divided
- 1   Medium Yellow Onion, chopped
- 1 tablespoon Fresh Ginger Root, grated
- 1   Serrano or Green Chili
- 2.5 teaspoons Salt, divided
- 2 teaspoons Ground Cumin
- 2 teaspoons Ground Coriander
- .5 teaspoons Ground Fenugreek
- 3.5 cups Water
- 1 cup Split Moong Dal
- 1 tablespoon Fresh Garlic, chopped
- .5 teaspoons Turmeric
- .5 Juice from 1/2 Fresh Lime
- 8 ounces Chopped Spinach (thawed box/bag of frozen spinach)
- 2 tablespoons Butter
- 3 tablespoons Chopped Fresh Cilantro

Direction

- Heat frying pan on medium heat. Add 3 tbsp. oil. Once heated add onion and sauté 1 min.
- Add ginger, green chili and 1 tsp salt and sauté 1 min.
- Add cumin, coriander, fenugreek and sauté a few min. Add remaining oil and sauté until onions become translucent, ensuring spices do not burn. Set aside.

- In a large soup pot heat water on high heat. Once boiling, add moong dal, garlic, turmeric and 1 tsp salt. Turn heat to low, cover pot with lid, leaving slightly uncovered. Stir occasionally. Cook lentils halfway, about 15 min.
- Add onion and spice mixture and 1/2 tsp salt and continue cooking 10 min. Stir occasionally.
- Add lime juice and spinach to pot and stir. Cook another few min., or until spinach heats through.
- Taste dal for softness. Dal should be soft but still retain its general shape. If more cooking needed and all the water has been soaked up, add 1/4 cup water. Taste for salt as well. You can always add more.
- Once dal is cooked add butter. Let butter melt into dal.
- Turn off heat and sprinkle cilantro on top.
- All done! Eat with jasmine or basmati rice and/or your favorite warm flat bread (roti/ chapati/ paratha/ naan/ pita/ tortilla) and yogurt on side.

118.   Delicious Beet And Ginger Soup

Serving: Serves 2 | Prep: | Cook: | Ready in:

Ingredients

- Mains
- 1,5 liters vegetable/herbal stock
- 2   cooked beets
- 1 tablespoon chopped ginger root
- 1   medium onion
- 2   garlic cloves
- 1/2   can of coconut milk
- 2 tablespoons olive oil
- Herbs
- 1/2   marjoram
- 1/2   savory
- 2 juniper berries
- 1/2   lovage

- 1/2 teaspoon dried parsley
- 1 bay leaf

Direction

- Cook herbal stock. Add vegetables, herbs (about 1/2 teaspoon savory, lovage, dried parsley, a teaspoon marjoram, 2 juniper berries, bay leaf, salt and pepper), olive oil and pour boiling water. Cook for 20-30 minutes. Season with soy sauce. 5 minutes prior finishing cooking, add chopped fresh parsley. Strain and throw veggies away.
- Heat olive oil, fry the chopped onion, garlic, beetroot and ginger for 10 minutes.
- Transfer to stock and cook for next 5-10 minutes. Pour it into a blender, add coconut milk and blend until smooth and creamy. Transfer back to pot and cook for a further 5-10 minutes.
- Seasoning to taste if necessary with salt, pepper and marjoram.

119.   Dill Pickle Soup

Serving: Serves 1 | Prep: | Cook: |Ready in:

Ingredients

- 1 medium sized cucumber, peeled
- 1 tablespoon plain yogurt (Heaping)
- 1 handful fresh dill weed
- 1/2 teaspoon kosher salt (be generous)

Direction

- Place all ingredients in the bowl of a food processor fitted with the metal blade, or into a blender. Cover tightly, process or liquefy until it reaches the desired consistency (I like it a little on the chunky side, but you may prefer it smooth). If serving immediately, put it individual bowls. If you're not quite ready, put it in the refrigerator... but not for too long. It separates quickly once made.
- Enjoy!

120.   Early Autumn Manhattan Clam Chowder

Serving: Serves 4 | Prep: | Cook: | Ready in:

Ingredients

- 24 Cherrystone clams, scrubbed
- 1 cup White WIne
- 1/2 cup Clam juice
- 1 cup Water
- 1 Yellow pepper, 1/4 inch dice
- 1 Celery rib, 1/4 inch dice
- 1 shallot, large, 1/4 inch dice
- 1 russet potato, medium, 1/2 inch dice
- 2 bacon strips, 1/2 inch dice
- 1 tablespoon butter
- 2 ripe tomatoes, roughly chopped
- 1 garlic clove, finely grated
- 2 teaspoons oregano, finely chopped

Direction

- Scrub clams thoroughly in cold water to remove as much sand as possible.
- Combine clams, wine, clam juice and water in a deep skillet with lid. Bring to a rapid boil, covered, shaking periodically, until clams are fully opened. Remove clams from liquid with slotted spoon and let cool.
- Simmer liquid over medium high heat and reduce by half. Strain through a fine mesh sieve and reserve.
- Wipe skillet with damp cloth to remove any remaining sand. Add bacon and butter over medium high heat, cook for 10 minutes or until mildly crisp. Remove bacon from skillet with slotted spoon, drain on paper towels and reserve.
- Pour off all but 2 Tbsps. of fat from pan, return to medium heat, add shallots, peppers and celery. Sauté until soft, not brown, about 10 minutes.

- Add potatoes to skillet, stir to coat, and cook for an additional 10 minutes until soft. Then combine tomatoes and garlic with other ingredients in the skillet. Toss to coat and soften, 1 minute.
- Transfer vegetable mixture to 3 Qt. sauce pan. Add reserve clam liquid, careful not to add any remaining grit accumulated in the bottom of the bowl, bring to medium simmer. Using an immersion blender, blend vegetable mixture, leaving some chunks. (A more pot-intensive solution is to remove ½ of the vegetable mixture and blend until smooth with a hand mixer or blender)
- Remove clams from shells and roughly chop. Add clams and reserved bacon to the soup, along with oregano. Let cook for 3-4 minutes to heat through. Serve accompanied by good bread.

121. Egg Ochazuke

Serving: Serves 1 | Prep: | Cook: | Ready in:

Ingredients

- 1/2-3/4 cups cooked short-grain brown rice
- 1/2 cup cooked shelled edamame (young green soybeans)
- 1-2 soft or hard boiled eggs (or use a poached or fried egg or two)
- 1 tablespoon natural pickled ginger, minced
- 1/2 sheet nori (toasted seaweed used for sushi), cut or torn into strips or small pieces
- 1-2 teaspoons toasted sesame seeds
- 1/2-1 cups hot green tea (sencha, hojicha or genmaicha are best; matcha is probably not the best choice)
- Pinch black lava sea salt or other coarse sea salt

Direction

- Mix brown rice and edamame in a small bowl.
- Sprinkle pickled ginger over rice/edamame.

- Place egg(s) on top (slice in half if using soft or hardboiled egg), and top with the nori and toasted sesame seeds.
- Pour in the green tea and sprinkle with the salt.
- Savor every bite!

122. Eleven Madison Park's Strawberry Gazpacho

Serving: Serves 4 to 6 | Prep: | Cook: | Ready in:

Ingredients

- 1 tablespoon plus 1/2 cup extra-virgin olive oil
- 2 cloves garlic, crushed but kept whole
- 1 1/2 cups whole grain bread, crusts removed, cut into 1-inch cubes
- 2 sprigs thyme
- 6 cups strawberries, hulled and quartered
- 2 1/4 cups English cucumbers, peeled, seeded, and diced
- 1 1/4 cups diced red bell pepper
- 3/4 cup diced green bell pepper
- 6 tablespoons tomato juice
- 3 tablespoons red wine vinegar
- 1 1/2 teaspoons salt
- Tabasco sauce
- 2 tablespoons extra-virgin olive oil
- 2 cloves garlic, crushed but kept whole
- 2 cups diced (1/4 inch) whole grain bread, crusts removed
- 3 sprigs thyme
- 1/2 teaspoon salt

Direction

- To make the soup: Heat a small sauté pan over medium-high heat. Coat the bottom with 1 tablespoon of the olive oil and add 1 clove of garlic. When the garlic begins to sizzle, add the bread cubes. Toss occasionally until the bread begins to color, being careful not to burn. Add the thyme and continue to toss until the bread is golden brown. Transfer the bread to a large bowl. Discard the garlic and thyme.

- Add the strawberries, cucumber, peppers, remaining garlic clove, remaining 1/2 cup of olive oil, tomato juice, vinegar, and salt to the bowl. Toss to combine and cover tightly with plastic wrap. Marinate at room temperature for 3 to 6 hours. Puree the ingredients and their juices in small batches in a blender on high speed until very smooth. Strain through a chinois and chill in the refrigerator until very cold. Taste and season, if necessary, with Tabasco sauce and additional salt and red wine vinegar.
- To make the garlic-thyme croutons for garnish: Heat a small sauté pan on medium-high heat. Coat the bottom with the olive oil and add the garlic. When the garlic begins to sizzle, add the diced bread. Toss occasionally until the bread begins to color, being careful not to burn. Add the thyme and continue to toss until the bread is golden brown. Quickly transfer to a baking sheet lined with paper towels. Discard the garlic and thyme and season with the salt. Once cool and dry, you may store in an airtight container lined with paper towels for up to 1 day.
- Serve chilled, garnished with garlic-thyme croutons. Tiny basil leaves and a swirl of olive oil make a nice additional garnish.

---
123. Fajita Stew

Serving: Serves 4-6 | Prep: | Cook: | Ready in:

Ingredients

- 2 1/2 pounds boneless beef top round steak
- 1 onion, chopped
- 2 cloves garlic, minced
- 14 ounces can of diced tomatoes, undrained
- 1 ounce fajita seasoning mix
- 2 red bell pepper, seeded & cut into 1" pieces
- 1/4 cup flour

- 1/2 cup chicken broth

Direction

- Trim excess fat from beef and cut into 2" pieces.
- Combine with onion in a 3-4 quart slow cooker.
- Mix together fajita seasoning mix and undrained tomatoes and pour over beef.
- Place peppers on top.
- Cover crockpot and cook on low for 7-9 hours until beef is tender.
- Add the broth to the flour to make a paste. Continue to add liquid until you have a slurry. Avoid lumps.
- Add the slurry to the crockpot gradually, stirring well to incorporate.
- Cover slow cooker and cook on high for 15-20 minutes until thickened, stirring occasionally.
- Serve hot.

---
124. Feta, Baby Spinach, Tomatoes, Lentils And Morrocan Spices
---

Serving: Serves 10 | Prep: | Cook: | Ready in:

Ingredients

- 2 1/4 cups French or Italian small lentils, picked over and rinsed
- 3 cups diced onions
- 1/4 cup extra virgin olive oil
- 1/4 cup minced garlic
- 3 tablespoons ground coriander
- 3 tablespoons ground cumin
- 1 teaspoon mustard seed
- 3 tablespoons ground fennel
- 1/8 teaspoon cayenne pepper
- 3 cups canned plum tomatoes chopped, with juice
- 6 cups a good veal or beef broth
- 4 cups baby spinach leaves

- Salt and pepper to taste
- 1/2 cup crumbled feta
- 1/4 cup chopped cilantro

Direction

- Place the rinsed lentils in a medium saucepan and cover with cool water by 4 inches. Bring to a boil over medium heat. Lower heat and simmer until done, about 10-15 minutes. Taste frequently and when al dente, strain, reserving both the lentils and liquid.
- Sauté the onions in the cup olive oil until translucent, about 5-10 minutes. Add the minced garlic, and sauté for five more minutes.
- Add the coriander, cumin, mustard seeds, fennel, and cayenne pepper. Stir and cook for one minute.
- Stir the canned tomatoes. Reduce heat to low and simmer for five minutes.
- Stir in the cooked lentils and 4 cups of the lentil cooking liquid and the broth. Bring to simmer.
- Stir in 4 cups or more of baby spinach leaves. Cook only until wilted.
- Add one tsp. of salt (much less if the broth is salted) and one tsp. pepper or to taste.
- Serve with crumbled feta and fresh chopped cilantro sprinkled on top.

125. French Mushroom Soup With Roasted Garlic Croutons

Serving: Serves 8 | Prep: | Cook: | Ready in:

Ingredients

- Roasted Garlic Croutons
- 2 Heads of Garlic
- 1/4 cup Olive Oil
- 8 Slices of Rustic Crusty Bread
- Kosher Salt
- French Mushroom Soup
- 4 tablespoons Butter

- 2 tablespoons Olive Oil
- 4 Large Sweet Onions, Sliced
- 8 ounces Cremini Mushrooms, Sliced
- 8 ounces Oyster Mushrooms, Sliced
- 1 pound Button Mushrooms, Sliced
- 6 ounces Shiitake Mushrooms, Stems Removed, Sliced
- 1 tablespoon Granulated Sugar
- 2 Cloves Crushed Garlic
- 2 tablespoons Flour
- 6 cups Beef Broth
- 1/4 cup Vermouth
- 2 tablespoons Balsamic Vinegar
- 1/2 cup Heavy Cream or Half and Half
- 2 Bay Leaves
- 1 teaspoon Fresh Rosemary, Chopped
- 1 teaspoon Fresh Thyme, Leaves Only
- Salt and Pepper to Taste
- 8 ounces Shredded Gruyere Cheese

Direction

- Roasted Garlic Croutons
- Turn oven on to 400 degrees. Create an aluminum foil pouch. Cut off the top of the garlic heads and discard. Place both garlic heads in the foil pouch and pour ¼ cup of olive oil into the pouch. Salt the garlic and place in oven. Roast for 30 to 40 minutes.
- Take out of oven and let garlic and oil cool. Reserve the olive oil for the bread. Slice 8 pieces of rustic bread around ½ inch thick. Spread the garlic olive oil on the pieces of bread. Then sprinkle with kosher salt. Broil the bread for about 5 to 10 minutes, until golden brown and hard. Keep an eye on them.
- Take bread out and spread the roasted cloves of garlic on top of the croutons. Reserve these croutons for the soup topper.
- French Mushroom Soup
- In a large soup pot melt the butter and add the olive oil on medium high heat. Add all the sliced onions and mushrooms to the pot and sauté until well caramelized, about 30 minutes. Add the crushed garlic, granulated sugar, salt and pepper. Continue to cook for another 10 minutes.

- Add the flour and stir. Add the vermouth, balsamic vinegar and beef broth to the soup pot. Stir and then add the bay leaves, fresh thyme and fresh rosemary
- Bring to a boil and then turn the heat to low and cook for 15 more minutes. Then turn off the heat and add the heavy cream. Stir and test soup, add more salt and pepper if needed.
- Turn on your oven broiler to high. In oven proof crocks pour soup into the crocks. Place roasted garlic crouton on top of soup and put 1 oz. of Gruyere cheese on top. Put into oven till cheese is melted and toasted. Serve immediately.

126. French Onion Soup

Serving: Serves 4-6 | Prep: 0hours20mins | Cook: 4hours20mins |Ready in:

Ingredients

- 3 pounds onions
- 3 tablespoons butter
- 2 tablespoons olive oil
- 4 cloves of garlic (up to 6)
- 1 generous pinch of salt
- 1 pinch black peppercorns
- 4 sprigs fresh thyme
- 1 bay leaf
- 4 cups beef, veal, and/or vegetable stock, preferably homemade (up to 6 cups)
- 2 cups red wine, preferably a burgundy, OR
- 2 cups beer, preferably a brown ale or stout (not chocolate)
- 1 baguette or other crusty bread
- 4 (up to 6) deli slices of cheese, OR
- 1/2 cup EACH of gouda, gruyere, parmesan & pecorino

Direction

- Slice & segment 3 pounds of onions.
- Melt together the butter and olive oil in a large stockpot.
- Crush and peel the garlic. You don't have to mince it; it will caramelize and turn soft and sweet as it cooks. Caramelize the garlic in the olive oil and butter.
- Pour in the onions, season with salt and pepper, and stir around just until the onions are all coated in the olive oil/butter.
- Add in the fresh thyme and the bay leaf and let the onions caramelize over low heat, stirring only often enough to move them around the pan. This will take at least an hour.
- Once the onions are caramelized and have cooked down, pour in the stock, about 4-6 cups depending on whether you prefer your soup more onion-y or more soup-y.
- Then, pour in the wine or beer and simmer, uncovered, for at least an hour and as much as three hours, tasting occasionally to adjust the flavors.
- Meanwhile, slice down your bread. Stale bread is perfectly okay for this, just heat it up a bit in a warm (250°F) oven first to soften it. Toast the bread; you can rub both sides with a cut clove of garlic first, if you like. You'll want 2 pieces of bread per person - one for the bottom of the bowl, and one for on top.
- If you're going for the mix of cheeses, grate together about 1/2 cup each of parmesan, pecorino, gouda, and gruyere. Alternatively, you can drape a deli-cut slice of cheese (emmentaler, gruyere) over the top of the bowls, but I like to do a grated mix. Get that ready, and set it aside.
- Preheat your broiler. Remove the thyme sprigs and bay leaf from the soup.
- Arrange your oven-safe individual serving bowls or coffee mugs on a baking tray with a thin lip.
- TO SERVE: drop a toast slice in the bottom of each bowl. Ladle in the soup and cover with a second slice of toast. Then cover the toast with cheese. Be generous! You want the cheese to seal in the soup and drape over the edge of the bowl.
- Broil for a few minutes, until the cheese is brown and bubbling on top. Garnish with a little fresh thyme, and serve.

127.   French Onion Soup For Two

Serving: Serves 2 | Prep: 0hours5mins | Cook: 0hours40mins |Ready in:

Ingredients

- 1 tablespoon butter
- 2 tablespoons extra virgin olive oil
- 1 clove garlic
- 1 red onion
- 1 shallot
- salt and pepper to taste
- 1-1/2 cups beef broth
- 1/4 cup red wine
- 2 slices of cheese (mozzarella or provolone)
- 2 slices French baguette
- Pinch parsley flakes for garnish

Direction

- Melt butter and extra virgin olive oil in medium saucepan.
- Add chopped garlic and cook until tender.
- Add chopped red onion and shallot to garlic in pan. Salt and pepper to taste. Sauté mixture until tender, about 15 minutes.
- Add beef broth and red wine. Bring to a boil and then reduce heat to medium-low to simmer for 20 minutes.
- Transfer soup to two oven-safe, broiler-safe crocks. Add French baguette slice to each crock and top with cheese. Broil until top is golden brown. Carefully remove from oven, garnish with parsley flakes, and serve.

128.   French Onion Soup In A Hurry

Serving: Serves 2 | Prep: | Cook: |Ready in:

Ingredients

- Caramelized Onions
- 12 yellow onions
- 1 stick butter
- 1 teaspoon kosher salt
- Beef broth and soup
- 5 pounds beef soup bones
- 1 teaspoon salt
- 1/2 teaspoon black pepper
- 1 onion, peeled and quartered
- 6 cloves garlic, crushed
- 2/3 cup red wine
- 2 slices good French bread or ciabatta
- 1 ounce gruyere or emmenthaler cheese

Direction

- Caramelized Onions
- Slice onions into half-moons and cram as many as you can into your slow cooker.
- Sprinkle salt over onions; put stick of butter on top.
- Turn slow cooker on low and walk away for 18 hours. It is well, if you have anyone sensitive to smells in your household, to do this in an outdoors or well-vented area; it will smell quite potent at about hour 8.
- Allow onions to cool, and portion into one or 1/2 cup servings, as fits your needs, in plastic bags. Squeeze out as much air as possible, and freeze.
- Beef broth and soup
- Arrange soup bones on sheet pan or cookie sheet.
- Sprinkle with salt and pepper. Roast at 350F for an hour and a half, or until deep brown.
- Move bones to stock pot. Add garlic cloves and quartered onion and cover with water. Bring to a boil and simmer for three hours.
- Strain solids from broth; package in pint containers and freeze.
- To make soup, put red wine and 1 cup frozen onions in saucepan. Heat over low heat until onions are thawed and wine reduced by half.

- Add 1 pint beef broth; heat on simmer until well blended. Taste and correct seasoning, add water if needed.
- While soup is simmering, grate cheese; pile onto sliced bread and toast until cheese is melted and bubbly. Remove and cut toast into 1 1/2 inch croutons.
- Float croutons on soup and serve immediately.

129.   French Onion Soup With Crostini And Brie

Serving: Serves 8 or more | Prep: | Cook: |Ready in:

Ingredients

- 4 Large sweet onions - thinly sliced
- 4 Large shallots - thinly sliced
- 4 tablespoons olive oil
- 4 cloves fresh garlic - finely chopped
- 1/4 cup organic, unbleached white flour
- 1 splash White wine
- 1 quart beef broth
- 1 quart chicken broth
- 1 1/4" slices of french bread per person
- 4 1/4" slices of brie
- 1 sprig fresh flat leaf Italian parsley
- 2 tablespoons fresh flat leaf Italian parsley - stems removed and chopped
- 1 pinch season with salt and pepper

Direction

- Place a large saucepan over medium heat, add oil and heat until hot but not smoking.
- Add onions and garlic. Cook until softened (about 10 minutes) stirring occasionally (lower heat if they begin to brown) and then add the flour and stir.
- Lower heat to medium/low and allow the flour to brown slightly, stirring occasionally for another 5 minutes or so.
- Add a splash of white wine, stir and then slowly add the beef and chicken broth. You

want to add the liquids slowly while stirring to avoid lumps.
- Add the sprig of parsley (keeping the stem on allows the herb to be infused in the soup and then later to be removed once the soup is done) and let the soup simmer for about another 30-45 minutes.
- In the meantime, toast the slices of bread under the broiler until golden, rub with garlic (optional)
- To serve, ladle into cups or bowl, top with the bread and the cheese and sprinkle with the chopped parsley

130.   Fresh Corn & Dungeness Crab Chowder

Serving: Serves 4 to 6 | Prep: | Cook: |Ready in:

Ingredients

- 1 pound Dungeness crab meat
- 2 cups fresh corn kernels (3 ears), cobs reserved
- 3 cups diced Walla Walla Sweet onion (or any sweet onion)
- 1/2 cup diced red bell pepper
- 1/2 cup diced fennel, plus a few fennel fronds for garnish
- 1 cup chicken stock
- 3 cups whole milk
- 3 tablespoons butter
- 2 tablespoons flour
- 1 bunch fresh basil leaves, thinly sliced
- salt
- pepper

Direction

- Cut the corn cobs into 2 inch chunks.
- In a large pot, heat the chicken stock until it begins to simmer. Add the corn cobs, cover and simmer for 10 minutes more.
- While the cobs are cooking, prepare a roux. Melt 2 Tbsp. of butter in a small sauté pan.

When the butter has melted, whisk in the flour and cook, stirring constantly, for one minute. Remove from heat and set aside.

- Strain the chicken stock mixture into a bowl and discard the cobs.
- Return the pot to the stove and add the remaining 1 Tbsp. of butter. When the butter is melted and sizzling, add the onion, bell pepper, and fennel. Cook, stirring occasionally, unit the onions are soft, about 3 minutes. Season generously with salt and pepper.
- Whisk the roux mixture into the onion mixture, then add the potatoes, corn, 1 cup of reserved chicken stock, and 3 cups of whole mile. Bring the chowder to a boil, then reduce heat and simmer until the potatoes are tender, about 10 minutes.
- Taste the chowder and adjust the seasoning as needed.
- Just before serving, stir in the crab (reserving a few nice pieces for garnishing), sliced basil, and fennel fronds. Garnish with additional crab and serve immediately.

131. Fresh Ginger And Carrot Soup

Serving: Serves 4-6 | Prep: | Cook: | Ready in:

Ingredients

- 2 tablespoons olive oil
- 1 large yellow onion
- 3 tablespoons fresh ginger, peeled and roughly chopped
- 3/4 teaspoon ground coriander
- 1/4 teaspoon ground cinnamon
- 1/8 teaspoon garam masala
- pinch red pepper flakes
- 5 cups carrots, peeled and diced
- 1/3 cup brandy or cognac
- 3 - 4 cups vegetable broth depending on whether you like it thinner or thicker
- 1 cup light coconut milk, canned and unsweetened

Direction

- Heat a large soup pot over medium heat and add olive oil.
- Add onions and cook until just beginning to soften, about 5 minutes. Add ginger and cook for another 5 minutes. Season with salt and pepper.
- Add coriander, cinnamon, garam masala, red pepper flakes and carrots. Stir well to incorporate and turn the heat to high. Add the splash of brandy and cook on high for about 2 minutes until the alcohol burns off. Season with salt and pepper and turn heat back down to medium.
- Add the vegetable broth. Cover and simmer until the carrots are fully softened, about 30 minutes.
- Once the carrots are soft, remove pot from the heat and blend the soup either in batches in a regular blender or right in the pot with an immersion blender. (If using a regular blender, be careful not to fill it too full because hot steam from the soup can create too much pressure in the blender and make the lid pop off.) Taste and season more as needed.
- Once blended, return soup to pot (if you used a blender, that is) and stir in coconut milk. Serve hot.
- This soup keeps well for up to five days and will freeze beautifully for up to three months if well contained.
- As a side note, garam masala is a ground spice mixture of Indian origin that you'll find in most Indian dishes. It's most commonly comprised of different peppercorns, cardamom, nutmeg, cloves and mace. It's beautifully aromatic and quite strong in flavor. Depending on the blend you use, it can provide a big punch of heat from the peppercorns so if you've never had it before and are unsure of the heat level, omit the red pepper flakes.

132. G.G. Rose's Matzo Ball Soup

Serving: Serves 6-8 | Prep: 1hours30mins | Cook: 1hours30mins | Ready in:

Ingredients

- Stock
- 2-3 chicken breasts, whole with skin and bone
- 4 quarts water
- 2 carrots, cut in half
- 1 large onion, quartered
- 2 stalks celery, halved
- 1 turnip, halved
- 1 bay leaf
- a few springs of parsley or dill
- Soup and Matzo Balls
- 2 large carrots, peeled and cut into medium dice
- 2 turnips, peeled and cut into medium dice
- 1 large onion, cut into medium dice
- 1/2 pound egg noodles
- 1/2 cup matzo meal
- 2 large eggs, lightly beaten
- 2 tablespoons vegetable oil
- 2 tablespoons seltzer water
- salt + pepper to taste

Direction

- Stock
- Begin your chicken broth several hours in advance. Add whole chicken breasts to a large soup pot and cover with water, 2 inches above top of breasts. This might be more or less than 4 quarts depending on size of pot and chickens.
- Add your veggies and herbs. These are optional and can be varied to your specific tastes. My mom never used vegetables when boiling the chicken, but it will help to flavor the broth. Veggies can be unpeeled, or peeled if that freaks you out.

- Boil for about 30 minutes. Chicken should no longer be pink in the middle and should remove easily from the bone. Remove veggies from broth and discard. Remove chicken breasts from broth and let cool.
- Take the meat off the bone and chop or shred into smaller pieces if desired. Skim any fat off the top of the broth.
- Soup and Matzo Balls
- In a small bowl, mix matzo meal, eggs, oil, seltzer, salt + pepper together. Let this mixture sit in the fridge for at least 30 minutes. The seltzer is a trick some people say helps to make the matzo balls fluffy. If you like your matzo balls dense (some do), my mom says using egg beaters instead of eggs will do the trick!
- Meanwhile, add diced veggies and salt + pepper to the pot with the broth, bring to a boil, and then simmer for about 30 minutes, until veggies begin to get tender.
- Bring broth back up to a boil. Take matzo ball mix from fridge and start rolling into small balls and dropping them into the boiling soup. You should be able to get about 10 balls out of the mixture and if they're too big they won't cook properly. Wet your hands a little before to keep the mixture from sticking.
- Cover the pot and boil for about 30 minutes (it's pretty hard to over-cook a matzo ball). Try not to open the pot or the matzo balls might deflate. At 30 minutes you can cut one open and see if it needs more time to cook, it should be the same texture the whole way through.
- When the matzo balls are done, add in the uncooked noodles and the chicken and boil for several minutes until the noodles are al dente and the chicken is hot.
- Ladle into bowls and enjoy!

133. Garlic Bread Soup With Clams

Serving: Serves 4 | Prep: | Cook: | Ready in:

Ingredients

- 1 pound onions, roughly chopped
- 1 cup garlic cloves, peeled and roughly chopped
- 1 tablespoon unsalted butter
- 1 tablespoon olive oil
- salt and white pepper, to taste
- 1 (4 inch) piece of parmgiano-reggiano rind only
- 1 tablespoon mixed herbs (parsley, thyme, etc)
- 4 slices stale garlic bread cut into 1-inch cubes
- 1 quart chicken stock, plus more if necessary
- 1 pound steamed clams per person (optional)
- 5 stems of thyme, leaves removed stems discarded
- additional parmgiano-reggiano for topping
- very good extra-virgin olive oil for drizzling

Direction

- In a medium-sized saucepan set over medium heat sauté onions and garlic in a mixture of butter and olive oil. Add a pinch or two of salt and a bit of white pepper. Do not let the mixture fry. Small gentle bubbles should form around the edge of the pan and are a good sign that the heat is just right. They will become a deep golden caramel color in about 30 minutes. Stir frequently, and watch them as they cook.
- Add the chicken stock, cheese rind, chopped herbs and the garlic bread cubes. Simmer another 15 to 20 minutes, stirring often. Taste for seasoning. It may need a bit more salt. If it does add a pinch and let it cook another 2 or 3 minutes. Remove what is left of the cheese rind and discard it.
- Puree the soup with an immersion blender. Adjusting consistency with more stock if necessary.
- You may make the soup a day ahead as it is often better on the second day. Serve this with steamed clams (optional) on the side and a hefty sprinkling of grated Parmigiano-Reggiano, a drizzle of good olive oil and some chopped thyme leaves.

134. Garlic, Green Onion & Glass Noodle Soup

Serving: Serves 2-4 | Prep: 0hours10mins | Cook: 0hours30mins | Ready in:

Ingredients

- ½ pound ground turkey
- 4 cloves garlic – crushed
- 1 clove garlic – very thinly sliced
- 1 bunch green onions (about 9 spears)
- 1 teaspoon hot chile flakes
- 32 ounces chicken stock (homemade if possible)
- 2 stems green garlic – finely chopped
- sea salt
- 2.4 ounces glass noodles (Mung Bean pasta – I like Eden Selected)
- dash of soy sauce
- 1-2 tablespoons lemon grass (minced) OR 2 teaspoons lemon juice
- 2 teaspoon fresh ginger – minced
- olive oil

Direction

- Sauté ground turkey w/ a sprinkling of salt in enough olive oil to cover bottom of pan. Make sure to break turkey up quite a bit so you get little tiny bits of turkey.
- Chop green onion and reserve ¼ cup.
- In separate small pan sauté green onions and 2 cloves crushed garlic until tender but still bright green (about 3-4 mins.). Add to turkey with oil.
- Add chile to turkey garlic green onion mixture.
- Bring stock to a boil in large pot w/ one clove of garlic sliced thin, green garlic & lemon grass (if using lemon juice instead add it at end with meat and ginger mixture). Add glass noodles and boil for about 4 minutes.

- Meanwhile sauté ginger and additional 2 cloves crushed garlic over med. low heat until soft and tender – about 3 minutes.
- Add turkey, ginger/garlic mixture, dash of soy sauce and reserved green onions to stock and boiling noodles. Serve immediately.

135. Gazpacho Poached Eggs

Serving: Serves 1 | Prep: | Cook: | Ready in:

Ingredients

- 1.5 cups Gazpacho-purchased or homemade
- 2 eggs
- Salt and Pepper

Direction

- Heat gazpacho to boiling in a small omelet pan. Reduce heat to simmer. Draw an imaginary line down the center of the pan to create two halves. At the center of one half, make a well with a wooden spoon; crack an egg into it. Repeat on the other "side" with second egg. Sprinkle the eggs with salt and pepper.
- Cover and let eggs cook gently 3-5 minutes or until done to your liking. You might want to slightly under cook the eggs as they'll continue to cook a bit in the hot soup. To serve, carefully tip pan's contents into a pasta or other shallow bowl. Serve with hot tortillas or cornbread.

136. Gherkin, Beef & Barley Broth (Рассольник | Rassol'nyk)

Serving: Serves 4 | Prep: | Cook: | Ready in:

Ingredients

- 500 grams (1 pound) pork ribs or beef short ribs
- 2 1/2 liters (4 pints) cold water
- 1 onion, peeled but kept whole
- 1 bay leaf
- 5 black peppercorns
- 5 allspice berries
- 100 grams (3 1/2 ounces) pearl barley or rice
- 1 onion, diced
- 2 tablespoons sunflower oil
- 1 carrot, peeled and grated
- 20 grams (3/4 ounce) parsley root, peeled and finely chopped, or parsley stalks, finely chopped
- 100 grams (3 1/2 ounces) gherkins, peeled and grated
- 200 milliliters (7 fluid ounces) gherkin brine from the jar, divided and used as needed
- 2 spring onions, finely chopped, to serve

Direction

- To make the stock, cut the ribs into individual ribs, place in a large saucepan, and cover with the water. Add the whole onion, bay leaf, peppercorns, and allspice and bring to the boil.
- Reduce the heat as soon as the water boils and skim the scum that rises to the surface. Simmer for a couple of hours while you watch your favorite TV series and eat leftover gherkins.
- When the meat is tender and falling off the bone, add the pearl barley or rice and cook for 15 minutes, until it is cooked but still has a bite.
- Meanwhile, sweat the diced onion in the sunflower oil in a frying pan over a medium heat for 5 minutes, then add the parsley root or stalks and carrot and continue to cook over a medium-low heat, stirring often, for 15 minutes or until everything is soft and starting to caramelize slightly. Add to the stock.
- Add the gherkins to the stock, taste and add 100 milliliters (3 1/2 fluid ounces) of the gherkin brine. Taste it and add more if you think it needs more salt. The broth should taste rich, but also a little salty, sweet, and

sour. Scatter with spring onions and serve with a huge hunk of good bread.

137.   Ginger Almond Soup With Broccoli, Tofu And Asparagus

Serving: Serves 4-6 | Prep: | Cook: | Ready in:

Ingredients

- 4 cups   Unsweetened ginger tea
- 1/4 cup   Almond butter (smooth)
- a few dashes   cayenne powder
- 1 tblsp.   Tamari soy sauce
- salt and fresh ground black pepper to taste
- 3 tblsp.   Olive oil
- 7 oz.   firm tofu, drained and cubed
- 2 large   Red shallots, finely chopped
- 2 cups   Broccoli, chopped
- 1 cup   fresh asparagus, chopped
- slivered almonds and chopped parsley to garnish (optional).

Direction

- Heat strained ginger tea to a simmer. Turn off heat and whisk in almond butter. Add cayenne, tamari and season to taste. Set aside.
- Heat oil in a large skillet. Add tofu and sauté over medium high heat until at least 2 sides of most cubes are lightly browned. Add shallots, broccoli and asparagus. Sauté another 5 minutes, or until vegetables are just tender.
- Add vegetables to broth and heat gently through. Garnish with slivered almonds and parsley, if desired.

138.   Ginger Scented Chicken Broth

Serving: Serves 2 1/2 to 3 quarts | Prep: | Cook: | Ready in:

Ingredients

- 4 pounds chicken bones (carcasses, or necks, backs, wings, etc.)
- 2 medium onions, cut in half
- 1 4-inch piece of ginger
- 2 carrots, peeled
- 2 stalks celery
- 3 star anise
- 1 bay leaf
- 2 teaspoons black peppercorns
- 4 whole cloves
- 2 cinnamon sticks
- 4 garlic cloves, peeled
- 6 quarts water
- Salt, to taste
- Lime juice, to taste

Direction

- Preheat oven to 425 degrees. Place chicken bones in a roasting pan. When oven comes to temperature, roast bones for 1 hour, or until thoroughly browned. Remove from pan and place in a 10-12 quart stock pot.
- Place onion halves (peels removed) over the open flame of a gas burner. Use tongs to turn onions when needed. When onions are blackened, place in stock pot. Repeat method with ginger, but cut ginger into 1-inch pieces before placing in pot. Add carrots and celery to pot.
- Make a sachet of spices: Pile star anise, bay leaf, peppercorns, cloves and garlic in a cheesecloth, and tie with kitchen string to make a little pouch. Add pouch to pot, as well as cinnamon sticks.
- Fill pot with 6 quarts of cold water, making sure to cover all ingredients (add more if you need to). Bring pot to a boil and immediately turn heat down to medium-low. Let the pot

simmer with the lid slightly ajar for 4 hours. Refrain from stirring here, so that you'll end up with a clear broth.

- Remove all bones, veggies and spices from pot. Turn heat up to medium-high, and reduce to about half of its current amount. Taste, and add salt if needed. When broth is full-bodied and flavorful (and this depends on personal preference), remove from heat and cool. Add a healthy sprinkle of lime juice, if desired.

---

139. Golden Cauliflower And White Bean Stew

Serving: Serves 6 | Prep: | Cook: | Ready in:

Ingredients

- 1 tablespoon olive oil
- 1 large sweet onion, diced
- 2 cloves garlic, minced
- 1 inch knob fresh ginger, peeled and minced
- 2 teaspoons ground cumin
- 1/2 teaspoon ground turmeric
- 1 large head cauliflower, cored and cut into bite sized florets
- 2 medium heirloom tomatoes, rustically cubed
- 1/2 cup raisins
- 4 cups vegetable broth
- 1 can (15 ounces) cannellini beans, thoroughly rinsed and drained
- 4 cups baby spinach
- salt & pepper to taste

Direction

- In a large Dutch oven or heavy pot, heat olive oil over medium-high heat until just hot. Add onion and garlic and sauté, stirring frequently, until onion is translucent and soft, but not browned (about 6 minutes). Add ginger, cumin, and turmeric and continue to sauté until spices are pungent (about 30 seconds).

- Stir in cauliflower, tomatoes, raisins, and broth and bring to a boil. Reduce heat to low, cover, and allow stew to simmer until all vegetables are fork tender (about 20 minutes). Uncover and stir in beans, spinach, and seasoning; stir until spinach is just wilted. Serve and enjoy!

---

140. Golden Gazpacho

Serving: Serves 6-8 as an appetizer | Prep: | Cook: | Ready in:

Ingredients

- 2 pints yellow cherry tomatoes
- 2 yellow bell peppers, seeded and chopped
- 1-2 jalapeno peppers (to taste), seeded and chopped
- 1/4 cup chopped fresh chives
- 2 tablespoons fresh tarragon leaves
- Juice of one lemon (about 2 tbsp)
- 2 tablespoons white wine vinegar
- Salt and freshly ground black pepper to taste
- Cold water as needed
- Extra-virgin olive oil for drizzling

Direction

- In a blender, combine tomatoes, bell pepper, jalapeno, chives, thyme, tarragon, lemon juice, vinegar, salt, and pepper, and puree until smooth. If you want a thinner soup, add cold water as needed. Cover and refrigerate for at least 2 hours, and up to 3 days.
- About 30 minutes before serving, place your soup bowls or cups in the freezer to chill. Strain the chilled gazpacho through a fine mesh strainer (for a finer result, line the strainer with cheesecloth). Taste and adjust the salt and pepper as desired. Serve ice-cold in chilled bowls, with a drizzle of olive oil on top.

141. Grad Student's Salmon Chowder

Serving: Serves 6 | Prep: | Cook: |Ready in:

Ingredients

- 3 tablespoons vegetable oil
- 2 teaspoons chopped garlic
- 1/2 cup white or yellow onion, diced
- 1/2 cup red bell pepper, diced
- 1 cup celery diced
- 1 1/2 cups potato, diced
- 4 cups chicken broth
- 1/4 cup tomato paste
- 1/2 cup fresh or frozen corn kernels
- 16 ounces canned salmon
- 8 ounces evaporated milk or light cream
- 1 teaspoon salt
- freshly ground black pepper

Direction

- Over medium high heat, sauté garlic, celery and onion in oil until translucent, about 3-5 minutes.
- Add potatoes, tomato paste and broth. Cover, bring to a boil, and reduce heat to medium.
- Allow to simmer until potatoes are tender. Add corn, salmon and evaporated milk. Stir gently. After adding salmon and milk, do not bring temperature above simmer. Add salt and pepper to taste. Add more broth as needed the next day. Serves 6.

142. Grass Fed Sweet Potato Chili

Serving: Makes 1 large pot | Prep: | Cook: |Ready in:

Ingredients

- 1 pound Lean Grass Fed Beef
- 1 Large Onion
- 1 Large Sweet Potato, peeled and cubed
- 2 Small Zucchini, diced
- 1 Can Black Beans
- 1 28 oz. Can Diced Tomatoes
- 1 Small Can Green Chilis
- 1.5 tablespoons Chili Powder
- 1 teaspoon Cumin
- 1 teaspoon Salt
- 1 teaspoon Orange Zest
- 1/2 cup Vegetable Broth
- 1/2 cup Beer, ale or amber
- Parmesan Cheese, grated

Direction

- Brown the Farmer Girl Ground Beef with the onion in a large soup pot over medium heat until the beef has lost its pink color.
- Peel and chop the onion, sweet potato, and zucchini.
- Once the ground beef is browned, add the chopped veggies and the ingredients from the black beans to the vegetable broth. Bring to a boil.
- Add ½ cup to 1 cup of beer, depending on how much liquid you like in your chili.
- Decrease the temperature to a low simmer and continue cooking until the sweet potatoes are soft, approximately 2 hours.
- Garnish with freshly grated parmesan cheese.

143. Green Lentil Soup With Curried Brown Butter

Serving: Serves 4 to 6 | Prep: 0hours15mins | Cook: 0hours57mins |Ready in:

Ingredients

- 2 tablespoons butter, ghee, or coconut oil
- 1 large yellow onion, chopped
- 3 cloves garlic, chopped
- 1/2 teaspoon red pepper flakes
- 5 1/2 cups good-tasting vegetable broth or water

- 1 1/2 cups green lentils or green split peas, picked over and rinsed
- 3 tablespoons unsalted butter
- 1 tablespoon Indian curry powder
- 1/2 cup coconut milk
- 1 pinch Fine sea salt
- 1 handful Small cubes paneer, pan-fried in ghee or coconut oil, for garnish (optional)

Direction

- Combine the butter, onion, garlic, and red pepper flakes in a large soup pot over medium heat, stirring regularly for a couple of minutes until the onions soften.
- Pour in the vegetable broth and the lentils and simmer, covered, until the lentils are tender; start checking after 20 minutes, but keep in mind that it may take as long as 50 minutes.
- While the lentils cook, heat the 3 tablespoons of butter in a small saucepan over low heat. Stir it constantly with a rubber spatula until it starts to foam and brown, about 5 minutes. Stir in the curry powder and sauté until the mixture is very fragrant, just 30 seconds to 1 minute. Set aside.
- When the lentils have finished cooking, take the pot off the heat and stir in the coconut milk and 1/4 teaspoon of sea salt.
- Purée the soup using an immersion blender, or transfer it in batches to a blender or food processor. I left the soup slightly chunky, but you can also purée it until it's very smooth (and strain it if you're looking for an even silkier texture).
- Stir in half of the curried butter and taste the soup for salt, adding more as needed. Serve the soup drizzled with the remaining curried butter and with cubes of pan-fried paneer, if you like.

144.   Green Vegetables Soup

Serving: Serves 6 | Prep: | Cook: | Ready in:

Ingredients

- 2 tablespoons butter
- 1 medium yellow onion
- 1 bayleaf
- 1 carrot
- 4 cloves of garlic
- 3 medium heads of broccoli
- 1 1/2 pounds wild cabbage and/or spinach
- 4 tablespoons chopped fresh chives
- 6 cups organic vegetable stock
- 1 1/2 tablespoons lemon juice
- 250 milliliters milk
- salt&pepper
- sour cream

Direction

- Start by preparing all the vegetables. Finely chop the onion, carrot, garlic, and chives. Roughly chop the broccoli heads and the kale and spinach.
- In a large soup pot heat the butter over medium heat. Once butter is melted, add the onion, carrot, and bay leaf. Cook, stirring occasionally until the onions become translucent.
- Add the garlic, cooking until the garlic becomes fragrant. Add the kale and spinach, season with salt and pepper and cook until the kale and spinach are just wilted.
- Add 2 tablespoons of chives stirring to incorporate. Pour in white wine and scrape the bottom of the pan to deglaze. Simmer for 2 -3 minutes.
- Pour in the vegetable stock and all of the broccoli. Bring to a boil, then reduce heat and let simmer until the broccoli is tender.
- Remove the bay leaf and carefully blend the soup in batches in a standing blender or directly in the pot.
- Return the pureed soup to the pot and bring to a simmer over low heat. Stir in the milk (or heavy cream), lemon juice and additional salt and pepper to taste if needed.

- Serve and garnish bowls with a dollop of sour cream and the remaining chives. Don't forget to serve with fresh bread!

145. Grilled Cheese And Fresh Tomato Soup

Serving: Serves 4 | Prep: 0hours5mins | Cook: 0hours30mins | Ready in:

Ingredients

- 6 tablespoons softened butter, divided
- 1 tablespoon tomato paste
- 8 plum tomatoes (about 2 1/2 pounds), quartered
- 1 sprig fresh thyme
- 1 pinch sugar
- 1 medium garlic clove, halved
- 2 pinches Kosher salt and freshly ground black pepper
- 1 splash White wine vinegar to taste
- 5 1 inch-thick slices white sandwich bread (2 ounces each)
- 4 ounces Raclette cheese, sliced

Direction

- In a medium saucepan, heat 2 tablespoons of butter and the tomato paste over medium heat. Cook, stirring until the butter is foamy and the tomato paste begins to stick to the bottom of the pan, about 2 minutes. Stir in the tomatoes, thyme, sugar, half a garlic clove, and 4 cups water. Season generously with salt and pepper. Crumble 1 bread slice into pan, stirring to combine. Bring the soup to a boil, reduce the heat, and rapidly simmer for 10 minutes until the tomatoes have broken apart.
- Heat a large cast iron skillet over medium heat. While the soup simmers, make the sandwiches: Rub the inside of the bread slices with the cut side of the remaining garlic clove. Stack the cheese on top of two of the pieces of bread and sandwich it with the remaining bread slices (garlic-rubbed sides of all bread slices should be facing the cheese). Spread the exposed side of the bread slices with the remaining butter. Add the sandwiches to the hot pan and place a second, heavy skillet over the top. Fry the sandwiches, turning once, until the cheese is melted and the outside of the sandwiches are crispy, about 8 minutes.
- Remove the thyme stems from the cooked tomato soup. Working in two batches, transfer the tomato soup to a blender and purée until smooth. Season the soup with salt, pepper, and vinegar. Serve the soup in bowls, each accompanied with half of a sandwich.

146. Guatemalan Hot Sauce

Serving: Makes 1 quart | Prep: | Cook: | Ready in:

Ingredients

- 4 tablespoons pickled Chili Pequin or Bird Peppers, stems removed
- 4 Celery Stalks, chopped
- 1 medium White Onion, chopped
- 1 handful Cilantro Leaves
- 1 handful Parsley Leaves
- 1 tablespoon Sea Salt
- 2 tablespoons Olive Oil
- 4 tablespoons Red Wine Vinegar
- 6 Garlic Cloves
- 3 Limes, juiced
- Pepper, to taste

Direction

- Place all ingredients in the blender. Fill the blender half way up with water and emulsify ingredients until smooth.
- Notes: Make sure that you use the same amount of Parsley and Cilantro. Don't use the stems only the leaves. You can always add more Garlic and Pepper to make it spicier. I made the recipe white girl mild. Make sure only to use fresh garlic. If the sauce is too thin

just add more celery. You can buy jarred Chili Pequin in Latin Markets. These tiny peppers are insanely spicy so use sparingly. The Vinegar is important to add because it preserves the sauce so that it will last for one month in the refrigerator.

147. Halloween Soup

Serving: Serves 4 | Prep: | Cook: |Ready in:

Ingredients

- 2 Carrots, chopped
- 2 Celery stalks, chopped
- 2 tablespoons Olive or vegetable oil
- 2 cups Black beans, cooked, with their liquid; equal to 2 cans of 15 oz. each
- 1 1/2 cups Chicken or vegetable broth
- 1/4 teaspoon Cayenne pepper
- 1/2 teaspoon Cumin, ground
- Salt and pepper to taste
- 1/4 cup Tomato salsa
- 1/2 cup cheddar cheese, orange and sharp!, shredded
- 1/2 cup Sour cream or plain Greek yogurt

Direction

- In a medium saucepan, heat the oil. Add the carrots and celery, and sauté until tender.
- Add the beans and their liquid, then stir in the broth. Add the cayenne, cumin, salt, and pepper. Heat gently till simmering.
- Divide the soup among 4 bowls. Let each diner top their spooky serving with a spoonful of salsa, festive orange cheese, and a ghost of sour cream. Serve with crusty bread or tortilla chips. Follow with candy for dessert!

148. Ham And Mushroom Soup

Serving: Serves 10 | Prep: | Cook: |Ready in:

Ingredients

- 1 Large onion chopped
- 3 cups Sliced fresh mushrooms
- 5 Sliced carrots
- 1 cup Butter
- 4 cups Bone Broth
- 6 Potatoes diced
- 3 cups Diced cooked ham
- 3 cups Heavy cream
- 1/4 cup All-purpose flour
- 2 teaspoons Dried thyme
- 1 tablespoon Dried parsley flakes
- 1 teaspoon Garlic powder
- 3/4 teaspoon Celery seed
- 1 1/2 tablespoons Salt
- 2 teaspoons Pepper

Direction

- Sauté the onion, mushrooms, and carrots in 1/2 cup butter. Stir gently for 3 minutes.
- In a large pot, pour the bone broth in with the sautéed vegetables, and the ham and potatoes. Let simmer for 10 minutes.
- In a small bowl, whisk together the flour and the cream. Slowly add to the soup, and stir until it is smooth. Then add the other 1/2 cup of butter.
- Add in the rest of the ingredients. Let simmer until the vegetables are soft and cooked through.

149. Ham, Cider And Butternut Squash Soup

Serving: Serves 6 | Prep: | Cook: |Ready in:

Ingredients

- 3 lbs. butternut squash, split and seeded (or, if you want to buy the already prepped and packaged kind (like they do at Whole Foods) use 2½ lbs).
- 3 apples (Fuji or Braeburn – Granny Smith tends to be too noticeably tart), peeled (if you want a more refined look) or unpeeled (rustic!) and sliced thin.
- 1 additional apple (also Fuji or Braeburn) peeled and diced into 1/4 inch cubes
- 1 stick unsalted butter
- 2 tablespoons olive oil
- 1 meaty smoked ham hock
- 1 medium onion, finely chopped
- 2 cloves garlic, finely chopped
- 1 celery rib, finely chopped
- 2 tablespoons kosher salt
- 1 teaspoon freshly ground black pepper
- 3 cups high-quality hard apple cider (French, if you can find it).
- 3 cups chicken or vegetable stock
- 2 cups water

Direction

- Preheat oven to 350°F.
- Heat a 9-quart (or larger, if you've been keeping fit – those things are heavy) Dutch oven over medium heat. Add the olive oil and place the squash in, cut side down. If it doesn't all fit, no problem – just make sure that the olive oil coats the cut side of the squash. If using already prepped squash, stir to make sure that all pieces are coated with oil. Add 1/2 cup water, and place in the oven (lid off!) until the squash is tender — about 45 minutes.
- When the squash is tender, take it out of the Dutch oven and let it cool on a plate. Pour off any remaining water and put the Dutch oven back on the stovetop. Melt the butter in the Dutch oven, add the onions, garlic, celery, a tablespoon of salt, and 1/2 teaspoon pepper and sauté until onions are soft, about 10 minutes. Add the apples and sauté until tender, about 3 to 4 minutes. Add the cider and bring to boil. Reduce heat and simmer uncovered until liquid is reduced by half.

- When squash is cool enough to handle, scoop out the flesh and add it to the soup. If you're using the prepped and cubed squash, it should be obvious that you just dump it into the soup at this point. Add the stock, the ham hock, the remaining water, and the remaining salt and pepper, and jack up the heat to bring the soup to a boil. Reduce heat to a simmer and partially cover the pot. Simmer for 45 minutes to an hour, stirring regularly.
- Remove the ham hock and – working in batches – purée the soup in a blender or food processor until very smooth (or use an in-the-pot blender) and bring the soup back to a simmer. Add the additional diced apple.
- When the ham hock is cool enough to work with, shred the meat off and discard the rest. Return the meat to the Dutch oven and simmer until the diced apple is tender, about 20-30 minutes, depending on the size of the dice. If the soup is too thick for your liking, add equal parts stock and water until it is at the desired consistency.
- Salt and pepper to taste, and serve with croutons, or with a nice, crusty bread.

150. Harvest Minestrone With Herb Lemon Pesto

Serving: Serves a big pot, about 8 | Prep: | Cook: | Ready in:

Ingredients

- Soup
- 1 cup Dried Beans (see headnote)
- 2 ounces pancetta, cubed small
- olive oil
- 1 large yellow onion, diced
- 2 stalks celery, diced
- 4 carrots, 2 diced and 2 sliced into thin rounds
- 3 garlic cloves, minced
- 3 ounces Parmigiano-Reggiano Rinds

- 7-8 cups chicken stock
- 1 tablespoon New Mexico Chile Powder (Rancho Gordo's is great)
- 6 ounces green beans, cut into bite size pieces
- 1 large or 2 small zuchinni, bite size cubes
- 1 large or 2 small summer squash, bite size cubes
- 5 ounces baby spinach
- juice of 1/2 lemon (reserve zest of the whole lemon for the pesto)
- salt & pepper
- Lemon Herb Pesto
- 2 cups loosely packed herbs, equal amounts of chives, thai basil, parsley and a small amount of tarragon and mint. This is very adjustable for whatever you have in the garden or fridge.
- 1/3 cup toasted pine nuts
- zest of one lemon
- 1 ounce parmesan cheese
- 3-4 tablespoons olive oil
- salt

Direction

- Soup
- Rinse the beans and pick out debris. Soak the beans for 4-6 hours or overnight in filtered water. The beans should be covered by 1-2 inches of water. If you forget, no big deal. The beans will just take a little longer to cook.
- Sauté the pancetta in a little olive oil over medium heat in a large Dutch oven or stock pot until crisp. Remove the pancetta with a slotted soup and set aside.
- Turn the heat up to medium high and add the onions, celery, diced carrot, and garlic to the pancetta drippings. Sauté approximately 8-10 minutes until soft.
- Drain the beans, reserving the liquid. Add enough chicken stock to the bean liquid so you have 8 cups of liquid. Add the combined liquid, beans, parmesan rinds, and chili powder to the pot. The chile powder adds a beautiful color and a light background flavor.
- Bring to a boil and hard boil for five minutes. Reduce the heat to low and simmer until the beans they are just about cooked through and

soft. It took me about 2 hours but it really depends upon your beans. If your liquid is evaporating too fast or you prefer a more brothy soup, add more stock or partially cover the pot.
- Add salt to taste (I used 1 TB but it depends upon the salt content of your stock), the carrot coins and simmer for 10 minutes. Then add the green beans, zucchini, and squash and simmer until cooked through, 5-10 minutes.
- Turn the heat to low and add the spinach and lemon juice. Cover until the spinach is just wilted. Season to taste with salt and lots of pepper.
- Serve topped with a dollop of the pesto and a sprinkling of the pancetta bits if your piggly wiggly husband hasn't already sneaked all the pancetta bits when you weren't looking!
- Lemon Herb Pesto
- Pulse all the ingredients in a food processor until coarsely blended. Start with 3 TB olive and add more if need to combine. Season to taste with salt

---

151.   Harvest Stew

Serving: Serves 6-8 | Prep: 0hours0mins | Cook: 0hours0mins | Ready in:

Ingredients

- 1 tablespoon olive oil
- 1 large onion (peeled & chopped)
- 1/2 head of garlic (peeled & minced)
- 1-1/2 pounds ground bison
- 2 pounds butternut squash (peeled & cubed)
- 30 ounces canned tomato sauce (I like Muir Glen)
- 2 cups vegetable broth
- 1/2 teaspoon sea salt
- 10 ounces fresh baby spinach

Direction

- Chop onion & garlic & place in large soup pot with olive oil. Cook over medium heat for a few minutes, to soften.
- Add bison & brown both sides, cutting meat into chunks in the process.
- Add tomato sauce, broth & salt. Bring to boil & then reduce to simmer.
- Peel & de-seed squash. Chop into cubes & add to pot. Simmer for 30 minutes
- Add baby spinach last, cooking for just 1-2 minutes, until wilted.
- Serve!

---

152. Healthy Broccoli Soup

Serving: Makes 6 cups | Prep: | Cook: | Ready in:

Ingredients

- 1 onion
- 2 celery stalks
- 2 garlic cloves
- 1 cup white wine
- 2 cups stock (chicken is best, but veggie works too)
- 12 oz broccoli, stems and florets seperated (about 1 1/2 heads)
- 1/4 cup cheese (optional)
- 2 tablespoons butter (optional)
- 1 cup spinach (optional)
- to taste   Salt & Pepper

Direction

- Roughly chop the onions and celery into medium sized pieces. Smash the garlic cloves. Sautee in a large pot over medium low heat until the onions are translucent and the celery is tender. Season generously.
- Add wine and turn the heat up to high. Simmer until almost all of the wine has evaporated.
- Add the stock and bring to a boil. Check for seasoning.

- Cut the broccoli stems into small pieces. Add the broccoli stems and cook until very tender, about 6 minutes.
- Add the broccoli florets and simmer until bright green, about 1 minute.
- Transfer the soup to a blender. Add the cheese and butter if desired.
- Carefully puree the soup. Start on low so the soup does not splatter. If the soup is too thick, add more stock or water. Gradually turn the speed up to high and puree until smooth.
- If the color is not perfectly green, add raw spinach and puree until smooth.
- The soup is ready to serve! Garnish with extra cheese and enjoy with crusty bread.

---

153. Heart Smart Bean And Barley Soup

Serving: Makes 8 servings | Prep: | Cook: | Ready in:

Ingredients

- 2 tablespoons canola oil
- 1 medium onion, diced
- 2 large parsnips, peeled and cut into 3/4-inch pieces
- 3 large carrots peeled and cut into 3/4-inch pieces
- 6 garlic cloves, minced
- 8 cups low sodium chicken or vegetable stock
- 2 medium russet potatoes, peeled and cut into 1-inch pieces
- 2 teaspoons minced fresh thyme
- 2 sprigs fresh rosemary
- 1 bay leaf
- 2/3 cup barley (uncooked)
- 3 cups kale (or spinach), stems trimmed and chopped
- 1 14.5 oz small white beans (navy beans), drained and rinsed
- 10 ounces package frozen peas
- salt and pepper to taste

Direction

- Heat oil in a large stockpot on high heat and add onion, parsnips, and carrots, and cook until lightly browned and softened, about 5 to 7 minutes. Add garlic and cook until fragrant, about 30 seconds more.
- Add broth, and then potatoes, uncooked barley, and herbs and bay leaf and bring to a boil. Reduce heat, and simmer for about 50 minutes, or until barley is tender.
- Remove and discard bay leaf and rosemary stems.
- With an immersion blender, pulse soup about 10 times, or until desired consistency is achieved. Alternatively, remove about 2 cups of the solids and liquid and puree them in a blender. Add pureed mixture back into the pot.
- Add drained beans, kale and peas, and simmer for another 10 minutes, or until peas are tender.
- Add salt and pepper to taste.

154. Hearty Sausage & Kale Lentil Soup

Serving: Serves 4 | Prep: | Cook: | Ready in:

Ingredients

- 12 ounces Pork Sausage, uncased
- 4 Campari Tomatoes
- 1 Roasted Red Pepper
- 1 Medium White Onion, minced
- 1 1/2 tablespoons Minced Garlic
- 1 cup Dry Lentils, washed & sorted
- 1 1/2 cups Organic Vegetable Broth
- 1 cup Water
- 1/2 teaspoon Ground Cumin
- 1/4 teaspoon Fresh Cracked Pepper
- 1 Bay Leaf
- 8 Baby Carrots
- 2 handfuls Chopped Kale

Direction

- In a large pot, brown the sausage on medium heat.
- Pulse the tomatoes and the roasted pepper in a food processor until you have a slightly chunky sauce.
- Add the tomato and red pepper mixture to the sausage along with the lentils, vegetable broth, water, cumin, black pepper and bay leaf.
- Mix and cover. Simmer on low heat for about 1 hour.
- Stir in carrots and add more broth if needed (based on your desired consistency)
- Cover and let simmer another 15-20 minutes before adding in kale.
- Simmer for 5-10 minutes. Lentils should be soft and kale wilted. Soup is ready to enjoy!

155. Hearty Sausage, Eggplant, And Bean Soup

Serving: Serves 8 | Prep: | Cook: | Ready in:

Ingredients

- 1 tablespoon olive oil
- 1 cup diced onions
- 1 pound Italian sausage links (chicken or pork both work well)
- 2 garlic cloves, minced
- 4 carrots, peeled and diced
- 2 cups chicken broth
- 1 14.5 oz can fire roasted crushed tomatoes, undrained
- 2 cups eggplant, peeled and diced
- 4 small red potatoes, unpeeled and diced
- 1 14.5 oz can cannellini beans, drained and rinsed
- 1 teaspoon dried thyme
- 2 bay leaves
- 1 tablespoon chopped fresh parsley
- 1/2 cup ditalini or other small pasta
- salt and pepper

Direction

- Heat olive oil in a large Dutch oven over medium high heat. Add onions and sausage. Cook until onions are translucent and sausage is browned, about 5 minutes, turning the sausage half way through. Add garlic and carrots and cook for 2 more minutes.
- Add broth, tomatoes, eggplant, potatoes, beans, thyme, bay leaves, and parsley. Bring to a simmer and cook on medium low for 10 minutes. Remove sausage links and slice into rounds. It's okay if the sausage isn't cooked all the way through when you slice it; it can break up a bit in the soup. Return to pot along with any juices from the cutting board and stir to combine.
- Simmer another 20 minutes or until eggplant begins to break down and the carrots are soft.
- Add pasta and cook for 10 more minutes. Season with salt and pepper.
- Spoon into bowls, grate some Parmigiano-Reggiano on top, and serve with your favorite bread. As my son says, "Deeeeeeeeeeeeeee-licious!"

---

156.   Hearty Turkey (or Chicken) Noodle Soup

Serving: Serves 8-10 | Prep: | Cook: | Ready in:

Ingredients

- 2 onions, roughly chopped
- 2 carrots, peeled and coined
- 4 stalks of celery, thinly sliced
- 4 garlic cloves, minced
- 2 bay leaves
- 1 teaspoon whole black peppercorns
- 1 roasted turkey (or chicken) carcass, leftover meat attached
- 3-4 cups cooked poultry meat, shredded
- 1 pound carrots, peeled and coined
- 4 garlic cloves, minced
- 6 stalks celery, thinly sliced

- 1 onion, chopped
- Package of dry pasta (your choice)
- salt and pepper to taste

Direction

- For the Broth: Place first 5 ingredients in a very large, heavy stock pot. Saute with 2 TB oil, on medium high until vegetables are soft. Add bay leaves, whole peppercorns, and poultry carcass. Add enough water to just cover entire carcass. (Broth will eventually be reduced to half, so if you know you want more broth, can add more water to begin with.)
- Bring stock pot to boil. Turn heat to low, and simmer uncovered until liquid is reduced to half its original amount (approx. 2-3 hours). Once liquid is reduced to half, set aside carcass and skim impurities and oil off top. Strain broth into a separate large pot.
- For the Noodle Soup: Season strained broth with salt and pepper to taste. Add carrots, celery, onions, and garlic. Bring to boil. Cook until veggies are very tender.
- Meanwhile, cook noodles in well-salted water in separate pot. Drain noodles. Add to broth. Add all shredded meat, including any additional meat from the boiled carcass.
- Season with additional salt and pepper to taste. Enjoy!

---

157.   Hearty Vegetable Stew

Serving: Serves 6+ | Prep: | Cook: | Ready in:

Ingredients

- 1 quart vegetable stock
- 1 quart water, more if needed
- 3-4 medium potatoes, cut into cubes
- 3-4 medium tomatoes, cut into eighths.
- 6 carrots, peeled and cut
- 2 cans of lentils
- 1 yellow squash, cut into thick pieces
- 1 zucchini, cut into thick pieces

- 1 bunch curly kale, chopped
- 2 cups corn, either canned or fresh.
- 4 garlic cloves, cut into slivers
- salt, to taste
- 2 tablespoons black pepper

Direction

- Pour vegetable stock and water into 5-quart pot or larger, Heat over medium setting.
- Add potatoes, tomatoes, garlic, lentils and carrots, cook for 25 minutes
- Add yellow squash and zucchini slices, cook for 10 minutes
- Add corn and kale, cook until Kale has lost most of its toughness. Add extra water if stew has gotten a little too thick. Turn off heat and let it rest for about 10 minutes, then serve.

158.   Heirloom Jewish Chicken Soup

Serving: Makes enough | Prep: | Cook: | Ready in:

Ingredients

- 1 small chicken, whole
- 8 carrots, peeled and cut into 2 inch pieces
- 1 bunch parsley, washed and trimmed
- 1 bunch dill, washed and trimmed
- 1/4 teaspoon turmeric
- 2 teaspoons salt
- 1/4 teaspoon white pepper

Direction

- Wash your chicken, inside and out. Especially all the brown things from inside the thigh. Trim excess fat and skin from the neck and bottom openings.
- Put your chicken in a big pot and cover totally with fresh water.
- Add salt.
- Bring to a boil over a high heat.

- Skim the soup. Any yucky stuff in the chicken will boil out and rise to the top in a brownish scum. You want to get this out. Holding your ladle straight up, press it gently into the surface of the soup where the most scum is. Tip one edge of the ladle in just a tiny bit. The scum will drizzle into the ladle. Throw that away. Repeat, moving the chicken around a little, until no more scum rises to the surface.
- Once all the scum is removed, add the carrots.
- Add the parsley and dill. Don't cut it. Just wash it and if necessary you can trim the excess stems. This allows you to serve the soup with or without greens, depending upon your guests' preference.
- Add turmeric and white pepper and add more water if necessary.
- Bring to a full boil.
- Taste and add more salt if necessary.
- Reduce heat to medium low and simmer for at least 30 minutes or longer. The longer you cook it, the richer the flavor (but not too long).
- Remove from heat and cool until you can handle the chicken.
- Wash your hands, reach into the soup and carefully pull out the whole chicken. Put it into a bowl.
- You're probably hungry after all that work, so you deserve to eat the wings now.
- Pull off the skin, add clean pieces of thigh and drumstick meat back into the soup.
- Clean off the breast and put it in the fridge to make chicken salad tomorrow.
- Before dinner, cook up some fine egg noodles and heat the soup.
- Serve by putting some noodles into each bowl. Ladle in the soup with a couple pieces of chicken, carrots and some greens. The soup should be very hot.
- Beautiful, golden, clean and delicious chicken soup like my mom, her mom and her mom and ... used to make.
- Note: I have a dog, so all the trimmings and skimmings goes into a separate pan for him. I'll cook it up and drizzle it over his dry food for a special treat.

159. Heirloom Tomato "Shorba"

Serving: Serves 2 | Prep: | Cook: |Ready in:

Ingredients

- 4 Chopped Heirloom Tomatoes
- 4-5 Roughly Chopped Fresh Cilantro stems
- 1/2 tsp Cumin seeds
- 1tbsp Chick peas flour
- 2 cups Veg./Chicken broth
- 2 tbsp Olive oil
- 1tsp Chopped fresh cilantro
- Dash Green Hot Pepper
- 4 cloves Chopped Garlic
- Salt & Pepper to taste

Direction

- Heat 1tbsp Olive oil in a pot and sauté the Garlic & Hot Peppers till golden brown
- Add chopped Tomatoes, Cilantro stems and cook while crushing the tomatoes
- Once the tomatoes are cooked and dried, stir in the Veg. /Chicken broth
- Make a slurry of 1tbsp Chickpeas flour with about 1/4th cup water (at room temp.) and stir into the pot. Add Salt & Pepper to taste
- Bring this to a boil and simmer till you get a desired consistency
- Strain the contents and keep aside
- For the "Tadka" - Heat 1 tbsp. Olive Oil in a small pan. Add Cumin seeds and wait till it crackles. Immediately add this to the strained liquid and stir
- If desired, the liquid can be boiled again. Transfer to soup bowls. Garnish with chopped Cilantro leaves and serve hot.

160. Hokkaido Style Salmon & Tofu Hot Pot

Serving: Serves 4 | Prep: | Cook: |Ready in:

Ingredients

- 4 cups water
- 1.5 teaspoons instant dashi powder (look for msg-free)
- 4 tablespoons white miso paste (or a red-white "awase" mix)
- 1 cup chopped shiitake mushrooms
- 2 cups chopped napa cabbage
- 1 block firm tofu, cubed
- 1 thin strip salmon fillet, cooked (see note for substituting fresh or thawed salmon)
- 2 fresh scallions, chopped finely

Direction

- Bring the water to a boil in a large pot and add the dashi powder, mix well until the powder is dissolved. Turn the heat down to a low simmer.
- Put the miso in a small mesh strainer and submerge it halfway into the simmering water. Use a spoon or chopsticks to swirl the miso and help it dissolve into the water through the strainer.
- If using fresh or thawed salmon, add it to the miso broth and simmer until translucent, 2-3 minutes.
- Add the mushrooms and cabbage and stir until just cooked through, about a minute. Then gently add the tofu (and salmon, if using cooked salmon) and cook until just heated through.
- Turn the heat off and sprinkle fresh scallions into the soup. Gently stir the broth to mix up the miso again, then spoon into bowls. Optional: serve with steamed rice and pickled daikon radish.

161. Home Sweet Home Buffalo Chili

Serving: Serves around 8 | Prep: | Cook: | Ready in:

Ingredients

- The Roux
- 2 tablespoons olive oil
- 2 tablespoons flour
- 1 tablespoon ground cumin
- 2 teaspoons dried oregano
- 2 teaspoons coarse black pepper
- 1 1/2 teaspoons white pepper
- 2 teaspoons crushed red pepper (cayenne or Thai)
- The Chili
- 2 cups onion, large dice
- 4 large garlic cloves, minced
- 1 cup bell pepper
- 1/2 cup garlic stems
- 1 (or 2) jalapeno pepper
- 2 pounds ground buffalo
- 28- ounces can fire-roasted tomatoes, undrained (Meir Glen my favorite)
- 12 ounces dark beer
- 15 ounces can black beans, drained, rinsed
- 2 squares baking chocolate (or Van Houten cocoa)
- salt, to taste
- tortillas or na'an

Direction

- Heat oil in a large cooking pot with a heavy bottom over medium heat. Add flour and stir until the roux is a light caramel color. Lower heat, add spices and stir for 1 minute.
- Add onion and sauté 7 minutes. Add garlic, garlic stems, and peppers, and cook for 3 minutes.
- Add buffalo meat, raise to medium heat and cook until pink is gone. Add tomatoes and beer, and bring to a boil. Cover, reduce heat, and simmer for 1 hour.

- Stir in beans and chocolate, stirring to melt. Add salt to taste. Cook, covered, for 15 minutes.
- Serve with tortillas. My hearty-appitite son likes to eat it with na'an.
- Leave out the beans, vegetarian still great chili. Goes great with toppings: sour cream, cheddar cheese, diced avocado, sliced green onions, or crunchy stuff like corn chips!
- Go Buffalos!

162. Hong Kong Style Spam & Egg Macaroni Soup (午餐肉通粉)

Serving: Serves 2 | Prep: 0hours10mins | Cook: 0hours30mins | Ready in:

Ingredients

- 2 cups macaroni
- 4 cups chicken broth
- 1/4 cup green peas
- 1 can of 13 oz. corn kernels
- 1 can of 12 oz. spam, cubed
- 1 egg
- 1 teaspoon soy sauce
- 1 pinch sea salt and black pepper to taste
- 1 dash sesame oil

Direction

- In a pot, cook the macaroni according to manufacturer's instructions until al dente. Drain and set aside.
- Pan-fry cubes of spam until crispy and one egg over medium.
- In another pot, boil chicken stock. Add macaroni, corn, green peas, corn kernels, and spam. Cook until it boils again. Add soy sauce, sea salt and black pepper.
- Drizzle with sesame oil. Serve hot with a fried egg on top.

163.   Hot And Sour Coconut Chicken Soup (Tom Kha Kai)

Serving: Serves 4 | Prep: | Cook: | Ready in:

Ingredients

- 2 stalks lemongrass, cut in rings
- 1" pieces galangal or ginger, sliced
- 2 cloves garlic
- 8 kaffir lime leaves (optional, but really adds to the fragrance)
- 2 serrano peppers, seeds removed dependent on how spicy
- 3 cups water
- 2 limes, juice (or to taste)
- fish sauce (to taste)
- 1 chicken breast, thinly sliced
- green onion (garnish)
- cilantro (garnish)
- 2 cups coconut milk

Direction

- Give the lemongrass, galangal, garlic a smash with the back side of a knife or in a mortar.
- Dice the shallot, thinly slice the kaffir lime leaves. Toast the ingredients to release the aroma.
- Add water and bring to a simmer for 30 minutes and allow the ingredients to steep for another 10-15 minutes.
- Add the sliced chicken and allow to cook in the soup until the chicken is cooked; about 10 minutes.
- Add the coconut milk and allow to boil. Lower the heat and scoop out the lemongrass, galangal, kaffir leaves.
- Squeeze in the lime juice to taste; add fish sauce and serrano pepper.
- Add mushrooms (optional) and allow to simmer for about a minute.
- Garnish with chopped green onion and cilantro.

164.   ICY MINT GAZPACHO SHOT THROUGH WITH GARLIC

Serving: Serves 6 | Prep: | Cook: | Ready in:

Ingredients

- ICY MINT GAZPACHO
- 1/2 cup ground raw almonds, preferably organic
- 3 cloves of garlic
- 1.5 large hothouse tomatoes, cut into approximate 1/2" cubes
- 1 unwaxed fresh cucumber, diced
- 1 celery stalk, leaves removed and diced
- 1 green bell pepper, seeded and cut into small narrow slivers.
- 1 yellow bell pepper, seeded and cut into small narrow slivers
- 2 slices of whole wheat bread
- 2 cups of cubed seedless watermelon
- 2 cups unsalted and unspiced tomato sauce
- 1 cup garlic croutons, recipe below
- 1 cup mini-ice cubes
- 3 limes, juicy
- 2 tablespoons kosher or sea salt
- 2 tablespoons olive oil, preferably extra-virgin organic
- 2 teaspoons freshly ground pepper, on the "fine" setting
- 7 sprigs mint leaves
- GARLIC CROUTONS
- 2 slice of whole wheat bread, lightly toasted
- 5 garlic cloves, chopped finely
- 1 tablespoon olive oil, preferably organic extra-virgin

Direction

- ICY MINT GAZPACHO
- Immerse the mint sprigs in a bowl of cold filtered water and add the kosher or sea salt to the bowl. Let stand for a half hour, then rinse out any impurities with cold filtered water.

- Mince the mint leaves. Reserve half for a topping, and place the other half in a large stainless steel bowl. Add to the bowl the tomato cubes, the diced cucumber and celery, the slivered bell peppers, and the watermelon cubes.
- Soak the whole wheat bread briefly in cold filtered water, then dry.
- Crush the garlic cloves and sauté in the olive oil, in a fry pan over moderate heat. Let the sautéed garlic cool, then mix thoroughly with the soaked whole wheat bread, and cut into half-inch-sized pieces.
- Add the garlic-infused whole-wheat pieces to the mixture, assimilating the ground almonds as well.
- Halve the limes, filter out any seeds, and squeeze them, raining the liquid into the bowl.
- Add the tomato sauce and 1 cup of cold filtered water. Divide into 6 bowls, and distribute the mini ice-cubes evenly among the bowls.
- Distribute the reserved minced mint leaves evenly among the bowls. Sprinkle the freshly ground black pepper on the soup in each bowl. Add the garlic croutons on top. Serve. Alternatively, this recipe can be made in advance, with everything except for the ice-cubes, black pepper, chopped mint, and croutons placed in a covered bowl and refrigerated for 24 hours. When ready to serve add the ice cubes, black pepper, reserved mint, and croutons.
- GARLIC CROUTONS
- Lightly heat the olive oil. Add the garlic cloves, sautéing them.
- Cut up the lightly toasted whole wheat bread into '/4" cubes, and mix with the sautéed garlic.

165.   Irish Fish Stew

Serving: Serves 4 | Prep: | Cook: | Ready in:

Ingredients

- Fish Stew
- 2 ounces thick-cut bacon, cut into ¼" cubes
- 1 medium onion, chopped into ¼" pieces
- 1 tablespoon flour
- 1/4 cup dry white wine
- 3 cups fish stock (recipe follows)
- 4 small new potatoes, red skin scrubbed and left on, cut into ½" pieces
- 1 medium turnip, peeled and cut into ½" pieces
- 1 branch of celery, cut into small pieces, about ¼" thick
- 1/2 teaspoon fresh thyme, minced
- 1 bay leaf
- Salt and freshly ground pepper to taste
- 1 pound cod fillets, rinsed, patted dry and cut into 3" chunks (they'll break up once cooked)
- 1/2 cup heavy cream
- 2 tablespoons parsley, minced
- 1 tablespoon chives, minced
- Fish Stock (makes about 8 cups; freeze leftover)
- 2 tablespoons olive oil
- 1 large onion, chopped
- 1 celery stalk, chopped
- 3 dried shitake mushroom (optional but good to keep in your pantry for flavor boosting)
- 2 cloves garlic, crushed
- 3 pounds fish heads, bones, fins – or whatever treats your fishmonger gives you… Rinse before using
- 3 cups dry white wine
- 6 cups water
- 1 fistful of parsley stems
- 2 sprigs fresh thyme
- 5 whole black peppercorns
- 1 bay leaf
- 1 teaspoon salt

Direction

- Fish Stew
- In a 4-quart heavy-bottomed pot, heat bacon over a medium heat until fat is rendered and bacon is browned. Remove cooked bacon to a

small bowl with a slotted spoon, setting aside for later.

- In the same pot, add chopped onion and cook 5 minutes, until softened, stirring occasionally.
- Add flour, stirring for 3 minutes, then add wine and ½ cup of fish stock. Continue stirring as the liquid thickens with the onions and flour. Continue adding the stock in ½ cup increments, stirring occasionally and waiting a few minutes between each addition. This ensures the stew base maintains some thickness.
- Once all the stock has been added, bring liquid to the boil and add the potatoes, turnips, celery, thyme and bay leaf. Season with salt and pepper. Lower heat to a simmer and cook for 15 minutes uncovered, or until the vegetables are just tender.
- Add the big chunks of fish and cook for 5 minutes. Gently stir in the cream, cooked bacon and parsley and heat through, just enough until the stew is piping hot and ready to serve. Garnish each serving with a pinch of minced chives.
- Fish Stock (makes about 8 cups; freeze leftover)
- Heat the oil in a large pot over a medium-low heat. Add the onion, celery, mushrooms, garlic, and fish bones. Increase the heat to high, cover, and cook about 10 minutes. Stir a few times. The ingredients will release their delicious liquid. Lower the heat to medium and continue to cook, stirring frequently and pressing on the fish bones/heads with a spoon to break them down, until the vegetables and bones are soft and aromatic, about 10 minutes longer.
- Add the wine, water, parsley, thyme, peppercorns, bay leaf, and salt, and bring to boil. Reduce the heat to low and simmer, uncovered, until stock is rich and flavorful, about 30 minutes.
- Strain the stock and discard the solids. The stock can be refrigerated in an airtight container for up to 2 days or frozen for several months.

166. It Quacks Like A Duck Won Ton Soup With Greens

Serving: Serves 4 | Prep: | Cook: |Ready in:

Ingredients

- 1 boneless duck breast about 16 ounces (the thickness of the skin and fat layer will determine how much flesh the breast will yield)
- Won ton wrappers
- 1/2 bunch collard greens, to yield 2 cups
- 1/2 bunch dandelion greens, to yield 1 cup
- zest from one small orange or tangerine
- 1/2 tablespoon Chinese five spice powder
- egg white from a single egg
- 1 tablespoon soy sauce or Maggi seasoning
- 3 ounces extra firm tofu diced
- 2 scallions, sliced on the bias
- chopped cilantro (optional)
- 1 1/2 quarts chicken stock (or duck stock if you have it)

Direction

- Stem your collard greens and cut each leaf in half down the middle. Stack the leaves and roll into cylinders. Slice crosswise into ribbons.
- Slice off the bottom stems of dandelion greens. The upper stems are tender when cooked. Slice these greens into ribbons as well.
- Season the ground duck with orange zest, salt and pepper, soy sauce and five spice powder.
- Using your clean hands work in the egg white to help bind the mixture.
- Have a bowl of water handy. Place no more than one teaspoon of the duck mixture in the center of a wonton skin. A melon baller works well for this. Don't over stuff or you risk won ton blow out. Dip your finger in the bowl of water and run it along the sides and far edge of the won ton skin. Fold and seal to your preferred method.* this should yield 20 or more won tons.

- Bring the chicken stock to a steady simmer. Add the greens to the pot and continue to simmer for 25-30 minutes or until very tender.
- Add the won tons. Simmer away until they begin to float. Taste one for doneness.
- Add the tofu dice and the cilantro if using. Finish with scallion and serve
- *A simple method for folding goes like this: place the filling in the center of the skin, wet the edges. Lift the edge of the skin closest to you and fold it all the way to the far end. Press edges to seal. Fold in half one more time. Bend the roll slightly to bring the far corners together. Wet the top of one corner and the bottom of the opposing corner. Press corners together. Roll on.

167.   Italian Colors Soup

Serving: Serves 2 | Prep: | Cook: | Ready in:

Ingredients

- 100 grams Pasta (fusilli)
- 1 bunch Spinach
- 100 grams Broccoli
- 2 tablespoons Chopped gree onions
- 50 grams Beans
- 8   Cherry tomatoes
- 2 tablespoons White wine
- 1 tablespoon Instant bouillon
- 1 pinch salt
- 1 pinch pepper
- 2 tablespoons Parmesan cheese
- 2 1/2 cups Water
- 1 tablespoon Olive oil

Direction

- Cut vegetables during boiling water in a pot.
- Once it boils, put those vegetables and all of ingredients.
- Add pasta (fusilli) in a pot and boil them.

168.   Japanese Beef Udon Soup Or Why Should Ramen Get All The Glory?!

Serving: Serves 2 | Prep: | Cook: | Ready in:

Ingredients

- 3 cups Dashi * (a fish broth)
- 1 c. shiitake broth** (or dashi)
- 2-4 T. tamari or Japanese Soy Sauce
- 2-4 T. Sake
- 2 teaspoon sugar
- 1 teaspoon kosher salt
- 2 T. canola oil
- 8-10 sliced fresh shiitake caps***
- 2 T. canola oil
- 3 scallions, rinsed, thinly sliced in rounds
- ½ lb. shaved beef, fresh and sliced or frozen and sliced
- 1 T tamari or Japanese soy sauce
- 1 T sugar
- pinch of kosher salt
- 1 -2 medium carrots, sliced in thin half rounds
- 1 medium zucchini, sliced in thin half rounds
- 1 c. snowpeas, sliced on diagonal
- 9-16 ou. fresh or frozen pre-cooked udon(I prefer Sanuki style, the white square chewy ones)
- ½ lb. soft tofu, in ½ inch cubes
- Toasted Sesame Seeds

Direction

- You will need two 2-quart saucepans on two front burners. Fill the right saucepan with 6-8 cups of water, cover, and bring to a boil. Meanwhile, heat a little oil in the left pan, add shiitakes and sauté 5 minutes till cooked through. Remove shiitakes to an empty saucepan or bowl.
- Add scallions to the hot oil in pan and stir fry over high heat 1 minute.

- Add meat, stirring quickly, then add soy- salt and stir-fry a few more seconds till still a little pink inside. Pour into shiitake bowl.
- Add dashi and shiitake broth to left pot, add soy- salt mixture to taste, cover and bring to boil; then turn to low simmer and cover.
- In the right pan, drop in carrots to boiling water, remove after 30-60 seconds, when carrots are easily pierced .Add them to the shiitake bowl.
- Add zucchini till cooked through, ~ 2 minutes, and remove to shiitake bowl.
- Finally, drop in the pre-cooked udon noodles and stir to separate. Remove in ~ 1- 3 minutes, after heated through. Be careful not to overcook the udon. Add to shiitakes bowl. (A bamboo-handle Chinese wire mesh scooper is ideal for all this blanching.)
- Divide the dashi and bring to a boil in the 2 saucepans. Divide the udon into the saucepans, cover and quickly bring each pot to a boil, then add all the vegetables and beef and quickly bring to boil. Immediately pour into 2 heated serving bowls. Top with cubed tofu and sesame seeds. Serve. If you are serving 4+ people, repeat all of the above for every 2 bowls. We serve udon soup in big (10 cup) pasta bowls with a flat bottomed white Chinese spoon.
- *DASHI :1 5 inch piece of kombu(a hard thick olive green dried seaweed) if you have it; 5 c. water; 2 1/2 c. bonito flakes; Dashi is so much easier to make than fish or chicken stock, but you do need to find its 2 ingredients at a Japanese store. I like a stronger dashi than most Japanese, so I cook it longer: Add Kombu to pot of water, remove it just as the water comes to a boil. Add bonito flakes and push down into the water. Turn off the heat. When bonito has sunk to bottom of pot, bring back to boil; turn down to simmer 10-30 minutes. Strain, pushing on solids. I yielded 3 c. dashi from 5 c. water. (I simmer the bonito flakes a second and longer time for myself. Then I compost the flakes or give them to the kitties. You can also buy tea bag-like dashi mix at Japanese stores.)

- ** SHIITAKE BROTH: Boil and then low simmer the stems from 1 lb. fresh shiitakes in 6-8 cups water. Simmer, covered, 1-2 hours, adding water to keep original level. Strain broth, pushing down on solids. Cook this down to intensify flavor. Whenever I sauté fresh shiitake, I make shiitake broth, and keep some in the freezer for soups and sauces. Like any stock, you can cook it down significantly so it takes up less freezer space.
- ***You can use dried shiitake/black mushroom caps, poached in water 1/2 hour till tender, then sliced, but make sure they are not too old (no scent.) I have come to prefer the silky and meaty texture of fresh sautéed shiitake.
- If you have leftovers, store the solids separated from the liquid so they don't get mushy.

169.   Jerusalem Artichoke Soup

Serving: Serves 6-8 | Prep: | Cook: |Ready in:

Ingredients

- 12   jerusalem artichokes,peeled and coarsely chopped
- 3/4 cup shallots, minced
- salt
- white pepper
- 1 tablespoon olive oil
- 4 cups vegetable stock
- 3 cups water
- 1/2 cup white wine
- 1   bay leaf
- 5   sprigs of parsley
- 1   clove garlic
- 1   medium carrot
- 6   mushrooms

Direction

- In a stock pot or pressure cooker sweat the shallots in olive oil then add the jerusalem artichokes and cook till tender. Add salt and pepper.

- Pour in the liquids and add the bay leaf, parsley, garlic and carrot. Bring to a simmer and cook for 30 -45 min or 7 minutes if you are using a pressure cooker.
- Remove the parsley and carrot and bay leaf. Puree the soup with an immersion blender.
- Slice mushrooms and sauté over high heat in butter or olive oil till tender. Place a few pieces in the bowl when serving the soup

170. Jerusalem Artichoke Soup With White Truffle Oil

Serving: Serves 6 | Prep: | Cook: | Ready in:

Ingredients

- 1 1/2 pounds Jerusalem artichokes
- 1/2 lemon
- 2 shallots, roughly chopped
- 2 cloves garlic, roughly chopped
- 1 baking potato, peeled and chopped into chunks
- 6 cups chicken stock
- 1 tablespoon white truffle oil, plus more to taste

Direction

- Peel the Jerusalem artichokes with a vegetable peeler. Save the peels and put the prepared artichokes into a bowl filled with water and the juice of 1/2 a lemon. Cut each artichoke tube into thirds.
- Dump the artichoke peels into the chicken broth and simmer for 2 minutes. Remove and discard the peels, saving the stock.
- In a clean soup pot over medium-high heat, sauté the shallot and garlic in 1 tablespoon truffle oil for just a moment. Add in the potato chunks and the chopped artichoke pieces, then pour in the chicken broth and bring just to a simmer. Cook for 20 to 30 minutes, until the

vegetables are very soft. Puree with an immersion blender or mash with a potato masher for a chunkier version. Taste and adjust seasoning with salt, if desired. Ladle the soup into warm bowls and drizzle with truffle oil.

171. Joan Nathan's Chosen Matzo Ball Soup

Serving: Serves 6 | Prep: 3hours30mins | Cook: 2hours45mins | Ready in:

Ingredients

- For the soup
- 1 whole chicken (about 4 pounds)
- 2 large onions (whole, unpeeled)
- 4 parsnips
- 2 stalks celery
- 6 carrots
- 6 tablespoons chopped fresh parsley
- 6 tablespoons snipped dill, divided
- 1 teaspoon salt
- 1/4 teaspoon coarse ground black pepper
- For the matzo balls
- 4 large eggs
- 4 tablespoons schmaltz (rendered chicken fat) or vegetable oil
- 4 tablespoons chicken stock
- 1 cup matzo meal
- 1/4 teaspoon ground nutmeg
- 1/2 teaspoon ground ginger
- 2 tablespoons finely chopped parsley, dill, or cilantro
- 1 teaspoon salt
- 1/4 teaspoon coarse ground black pepper

Direction

- For the soup
- Put the chicken and enough water to cover by two inches (about 4 quarts) in a large pot and bring the water to a boil. Skim off the froth as it rises to the top.

- Add the onions, parsnips, celery, carrots, parsley, 4 tablespoons of the dill, and the salt and pepper. Half-cover and simmer for at least an hour and up to 2 hours, adjusting the seasoning to taste.
- Refrigerate for 2 to 3 hours or overnight so the liquid solidifies. When the fat rises to the top, skim it off and reserve for the matzo balls.
- For the matzo balls
- Using a spoon, gently mix the eggs, schmaltz, stock, matzo meal, nutmeg, ginger, and parsley, dill, or cilantro in a large bowl. Season with salt and 2 to 3 grinds of pepper. Cover and refrigerate until chilled, at least an hour or overnight.
- To shape and cook the matzo balls, bring a wide, deep pot of lightly salted water to a boil. With wet hands, take some of the mix and mold it into the size and shape of a golf ball. Gently drop it into the boiling water, repeating until all the mix is used.
- Cover the pan, reducing heat to a lively simmer. Cook for about 20 minutes for al dente matzo balls, or closer to 45 for lighter matzo balls. To test their readiness, remove one with a slotted spoon and cut in half. The matzo ball should be the same color and texture throughout.
- Strain the soup. Set aside the chicken for chicken salad and discard the vegetables. Just before serving, reheat the soup. Spoon a matzo ball into each bowl, pour soup over each matzo ball, and sprinkle with the remaining snipped dill.

172.   Just Good Chili

Serving: Serves many | Prep: 0hours20mins | Cook: 3hours15mins | Ready in:

Ingredients

- 1 tablespoon oil (i prefer olive veg is fine)
- 1 pound sirloin, cubed

- 1 pound ground meat (I prefer buffalo; turkey or beef fine)
- 1 large onion, finely chopped
- 1 Bottle of beer (my choice is Fat Tire)
- 1 14.5 ounce can diced tomatoes
- 1 cup coffee (strong is best)
- 1 tablespoon tomato paste
- 1 tablespoon chili sauce
- 1 tablespoon cocoa powder
- 1/2 finely chopped chili of choice (i use seeded serrano)
- 1/4 cup brown sugar
- 1 tablespoon heaping of cumin
- 1 teaspoon heaping of coriander
- 1 teaspoon cayenne pepper
- 1 teaspoon salt
- 2 15 ounce cans kidney beans
- 1 15 ounce cans white beans
- 5 large carrots, chopped into discs (OPTIONAL)

Direction

- In large stock pot or Dutch oven, heat oil over med. flame and brown meat, sirloin chunks first then ground.
- When meat is lightly browned, throw on the onions.
- Take two large sips from the beer.
- Add remaining beer plus, tomatoes, coffee and tomato paste.
- Add sugar, spices and kidney beans. Reduce flame to low and let simmer for an hour.
- Add white beans and carrots simmer for another hour or two; longer will be better. Season as needed.

173.   Kale & Borlotti Bean Soup With Poached Eggs

Serving: Serves 4 | Prep: 0hours5mins | Cook: 0hours15mins | Ready in:

Ingredients

- For the soup
- Extra-virgin olive oil
- 1 medium onion, cut into quarters
- 2 large cloves garlic, cut in half
- 7 ounces (200g / approximately 1 bunch) trimmed kale leaves, cut into strips
- 5 1/4 cups (1.25 liters) homemade or quality store-bought duck, chicken, or vegetable broth, hot
- 1 bunch fresh thyme
- 1 sprig fresh rosemary
- 1 bay leaf
- Fine sea salt
- Finely ground pepper
- 1 1/4 cups (250g) drained and rinsed canned borlotti (cranberry) or pinto beans
- For the topping
- 4 to 8 large eggs
- Coarsely ground pepper

Direction

- For the soup, in a large pot, heat a splash of olive oil over medium heat and sauté the onion and garlic, stirring, for a few minutes or until golden and soft. Add the kale, stir, and cook for 1 minute then add the hot broth, thyme, rosemary, and bay leaf. Season to taste with salt and finely ground pepper, reduce the heat, and simmer for 20 minutes or until the kale is tender. Remove and discard the herbs then add the borlotti beans and cook for 1 minute. Season to taste with salt and finely ground pepper and keep warm.
- For the topping, bring a small saucepan of salted water to a low simmer. Crack 1 egg into a small bowl. Hold a large spoon just over the surface of the water and gently pour the egg onto the spoon. Lower the spoon into the water and hold until the egg white starts to turn white then use a tablespoon to gently scoop the egg off the large spoon. Poach the egg for 3 minutes. Using a slotted ladle or spoon, transfer the egg to a plate. Poach the remaining eggs the same way, adjusting the heat as needed to maintain a low simmer. It's

best to poach 1 egg at a time, but you can cook 2 at once.
- Divide the soup among 4 bowls, place 1 to 2 eggs in the middle of each bowl, and sprinkle with a little coarsely ground pepper. Cut the tops of the eggs with a sharp knife and serve immediately.

174.   Kickin Squash Soup

Serving: Serves 2 | Prep: | Cook: | Ready in:

Ingredients

- 2 tablespoons coconut oil
- 1 small squash - I used red kuri - about 1kg whole
- 4 cloves garlic
- 2 carrot, diced
- 1 small leek, washed and sliced
- 1 small onion, sliced
- 1 inch ginger
- 1 inch turmeric
- 1 red chilli, deseeded
- 700 milliliters vegetable stock or water

Direction

- Cut your squash into wedges, deseed and place on a roasting tray with the unpeeled garlic cloves. Cover with 1 tablespoon of the coconut oil. Roast for about 30 minutes at 200c, until the squash is soft and has a nice colour.
- While you're roasting, heat a medium saucepan, add the rest of the coconut oil. Add your leeks and onion, cook for 5 minutes until softened. Add the carrots, ginger, turmeric and chili to the pan, mix and cook for a couple of minutes. Add the stock, scoop the flesh of the pumpkin and garlic out of their skin and add. Cook on a low heat until everything is tender, about 10 minutes.
- Blitz in a high powered blender until smooth. Check for seasoning and that it's the right

thickness for you. Add a little water or stock if necessary.

- Top with your favourite roasted vegetables. Beetroot, cherry tomato, aubergine, cauliflower would all be lovely.
- Here I steamed beetroot until almost cooked, peeled, cut into wedges and slow roast at 160c, for an hour. The results are chewy and tender, along with the sweet burst of cherry tomato. Add these to the oven 20 minutes before the beetroot are ready.   Enjoy!

175.   Kimchi Jjigae (Kimchi Stew) 김치찌개

Serving: Serves 4-6 | Prep: | Cook: | Ready in:

Ingredients

- 2 tablespoons vegetable or canola oil
- 1 pound pork belly, loin, or shoulder, sliced thinly
- 1/2 teaspoon sea salt
- 1/4 teaspoon ground black pepper
- 4 cups ripe kimchi
- 3.5 cups water
- 1 tablespoon sesame oil
- 1 bunch green onion, chopped finely

Direction

- In a large, heavy-bottomed pot, heat the oil on medium-high heat.
- Add pork slices, and sauté with the salt and black pepper until golden and cooked through.
- Add the kimchi and stir together until kimchi has cooked through, around 3-5 minutes.
- Add water, just enough to barely cover the kimchi and pork. Cover, and reduce heat to medium and simmer for 40-45 minutes.
- Turn off the heat and add sesame oil and green onion and stir to combine.
- Enjoy with a bowl of hot, white rice.

176.   Kitchen Sink Green Soup

Serving: Serves 4 | Prep: | Cook: | Ready in:

Ingredients

- 1 bunch green onions sliced (set aside dark green part)
- 1/4 cup yellow onion diced
- 1 celery stalk diced
- 1 garlic clove sliced
- 2 pinches herbs de provence
- 1 bay leaf
- 1 tablespoon extra virgin olive oil
- 2 cups vegetable or chicken broth
- 2 cups water
- 1 new potato diced
- 1 pinch salt to taste
- 1 handful green beans sliced
- 2 cups kale torn into bite size pieces
- 1 zucchini sliced into half moons
- 1/4 cup frozen peas
- 1 cup baby spinach chopped
- 1 pinch cracked pepper
- 1 tablespoon grated Parmesan or Parmela nut cheese

Direction

- Place first seven ingredients into soup pot and sauté over medium low until onions and celery soften.
- Add broth, water and diced potatoes and bring to a simmer. Continue simmering until potatoes are nearly done (about 15 minutes). This is a good point to taste and add a pinch of salt if needed.
- Add kale and green beans, bring back to a simmer for 2 more minutes.
- Add zucchini, frozen peas, the remaining sliced green onions and simmer for 3 more minutes. Remove from heat, cover and add baby spinach until wilted.
- Spoon into bowls and garnish with cracked pepper and cheese (optional).

177.   LENTIL, CHILI & THAI BASIL SOUP

Serving: Serves 4 | Prep: | Cook: |Ready in:

Ingredients

- For the soup
- 1 cup brown lentils
- 1/2 cup short grain brown rice
- 3 bay leaves
- 5 cups filtered water
- 20 grams Thai basil
- 2 red birds eye chili, optional
- Chili oil
- 20 grams dried whole long red chili
- 1 bulb garlic, peeled and finely chopped
- 150 milliliters olive oil / avocado oil

Direction

- Rinse the rice and lentils and place in a large pan with the water and the bay leaves. Bring the pan to the boil and cook on a low heat with the lid on for about 30-40 minutes until the rice and lentils are tender. Adding more water if the soup becomes too thick.
- While they're cooking make your chili oil.
- In a small pan on low heat* add your oil, then the garlic and cook for about 8 minutes until the garlic just begins to turn golden and crisp up. Make sure you don't take this too far as the garlic will become bitter if it browns. Transfer the garlic & oil to a bowl.
- Grind the chilies in a spice grinder until you have a rough powder. – You could use chili flakes here but I find grinding your own is fresher, spices can get a little stale sitting in your cupboard too long. Mix the chili flakes into the garlic oil & season with a pinch of salt.
- *You should keep the heat on low here as olive oil has a low smoking point, which means it burns easily. Avocado has a very nice flavor and has a very high smoking point so you can turn it up a little but be careful not to burn the garlic.

- To finish the soup season with salt and pepper. Stir through chopped Thai basil and birds eye chilies, if using and 2 tablespoons of the chili oil. Serve the remaining on the side to add more as desired.

178.   Lasagna Soup With Ricotta Parmesan Cream

Serving: Makes 4 quarts | Prep: 0hours10mins | Cook: 0hours20mins |Ready in:

Ingredients

- 1 pound lasagna noodles
- 2 tablespoons olive oil
- 1 pound ground beef
- 1 onion, chopped
- 4 cloves garlic, chopped
- 1 tablespoon salt
- 1 1/2 teaspoons dried oregano
- 1/2 teaspoon red pepper flakes, or more if you like it spicier
- 2 tablespoons tomato paste
- 1 28-ounce can crushed tomatoes
- 1 28-ounce can diced tomatoes
- 1 16-ounce container ricotta
- 1/4 cup heavy cream
- 1/2 cup finely grated Parmesan, plus more for topping
- Parsley, chopped, for topping
- Basil, for topping

Direction

- Four or five pieces at a time, wrap the lasagna noodles in a kitchen towel. (The towel will prevent noodle fragments from flying across the room when you break them.) Using the edge of the counter as leverage, press the towel into the counter to break the noodles into roughly 1-inch to 2-inch shards. Repeat with remaining pasta. Set aside.
- In a large Dutch oven, heat olive oil over high heat. Once hot, add the ground beef and cook

until brown, breaking it up as it cooks. Once brown, add the onion and garlic. Cook, stirring occasionally, until onions become soft. Season with oregano, salt and red pepper flakes. Add the tomato paste and stir to combine. Add the can crushed tomatoes and can of diced tomatoes. Fully refill one of the empty cans with water and add it to the pot. Bring the mixture to a bubble. Once bubbly, add the lasagna noodles and stir to combine. Turn then heat down to medium-low, and cook, stirring occasionally, for 10 minutes. Meanwhile, make the ricotta mixture.

- In a small bowl, using a fork, mix ricotta with the heavy cream until smooth. Once smooth, add the Parmesan cheese. Set aside.
- Once the noodles are tender, serve the soup. Ladle into bowls and top with a dollop of the ricotta cheese, a few Parmesan cheese shavings, torn basil and chopped parsley.

---

179. Lemon & Herb Chicken Soup With Spinach Pasta

Serving: Serves 4-6 | Prep: | Cook: | Ready in:

Ingredients

- Spinach pasta dough
- 6 ounces Frozen Spinach, Squeezed Dry
- 3 eggs
- 1 egg Yolk
- 2 cups All Purpose Flour
- 1/4 cup Whole Wheat Flour, just to make it extra heart healthy
- 1 teaspoon Salt
- Lemon Chicken Soup
- 1 Pre Cooked Turkey Carcass (optional)
- 2-3 Raw Chicken Carcasses with giblets
- 1/2 cup Tomato Paste
- 4 of each: Carrots and or parsnips, Onions and or Leeks, and Celery, Divided
- 4 Cloves of Garlic, Minced
- 4 Lemons, Halved

- 4 Sprigs of rosemary and thyme
- 1 tablespoon Each: Whole Coriander, Fennel, and celery Seed, red pepper flakes and peppercorns. Toasted and lightly cracked with mortar and pestle to release aromas
- 2 Large Bay Leaves, Preferably Fresh
- Splash White Wine
- 4 Chicken Quarters, seasoned with S&P
- 1 tablespoon Duck Fat, (or grapeseed/canola oil)

Direction

- Spinach pasta dough
- Using a Food processor, pulse your spinach as fine as possible. Add your eggs and puree to combine. Next, add your flours and salt and continue to pulse until the dough comes together. If it's a bit clumpy that's okay.
- Knead your dough for about 10 minutes or until soft and smooth. Wrap your dough in plastic and allow to rest, for at least 20 min. This helps to hydrate the flour and to keep it from being too elastic.
- Once it has rested, roll your dough out in a pasta machine going from 1 -6 or 7. Folding in thirds each time and dusting with flour. Once it is rolled out long and smooth, cut your pasta into whatever noodle you prefer. I like wide noodles (pappardelle) or cut into 2" x 1" rectangles. (Using the fluted cutter) and pinched in the middle for cute little bow ties (farfalle). Dust your pasta with rice flour to prevent them from sticking together.
- Have your pasta water boiling and salted. Cook your pasta when you are ready to serve your soup!
- Lemon Chicken Soup
- Roast your Bones for Stock: Baste your RAW Chicken Carcasses and most of your Chopped Veggies (3 carrots, 3 onions, 3 Leeks, 3 celery sticks or whatever it is that you have) with tomato paste. Roast in a 400 degree oven until browned and beginning to caramelize, approx. 45 min. In the last 5 minutes add your lemon halves to give it a sear. This helps to release some juices and deepen their flavor just a bit.

- Transfer your roasted veggies and chicken to a stock pot. Be sure to scrape up all the yummy cracklings on the bottom. Deglaze with a splash of wine to help scrape it up. Also add your pre-roasted turkey, lemon halves, and make your bouquet garni with the fresh herbs and seeds. Fill pot with cold water just enough to cover your chickens. Bring to a soft boil (NOT a Roiling Boil). Reduce heat and simmer for as long as you can stand. 6 hours or so. The longer the better. Skim the fat and foam from the top but resist the urge to stir. We don't want a cloudy broth!
- Strain your broth with a mesh sieve lined with cheesecloth several times for the best clarity. Reserve your stock. You will probably only need about half of it for the actual soup, so the rest of what you don't use can be saved for later use.
- Now that we have stock, let's make the actual Soup! In a large Dutch oven, heat duck fat (or oil) at medium high. Brown your chicken quarters. Remove from pan and add the other half of your chopped veggies. Once they begin to soften add your garlic. Deglaze your pot again with a splash of white wine, because white wine is good for you when you feel sick.
- Add your delicious fresh stock to your pot. Bring to a boil and allow to simmer and let those flavors start reducing and melding. Taste, if it seems a little lack luster allow to simmer uncovered to reduce for a richer flavor. Maybe add a little more lemon? Fresh Thyme, Red Pepper Flakes? Try to refrain from adding salt until the VERY end. Once your broth is perfect return your chicken quarters and allow to simmer covered until they are about fall off the bone.
- Serve your hearty chicken and broth over your spinach pasta and enjoy a hard day of work!

180. Lentil & Chorizo Stew With Saffron & Cinnamon

Serving: Serves 8 | Prep: | Cook: |Ready in:

Ingredients

- 2 tablespoons extra virgin olive oil
- 1 large onion, medium dice
- 2 large garlic cloves, minced
- 1/2 pound Spanish chorizo, thinly sliced
- 1/4 teaspoon pure saffron, crushed with a mortar and pestle
- 1 teaspoon ground coriander
- 1/2 teaspoon ground cinnamon
- 1/2 teaspoon ground ginger
- 1 14-ounce can fire-roasted tomatoes, preferably Muir Glen, or regular canned diced tomatoes
- 1 red bell pepper, medium dice
- 1 yellow bell pepper, medium dice
- 2 cups brown Spanish lentils (padrina) or French green lentils (puy), cooked until tender
- 2 cups dried chickpeas, soaked overnight and cooked until tender, or 2 14-ounce cans, rinsed and drained
- 5 to 6 cups low-sodium commercial chicken stock
- extra virgin olive oil, for drizzling
- cilantro leaves, for garnish
- crusty bread, for serving

Direction

- In a soup pot, over medium heat, add the olive oil. Add the onion and sauté' about 3 to 4 minutes, or until onion has softened. Add the garlic, stir for 30 seconds, and add the chorizo. Sauté for another minute or two, then add the saffron, coriander, cinnamon and ginger. Stir to combine. Add the tomatoes, red and yellow bell peppers, lentils and chickpeas. Stir to combine. Add 5 cups chicken stock, cover and cook over medium-low heat for 20-25 minutes to allow the flavors to meld. If the stew seems too dry, add a little more stock.

- To serve, ladle into warm soup bowls, drizzle with olive oil and top with cilantro leaves. Serve hot with warm crusty bread

181. Lentil And Sausage Soup With Kale

Serving: Serves 6 | Prep: 0hours10mins | Cook: 0hours40mins |Ready in:

Ingredients

- 1 tablespoon olive oil, plus more for browning the sausages
- 1 tablespoon bacon fat (or add another tablespoon of olive oil)
- 1 cup chopped carrots
- 3/4 cup chopped celery
- 1 medium onion, chopped
- 3 cloves garlic, chopped
- 1 pinch Salt
- 1 1/2 cups french green lentils, rinsed
- 28 ounces canned chopped tomatoes (I use tetra-pack)
- 2 sprigs thyme
- 1 sprig rosemary
- 4 chicken sausages (or substitute another kind of sausage)
- 1 1/2 cups chopped kale

Direction

- Heat the olive oil and bacon fat over medium heat in a large, heavy pot and add the carrots, celery, onion and garlic. Add a big pinch of salt. Cook until softened, about 5 minutes.
- Stir in the lentils, tomatoes and 4 cups water. Add the thyme and rosemary and a couple more pinches of salt. Bring to a boil and then lower the heat to a simmer. Cook until the lentils are tender, 15 to 20 minutes, adding more water if necessary to cover the vegetables.

- Meanwhile brown the sausages in about a teaspoon of olive oil in a small pan and then slice them into quarter moons.
- When the lentils are just tender, taste the soup and add more salt if necessary. Add the kale and cook for about 3 minutes, until the kale is tender but still green. Stir in the sausage, make sure everything is heated through, and serve.

182. Lentil And Sausage Stew

Serving: Serves 4 to 6 | Prep: | Cook: |Ready in:

Ingredients

- 2 cups green or brown lentils
- salt, to taste
- 2 tablespoons butter or olive oil, divided
- 4 sausages
- 1 onion, chopped
- 2 carrots, chopped
- 2 sticks of celery, chopped
- 1 green bell pepper, chopped
- 2 cloves of garlic, minced
- 1 tablespoon flour
- one 28-ounce can chopped tomatoes
- cheese, grated (optional)

Direction

- Bring the lentils to a boil on medium heat in 6 cups of water (you'll let these cook while you proceed with the rest of the recipe for maximum efficiency). Sprinkle about 1/2 teaspoon of salt into the water with the lentils. Once the water is boiling, turn the heat down to simmer and cook for 20 minutes, or until the lentils are soft all the way through. Once they are soft, turn off the heat and drain any excess water. Taste and add more salt if needed. Try not to leave the lentils cooking for too long because they can easily end up getting overcooked and mushy. They are still totally edible and even delicious when they get overcooked and fall apart—they just don't have quite as nice a texture.

- If you want to do the extra step of melting cheese on the top of your stew, then use an ovenproof pot or Dutch oven for this next step. Also set your oven to 375° F. Otherwise, use any large pot.
- While the lentils cook, melt 1 tablespoon of the butter in another large pot on medium heat. Cook the sausages, flipping to brown on all sides, about 5 minutes. The chorizo I used was already pre-cooked so the browning just took a few minutes. If you are using fresh sausage, cook for as long as you need for the sausage to be cooked through—sometimes with larger fresh sausages, they can take 15 minutes or more so be patient.
- Once the sausages are cooked, remove them from the pot onto a side plate. My chorizo let off a lot of oil, so I didn't need to use the second tablespoon of butter to cook my vegetables, but add more butter to the pan now if there isn't much left.
- Add the onion, carrots, celery, and green pepper and cook for about 5 minutes with the lid on, stirring occasionally. Sprinkle a bit of salt over everything, about 1/2 teaspoon or so to start. Once the vegetables are softened and the onion is translucent, add the garlic and stir, cooking for another 2 minutes. Sprinkle the flour over everything and stir until it disappears into the vegetables and oil.
- Add the chopped tomatoes and the cooked lentils to the pot and stir to combine. Let it cook for about 5 minutes, until some of the water from the tomatoes has cooked off and it's a little thicker.
- Slice the sausage into bite-sized pieces and add them back into the pot. Stir. Taste and add salt if needed. If it tastes delicious, you're done and can serve it now, or go onto the optional last step.
- Set the oven to 375° F. Grate or blob your favorite melt cheese over top of the stew. Bake for 20 minutes or until all the cheese is melted.

Serving: Serves 6 to 8 | Prep: | Cook: | Ready in:

Ingredients

- 1/2 pound sweet Italian sausage (cut into rounds then quartered)
- 1 large onion, chopped
- 1 stalk celery, finely chopped
- 1 tablespoon chopped garlic
- 1 ounce (16 ounce) package dry lentils
- 1 cup chopped carrot
- 8 cups water
- 2 (14.5 ounce) cans chicken broth
- 1 (28 ounce) can diced tomatoes
- 1 tablespoon chopped fresh parsley
- 2 bay leaves
- 1/2 teaspoon dried oregano
- 1/4 teaspoon dried thyme
- 1/4 teaspoon dried basil
- 1 teaspoon salt, or to taste
- 1/1 teaspoon black pepper

Direction

- Cover lentils in boiling water for 30 minutes, drain. Place sausage in a large pot. Cook over medium high heat until evenly brown. Set aside. Add onion, celery and chopped garlic, and sauté until tender and translucent. Stir in sausage, drained lentils, carrot, water, chicken broth and tomatoes, parsley, bay leaves, oregano, thyme, basil, salt and pepper. Bring to a boil, then reduce heat. Cover, and simmer for 2 1/2 to 3 hours, or until lentils are tender.
- Serve with crusty Italian bread

184. Lentils Once, Twice, And Thrice: Lentils Once With Brown Rice, Lentils Twice In Soup, And Lentils Thrice As Lentil Cakes

Serving: Serves 4, with enough left over for 4 bowls of soup and 4 large lentil cakes | Prep: | Cook: | Ready in:

Ingredients

- Lentils Once, Base Recipe: Lentils with Rice
- 3 c brown lentils (or French lentils)
- 4 slices bacon or ham, chopped, fine dice
- 2 - 4 T olive oil, as needed
- 2 medium onions, chopped, small dice
- 2 large carrots, peeled and chopped, small dice
- 2 stalks celery, chopped, small
- 6 cloves garlic, minced
- 2 medium potatoes, peeled and chopped in small dice
- 3 - 4 quarts broth (I like a chicken/poultry or pork broth that has been made with bones that have been smoked, but beef or vegetable stock is fine too)
- 2 c chard, spinach, or other leafy greens, washed well and chopped into ½" pieces
- 1 ½ tsp garam masala
- Pinch of cayenne
- Salt and pepper to taste
- 2 T minced parsley
- 2 c short grained rice, brown or white
- Olive oil and balsamic or malt vinegar for serving
- 4 t Sour Cream for serving
- Lentils Twice: Lentil Soup
- Per serving:
- ½ c Lentils Once
- 1 T cooked rice, optional
- 1/3 – ½ c broth of your choice
- A generous pinch of dried Herbes de Provence, or two large pinches of fresh oregano, minced and one large pinch of fresh thyme, minced (or a bit less of dried oregano and thyme).
- 1 T Sour Cream

Direction

- Lentils Once, Base Recipe: Lentils with Rice
- Rinse lentils thoroughly, removing any pebbles, etc., that there might be. Place in a glass bowl, cover by one inch with water, and allow to soak for 30 minutes.
- In large soup pot fry bacon or ham over medium heat for a minute or two, until it starts to brown. Add a tablespoon or two of olive oil and onions and cook for a minute, then add carrots; cook for another minute, then add celery and garlic, stirring gently occasionally.
- Drain lentils and add to vegetable mixture with potato and garam masala and cayenne. Add 3 quarts broth. Raise heat and just as it begins to boil, turn heat down and simmer, uncovered, for 30 or 40 minutes or so, adding more broth if needed, until lentils and vegetables are soft but not falling apart, and it has thickened up a bit. Stir in chard or spinach and parsley. Add salt and pepper to taste.
- While lentils are cooking, cook rice according to package directions. 2 cups dry rice cooked should be plenty, with extra for lentil cakes.
- To serve, spoon over rice with a bit of olive oil and a drop or two of vinegar, and top with a tablespoon of sour cream
- Lentils Twice: Lentil Soup
- Mix Lentils Once with rice, if using, broth and herbs. Heat for a few minutes, add salt and pepper if needed, and serve with sour cream.
- Lentils Thrice: Lentil Cakes To make 2 large or 3 small cakes, use ½ c Lentils Once ½ c cooked rice 1 slice stale bread or toast, coarsely ground by hand or in food processor to make crumbs ¾ tsp curry powder 2 - 4 T warm water Bacon grease or canola oil for frying 1 - 2 T Sour Cream Chutney Shredded lettuce, greens, or cabbage. Blend Lentils Once, cooked rice, bread crumbs, and curry powder together. A tablespoon at a time, add warm water until mixture comes together and can be easily formed into two 3" cakes or three 2" cakes. Heat bacon grease or canola oil in heavy frying pan. Fry on medium heat 2 – 3 minutes

per side, until cakes brown and form a light crust, and are heated through. Serve on shredded greens with sour cream and chutney.

cornbread. Hope you enjoy, and happy New Year, y'all!

185. Lucky Black Eyed Pea Soup – Southern Secret

Serving: Serves 6 easily | Prep: | Cook: | Ready in:

Ingredients

- 2 15-oz cans of black-eyed peas
- 1.5 cups diced celery stalks
- 1.5 cups diced carrots – about 2 large
- 2.5 tablespoons fresh parsley – minced
- 2 cups diced red onion
- 4 large garlic cloves – minced
- 1 bay leaf
- 1 quart vegetable stock
- 2.5 tablespoons olive oil
- 1.5 teaspoons salt
- 1 teaspoon freshly-ground black pepper
- .5 teaspoons ground cumin
- cornbread – optional!

Direction

- Start by warming up the 2 Tbsp. of olive oil in a big saucepan or cast-iron skillet. Once fragrant, toss in the diced onion and minced garlic. Lightly sauté for 3 minutes; if they go dry, add in water (I added about 1/4 cup).
- Add the vegetable stock, beans, carrots, celery, parsley, bay leaf, and spices. Stir to mix evenly. Turn up heat and bring to a simmer; cook for 20 minutes or until the vegetables are nicely tender. Stir in the remaining 2 tsp of olive oil, and remove the bay leaf lest your kid tries to eat it.
- Here's the trick to good soup: let it sit overnight so the flavors meld. If you're looking to eat this tonight, let it sit for at least 30 minutes. Before eating it, gently reheat the soup on the stove and serve with fresh

186. Manestra

Serving: Makes about 3 quarts | Prep: 0hours0mins | Cook: 0hours0mins | Ready in:

Ingredients

- 1/4 cup extra virgin olive oil
- 1 medium onion, finely diced
- 3 large cloves garlic, minced
- 2 tablespoons dried oregano (preferably Greek)
- 1 teaspoon salt
- 1 teaspoon coarse ground black pepper
- 1 28 ounce can crushed tomatoes
- 6 cups vegetable broth or water
- 1 1/2 cups orzo
- Grated Kefalotyri or Parmesan cheese for garnish (optional)

Direction

- Heat the olive oil in a 4 quart soup pot and add the diced onion. Sauté for a few minutes and then add the minced garlic and oregano. Continue to sauté until the garlic smells fragrant.
- Stir in the crushed tomatoes and simmer for about 5 minutes. Add the broth or water and bring up to a boil. Stir in the orzo and simmer for about 8 to 10 minutes, stirring often so the orzo doesn't stick to the bottom of the pot. Serve nice and hot in bowls garnished with the cheese if you like.
- NOTE: If re-heating you may need to add a little extra broth or water as the orzo soaks up so much liquid.

187. Marcella's Broccoli And Potato Soup

Serving: Makes 6 servings | Prep: | Cook: | Ready in:

Ingredients

- 3 tablespoons unsalted butter, divided
- 1/4 cup extra virgin olive oil
- 2 cups yellow onion, julienned
- Kosher salt and freshly ground black pepper
- 3 garlic cloves, peeled and minced (about 1 tablespoon)
- 2 cups Yukon Gold potatoes, peeled, medium dice
- 2 1/2 cups broccoli florets, no stems
- 3 1/2 cups stock, chicken or vegetable
- 6 smallish fresh basil leaves, torn
- 1/2 cup Parmesan, grated

Direction

- In a 3 1/2-quart heavy-bottomed pot, combine the olive oil and half the butter. Place the pot over medium heat. Once the butter begins to melt, add the onions. Season them with a pinch of salt and freshly ground black pepper.
- Sauté the onions until they become golden. Don't rush this step and adjust the heat as necessary to keep them from browning too fast. Add the garlic and cook until fragrant.
- Add the potatoes. Stir them to coat with oil and let them sizzle away for a minute or two. Add the broccoli and do the same as you did with the potatoes. Add the stock.
- Bring the stock to a boil. Taste the broth and adjust the seasoning. Go easy on the salt though because the Parmesan has lots and will act as seasoning as well.
- Simmer the soup until the broccoli and potatoes are tender. The broccoli is not going to remain vibrant green, but if it is good broccoli it won't be olive drab either.
- Once the potatoes have cooked through, add the parmesan, the remaining butter, and the basil. Stir to combine and serve with more black pepper.

188. Mashed Sweet Potato And Kale Soup

Serving: Serves 6 | Prep: | Cook: | Ready in:

Ingredients

- 1 tablespoon coconut oil
- 1 large yellow onion, diced
- 1 large clove garlic, minced
- 2 sprigs fresh thyme, destemmed
- 1 dried bay leaf
- 2 large (about 2 pounds total) sweet potatoes, peeled and rustically cubed
- 4 cups kale, destemmed and roughly chopped
- 6 cups filtered water
- salt & pepper to taste

Direction

- In a large Dutch oven or heavy pot, heat coconut oil over medium-high heat. Add onion, garlic, thyme, and bay leaf and sauté, stirring frequently, until onion has just softened, but not browned (about 4 minutes). Add sweet potato, kale, and water, then bring to a boil. Cover pot, reduce heat to low, and allow soup to simmer for 15-20 minutes, or until sweet potatoes are completely soft.
- Remove from heat, remove bay leaf, then using a vegetable masher or strong fork, and mash the sweet potato into a lumpy soup. Season with salt & pepper and enjoy!

189. Mason Jar Gazpacho

Serving: Serves 6 | Prep: | Cook: | Ready in:

Ingredients

- 1 1/2 pounds ripe summer Tomatoes, quartered

- 1 stalk Celery, chopped
- 1/2 small Cucumber, seeded and chopped
- 1 medium Shallot, peeled and chopped
- 1 clove Garlic
- 2 cups Tomato juice
- 4 leaves Basil, chiffonade
- 2 tablespoons finely chopped Parsley
- 1/4 cup Balsamic Vinegar
- 1/4 cup Extra Virgin Olive Oil
- 1/4 cup Dry White Wine
- 1/2 teaspoon Salt
- 1 teaspoon Pepper
- 1/2 Lime

Direction

- Process the tomatoes, and celery separately and put them in a large bowl. Process the cucumber, shallot and garlic together and add to the bowl with the tomatoes and celery.
- Add the tomato juice and next 4 ingredients. Squeeze the juice from the lime into the bowl.
- Ladle the mixture into 6 1/2-pint Mason jars. Seal and refrigerate for at least 4 hours or preferably overnight.

190.   Meatball Soup

Serving: Serves 6-8 | Prep: | Cook: | Ready in:

Ingredients

- For the Meatballs
- 1 pound lean ground beef
- 1/2 cup white long grain rice
- 1 small onion finely chopped
- 1/2or1/3 of a parsley bunch finely chopped
- salt and pepper
- 1/2 cup all purpose flour
- For the Soup
- 1.5-2 liters water
- 1/3 cup extra virgin olive oil
- 2 medium potatoes cut into big pieces
- salt and pepper
- 2 eggs (for the egg-lemon sauce)

- 1 lemon juice (for the egg-lemon sauce)

Direction

- Pour the water in a soup pan and bring it on medium heat.
- Meanwhile, in a medium bowl place the ground beef, onion, ¼ rice, parsley, salt and pepper.
- Mix the ingredients and shape the mixture into small balls (about 1,5 inch d).
- Place the flour in a big shallow plate and roll the meatballs over.
- When the water starts boiling add the olive oil and the meatballs, reduce the heat and simmer for 15'.
- Add the potatoes and simmer for 10', then add the rice, some salt and pepper and simmer for another 10'-15'.
- Once you finish cooking the soup, whisk (in a medium bowl) the egg whites for 1'-1.5', add the egg yolks, whisk for a minute and add the lemon juice. Whisk for a few seconds.
- Using a ladle pour into the egg-lemon mixture about 2 cups of the soup (liquid only) little by little, stirring continuously.
- Pour the egg-lemon-soup liquid sauce back into the soup pan and stir slowly.

191.   Mexican Cucumber Tomato Gazpacho

Serving: Serves 6 | Prep: | Cook: | Ready in:

Ingredients

- 1 slice country-style bread, crusts removed
- 3 cucumbers, peeled, seeded and chopped
- 2 pounds vine-ripened tomatoes, seeded and chopped
- 1 clove garlic, peeled and chopped
- 3 tablespoons cilantro
- 1 jalapeño, seeds removed and chopped
- 2 tablespoons sherry vinegar
- 1/2 cup extra virgin olive oil

- 1/2 cup water
- 1 tablespoon Mexican-style hot sauce
- 1/2 jicama, peeled and small diced
- 1/2 cup fresh corn kernals
- 2 tablespoons pickled jalapeno, minced
- Mexican crema (optional)
- salt & pepper, to taste

Direction

- Soak the bread in water to soften. Squeeze out the moisture with your hands and place in a blender.
- Add the cucumbers, tomatoes, garlic, cilantro, jalapeño, vinegar, olive oil, hot sauce, and water. Puree until smooth. Season with salt and pepper, to taste.
- Chill the gazpacho for about 2 hours in the refrigerator before serving.
- Serve in bowls topped with the garnishes - jicama, sweet corn, pickled jalapeno, and Mexican cream.

---

192. Minestra Of Spring Greens And Herbs With (Optional) Truffled Polenta Croutons

Serving: Serves four | Prep: | Cook: | Ready in:

Ingredients

- For the truffled polenta croutons:
- 3/4 cup medium fine stoneground cornmeal
- 3 1/4 cups water
- 1/2 teaspoon salt
- 1/4 cup fresh grated parmesan cheese
- 2 tablespoons white or black truffle oil
- 1 tablespoon unsalted butter
- For the soup:
- 4 ounces piece of trimmed leek, halved lengthwise, thickly sliced so they don't disintegrate completely, rinsed and shaken dry

- 1 spring onion bulb or 2 scallions, roots trimmed, chopped
- 1 green garlic bulb or 1 fat garlic clove, chopped
- 4 ounces trimmed fennel bulb, halved lengthwise, sliced about 1/8" thick
- 1 tablespoon olive oil
- 1 2" serrano pepper with seeds, minced
- 1 quart broth from cooked beans (see note)
- 2 cups chicken or vegetable broth
- 1 packed cup loosely chopped cleaned cilantro leaves and tender stems, plus a bit more for the garnish
- 1/2 cup packed loosely chopped cleaned flat leaf parsley leaves, plus a bit more for the garnish
- 2 cups cooked cranberry or borlotti beans (see note)
- 1 or two bunches swiss chard, (you'll need a packed quart of leaves) rinsed, leaves cut into ribbons, stems chopped into 1/2" pieces (keep stems separate)
- salt to taste
- extra virgin olive oil for the garnish
- the rind of one preserved lemon (regular or meyer is okay)

Direction

- For the truffle polenta croutons:
- Line a 12" x 12" baking sheet or other plate that's at least 1/2" deep with parchment. Bring 3 1/4 cups of water to a boil in a medium saucepan. Whisk in cornmeal while pouring in a slow steady stream. Whisk in salt. Reduce heat to low and cook 25 minutes, stirring fairly frequently to prevent sticking. Polenta should be thick but pourable so you may need more boiling water during the cooking time. Add the cheese and truffle oil, taste for salt and then pour onto the baking sheet. Spread evenly. Cool until completely set, a day in advance is good.
- While the soup is cooking, cut the polenta into squares, as many as you like. In a skillet, melt the butter over medium heat. Add the squares

and brown both sides in the butter. Remove to a plate and reserve.

- For the soup:
- In a 5-7 quart stockpot, heat the oil over medium heat. Add the leeks, onion/scallion, garlic and fennel. Stir to combine, add a pinch of salt, stir again, then reduce heat and partially cover pot. After 5-7 minutes, uncover, stir, and add the serrano pepper and chard stems. Cook 5 minutes on low, then add the bean broth, chicken or vegetable broth increase heat to medium and bring to a boil. Stir in cilantro and parsley, reduce heat to low, cover and simmer 15 minutes. Add the cooked beans, cover and simmer 5 minutes. Uncover and add the ribbons of chard or other greens. Simmer uncovered for 10 minutes or longer, until the chard is tender and almost silky. Taste for salt and pepper.
- Thinly julienne the preserved lemon rind and mix with some extra virgin olive oil and a 1/2 teaspoon each of finely minced parsley and cilantro leaves. The soft rind kind of melts and makes a "pesto-like" mixture with distinct pieces of lemon rind.
- To serve, ladle the soup into shallow bowls, add some of the truffle polenta croutons (or not), and place a dollop of the lemon garnish in the middle of each bowl.
- Note: Since this isn't a "bean" soup, I didn't feel it necessary to include a recipe for that process. I did cook the beans with a strip of Kombu which I think contributes mightily to a good bean broth as well as half a small onion, a bit of carrot, celery leaves and parsley stems. I added salt to the beans and broth about 15 minutes before they were finished cooking and then I let them sit an additional 1/2 hour uncovered off the heat before draining them.

193. Miso Thyme Potato Soup

Serving: Serves 4 | Prep: | Cook: |Ready in:

Ingredients

- 1 cup Miso Paste (white preferably)
- 2 handfuls russet or other potatoes, about four medium-sized
- 4 sprigs fresh english thyme
- 3 cups water
- 1 teaspoon salt
- 1 tablespoon olive oil (optional)

Direction

- Begin with a clean French oven or Dutch oven and place upon the stovetop, with the heat on low. Gather your ingredients: fresh miso paste, two handfuls of russet potatoes, and 4 sprigs of English thyme.
- Measure out 1 cup Miso Paste. If a salty result is not your goal, omit the added salt. If not, place miso, salt and 3 cups water in the warmed French oven. Begin stirring, gently with a whisk, until the paste forms a smooth broth.
- Rinse potatoes, cut into halves, and then dice into quarters. Bring a second pot of water to a boil, add the potatoes, and simmer on medium-high heat for up to 20 mins, or until cooked through. Drain potatoes in a colander, and then carefully tumble them into the warmed miso broth. At this point, you may want to raise the heat of the Dutch oven to just below medium heat to prepare for serving.
- Now, once the potatoes and broth are at a sufficiently heated state, add the thyme sprigs, cover and remove from heat. Let sit, ten minutes more.
- The soup should now be ready to serve. Remove the thyme sprigs, and sprinkle the thyme leaves back into the soup to garnish.
- For a richer result, drizzle on 1 tbsp. olive oil to garnish. The olive oil can also be added to the broth early on with the potatoes.

194. Mock Chicken Stock

Serving: Makes about a quart | Prep: | Cook: |Ready in:

Ingredients

- 1/3 cup red lentils
- 1/4 cup yellow split peas or chana dal
- 1 small onion or 1/2 large onion, coarsely chopped
- 1/4 teaspoon ground turmeric
- 4.5 cups water
- 1/2 teaspoon salt

Direction

- Combine the lentils and wash them in several cold changes of water.
- Combine the onion and lentils in a pot and add the water.
- Add the turmeric and salt.
- Bring to a boil, cover and simmer for a half hour.
- Strain out the liquid into a separate container and season with salt if necessary. Discard the lentils and onions or use for another purpose.

195. Mushroom And Seaweed Soup

Serving: Serves 2, generously | Prep: | Cook: |Ready in:

Ingredients

- For the broth, which is sort of a fortified dashi
- 1/2 cup dried mushrooms, wiped clean (Polish or porcini are terrific if you have them, but any dried mushroom will be fine)
- Six strips of Kombu seaweed, wiped clean
- 1 or 2 cups of bonito flakes, depending on how intense you'd like the broth
- 1 clove of garlic
- 1 can of red kidney beans, or adzuki beans, rinsed well
- 2 or 3 tablespoons white miso paste
- For the soup and garnish
- 6 pieces of Wakame seaweed, chopped or broken into bits, soaked in warm water for 10 minutes
- 2 tablespoons of chopped Dulse seaweed
- 1 cup of Enoki mushrooms, end trimmed off and wiped clean
- 2 cups of assorted mushrooms such as Crimini , Hen of the woods, or Oyster, wiped clean and thinly sliced
- Sesame oil, 1 Tablespoon for sautéing and 1 teaspoon for garnishing
- 6 pieces of Korean dried seaweed, sliced into thin strips
- Thinly sliced scallion
- Soy sauce
- Sea salt
- White pepper

Direction

- Soak the dried mushrooms and the Kombu in 4 cups of water in a large soup pot for 20 minutes. Add the garlic and the beans. Simmer for 20 minutes. Add the bonito flakes and simmer for 10 more minutes. Using a potato masher, smash the solids in the broth to pulverize any beans or garlic that have not cooked down into the broth. Strain the broth through a fine sieve and discard the remaining solids. (The Kombu strips can be reserved, rinsed and chopped up for later use. It is lovely in a salad of delicate lettuce, sesame oil, and sesame seeds.) Return the warm broth to the pot. Add the miso paste to the broth and stir. You will have a cloudy, savory, rich broth. Keep the broth warm at a gentle simmer while you make the body of the soup. If the broth reduces too much, add a cup or so of water and an additional tablespoon of miso paste to create the volume of broth you would like.
- Add the Wakame and the Dulse to the broth and simmer. In a skillet, gently sauté the assorted mushrooms in the sesame oil until they become almost tender. Add the enoki mushrooms and sauté for an additional minute. Add all the sautéed mushrooms to the

seaweed and broth. Taste, adding soy sauce and additional miso paste to taste. Simmer for 5 minutes to allow the flavors to combine.

- Ladle the soup into 2 large bowls, using as much or as little of the broth as you like. Drizzle sesame oil and soy sauce to taste into the soup. Sprinkle the Korean dried seaweed strips atop the soup, and garnish with scallion, sea salt and white pepper.

---

196.   Mushroom And Vegetable Pho

Serving: Serves 4 | Prep: | Cook: | Ready in:

Ingredients

- For the mushroom and vegetable pho:
- 2 carrots
- 6 cups (1 1/2 liters) rich mushroom stock (see recipe below)
- 1 generous handful of baby spinach
- 1 splash rice wine vinegar
- 3 1/2 ounces (98 grams) Chinese noodles, prepared according to package directions
- 1/4 small head of savoy cabbage, thinly sliced
- Handful of fresh cilantro
- Handful of fresh mint leaves
- 1 Fresh red chili pepper, chopped fine (optional)
- Slow Roasted Crispy Mushrooms (see recipe below)
- For the rich mushroom stock and slow-roasted crispy mushrooms:
- 1 1/2 pounds Crimini mushrooms, sliced thin and divided (use both the stems and caps)
- Olive oil
- Sea salt, to taste
- 6 carrots, cut into coins
- 1 medium yellow onion, cut into quarters
- 4 garlic cloves, crushed
- 8 cups (2 liters) water
- 4 dried bay leaves

- 6 sprigs of fresh thyme
- Handful of flat-leaf (Italian) parsley
- 2 to 3 splashes soy sauce

Direction

- For the mushroom and vegetable pho:
- Peel the carrots into ribbons. (Either store the cores in a container or use them to make the vegetable stock, or each them as-is.)
- Combine the stock, carrots, spinach, and rice wine vinegar in a medium pot. Bring to a boil, and then reduce heat to a simmer. Cook for 5 to 7 minutes, until the carrots are tender.
- Divide the cabbage and noodles amongst four deep soup bowls. Ladle the soup into the bowls. Top with the herbs, chili pepper, and Crispy Mushrooms. Serve hot.
- For the rich mushroom stock and slow-roasted crispy mushrooms:
- To prepare the slow-roasted mushrooms: preheat the oven to 300° F. Line a rimmed baking pan with parchment paper; set aside.
- Add 8 ounces (224 grams) of mushrooms to a medium bowl. Drizzle with a bit of olive oil, just enough to coat the mushrooms. Season with salt, and toss well to mix. Spread them in a single layer onto the prepared sheet pan. Bake for 1 hour and 15 minutes, give the mushrooms a stir, and bake for 45 to 60 minutes more, until crisp. Let the mushrooms cool completely before using, or store the cooled mushrooms in a tightly sealed container in the fridge for up to 2 weeks.
- To prepare the stock: place a 4-quart pot over medium-high heat. Swirl in just enough oil to coat the bottom of the pan. Add the remaining mushrooms, season with salt, and sauté, stirring occasionally, until deep, golden brown, 7 to 8 minutes.
- Add the onions, using a wooden spoon to scrape up any browned bits of mushroom. Cook until the onions begin to slightly soften, about 2 minutes. Give the mushrooms and onions a taste, and add more salt if necessary.

- Add the carrots and garlic, giving everything in the pot a good stir. Cook for 2 more minutes.
- Use a wooden spoon again to scrape up any browned bits on the bottom of the pot. Pour in the water, and add the herbs, and soy sauce. Increase the heat to high, and bring to a boil. Reduce the heat to low, and simmer until the liquid has reduced by 1/3, roughly 35 to 40 minutes.
- Place a sieve, or fine meshed strainer, over a deep pot. Pour the stock through the sieve, to strain out the vegetables and herbs. The stock is now ready to use, or you can portion it into smaller containers for use later on. Store it in the fridge, covered, for up to one week, or the freezer for up to two months.

197.   New World Symphony: Turkey Chile Verde Soup With Beans, Corn , Almonds And Lime

Serving: Serves 20, 1 1/2 cups each as entree | Prep: | Cook: | Ready in:

Ingredients

- oil
- 3 turkey thighs,bone-in, total 3+ lb.
- 2 T evoo
- 2 T bacon fat
- 1 medium large yellow onion, chopped, ~ 10 ou.
- 4 cloves garlic, minced
- 5-6 10 ou. jars salsa verde (I use Trader Joe's)that are mild to low heat
- 16 ou. homemade hot/spicy chile verde sauce (I get mine from Anna's Taqueria in Boston) or more salsa verde, or salsa
- 4-8 c.chicken stock
- 3 medium yukon gold potatoes, cubed and steamed or roasted til done, total ~ 28 ou., skin-on
- 1-2 c.corn, fresh or frozen
- 29 ou. canned pinto beans* plus their liquid (or 10 ou. dry beans, soaked and cooked in water til tender)
- 1 lb fresh or frozen whole okra, cut across in 1/2 inch pieces (if frozen, spread out on cutting board for a few minutes- to slightly soften; cut as for fresh okra)
- 1 4 ou.can whole green chiles, chopped (or 3 poblano chiles, roasted and skinned)
- 1 tsp.good quality chili powder (not supermarket brands which contain alot of salt)
- 2 tsp toasted and ground cumin
- 2 tsp mexican oregano or regular, rubbed between your palms to release flavors
- 1/2-1 cup ground toasted pumpkin seeds
- 1/2-1 c. toasted almonds, chopped to pea-size
- 1/2 bunch cilantro, chopped
- (No salt because salsa verde is already salty)
- Freshly ground black pepper
- more salsa verde and chicken stock as needed for soupy quality
- optional 1-3 minced jalapeno chiles, seeds and ribs removed (may not be needed)
- bunch red chard, sliced crosswise in 1/2 inch pieces and strips
- fresh lime juice, ~12 limes
- garnish with chopped fresh cilantro
- tortilla chips

Direction

- In a little hot oil in a saucepan just big enough to fit the thighs, place the turkey, skin side down. Cook ~ 5-8 minutes over medium high heat till skin has browned. Turn thighs, skin-side up; peel off the skin and reserve for a treat later. Brown second side. Pour over the thighs enough Salsa Verde to cover them. Top with a lid and turn down to Simmer for 1-2 hours, till meat easily pulls away from the bone. (But don't overcook or turkey will get shreddy and somewhat disappear.) In the meantime, in an 8 quart pot, chop onion and sauté in some hot oil and/or bacon fat, until translucent, adding garlic for last few minutes. Add about 2/3 of the remaining salsa verde, chili verde and chicken stock, and all of the potatoes- oregano. Remove the thighs to a cutting board, discard any remaining skin. Cut the turkey into 3/4" cubes and add the meat, the bones and the cooking Salsa verde- into the large pot. Stir well. Add ground pumpkin seeds and almonds. Add some or all of the remaining liquids to have a soupy quality. Simmer, uncovered, 1 hour, to meld flavors, stirring occasionally and adding liquids if needed to keep pan bottom from scorching. Add cilantro - chard and simmer 10-20 minutes, till greens are wilted into the soup but are still a bit chewy. Taste and add liquids, seasoning or solids as needed. Discard bones.

- Add ~ 1/2 lime's juice to each 12 ou. Serving. Serve with tortilla chips and chopped cilantro.
- * Perhaps canned beans vary, but I was surprised recently when I taste-compared Goya canned white beans and Goya pinto beans, and I found the pintos more flavorful and creamy! Of course, you may have another fav bean you prefer.

- After hard veggies soften, add stock, salt and pepper. I add a big dash of cayenne because it wakes up bland vegetables. At this point I add any dried fruits I might have. They add great flavor and texture. Add additional water if necessary and simmer another 30 min.
- Remove from heat and allow to "rest" about 20 minutes. Meanwhile, line up your soup bowls. Place chunks of bread in bowls. Ladle soup over bread. Cover the top of the soup with various pieces of cheese.
- Let everyone decide to either melt the cheese in the soup or fish it out and eat it just warmed.

---

198.   New Year Soup

Serving: Serves a hoard... | Prep: | Cook: | Ready in:

Ingredients

- all   marinated vegetables
- all handfuls cut up cheese
- 1 handful garlic cloves
- 1 cup chick peas
- 1 quart vegetable stock
- 2 cups water
- Cut up bread. Preferably hard or slightly stale.

Direction

- In a large soup pot add water and vegetables and simmer on a low flame about 30 minutes. Add whatever cut vegetables you have on hand in any condition short of gross. Add the chickpeas. (Your protein shot).

---

199.   No Time Rosemary/Lemon Roast Chicken And Chicken Soup

Serving: Makes 1 great chicken and a quart of chicken soup | Prep: 0hours20mins | Cook: 0hours50mins | Ready in:

Ingredients

- Roast Chicken
- 5 pounds chicken
- 1   stick of butter
- 1   lemon
- 1 packet fresh rosemary sprigs
- 1 teaspoon sea salt
- 1 teaspoon pepper
- Chicken soup
- 1   chicken carcass
- 1/2 cup celery
- 1/2 cup carrots
- 1/2 cup onions
- bay leaves
- 1/2 cup dry white wine
- 1 tablespoon chopped ginger
- 1/4 cup lemon juice

Direction

- Roast Chicken

- Buy a chicken. Mine was about 5 pounds, which was fine for me. Assemble these ingredients: a stick of unsalted butter, sea salt, pepper, fresh rosemary sprigs, and a lemon.
- Preheat the oven to 375. While it's heating up, take the giblets from the cavity of the chicken and rinse it out with cold water. I actually rinse the whole chicken. Afterwards, pat your bird down with a paper towel on both sides, and do a little pat in the cavity so that it's not waterlogged. Place it on a sheet pan.
- Cut the lemon in half, and rub one half all over the chicken. Cut the used half into quarters. Stuff the chicken cavity with rosemary sprigs and the lemon quarters. If you need more lemon, cut up the other half. Sprinkle the chicken with salt and pepper, and sprinkle some rosemary leaves on it, too. Cut up the stick of butter and place pats all over the chicken, then stick some butter into the cavity with the lemon and rosemary.
- *Cut up some potatoes or yams and put them on the sheet pan. Prep the veggies of your choice (heirloom carrots would be lovely) and put them on the sheet pan. Put a little butter or olive oil on them. When your sheet pan is loaded, put it in the oven, close the door, and leave everything alone for half an hour.
- Come back and baste your chicken with the juices on the sheet pan. If vegetables are cooked to your satisfaction, put them on a platter. Slide the chicken back in the oven for ten minutes. Once it's done, turn the broiler on low and hit the chicken with that for 10 minutes, which should net you a deliciously crackly skin. Carve and serve, or if it's just you, eat half of the chicken with your delicious veggies. Remove all the breast meat, wings and chicken legs from the carcass and leave the bones on the sheet pan.
- Chicken soup
- Put the carcass in a Dutch oven and pour in enough water to cover it. Scrape the sheet pan into the pot. Use a little cooking wine to get the last of the lemony chicken drippings up. Throw in a few bay leaves, a chopped onion, carrots and celery and boil the carcass for an hour.
- Remove the bones and discard. Add a tablespoon of chopped up ginger, 1/4 cup of lemon juice, some leftover breast or thigh meat, Add any veggies that you might like. Frozen peas, chopped mushrooms, etc.
- Once you've added everything you want, bring the soup to a boil and then turn the flame down. Cover and simmer for an hour to an hour and a half. Season to taste, give yourself a cup then pour the rest into plastic bowls and freeze.

---

200.   Nordic Pea Soup

Serving: Serves 6–8 | Prep: | Cook: | Ready in:

Ingredients

- 1 pound dried whole green peas, picked over, rinsed, & soaked for 10 hours
- 2 tablespoons olive oil
- 1 onion, chopped
- 10 ½ cups water
- 2 teaspoons fine sea salt
- 2 teaspoons dried marjoram
- ¾ pounds smoked pork shank with bone
- optional: mustard, for serving

Direction

- In a big pot, heat the olive oil on medium heat. Add the onion and cook until soft. Add the water, salt, marjoram, peas, and pork shank. Bring to a boil and let simmer for at least an hour.
- Remove the shank. Shred meat and discard skin and fat. Return the meat and bone back to the pot. Cook for at least another hour. Add more liquid if necessary. Should the soup look too thin, cook it without a lid for a while.
- Taste and season. Discard the bone before serving.

- Serve with mustard if preferred and rye bread or crisp bread.

---

201. Not Your Grandmother's Cabbage Roll Soup

Serving: Serves 6 | Prep: | Cook: | Ready in:

Ingredients

- For the soup
- 1 large onion, chopped
- 2 garlic cloves, minced
- 2 tablespoons olive oil
- 1 head of cabbage, shredded
- one 28-ounce can diced tomatoes
- one 15-ounce can tomato sauce
- 1/3 cup brown sugar
- 1/3 cup lemon juice
- 1/2 cup dried cranberries
- 5 cups water
- For the meatballs
- 1 pound ground round
- 2 tablespoons grated onion
- 2 tablespoons milk
- 1 teaspoon salt
- 1/4 teaspoon freshly ground black pepper
- 1 egg, beaten
- 1/2 cup uncooked rice
- 1/2 cup plain bread crumbs

Direction

- In a large Dutch oven, sauté onions and garlic over medium heat in olive oil until soft. Add salt and pepper. Add shredded cabbage and lightly sauté until soft. Add tomatoes with their liquid, tomato sauce, brown sugar, lemon juice, cranberries and 5 cups of water. Stir to blend.
- In a separate bowl, mix all meatball ingredients. Form cocktail size meatballs from mixture and add to liquid. Bring to a boil. Cover, reduce heat to low, and cook for 1 to 1 1/2 hours.

---

202. Okroshka

Serving: Serves 4 | Prep: | Cook: | Ready in:

Ingredients

- 1 cucumber, peeled and diced
- 2-3 hard-boiled eggs, diced
- 400 grams / 14 oz. / 1¼ cup sour yogurt (or Greek yogurt + the juice of half a lemon)
- 200 grams / 7 oz. cooked shrimp or crab meat, chopped
- 1 bunch fresh dill or fennel leaves, chopped

Direction

- Combine all in the ingredients, except the ice cubes, in a large bowl.
- Chill in the fridge for 1 or 2 hours.
- Serve with ice cubes.

---

203. One Pot Surf And Turf

Serving: Serves 4 | Prep: | Cook: | Ready in:

Ingredients

- 10.6 ounces giant king prawns (300g)
- 17.6 ounces mussels, cleaned (500g)
- 4 pieces salsiccia sausages (casings removed & meat separated into small pieces)
- 1 medium yellow onion, cubed
- 1 small fennel bulb, thinly sliced
- 2 garlic cloved, minced
- 1 package of mussel seasoning
- 250 milliliters dry white wine
- 3 tablespoons Pernod
- 8 sprigs fresh tarragon leaves
- 2 small crushed chilies
- 250 milliliters heavy cream
- 2 tablespoons fresh dill
- 6 tablespoons extra-virgin olive oil

- freshly ground pepper & salt
- 1 lemon, sliced

Direction

- Fill a large pot with the broth or salted water. Bring to the boil. Add the potatoes and corn and cook until slightly tender. Note: you could actually add the potatoes and corn after the 3. Step into the stockpot.....but I think the potatoes taste better if they are cooked separately.....
- In a large heavy bottomed stockpot heat the olive oil over medium heat. Add the onions and cook, until soft about 4 minutes. Add the garlic and fennel and cook for another 3-4 minutes. Add the sausage meat and cook for another 5 minutes, until the meat is nicely browned.
- Add the wine and Pernod and bring to the boil. Add the mussel seasoning, a bit of salt, chili flakes and tarragon.
- Add the prawns, mussels and lemons slices and cover with the lid and cook, shaking the pan from time to time until the clams are open for about 6 minutes.
- Add the heavy cream, gently stir with spoon to mix and simmer uncovered for another 2-3 minutes.
- With a slotted spoon add potatoes and corn to the pot and gently stir that all is covered in broth. You might want to add a little bit broth as well.
- Spoon into bowls or soup plates. Garnish with cut dill. Season again with pepper. Serve with fresh French country bread or baguette.

204. Our Favorite Chicken Noodle Soup With Homemade Noodles

Serving: Serves 8 to 10 | Prep: | Cook: | Ready in:

Ingredients

- The Soup
- 1 tablespoon butter
- 1 tablespoon olive oil
- 2 carrots, peeled and chopped
- 1/2 onion, fine dice
- 1 celery heart including leaves, diced
- 2 garlic cloves, minced
- 1 gallon homemade chicken stock or high quality store bought stock
- 2 tablespoons parsley, chopped
- kosher salt
- pepper
- 1 pinch red cayenne powder
- 2 oven roasted chicken breasts, cut into cubes
- 5 drops lemon juice
- The Noodles
- 2 cups flour
- 1 tablespoon kosher salt
- 4 large eggs

Direction

- The Soup
- Add the oil and butter to the soup pot over medium heat. Sweat carrots, onion, celery, and garlic with 2 teaspoons of kosher salt for 8 to 10 minutes. Add chicken stock. Bring to a boil and then drop to a simmer. Cook for thirty minutes.
- The Noodles
- Combine the salt and flour in a bowl with a whisk. Make a well in the center of the flour. Break eggs into the flour well. Stir together with a spoon or your hand. Stir until it becomes a sticky dough. Place dough on a lightly floured cutting board or counter. Knead the dough adding flour as you go until the dough becomes smooth and dense. Then let it rest for 20 minutes.
- Cut your dough into four sections. Roll them into balls and set aside. Roll out one ball of the dough at a time with a rolling pin using flour as needed. Roll it out as thin as you can comfortably get it. Add a little flour to the round and roll it up like a sleeping bag. Then cut into slices, ¼ inch wide for company or ¾ inch wide for the big fluffy noodles. Unroll

the noodles and put them onto a plate or another cutting board. Repeat with the rest of the dough balls.

- Bring your soup back to a full boil and start dropping noodles into the soup pot, a few at a time, and stirring them to keep them from sticking together. Add all the noodles, add parsley and cubed chicken meat in, stir, and cook for 15 minutes or so. Taste and adjust seasonings. Stir in the five drops of lemon juice. Serve.

---

205.   Oven Roasted Chicken Broth

Serving: Serves 1 - 2 quarts. | Prep: | Cook: | Ready in:

Ingredients

- 1 chicken carcass
- 1 carrot scraped, washed, halved.
- 3 celery stalk. Cut to fit in pot.
- 2 medium onions quartered
- 3 sprigs parsley
- 1 dry bay leaf
- 6 black peppercorn
- 1/2 teaspoon kosher salt
- Enough water to cover the chicken and vegetables plus 2 inches.

Direction

- Preheat oven to 450F
- In oven safe pot (big enough for the whole recipe) place chicken carcass, onion, celery and carrot. Toss them all to coat veggies with the chicken fat. Into oven uncovered. Roast for 30 to 45 minutes or until all are lightly browned and veggies are wilted.
- Remove pot from oven and onto stove burner. Turn heat to high and add remaining ingredients. Cover pot to help bring broth to boil. When boiling starts, turn down heat to lowest setting so that broth barely bubbles. Continue cooking at this temp for 2 hours.

- Pour broth through sieve and into container. When cooled a bit move container to fridge and leave overnight. Fat will collect on top. The next day remove fat, reheat broth, adjust for salt.
- Now is the time to think about eating. What shall it be? Cup of broth with grilled cheese. Fresh dill and sautéed mushrooms with a cup of cooked barley, maybe create a jambalaya.

---

206.   Oven Roasted Summer Tomato & Rosemary Bisque

Serving: Serves 4 | Prep: | Cook: | Ready in:

Ingredients

- 3 pounds tomatoes
- 6 pieces garlic, unpeeled
- 3 sprigs rosemary
- 3 tablespoons oliv oil
- 3 cups vegetable stock
- 1-2 teaspoons to taste
- 1 handful fresh basil, chopped
- 1 teaspoon freshly ground black peppar

Direction

- Preheat the oven to 400 F.
- Cut the tomatoes into quarters and place in an oven-proof dish.
- Cut the garlic gloves in half and add to tomatoes, along with 2 springs of rosemary and drizzle with olive oil.
- Roast the tomatoes in the upper side of the oven for about 25 minutes.
- When done, separate the roasted garlic gloves from the skin by squeezing them out. Place all the tomatoes, garlic and rosemary in a large pot. Add 3 cups of vegetable stock and bring to a boil. Then turn of the heat, add basil and blend with an immersion blender. Season with salt and pepper. Serve with a drizzle of olive oil.

207. Oyster Chowder

Serving: Serves 4 | Prep: | Cook: | Ready in:

Ingredients

- 1/4 pound bacon, cut into 1/4-inch strips
- 1 cup chopped onion
- 1 cup chopped celery hearts
- 3 white potatoes, peeled and cut into 1/2-inch cubes (about 4 cups)
- 14 to 16 large oysters and their liquor
- Salt
- Cayenne pepper
- 2/3 to 1 cups whole milk
- 1 tablespoon chopped Italian parsley

Direction

- Spread the bacon in a soup pan and place over medium heat. Cook until browned and its fat has rendered. Drain. Discard all but 1 tablespoon of fat and put the pan back on the heat. Scrape the onion and celery into the pan and sauté until softened. Drop in the potatoes. Add enough water to cover, about 3 cups. Bring to a boil, then reduce the heat and simmer until the potatoes are tender, 15 minutes.
- Take the pan off the heat and, using a masher, lightly crush the potatoes to thicken the chowder. Add the oysters and oyster liquor and season to taste with salt and cayenne pepper. Simmer until the oysters curl, 3 to 5 minutes.
- Pour in the milk (use 2/3 cup if you prefer it less rich), bring to a boil, then shut off the heat. Crumble in the bacon and stir in the parsley.

208. PB & J Pumpkin Soup

Serving: Makes 5 1/2 cups | Prep: | Cook: | Ready in:

Ingredients

- 2 teaspoons olive oil
- 1/2 cup chopped onion
- 1 garlic clove, chopped
- 1 teaspoon fresh chopped ginger
- 1 cup chicken stock
- 2 cups coconut milk
- 1 tablespoon fresh lime juice
- 1 tablespoon fish sauce
- 1 cup peanut butter
- 1 cup pumpkin puree
- 2-3 tablespoons pepper jelly
- peanuts for garnish

Direction

- In a small skillet, heat olive oil over medium heat. Add onion, and cook for a few minutes. Add garlic and ginger and continue to cook a few more minutes until onion is softened. Remove from heat and place in blender. Add the chicken stock, coconut milk, lime juice, fish sauce, peanut butter and pumpkin to the blender and blend on high until smooth.
- Strain mixture into a medium saucepan and heat thoroughly. When serving, ladle soup into individual bowls and garnish with a teaspoon or 2 of pepper jelly and peanuts. Stir to combine and enjoy!

209. Paleo Pho With Turkey

Serving: Serves 2 | Prep: 0hours10mins | Cook: 0hours10mins | Ready in:

Ingredients

- The Pho
- 1 tablespoon Avocado oil
- 1/4 Inch Fresh Ginger - Lightly smashed
- 2 Cloves Garlic - Smashed
- 1 Whole Star Anise
- 6 cups Turkey bone broth
- 3 tablespoons Coco Aminos

- 2 Medium Zucchini - Spiralized or julienned
- 1/2 Onion Sliced - thin
- 1 cup Turkey - Shredded
- 1 teaspoon Salt
- 1 teaspoon Pepper
- Optional Toppings
- Green onion ribbons
- Basil leaves
- Sriracha
- Lime wedges
- Jalapeno slices

Direction

- Place a large pot over med-high heat and pour in the Avocado oil. Once this is hot add in the garlic, ginger, and star anise. Let this cook for a few minutes to release the flavors, stirring every so often so nothing burns. Then add in the Turkey stock. Let this simmer while you prepare the other ingredients.
- Set out two deep soup bowls and divide the zoodled zucchini into each bowl. Then divide out the shredded turkey and top it with the onions slices.
- Strain out the solids from the broth and add in the coco aminos. Pour the broth into the bowls and let it sit a few minutes so the broth can warm the zoodles and meat. Divide and sprinkle the salt and pepper over the bowls. Serve with optional toppings
- You have 2 options for bone broth. 1. Use a pre-made, paleo approved, bone broth2. Make it in the crock pot the night before. Stuff all the turkey bones in a large crock pot with 2 tsp apple cider vinegar and cover with water. Set on low for 8-12 hours. After that add in a quartered onion and several smashed cloves of garlic. Continue to cook on low for another 2-4 hours. Strain everything and use or store the resulting bone broth.

<table>
<tr><td>210.</td><td>Paleo Friendly Pumpkin Soup With Bacon</td></tr>
</table>

Serving: Serves 3 | Prep: | Cook: |Ready in:

Ingredients

- 1/2 pound Bacon, cut into 1 inch chunks
- 2 cups Pumpkin puree
- 1/2 Onion, diced
- 2 Celery stalks, diced
- 4 Carrots, peeled and diced
- 2 Apples, peeled, cored and diced
- 3 Garlic cloves, minced
- 1/2 teaspoon Ground cinnamon
- 1/4 teaspoon Ground ginger
- 1 tablespoon Olive oil
- 4 cups Chicken stock
- 1/4 cup Toasted pumpkin seeds
- Salt and pepper to taste

Direction

- Cook the bacon until crispy in a large stock pot over medium high heat. Remove from the pot and place on a paper towel lined plate to cool. Set aside.
- Drain most of the bacon fat from the pot. Add the olive oil, onions, carrots, and celery. Sauté until translucent, about 5-7 minutes.
- Add the apples and cook for another 3-5 minutes, until they begin to caramelize. Add the garlic, cinnamon, and ground ginger and cook for another 1-2 minutes, until fragrant.
- Add the chicken stock and pumpkin puree. Turn the heat to high and bring to a boil. Reduce heat and simmer for 20 minutes.
- Either transfer the soup to a food processor or use an immersion blender to blend the soup until smooth.
- Season with salt and pepper to taste.
- Spoon into bowls and garnish with the crisp bacon and pumpkin seeds.

211.   Parmesan Broth

Serving: Makes 10 cups | Prep: | Cook: |Ready in:

Ingredients

- 12 cups cool water
- 1 tablespoon unsalted butter
- 2 cups medium-diced onions
- 1 cup coarsely chopped carrots
- 1 cup coarsely chopped celery
- 1/4 ounce dried mushroom, such as porcini or shiitake
- 2 bay leaves
- 3 sprigs fresh thyme
- 3 sprigs fresh flat-leaf parsley
- 1 cup (or so) leftover bits of hard cheese and natural rind

Direction

- In a large pot, bring the water to a simmer over medium-high heat.
- While the water heats, in another large pot, melt the butter over medium heat. When it's melted, add the onions, carrots, celery, mushrooms, bay leaves, thyme, and parsley. Cook until the onions are translucent and the carrots, celery, and mushrooms are soft, about 8 minutes. With a wooden spoon, stir in the cheese bits. Let the cheese and vegetables sit on the bottom of the pot for short periods of time, no longer than 10 seconds; this will allow the vegetables and the cheese to brown the bottom of the pot a little. (You don't want all the vegetables browned, but just the bottom surface needs a little color.) Stir often.
- When the vegetables and cheese at the very bottom of the pot show some brown and the cheese is beginning to melt, slowly introduce the simmering water to the pot, stirring in just 1 cup/240 ml to start. Stirring constantly, deglaze the pan's bottom with the hot water to loosen any browned bits. When the pot bottom is clean of any brown, pour in the remainder of the water. Decrease the heat to medium-low and monitor the heat, adjusting the flame so the broth stays at a gentle simmer.
- Simmer for 40 to 50 minutes, stirring every 3 to 5 minutes, so the broth doesn't pick up a scorched flavor. Strain the broth into a very large container or another clean pot and allow it to cool. Once it's cool, you can easily skim the top of any fats. Store this in your refrigerator for up to 3 days or in your freezer for up to 3 months.

212.   Pasta Fagioli~

Serving: Serves a large pot fill | Prep: | Cook: |Ready in:

Ingredients

- 2 tablespoons Olive Oil
- 1 Medium Onion Diced
- 2 Garlic Cloves Chopped
- 1 pound Ground Beef or (1/2 lb. ground beef~1/2 lb. Sausage)
- 2 Celery Stalks Chopped
- 2 Carrots Diced
- 1 can of Pinto Beans (15oz)
- 1 can of Roman Beans (15oz)
- 1 can of Cannellini Beans (15oz)
- 1 pound can of Crush Tomatoes
- 2 cups Beef Broth
- 1/2 cup Red Wine
- 1 tablespoon Balsamic Vinegar
- 1 Bay Leaf
- 2 tablespoons parsley
- 1 tablespoon Rosemay Chopped
- 1 pinch Red Pepper Flakes
- 1 teaspoon Sea Salt
- 1/2 teaspoon Black Pepper
- 1 pound Ditalini Pasta

Direction

- In a large pot, (soup pot) on medium heat warm oil.
- Add onions and garlic, cook until soft.
- Add ground beef and brown with onions and garlic.

- Add celery and carrots, and beans combination to beef mixture.
- Stir in the crush tomatoes, beef broth, red wine, balsamic vinegar, bay leaf, parsley, rosemary, red pepper flakes, sea salt and black pepper. (The seasons may be use at your taste liking.)
- Cook on low heat gently for 2 hours~~ you may use it now or let sit, on stove, with no heat and rewarm later or put in refrigerator overnight to flavor even more.
- When ready to serve, cook ditalini pasta, in salted water "al dente" and drain then add to warm soup and serve. Garnish with grated cheese.

213.   Pea Soup

Serving: Serves 4 | Prep: | Cook: |Ready in:

Ingredients

- 2 medium leeks–rinsed and sliced
- 1 tablespoon minced garlic–about 6 cloves
- 1 tablespoon olive oil
- 1 quart low sodium vegetable broth
- 2 1 pound bags of frozen peas–thawed

Direction

- Heat olive oil in a large pot over medium high heat. When hot, add leeks and sauté until translucent–about 5 minutes. Add the garlic and cook for another minute.
- Add peas, vegetable stock, and salt and pepper to taste. Bring the soup to a boil, then reduce the heat and simmer for 5 minutes.
- Blend soup until smooth in a blender or in the pot with an immersion blender.

214.   Pea Soup With Meyer Lemon Cream And Fried Shallots

Serving: Serves 8-10 | Prep: | Cook: |Ready in:

Ingredients

- For the soup
- 1 1/2 cups Canadian bacon or thick-cut pancetta, cubed
- 2 Standard-size bags frozen peas
- 1 Bulb fennel
- 2 Shallots
- 3 Garlic cloves
- 3 cups Chicken broth
- 1 cup Dry sherry (or white wine)
- 1/4 cup Half & half
- 1 teaspoon Dried dill
- For the toppings
- 2 tablespoons Creme fraiche
- 4 Shallots
- 1 tablespoon Flour
- 1 Meyer Lemon

Direction

- Start by prepping the veggies. Slice the fennel bulb into thin pieces and roughly chop. Mince garlic cloves and two shallots.
- Place bacon into a large pot with some olive oil. Once the bacon is sizzling and slightly browning, remove from the pot and set aside for now.
- In the same pot, add the garlic, shallots, fennel, dill, kosher salt and pepper and a bit more olive oil if needed. Simmer on medium-low heat until the fennel begins to soften, about 10-15 minutes.
- Add the sherry to the pot, bring to a boil. Add the chicken broth and peas to the pot. Season again with salt and pepper. Let the soup reach a boil again, and then remove from the heat.
- While soup is cooling, work on the toppings. For the shallots, slice the remaining shallots into about 1/8 inch slices. Dress with oil, kosher salt, flour and cornmeal. In a small

saucepan, heat olive oil to high heat and place shallots in the pan turning once to brown each side. For the cream, mix the crème fraiche, lemon juice and zest in a small bowl.

- Go back to the soup pot and use an immersion blender to blend into a smooth mixture. You can also ladle the soup into a regular blender. Once blended, add the half and half and the bacon back into the soup, stir. Season again to taste.
- To serve, reheat soup, drizzle with the lemon cream and top with the fried shallots.

215.   Pea And Lentil Soup

Serving: Serves 6 - 8 | Prep: | Cook: | Ready in:

Ingredients

- 16 ounces dried, split peas
- 1 cup dried, green lentils
- 3 cloves   garlic, pressed or minced
- 1 onion, diced
- 2 teaspoons cumin, ground
- 1/2 teaspoon coriander, ground
- 6 pods cardamom
- 2 tablespoons curry powder
- 2/3 to 1 gallons low sodium chicken stock
- 1 ham bone with meat (left over spiral cut ham bones are perfect)
- salt & pepper, to taste

Direction

- Rinse peas and lentils and put them in the bottom of a crock pot.
- Place the ham bone on top of the peas and lentils and then layer the onions, garlic and spices over the ham, peas and lentils.
- Add the stock, reserving a bit for thinning out later, if necessary.
- Cover and cook on high for approximately 6 hours. The ham should be falling off the bone, the lentils tender after that time. If you give it a stir, the peas should break up and thicken

the soup. If it still seems a bit undercooked, give it another hour.

- Once the soup is cooked, fish out the ham bone and meat. Shred the meat into chunks and return the meat to the soup.
- Give the soup a good stir, which will incorporate the peas into the broth. If the soup is too thick, stir in some more stock. Taste for seasoning and add any salt or pepper, if desired.

216.   Pea And Taragon Soup

Serving: Serves 4 | Prep: | Cook: | Ready in:

Ingredients

- 4 shallots, roughly chopped
- 2 tablespoons olive oil
- 16 ounces frozen petite peas
- 1/4 cup roughly chopped fresh tarragon
- 2 cups chicken or vegetable broth
- 1 cup whole milk
- salt and pepper to taste

Direction

- Heat the olive oil in a large soup pot over medium heat. Sauté shallots until translucent.
- Add frozen peas, and stir to defrost and lightly cook. Add broth, milk, and tarragon and simmer for about 10-15 minutes.
- Process with an immersion blender and season with salt and pepper to taste.
- Serve either hot or chilled, garnished with fresh tarragon leaves.

217.   Pinto Beans And Turnip Greens

Serving: Makes a big potful of stew | Prep: | Cook: | Ready in:

Ingredients

- 1 cup dried, uncooked pinto beans
- 3-4 tablespoons olive oil
- 1 onion, chopped
- 2 cloves garlic, or to taste, minced
- 12 sprigs fresh parsley, or to taste, chopped
- 1 28 oz can whole tomatoes, with juice, chopped or smushed (or, in season, 3 or 4 large tomatoes, chopped)
- 1 sweet bell pepper, chopped
- 3 large carrots, chopped
- 2 dried bay leaves
- 2 bunches turnip greens, coarsely chopped or torn
- salt and pepper, to taste
- juice of half a lemon

Direction

- Start by cooking the pinto beans according to package directions: soak them overnight, or boil and do a quick 1-hour soak, and then simmer them in fresh water until they're almost cooked. You can buy canned beans and skip this step, but if you have time, I tend to prefer dried to canned. If using canned, just rinse the beans before you add them (later on); if you cook dried beans, once they're at the almost-cooked stage, drain them to stop them from getting mushy while you cook the veggies, but save the cooking liquid.
- Take out a big soup pot and heat the olive oil in it. When it's hot, add the onion and garlic and sauté for a few minutes; when the onion gets soft, add the parsley and stir. Then, dump in the carrots, sweet pepper, and tomatoes. Break the bay leaves in half and throw them in, too. Watch until the tomato juice heats up and starts to bubble, and then let it all cook for 3 or 4 more minutes to start the carrots softening.
- To the tomato-y base, add bean cooking liquid (or a cup or two of water or stock, if you used canned beans) and let it all come back to a boil. Then, with the heat up high, add the turnip greens by the handful, stirring them in and

waiting for each handful to begin to collapse before adding the next. It may take a while to incorporate all the greens, and you may need to add more liquid to the pot to make sure they're all covered; go ahead and add what you need. Once they're all in, stir in the cooked pinto beans, bring the whole pot back to a boil, and then turn the heat down to a simmer level. Taste for salt and pepper, and adjust the seasoning to your liking. I find the amount of salt I add often depends on the brand of canned tomatoes I use, but it's a safe bet that you'll need to add *some* salt. Stir in the lemon juice now, too.

- Simmer the stew, stirring occasionally, until the carrots are tender and the liquid is as reduced as you like. Serve hot, maybe with a poached egg on top or some toast on the side. I find that the leftovers, reheated or just eaten cold, get better and better throughout the week, too.

---

218.   Pork Kimchi Chili

Serving: Serves 4 + leftovers | Prep: 0hours30mins | Cook: 0hours15mins |Ready in:

Ingredients

- 1.5 pounds pork tenderloin, thinest slices
- 1 onion, peeled
- 1 red bell pepper, deseeded
- 1 1/2 cups kimchi, (300 grams)
- 2 whole chili peppers, (Thai or your choice)
- 8 cloves of garlic, peeled
- 3 cups chicken broth (or vegetable broth)
- 1 package silken tofu, Morinaga recommended
- 2 bunches spring onions, cut in 1-inch lengths
- 1 package bean sprouts, rinsed (whole bean attached, if available))
- 1-2 tablespoons soy sauce (optional-depends on how salty the kimchi)
- prepared rice, to serve with chili

Direction

- Ask butcher to slice on thinnest setting. If not, freeze pork. Two hours before cooking, start defrosting until about 25% thawed. (Easy to cut if middle is still hard). Sharpen knife, and slice. You can do it!
- Cut onion in half, then cut slices from top to bottom. Cut bell pepper in thin strips.
- Prepared kimchi from Asian market is great, but bottled is fine too. If you're trying kimchi for the first time, buy Japanese-type. (Korean is more 'vibrant'). Chop in 1-inch lengths.
- Morinaga Tofu comes in packaging that lasts for months, so it's not in the fridge section at the store, try the bean or Asian section. Regular American tofu is almost like cheese in texture, so add a little water, and smash with a fork or hand-held blender. Some chunks are fine.
- Prepare all ingredients and put on platter. Everything will be cooked directly before eating. (Or prepare on stove, and carry pot to table to serve.) Set out one little bowl per person. The 'pot' needs one large spoon and fork.
- Heat the broth to boiling. Add onions, whole garlic cloves, whole chilies, and kimchi. Stir, and cook until onions are soft, about 5 minutes. Add smashed tofu, mix and bring to boiling.
- Now add pork, one by one, so pieces don't stick together. When pork color changes, add spring onions and bean sprouts. When they are soft, everything is ready.
- Each person helps themselves to their preferences. Spoon some 'chili soup' in your bowl too. Serve with rice in separate bowls.
- When everyone is 'beginning-to-be-full' you can add extras like udon noodles, harusame (glass) noodles, bean-thread noodles or pounded rice cakes.
- Save leftovers for 'Breakfast Nabe Leftovers'.

219. Porridge And Red Lentils Spilt Soup

Serving: Serves 2/3 | Prep: | Cook: |Ready in:

Ingredients

- 1/2 cup porridge
- 1/2 red lentils
- 1 cup fresh tamatoes puree
- 1 teaspoon cumin seeds
- 1 tablespoon olive oil
- 1/4 teaspoon salt .add more if requried
- 1/4 cup fresh peas
- 1/8 cup raisins
- 1/8 cup cashews

Direction

- Soak red lintels and porridge in cold water for an hour .Then boil them together with two cups of water .once cooked keep it aside.
- In a medium size saucepan add olive oil, cumin seeds and tomatoes and sauté for 2 to 3 minutes. Add fresh peas , cashews and green raisins and slowly add the porridge and red lentils split boiled mixture .Add salt to your taste .Let it cook until peas are soft , then remove the pan from the heat .Garnish it with some raisins and cashews. Serve hot. Enjoy!!

220. Portuguese Chicken Soup Aka Canja

Serving: Serves 6-8 | Prep: 0hours15mins | Cook: 2hours0mins |Ready in:

Ingredients

- 1 Yellow onion diced
- 1 Carrot sliced
- 1 Stalk of celery sliced
- 2 Bay leaves
- 1 Stewing hen or whole chicken with legs and thighs removed

- 2 teaspoons Salt
- 1 cup Rice or soup pasta
- 2 Lemons
- Salt and black pepper to taste
- 2 sprigs thyme (optional)

Direction

- Place onion, carrot, celery, bay leaves and salt in a large pot. Add the whole stewing hen. If using a regular chicken, remove the legs and thighs for another use and place the remaining chicken, bones and all, in the pot. Add enough water to cover the chicken (about 8 cups). Bring to a boil then simmer for 1.5 - 2 hours.
- Remove chicken from pot and set aside. Add rice or soup pasta to pot and stir. Cook until rice or pasta is done to your liking. Meanwhile, shred chicken, disposing of skin and bones. If using a stewing hen, you may only want to shred the white meat.
- When rice or pasta is to your liking, add shredded chicken back to pot along with the juice of 1 lemon. Season with salt and pepper. Sprinkle thyme leaves on top (optional). Serve with remaining lemon cut into wedges.

221. Pot Pie Soup With A Little Warmth (or A Big Kick!)

Serving: Makes about 3 quarts | Prep: | Cook: | Ready in:

Ingredients

- 1/4 cup butter
- 1/4 cup vegetable oil
- 1/2 cup flour
- 1 medium onion, diced
- 3 small carrots, diced
- 1 stalk celery, diced
- a pinch of ground thyme
- 2 teaspoons black pepper
- 2 medium potatoes, peeled and diced
- 8 cups chicken or turkey broth
- 2 cups fresh or frozen corn kernels

- 2 cups fresh or frozen peas
- 4 cups diced cooked turkey or chicken
- 1/2 cup cream
- 1/2 cup chopped parsley
- 5 tablespoons finely grated fresh horseradish plus more for passing (optional) at the table
- more pepper and salt to taste
- 1 sheet of puff pastry from a 17.3 ounce package, cut into 9 squares and baked at 400F for about 20 minutes

Direction

- In a soup pot, melt the butter and oil and sauté the onion, celery and carrot until the onion softens a bit.
- Add the thyme, black pepper and flour and cook while stirring for a couple of minutes until the mixture forms a tight roux.
- Slowly add the broth, stirring constantly, until the roux mixture is incorporated. Add the potatoes. Bring to a boil and simmer for 15 minutes.
- Add the corn, peas and chicken or turkey and bring back to the boil.
- Turn off the heat and stir in the cream, horseradish and parsley. Re-season with salt and pepper, if desired.
- Serve each bowl with a puff pastry square floating on top.

222. Potato And Spinach Soup With Bacon And Jalapeño

Serving: Serves 3 or 4 as main up to 6 to 8 as first course | Prep: | Cook: | Ready in:

Ingredients

- 3 strips bacon, diced
- 1 teaspoon butter
- 1 teaspoon reserved bacon grease
- 1/2 cup diced onion
- 1/2 large jalapeño, seeded and minced

- 1 pound potatoes peeled and chopped (I used Russet Idahos!)
- 5 to 6 cups homemade or low-sodium chicken broth
- 10 to 12 ounces fresh or thawed frozen spinach
- Sour cream or cream fraiche, for serving

Direction

- Cook bacon in a Dutch oven or stockpot until browned and crispy. Remove, drain on paper towels and set aside. Drain all but about one teaspoon of the grease from the pot.
- Add 1 teaspoon of butter, then stir in the onion and jalapeño and cook until the onion is translucent, about 5 minutes. Add the potato chunks, then give it a good mix.
- Pour in the chicken broth, cover, and bring to a simmer. Simmer for about 30 minutes, or until the potatoes are cooked through all the way.
- Stir in the spinach and bacon (reserving some bacon for garnish), and simmer another 5 minutes. (If using fresh spinach, simmer until it wilts.)
- Puree the soup with an immersion blender (I don't have one) or in batches in a blender or food processor until completely smooth. Serve the soup with a dollop of sour cream and bacon pieces as additional garnish. You may salt to taste at this point, but the bacon and sour cream made it plenty salty for our tastes.

223. Potato Soup With Pomegranate Seeds And Almonds

Serving: Serves 6 | Prep: | Cook: | Ready in:

Ingredients

- 1 1/2 cups white onions
- Yukon Gold potatoes
- 3/4 cup slivered almonds

- 1/2 cup lime, juice and 2 tsp zest
- 500 milliliters milk
- 400 milliliters water (approx)
- 1 pinch cumin
- 1 pinch nutmeg
- 1/2 cup arugula leaves
- 1 pomegrenate
- salt and pepper, to taste
- 1-2 tablespoons olive oil

Direction

- Slice the onion in half and cut into fine, small slices. Peel the potatoes and cut into cubes
- Wash the arugula and drain well. Cut the pomegranate in two, carefully remove the seeds. You can do this in a bowl filled with water so as not to make a mess. Set aside.
- In a dry pan, roast 1/4 cup of the slivered almonds on low-medium heat
- Melt the butter in a large pot and cook the onions for 4-5 minutes, until translucent. Add the remaining slivered almonds and the potatoes. Cook for 3-4 minutes, steering often. Pour in the milk and 400 ml of water. Cover and let cook for 25 minutes until the potatoes are cooked. Add the spices, salt and pepper. Then add the line zest and lime juice.
- Puree the soup with a hand mixer and run through a sieve. Season with salt and more pepper if needed. Return to the pot, puree more if desired and cook for another 3-4 minutes. Adjust the water if you want a more liquid soup.
- Serve the soup warm topped with a few arugula leaves, roasted slivered almond, a sprinkle of olive oil and pomegranate seeds.

224. Pumpkin Soup With Cranberries & Sage

Serving: Serves 6 to 8 as a first course | Prep: | Cook: | Ready in:

Ingredients

- 1 pound Sugar Pumpkin or Butternut Squash
- 2 tablespoons Olive Oil
- 1/2 cup Onion- chopped
- 1/2 cup Celery- chopped
- 1/2 cup Carrot- chopped
- 1 cup Apples- peeled and chopped
- 1 cup Cranberries- fresh or frozen
- 2 teaspoons Ginger- freshly grated
- 2 tablespoons Sage- fresh and chopped
- 1 pinch each- Cinnamon, Allspice and Nutmeg
- 1 quart Chicken Stock
- Salt & Pepper- to taste
- 1 cup Cranberry Juice- (optional)

Direction

- Peel and chop the pumpkin or squash. Heat the oil in large pot over medium heat and add vegetables, including pumpkin. Then add the apples and cranberries, stirring often. After a couple of minutes, add the seasoning, stock, and juice (if you use it) and bring to a boil. Reduce heat and cook until vegetables are tender. Puree in a blender, or use a blender stick to make a creamy puree. Put back on the stove to heat. If the soup is too thick, thin down with a little more stock or white wine. Taste and adjust seasonings as necessary. You can serve it with a dollop of sour cream, if desired.
- Enjoy!

225.   Pumpkin Soup With Polenta Croutons

Serving: Serves 4 | Prep: | Cook: |Ready in:

Ingredients

- Pumpkin Soup
- 28 ounces peeled pumpkin, coarsely chopped in to small cubes (1/2 inch)
- 2 medium size skinned yams or sweet potatoes, coarsely chopped into small cubes (
- 1 finely chopped white onion
- 4 tablespoons extra virgin olive oil
- 3 1/2 ounces unsalted butter
- 4 cups vegetable stock
- 6 finely chopped basil leaves
- 1 teaspoon sugar
- salt and pepper to taste
- Corn Polenta Croutons
- 10 1/2 ounces cornmeal
- 4 cups water
- 1 1/2 teaspoons salt
- 1 tablespoon unsalted butter
- Peanut Oil

Direction

- Pumpkin Soup
- Add the olive oil to a deep saucepan, and cook the onion on low-medium heat until soft and translucent, approximately 8–10 minutes.
- Add the potatoes and the pumpkin, and cook together with the onion for about 5 minutes, then cover with the vegetable stock.
- Add the sugar and the basil leaves. Cover and simmer for about 1 hour on low heat. Stir periodically.
- After one hour, add the butter and whisk everything until you obtain a smooth and delicious creamy soup.
- Add salt and pepper to taste. Serve with croutons.
- Corn Polenta Croutons
- Boil a pot of water. At the boiling point, add the salt and then the corn meal, continually stirring to prevent it from sticking or burning. Stir the polenta continuously until very thick, about 20 minutes, although time varies depending on the corn meal used (you may add some additional water if it thickens very quickly).
- Coat a glass ovenproof dish (7" x 11"x 1-1/2") with the butter. When the polenta is ready, pour the polenta into the dish and spread so it is no more than 1/3 of an inch deep and let it

cool for several hours (after it reaches room temperature place pan in the fridge).

- Slice the polenta in strips, and then into small cubes, Dust them in flour and deep-fry them in peanut oil (use a deep pot with at least an inch of oil). Cook for 8 minutes or until polenta has browned and become crispy.
- Add the warm, fried corn polenta cubes to the creamy pumpkin soup, and enjoy!
- Author's Note: Pumpkin is available only in the fall, but this soup is delicious much of the year. Try substituting butternut squash, which is available for longer periods, and prepare the same way. If you are looking for an appropriate wine, this dish pairs particularly well with an off-dry Gewürztraminer or Riesling from France or Austria.

226. Purple Carrot Soup + Turmeric Tahini Dressing

Serving: Serves 2 | Prep: | Cook: | Ready in:

Ingredients

- Purple Carrot Soup
- 3 cups vegetable broth
- 1   yellow onion, quartered
- 4-5 carrots, quartered
- 1   head of garlic
- 1/2   head of cauliflower, coarsely chopped
- 1/2 cup non-dairy milk, unsweetened almond or cashew
- 1/2 cup hazelnuts, toasted
- 2 tablespoons olive oil
- Tahini Turmeric Dressing
- 1 tablespoon nutritional yeast
- 11/2 tablespoon tahini
- 1 teaspoon turmeric
- 1/2   lemon, juiced

Direction

- Preheat oven to 425°.

- Line a baking pan with parchment paper and set aside. In a large bowl mix together coarsely chopped cauliflower and quartered onions and carrots in 2 tbs of olive oil. Season with fresh cracked pepper and sea salt. Pour onto prepared baking sheet and nestle 1 head of garlic in to the center of the veggies. On a separate baking sheet, pour 1 cup of hazelnuts for toasting. Roast the vegetables for 30-35 minutes, or until you can pierce the carrots with a fork, and the hazelnuts for 8-10 minutes, or until they release a nutty aroma.
- In a bowl or small jar, mix together nutritional yeast, tahini, soy sauce, turmeric, and lemon. Add cracked pepper for additional flavor and 4-6 cloves from the roasted garlic.
- After 20-25 minutes of roasting, bring three cups of vegetable broth to boil in a large soup pot. Turn to simmer and add roasted veggies and 4-6 cloves of roasted garlic. Puree with an immersion blender. Pour into bowls and top with chopped roasted hazelnuts and turmeric tahini dressing.

227. Purple Cauliflower Soup

Serving: Serves 4 | Prep: | Cook: | Ready in:

Ingredients

- 1 1/2 pounds purple cauliflower
- 2   small shallots
- 2   garlic cloves
- 3 - 4 cups veggie stock
- 2 tablespoons olive oil
- kosher salt, to taste
- good quality olive oil, garnish
- ezpeletako bipera or smoked paprika, garnish

Direction

- Remove outer leaves of cauliflower. Wash and cut cauliflower into chunks.
- Cut shallots and garlic into medium sized pieces.

- Heat olive oil over medium heat in a large saucepan or Dutch oven. Add shallots, cook over low heat, until soft. About 5 minutes.
- Add cauliflower. Stir to coat with olive oil. Cook for about 5 minutes over low heat.
- Add stock and garlic. Bring to boil. Do not cover with a lid.
- Bring heat to a low simmer. Season to taste with salt.
- Cook until cauliflower is soft, about 25 - 35 minutes. It all depends on how large you cut the pieces of cauliflower.
- Remove from heat and let cool about 10 minutes. Puree in batches, using either a blender or food processor. Return to cooking pan.
- Gently reheat over low heat. If necessary season with a bit more salt.
- Ladle into serving bowl. Drizzle good quality olive oil over the top and sprinkle with ezpeletako bipera or smoked paprika.
- Serve. Eat.

228. Purple Sweet Potato Mini Tangyuan

Serving: Serves 4 people | Prep: 0hours10mins | Cook: 0hours10mins |Ready in:

Ingredients

- 1/2 cup mashed purple sweet potato
- 3/4 cup glutinous rice flour
- 1/4 cup water

Direction

- Steam or microwave your sweet potato until fork tender. If you choose the microwave, make sure to put some water in the bowl to prevent burning. Also, peel the skin off, or poke holes so that it doesn't burst.
- Mash the purple sweet potato and then mix the rest of the ingredients in.

- Form into balls of whatever size you desire. I like bigger ones.
- Boil a pot of water, enough water so that when you put them in, they float.
- Carefully place all of the purple sweet potato balls in and boil until they can be squished with chopsticks or a spoon. They should all float as well.
- Enjoy warm with a bit of sugar or maple syrup (honey if you like it)!

229. Quick And Easy Minestrone Soup

Serving: Serves 6 | Prep: | Cook: |Ready in:

Ingredients

- 1 tablespoon olive oil
- 5 bacon slices, cut to bite sized
- 1 cup onion, chopped
- 2 celery stalks, chopped
- 1 medium carrot, chopped
- 5 garlic cloves, minced
- 6 cups chicken stock
- 2 15 oz cans diced tomato
- 10 ounces can Kidney Beans
- 10 ounces can Cannellini Beans
- 9 ounces can Garbanzo Beans
- 1/2 cup Italian parsley, chopped
- 6 large basil leaves, chopped
- 2 tablespoons oregano, chopped
- 1 1/2 cups shaped pasta

Direction

- Sauté the bacon until crisp in 1 tablespoon of olive oil, about 5 minutes. Remove the oil and fat from the pan leaving about 1 tablespoon.
- Add the chopped onion, celery and carrot and sauté until the vegetables begin to get soft. About 5 minutes. Add the garlic and sauté for 1 minute more.

- Add the broth, tomatoes, beans and chopped herbs and bring to a boil. Turn down the heat and simmer for 20 minutes.
- Add the pasta and cook for 8 minutes more.
- Serve in big bowls with Parmesan cheese and crusty bread.

230. Quick And Healthy Chicken And Dumplings

Serving: Serves 8 | Prep: | Cook: | Ready in:

Ingredients

- For the Dumplings
- 1/2 cup all purpose flour
- 1/2 cup white whole wheat flour
- 1 pinch salt
- 3 tablespoons Vegetable Oil
- 3-4 tablespoons cold water
- additional flour for rolling
- For the chicken stew
- 1 tablespoon vegetable oil
- 1 yellow onion, washed peeled, and chopped
- 2 medium carrots, washed, peeled, and chopped
- 2 ribs celery, washed and chopped
- 3 boneless skinless chicken breasts, cut into 1 inch cubes
- 4 cups chicken stock, hot
- 1 teaspoon dry thyme
- 1/4 teaspoon ground black pepper
- 2 pinches salt
- 1 tablespoon chopped fresh parsley

Direction

- In a medium bowl, combine the all-purpose and whole wheat flours and the salt. Add the oil and stir well. Add the cold water 1 tablespoon at a time and stir until a dough just barely comes together. Place the dough on a piece of plastic wrap and wrap well. Refrigerate the dough while you prepare the stew.
- Heat a stock pot over medium high heat. Add 1 Tablespoon oil and swirl to coat the bottom of the pot. Add the onion, carrot, and celery to the oil and stir until just softened. Add the chicken and stir until the color changes from pink to white, but not cooked through. Add the thyme and the hot stock and stir. Bring the stew to a simmer for ten minutes.
- Remove the dough from the refrigerator and place onto a lightly floured counter. Dust the top of the dough with a little flour. Also flour the rolling pin. Roll the dough out to ¼ inch thickness. Cut the dough with a knife or rolling pastry cutter into ½ inch strips.
- Drop the dough strips into the simmering stew and stir gently. Simmer, stirring every so often, for another 10 minutes or until the broth is thickened and the dumplings are puffed and the chicken is tender. Add salt and parsley and stir. Serve hot.

231. Quick Vegan Thai Coconut Soup (tom Kha)

Serving: Serves 2 | Prep: | Cook: | Ready in:

Ingredients

- 2 garlic cloves, grated
- 2 stalks of lemongrass, mashed in a mortar and pestle
- 1 thumb-sized piece of ginger, grated
- 1 small chilli, sliced
- 1/2 cup sliced dired shiitake mushrooms
- 2 cups vegetable stock
- 270 grams coconut milk
- 1 tablespoon tahini
- 1 tablespoon maple syrup
- 2 tablespoons gluten-free soy sauce
- 150 grams fresh enoki mushrooms
- 1 lime, juiced
- 1 large handful coriander, finely chopped
- 200 grams rice noodles, cooked

- 1 sheet of nori, cut into small pieces (optional)
- Cooked tofu squares (optional)

Direction

- Add garlic, lemongrass, ginger and chili to a saucepan on a medium heat. Cook until fragrant and starting to catch on the bottom of the pan. Add the dried shiitake mushrooms and the vegetable stock and gently simmer for five minutes.
- Whisk in the coconut milk and simmer for 10 minutes before whisking in the tahini, maple syrup and gluten-free soy sauce, and simmer another five minutes.
- Remove from the heat and add enoki mushrooms, lime juice and coriander. Add cooked rice noodles into a bowl, and top with the soup and mushrooms. Add some of the nori pieces and tofu (if using) and some lime slices.

232.   Quick, Easy And Healthy Chilli Chicken

Serving: Serves 2 | Prep: | Cook: | Ready in:

Ingredients

- 250g Boneless, skinless chicken breast
- 400g Can drained chickpeas
- 1/2 Courgette cut into chunks
- 1 Onion cut into chunks
- 4 Button mushrooms quartered
- 2 teaspoons Rapeseed/canola oil
- 1 teaspoon Minced garlic
- 1 teaspoon Ground coriander
- 1/4 teaspoon Oregano
- few drops Tabasco
- 1 cup Water with 1/2 low salt chicken stock cube
- Seasoning
- 1 Nest (50g) buckwheat noodles
- 100g Finely shredded cabbage

- 1/2 Courgette finely shredded

Direction

- Heat oil in a wok and add the chicken. Sauté for 5 minutes, turning until browned, before adding onion, mushroom, courgette, garlic, cumin, coriander, oregano, red pepper and tobacco. Stir-fry for 3 minutes over a medium heat before adding the chickpeas and pouring in the stock. Season to taste and bring to boil. Cover and simmer for 5-10 minutes.
- Meanwhile, cook noodles in boiling water for 4 minutes. For the last 2 minutes, add the cabbage and courgette to a steamer and place on top of the noodle pot to steam. Drain noodles over the cabbage and courgette and divide amongst two bowls. Top with chili chicken and broth.
- A little hint; it tastes so much better when eaten with chopsticks. But then in my opinion, so does everything!!

233.   Rainbow Congee

Serving: Serves 4-6 | Prep: | Cook: | Ready in:

Ingredients

- 1 cup short grain brown rice
- 8 cups water or vegetable stock
- 3 sweet potatoes, one purple, one red, one white or 2 medium orange sweet potatoes
- 1 tablespoon grapeseed oil
- 3 garlic cloves, minced
- 2 inches ginger root
- 1 bunch kale
- 1/2 pound mushrooms
- 1 1/2 tablespoons mirin
- 2 tablespoons soy sauce
- 1/2 teaspoon sesame oil
- 3 shallots
- 1 handful of marble sized Yukon gold, blue and red skinned potatoes or two Yukon Gold potatoes

Direction

- Bring rice and stock or water to a boil in a large saucepan. Turn down and simmer for 25 minutes.
- Thinly slice the shallots. Use half the oil to frizzle them in a small saucepan. Set aside.
- Chop the sweet potatoes into 1/2 inch dice. Leave the skins on. Slice the Yukon gold, red and blue potatoes in half. Leave their skins on, too. After the rice mixture has cooked for 25 minutes, add the potatoes. Continue to simmer, partly covered.
- Heat the remaining oil in a small frying pan. Mince the garlic cloves and peel and mince the ginger. Warm the garlic and ginger gently until they are softened. Wash the kale well and slice into thin ribbons. Add to the pan and cover. Wash and chop the mushrooms and add them to the kale. Let them cook down until the kale loses its bright green color and the mushrooms give up their liquid and brown. If the mixture becomes too dry, add a ladle of liquid from the rice so there isn't too much oil in the finished dish.
- Add the mirin and soy sauce to the kale and mushrooms and stir well. When the potatoes are tender, stir the sesame oil into the rice mixture.
- Rice and put a spoonful of greens into the bottom of each soup bowl. Ladle over the rice and stock. Top with a bit of the frizzled shallot. Enjoy!

234.   Red Lentil Soup

Serving: Serves 4-6 | Prep: | Cook: | Ready in:

Ingredients

- 2-4 tablespoons butter or olive oil
- 1 large onion, finely chopped
- 1 celery stalk, finely chopped
- 4 carrots, diced
- 1 cup zucchini, peeled and finely diced

- 3 tablespoons cilantro stems, minced
- 2 garlic cloves, minced
- 1 cup canned tomatoes with their juice, chopped
- 1 teaspoon ground turmeric
- 1/2 teaspoon ground cumin
- 1-1 1/2 teaspoons sea salt
- 1 1/2 teaspoons freshly ground pepper
- 1-2 pinches chile powder
- 1 cup dried red lentils, well rinsed
- juice of 1/2 lemon
- 1 quart chicken broth
- 4-5 chopped scallions
- Optional: dollop of Greek yogurt

Direction

- Melt/heat butter and/or olive oil, add onion and stir.
- Add celery, carrots, zucchini, cilantro, garlic and sprinkle with salt, turmeric, cumin and cook about 5 minutes.
- Add tomatoes, lentils and chicken stock (you may need to add more as the soup cooks). Bring to a boil, lower heat and simmer partially covered for 20-30 minutes until the lentils are soft.
- Taste for salt and add the pepper and chili powder. Add lemon juice.
- Garnish with lightly sautéed chopped scallions.
- Optional: My daughter recommends a dollop of Greek yogurt to "cool the heat".

235.   Red Lentil Soup

Serving: Serves 4-6 | Prep: | Cook: | Ready in:

Ingredients

- 3 tablespoons extra virgin olive oil,plus extra to serve
- 1 large onion, coarsly chopped
- 4 garlic cloves,crushed
- 2 cups red lentils, washed and drained

- 1.5 teaspoons ground cumin, plus extra to serve
- 1 teaspoon seasalt, plus more to taste
- 1 tablespoon tomato paste
- 6.5 cups filtered water
- Pinch freshly ground pepper to serve
- 2 tablespoons fresh lemon juice

Direction

- Warm olive oil in a deep pan over low to medium heat
- add chopped onions and stir for 3 mins, or until soften, then add crushed garlic and stir for 2 more minutes or until garlic starts to sizzle.
- Add water and stir gently, and bring to boil over high heat. Reduce heat to lowest, cover the pan and leave to simmer for 30 mins, stir twice or 3 times during cooking and check if it needs more water. Make sure the pan is covered while simmering.
- When lentils are completely cooked, the soup will look creamy and the lentils will dissolve in the liquid. Turn the heat off. Check seasoning, add a pinch of salt if needed. Leave to cool down before blending.
- Blend all ingredients in a blender for 1-2 mins, or until soup is smooth and creamy.
- Warm it up if cold then add a dash of lemon juice, and serve in separate bowls with a drizzle of olive oil, a pinch of ground cumin and some freshly ground black pepper.

236.   Red Lentil Soup With Mint And Beet Greens

Serving: Serves 6 | Prep: | Cook: | Ready in:

Ingredients

- 1 tablespoon olive oil
- 1 onion, chopped
- 4 cloves garlic, chopped
- 2 stalks celery, chopped

- a dozen or so mint leaves, chopped
- 1 teaspoon salt
- 1/4 teaspoon coriander
- beet greens, removed from one bunch of beets (use the beets for something else), cleaned and sliced
- 1 small tomato, chopped
- 1 cup red lentils
- 1/3 cup bulgur wheat
- 1 egg, lightly beaten
- extra mint, for garnish, optional

Direction

- Heat the oil in a medium soup pot. Add the onion and sauté for a few minutes, till translucent. Add the garlic and celery and cook for a few minutes longer, stirring frequently.
- Now, add the mint, salt, and coriander. Mix well and cook for another minute or two.
- Add the beet greens and cook for a few minutes till they are softened and heated through.
- Add the lentils, bulgur and about 6 cups of water. Bring to a boil and reduce to a very gentle simmer. Simmer for 30 minutes, adding water as needed if it seems too thick.
- After the 1/2 hour of cooking, add the tomato and cook for about 10 minutes longer.
- Immediately before serving, whisk in the egg. Serve, garnished with mint if desired.

237.   Red Miso Udon With Onsen Tomago

Serving: Serves 2 | Prep: | Cook: | Ready in:

Ingredients

- 1 cup boiling water
- 2 dried shitake mushrooms
- 4 cups water
- 4 teaspoons dashi granules
- 4 tablespoons red miso

- 400 grams fresh udon noodles
- 2 soft poached eggs
- 8 pieces slices of Chinese BBQ Pork
- 1 bunch baby bok choy, halved
- 1 scallion, thinly sliced
- 3 teaspoons wakame or dried seaweed
- furikake for optional garnish

Direction

- Cover the dried shiitakes with the cup of boiling water and set aside to soak for at least 20 minutes.
- Get all of your soup garnish ingredients prepared and set aside so that you can assemble the soup at the last minute right in the bowl.
- Bring a medium sized pot of water to a boil and add the shiitakes to the water so you can let them cook while you blanch the bok choy and the udon. Reserve the mushroom soaking liquid.
- Submerge both halves of the bok choy in the boiling water and blanch for one minute. Remove with a slotted spoon and set aside. Be careful to leave the mushrooms in the water and keep the water boiling. Have your sliced scallion, poached eggs and sliced pork handy.
- In a smaller pot, bring the 4 cups of water to a boil. Add the dashi granules, the wakame and 1/2 cup of strained mushroom soaking liquid and simmer for a few minutes to make your dashi broth.
- Put the miso paste in a small bowl and ladle about 1/2 cup of hot dashi into the bowl and whisk until the miso is dissolved.
- Take the dashi pot off of the heat and add in the miso, giving a good whisk and then set aside with a lid on the pot. Don't boil it again after adding the miso.
- Cook the udon noodles for three in the same pot of water that you boiled the bok choy in (you have kept it simmering this whole time).
- While the noodles cook, put out your soup bowls

- Fish the shitakes out of the pot before you drain your noodles and set the mushrooms aside.
- Divide the udon among the two bowls. Slice your mushrooms and arrange on the noodles, lay out the pork slices and snuggle in the bok choy. Lay the poached egg on the top and then, after giving one last stir, ladle the miso soup over the whole thing until you have just covered the noodles.
- Sprinkle the chopped scallion and furikake (if using) over each bowl.

| 238. | Red Potato And Leek Chowder With Bacon |

Serving: Serves 4 to 6 | Prep: | Cook: | Ready in:

Ingredients

- 8 strips thick-cut bacon (about 12 ounces), diced
- 2 tablespoons unsalted butter
- 2 cloves garlic, minced
- 1 medium leek, white and light green parts only, thinly sliced
- 3 sprigs fresh thyme
- 1 bay leaf
- Kosher salt and freshly ground black pepper, to taste
- ¼ cups all-purpose flour
- 3 cups chicken stock
- 2 cups half-and-half
- 1½ pounds medium red potatoes (about 6), scrubbed and cut into ½-inch cubes
- ½ cups frozen peas, thawed (optional)

Direction

- Cook the bacon in a large stockpot or Dutch oven over medium heat until browned and crispy, 13 to 15 minutes. Using a slotted spoon, remove half the bacon and transfer to a paper towel-lined bowl; set aside. Drain off excess bacon fat from pot, leaving 1 tablespoon.

- Melt butter in remaining bacon fat and add garlic and leek. Cook until slightly softened, about 3 minutes. Stir in thyme and bay leaf and cook until thyme is fragrant, about 1 minute more. Season to taste with salt and pepper. Sprinkle flour over vegetable mixture and stir to combine. Cook 2 to 3 minutes until flour is no longer raw.
- Gradually whisk in stock and half-and-half. Add potatoes and bring mixture to a boil. Reduce heat to medium-low and cook, stirring occasionally, until chowder is thickened and potatoes are tender when pierced with a knife, 20 to 25 minutes. Stir in peas, if desired, and season to taste. Ladle chowder into individual bowls and garnish with reserved bacon.

239. Research Chili

Serving: Makes 1 large pot full | Prep: | Cook: |Ready in:

Ingredients

- 4 cloves of garlic
- 1 tablespoon of olive oil, divided
- 7 pieces of applewood smoked bacon, thinly sliced
- 1 white onion, diced
- 1 large carrot, peeled and sliced
- 4 celery stalks, sliced
- 1 tablespoon light brown sugar
- 1.5 tablespoons Rye whiskey
- 1 pound ground beef
- ½ pound ground lamb leg
- 2 teaspoons cumin
- 2 teaspoons smoked paprika
- 1 teaspoon oregano
- 1 teaspoon cayenne
- 1 teaspoon dried mint
- 1 teaspoon nutmeg
- 1 teaspoon dried parsley
- 1 teaspoon ground thyme
- 1 teaspoon dried basil
- 1 clove

- 1 teaspoon Dijon mustard
- 1 serrano chili, halved, seeded and sliced
- 1 6-ounce can tomato paste
- ¼ cup cider vinegar
- 1 tablespoon black coffee
- 1 ¼ cups dark stout beer
- 1 square dark chocolate, shaved with a vegetable peeler
- 2 bay leaves
- 1 28-ounce can crushed tomatoes
- 1 can kidney beans, rinsed
- 1 sprig fresh thyme
- 4 cups low-sodium chicken stock
- sea salt, black pepper
- scallions, sliced
- goat-cheddar cheese, grated

Direction

- Preheat the oven to 375F. Rub the garlic cloves with a little olive oil and roast for 20 minutes, or until soft.
- Heat the rest of the olive oil in a Dutch oven over medium heat. Add the bacon, in batches if you have to, so as not to crowd. Cook for about 5 minutes, until crispy, and then set the bacon aside. (You want about 2 tablespoons of bacon fat; remove any excess.)
- Add the onion. After a few minutes, add the carrot and then the celery until they start to soften. (This should take about 15 minutes.) Add the brown sugar, and then the Rye, and stir to combine.
- Add the meat. After a minute or two, add the cumin, paprika, oregano, cayenne, mint, nutmeg, parsley, dried thyme, basil, clove, mustard and the garlic, and stir into the meat. Stir in the serrano chili. Cook until the meat is no longer red.
- Add the tomato paste, the cider vinegar, the coffee, the stout and the chocolate; stir to combine. Add the bay leaves. Raise the heat, to reduce the beer a little. After a few minutes, add the crushed tomatoes, the kidney beans, the fresh thyme and the chicken stock. Add back the bacon.

- Lower the heat to a simmer. Cook, partially covered, for about an hour. (Check it after 30 minutes–if it looks a little dry, you can add another 1/2 cup of chicken stock or water.) Check the seasonings, and adjust salt and pepper accordingly.
- Serve the chili topped with the scallions and the goat-cheddar cheese.

240. Rice Soup With Egg, Thyme And Lemon Sauce

Serving: Serves 4-6 persons | Prep: | Cook: | Ready in:

Ingredients

- 1 cup whole grain rice
- 4 cups water
- 2 or 3 fresh organic eggs in room temperature
- the juice of 1 large lemon
- some thyme flowers
- salt
- olive oil

Direction

- First bring the rice and water to a boil, then lower the fire
- Add the salt, cover the pan and let the rice cook. Whole grain rice can take up to one hour for cooking, but it's safer to follow the instructions on the packaging
- Whisk together the eggs and lemon juice
- Sprinkle the thyme flowers on top and continue whisking while pouring spoons of warm soup in the sauce
- When the two liquids have reached the same temperature pour the sauce in the pot with the soup
- Stir again and serve warm with a freshly sprinkled thyme flower on top. Bon appetit!

241. Roast Broccoli Soup

Serving: Serves 3 - 4 bowls | Prep: | Cook: | Ready in:

Ingredients

- 2 1/2 heads of broccoli
- 2 tablespoons olive oil
- 1 clove garlic (minced)
- 1 teaspoon salt
- 1 dash pepper
- 6 cups chicken broth

Direction

- Cut broccoli into florets and sliced stems. Toss in olive oil, garlic, salt, and pepper. Roast broccoli at 350°F for 15 minutes.
- Boil roasted broccoli florets and stems in 6 cups of chicken broth on the stove. Cook until sliced stems can be easily pierced with a knife. Remove from heat and allow mixture to cool.
- Puree mixture in a blender until smooth.
- Possible additions: sour cream and fried shallots for garnish

242. Roasted Acorn Squash Soup

Serving: Serves 5 | Prep: | Cook: | Ready in:

Ingredients

- 5 pieces Bacon
- 3.5-4 pounds Acorn Squash
- 1 onion
- olive oil for brushing
- 4-5 cloves garlics, skin on
- 2 stalks celery
- 1 golden delicious apple, chopped
- 2-3 cups chicken broth
- 1/4 cup evaporated milk
- 1 tablespoon good quality curry powder
- 4 tablespoons brown sugar, divided
- 1/2 teaspoon cayenne

- a pinch of cumin
- salt and pepper to taste
- 1 bunch scallion, for garnish

Direction

- Fry bacon strips in pan with half a tablespoon of olive oil in medium heat until crispy, then set aside on a paper towel
- Roasting of Squash: Preheat oven to 425F
- Halve squash and brush both sides with a mixture of olive oil, a little salt, and the divided 2 tablespoon of brown sugar
- Place squash cup side down and roast for 50 min
- Let squash cool until can be handled by hands
- Remove charred squash skin
- In a medium pot, saute onion, celery, and apple until tender
- Add curry powder, cayenne, cumin, salt and then add squash into the pot and stir thoroughly
- Transfer squash mixture into blender and puree it
- In the same medium pot, heat 2-3 cups of chicken broth, depending on the consistency of your preference
- Transfer the squash puree back into the warm broth and mix
- Just before boiling, add evaporated milk
- Serve immediately with crumbled crispy bacon and chopped scallions
- This recipe is very versatile. Using butternut squash is just as tasty!

243. Roasted Butternut Squash Soup With Gorgonzola Walnut Toasts

Serving: Serves 3, with leftover butter | Prep: | Cook: | Ready in:

Ingredients

- Soup
- 1 1.5 pounds butternut squash
- 4-5 sprigs thyme, leaves stripped
- salt
- freshly-ground pepper
- 4 tablespoons vegetable oil
- 1 onion, chopped
- 2 garlic cloves, thinly sliced
- 1 quart vegetable stock
- 2 tablespoons maple syrup, optional
- Butter
- 3.5 ounces gorgonzola
- 1 ounce salted butter
- 1.5 ounces walnuts, toasted

Direction

- Soup
- Preheat the oven to 200C/400F.
- Cut the top and bottom off of the squash, then slice it in half lengthways. Scrape out the seeds like it's a miniature version of a Halloween pumpkin. Then peel each half. After all that palaver, cut the remaining flesh into 2cm/1-inch cubes. Toss the squash in a roasting pan with the thyme leaves, salt, pepper, and two tablespoons of the oil. Roast in the oven for an hour.
- 20 minutes before the squash is done, warm the remaining oil in a medium saucepan over a medium flame. When hot, add the onion and turn the heat down to medium-low. Sauté the onion slowly until it's very soft and just starting to go brown, around 15 minutes. Then add the garlic slices and sauté for another 2-3 minutes.
- Add in the roasted squash and the stock, and bring everything up to a simmer. Then remove from the heat and blitz with an immersion blender until completely smooth. Taste for seasoning; if your squash isn't sweet enough for your palate, stir in some maple syrup. Serve with toast, optionally spread with gorgonzola-walnut butter.
- Butter
- If not using a food processor, finely chop the walnuts. Then put all ingredients in either a mixing bowl or the bowl of a food processor.

Pulse in the machine until well-combined and a little fluffy, or mash with two forks until mixed.

244. Roasted Cauliflower Buttermilk Soup

Serving: Serves 4-6 | Prep: | Cook: |Ready in:

Ingredients

- 1   med head cauliflower, cut into florets
- 1   med onion, rough chopped
- 3   cloves of garlic, minced
- 3   small red potatoes, cubed
- 1 teaspoon dried dill
- 1/2 teaspoon paprika
- 1 tablespoon butter
- 3 ounces large handfulls baby spinach
- 4 cups chicken stock
- 1 cup buttermilk
- 1 cup white cheddar, shredded

Direction

- Preheat oven to 450. Combine the first 6 ingredients in a roasting pan with some olive oil and season with salt and pepper. Roast in the top third of the oven for about 40 minutes or until a nice golden brown color is achieved.
- In a large pot melt the butter on medium heat and sauté the spinach until wilted. Add the roasted vegetables and stir until well mixed. Add the chicken stock, bring to a simmer then reduce heat to low, cover and cook for 20-30 minutes.
- After the vegetables are tender remove from heat and use an immersion blender to roughly puree soup (I like to leave it a chunky texture, but you could puree it smooth if you prefer). Blend in the buttermilk and shredded cheese then season to taste with salt and pepper (and more dill if you like). Enjoy!

245. Roasted Cauliflower And Harissa Soup

Serving: Serves 2 - 3 | Prep: | Cook: |Ready in:

Ingredients

- 500 grams cauliflower, chopped into florets
- 1 teaspoon cumin seeds
- 1/2 teaspoon harissa paste (or more, to taste)
- 3   cloves of garlic, finely chopped
- 1/2 an onion, finely chopped
- 3 tablespoons olive oil
- 1/4 teaspoon turmeric powder
- 1/4 cup milk
- Freshly ground black pepper
- Salt

Direction

- Line a baking tray with aluminum foil. Toss the cauliflower with 2 tablespoons olive oil, cumin seeds, turmeric powder, and harissa until evenly coated. Spread in a single layer and bake at 180°C/360°F for 45 to 50 mins, or until they've browned. Remove and set aside. Taste and check the fieriness of the harissa at this stage; add more if you'd like and return to the oven for 5 more minutes.
- Pour 1 tablespoon of olive oil in a pot and sauté the onion and garlic until translucent. Add the roasted cauliflower along with any of the remaining cumin on the foil to the pot, and pour in 2 cups of water. Season with pepper and salt. Cover and bring to the boil, then simmer for 10 to 15 minutes, until the florets and tender. Take off the heat and let it cool slightly.
- Once cooled, add to a blender/use an immersion blender and blend until smooth. Check seasoning and add milk and more water to get the right consistency. Return the soup to a clean pot and gently reheat. Best served hot.

246. Roasted Cauliflower And Moroccan Spiced Almond Soup

Serving: Serves 4 | Prep: | Cook: | Ready in:

Ingredients

- 1 large head of cauliflower
- salt and pepper, to taste
- 4 tablespoons extra virgin olive oil, divided into 2 parts
- 1 onion, chopped roughly
- 2 tablespoons unsalted butter
- 1/4 teaspoon ground cinnamon
- 1/4 teaspoon ground cardamom seeds (shells removed)
- 1/4 teaspoon cumin
- 1/4 teaspoon ground coriander
- 1/4 teaspoon ground ginger
- 1/4 teaspoon paprika
- 1/4 teaspoon salt
- 2 cloves of garlic, crushed
- 1 cup sliced almonds
- 1 russet potato, peeled and sliced into 1-inch pieces
- 1 cup heavy cream
- 6 cups chicken stock (or vegetable stock for a vegetarian version), plus more to suit preferences
- 1-3 teaspoons of salt, depending on taste preferences
- harissa , for garnish
- cilantro , for garnish

Direction

- Preheat oven to 400 degrees F.
- Chop the cauliflower in half and then cut the florets off the stalk. Place on a baking sheet, drizzle with 2 tablespoons of the olive oil, salt, and pepper and roast for 30-45 minutes, or until cauliflower begins to turn golden brown along the edges.
- While the cauliflower is roasting, chop the onion. Add the remaining 2 tablespoons of olive oil to a medium skillet and heat over medium heat. Add onions and cook until onions are soft and nearly translucent, about 8 minutes. Add garlic and continue to cook for an additional 2 minutes, or until garlic is fragrant. Remove from heat and transfer to a plate.
- In the same skillet, over medium heat, add 2 tablespoons of butter. Once butter is melted, add the spices and sliced almonds and toast until fragrant and almonds turn a light golden color, about 3-4 minutes, stirring frequently. Be careful not to let any of the contents (including the butter) burn. If anything begins to burn, reduce heat to low and continue cooking. If they begin to look too dry, add 1-2 tablespoons of olive oil, a little bit at a time. Remove from heat when almonds are golden and set aside.
- In a large pot, bring the chicken stock to a boil. Add potatoes, roasted cauliflower, onions, garlic, and salt and boil for 10 minutes, or until potatoes are tender. Once potatoes are tender and able to be pierced easily with a fork, add cream. Using an immersion blender, blend (or puree in a food processor) until soup is thick and creamy. If too thick for your tastes, add stock, one cup at a time, until you reach your desired consistency.
- Serve in bowls and garnish with spiced almonds, harissa, and cilantro.

247. Roasted Chestnut Bisque

Serving: Serves 4 - 6 | Prep: | Cook: | Ready in:

Ingredients

- The Bisque
- 1 medium onion
- 2 carrots
- 3 celery stalks
- 1 medium leek
- 1/4 cup olive oil
- 6 tablespoons cognac or brandy

- 4 cups chicken stock
- 2 7.4 ounce jars roasted and peeled chestnuts
- 6-7 sprigs marjoram
- 1 1/2 cups heavy cream
- salt and pepper to taste
- Marjoram Oil
- 6 tablespoons olive oil
- 4 sprigs marjoram

Direction

- Dice the onion, carrot, celery and leek. I do this in the food processor pulse just until everything is chopped. In a large Dutch oven, sauté the vegetables in ¼ cup olive oil over medium-high heat until soft and tender, and the onion and leeks are translucent. Add the cognac and stir, scraping up and bits from the bottom of the pan, and cook until the cognac is evaporated. Add the stock, the chestnuts and the marjoram sprigs (count how many so you can take them out later). Bring to a boil, lower the heat, cover and simmer the soup for 45 minutes. Leave the soup to cool until it's safe to put in the blender. Meanwhile, prepare the marjoram oil (see below).
- Fish out the marjoram stems, then transfer the soup to a blender in batches and puree until smooth. After blending each batch, pour the soup through a wire mesh strainer set over a large bowl and push the soup through with a wooden spoon or spatula. There won't be much in the way of solids left behind, but straining the soup creates the velvety texture that makes this bisque so elegant. (For an even more velvety texture, you could push the soup through the strainer a second time). When you have strained all the soup, wipe out the Dutch oven and return the soup to the pot. At this point, you can cover the soup and refrigerate it for up to two days before completing it.
- When ready to serve the soup, heat it gently over medium heat, stirring occasionally, but do not let it boil. Slowly stir in the cream, incorporating it fully into the soup, then warm

through. Serve immediately drizzled with marjoram oil.
- Heat the olive oil in a small saucepan just until bubbles appear on the surface and the oil is shimmering. Remove from the heat and leave to cool for two minutes, then drop in the marjoram sprigs, cover the pan and leave to cool. Strain the cooled oil into a jar or small spouted measuring cup for drizzling on the soup. The oil can be kept in an airtight jar for up to a week.

248. Roasted Chickpea Calder Verde

Serving: Serves 4 | Prep: | Cook: |Ready in:

Ingredients

- 1 can of chickpeas, drained
- 1 medium yukon gold potato, peeled and cut into 1/2 inch dice
- 1/2 teaspoon kosher salt
- 1/2 teaspoon whole cumin seed
- 1/2 teaspoon whole dill seed
- 1/2 teaspoon sumac
- 1/2 teaspoon smoked paprika
- 2 tablespoons extra virgin olive oil, divided plus more for roasting kale
- 1 head curly kale (8-9 leaves), washed and thoroughly dried (do not remove stem)
- pinch kosher salt
- 1 medium onion, diced
- 2 garlic cloves, minced
- 2 3/4 cups chicken stock (or vegetable stock to make it vegetarian)
- 2 cups unsweetened organic rice milk
- Chopped Italian parsley
- Chopped (and rinsed) preserved lemon (optional)

Direction

- Preheat the oven to 400 degrees F. Arrange racks in the middle and bottom third of oven.

- Get out two large rimmed baking pans. Line one with parchment paper.
- In a medium bowl, combine well drained chickpeas with diced potato. Add salt, spices and 1 T extra virgin olive oil. Using a spatula, fold together to thoroughly combine. Spread seasoned chickpeas and potato in a single layer on lined baking sheet.
- Place curly kale leaves on the remaining baking sheet. Drizzle 1/2 T or so of extra virgin olive oil on to kale and add a pinch of salt. Massage leaves with hands until kale is coated with oil and salt. Evenly spread out leaves on pan, alternating the direction of each leaf.
- Place kale pan on the middle rack and chickpea/potato pan on the lower rack. Roast kale for about 10 minutes, turning pan once midway through. You want the leaves to be roasted, but still have a hint of green. They do not have to be completely crispy. When kale is finished, turn chickpea pan and continue to roast chickpeas and potato until chickpeas are slightly crispy and potatoes are tender (yield easily when poked with the tip of a knife) about 15-20 minutes more.
- While kale is cooling and chickpea/potato mixture is finishing roasting, heat remaining tablespoon of olive oil in a soup pot over medium heat. Add onion and garlic and cook until fragrant and beginning to be translucent, about 5 minutes. Lower heat, add liquids and continue to cook until chickpea/potato mixture is done. Scrape roasted chickpeas and roasted potato into pot. Stir to combine.
- Remove kale from stems by holding leaves stem side up, grasping on either side and pulling leaves down, away from the stem. Repeat with remaining leaves. Place leaves in a blender.
- Working in batches, carefully add soup mixture to blender and puree until smooth. Add pureed soup back to original pot and warm until heated through. Serve soup garnished with chopped parsley, and a sprinkle of sumac. I also enjoyed it with chopped preserved lemon. Enjoy!

249. Roasted Kabocha Squash And Parmigiano Soup

Serving: Serves 6 | Prep: | Cook: | Ready in:

Ingredients

- 2 kabocha squash with skin
- 1 tablespoon olive oil
- 1/2 onion, chopped
- 2 garlic cloves, minced
- 1 teaspoon fresh minced ginger
- 1 teaspoon salt+sprinkle black pepper
- 3 cups vegetable stock (or other kind)
- 1/2 cup water
- 1/4 whipping cream
- 1/2 cup grated parmigiano
- chopped   parsley for garnish

Direction

- Preheat oven to 450 F (232 Celsius). Place Kabocha on a baking pan and roast for approximately 45-50 minutes, or until the flesh inside is tender when poked with a fork. Set aside to cool.
- In a large pot over medium fire, cook onion in olive oil until slightly translucent. Then add garlic, ginger, salt and pepper, and sauté for another 4 minutes. Turn off the stove. Peel the skin off the squash which is really easy to do as it comes right off, scrape off the seeds, and set seeds aside if you choose to roast them. You can use those as a topping later on if you like the extra crunch. Add the cooked squash into the pot, turn fire on low-medium, then pour vegetable stock, water, and cream. Simmer for about 10 minutes stirring often. Add grated Parmigiano and cook for another 5 minutes. Transfer to a bowl and garnish with more cream (if desired) and chopped parsley leaves.

250.   Roasted Leek And Cauliflower Soup With Green Apple Vinaigrette

Serving: Serves 4-6 by the bowl, or many as a starter |
Prep: | Cook: | Ready in:

Ingredients

- For the Green Apple Vinaigrette:
- 1 tablespoon extra virgin olive oil
- 1 tablespoon plus 1 teaspoon sherry vinegar
- 1 teaspoon fish sauce
- 1/2 teaspoon Dijon mustard
- 1/4 cup Granny Smith apple, diced very small (brunoise, 1/8 inch cubed)
- For Soup:
- 4 large leeks
- 3 cups cauliflower florets with stems
- 2 tablespoons extra virgin olive oil
- 1/2 teaspoon coriander seeds
- 1/2 teaspoon cumin seeds
- Pinches of kosher salt, plus more to taste
- 1/4 cup calvados (apple brandy)
- 3 cups good chicken stock
- 1/2 cup half-and-half

Direction

- For the Green Apple Vinaigrette:
- In a small bowl, emulsify the olive oil, vinegar, Dijon and fish sauce. Add diced apple and stir to combine. Cover with plastic wrap and set aside until soup is ready, about one hour.
- For Soup:
- Preheat oven to 400°F.
- Thoroughly wash and trim ends of leeks -- root and dark green tops -- so you just have white and pale green stalks. Cut into 4-inch sections, then slice in half lengthwise and rinse again under running water, separating edges where you can see dirt. Place pieces in a large bowl of water and agitate to release any remaining dirt. Scoop leek halves out of water (do not pour out or dirt will just go back onto

leeks) and thoroughly dry in a salad spinner or clean towels.
- Spread cauliflower florets and leek sections out on a large rimmed baking pan (jelly roll pan) and evenly toss with olive oil, coriander seeds, cumin seeds, and a few good pinches of kosher salt. Cover pan tightly with foil; roast for 30 minutes until leeks are melted and the cauliflower is tender.
- Transfer roasted vegetables to a large saucepan. Over medium heat, add calvados and cook until almost completely evaporated, about 5 minutes. Add chicken stock and simmer for 10 minutes. Add half-and-half and simmer for 5 minutes more, stirring. Taste for salt, remembering that vinaigrette will add some salt (I did not add any additional salt).
- Divide soup in half between a blender and large Pyrex measure, reserving saucepan. Allow to cool slightly before puréeing batch in blender. Transfer puréed soup back to saucepan. Repeat with remaining soup in Pyrex measure before returning to saucepan. Serve immediately, topping each bowl with about a teaspoonful of green apple vinaigrette. Enjoy.

251.   Roasted Mushroom Soup

Serving: Serves 1-2 | Prep: | Cook: | Ready in:

Ingredients

- 10 ounces baby portobello mushrooms, sliced
- 2 tablespoons extra virgin olive oil
- Freshly ground black pepper
- 2 cups low-sodium beef stock
- 1 tablespoon unsalted butter
- 1/2 shallot, thinly sliced
- Salt, to taste
- 1 small clove garlic, finely minced
- 1 teaspoon chopped thyme, plus extra for garnish
- 2 tablespoons white wine
- 2 tablespoons flour

- 1/4 cup heavy cream

Direction

- Preheat oven to 425°F. Place mushrooms on a baking sheet and drizzle with olive oil. Season with pepper and roast for 15-20 minutes, until softened. Transfer to a blender (reserving 1 tablespoon of mushrooms for garnish), along with 1/2 cup stock and purée until smooth.
- Meanwhile, in a medium sauté pan, heat butter over medium heat. Add shallot and cook until softened, about 5 minutes. Season with salt and pepper. Add garlic and thyme and cook for another 1-2 minutes. Deglaze pan with wine and cook for 1-2 minutes. Stir in flour until incorporated, about 2 minutes. Add puréed mushroom mixture to pan, along with remaining 1 1/2 cups stock and cream to bring to a boil. Reduce heat to medium-low and simmer for 10-15 minutes until soup is thickened and warmed through. Top with reserved mushrooms and a sprig of thyme and serve warm.

---

252. Roasted Pecan And Acorn Squash Soup

Serving: Serves 8 | Prep: | Cook: |Ready in:

Ingredients

- 1 acorn squash
- 1 tablespoon olive oil
- 1 1/2 teaspoons salt, divided
- 1/2 teaspoon black pepper, divided
- 1/2 teaspoon chipotle chile powder, divided
- 1 cup chopped pecans
- 3 cups chicken or vegetable broth
- 3 tablespoons honey
- 1/4 cup heavy cream, plus more for garnish
- 1/2 cup grated Parmesan cheese

Direction

- Preheat the oven to 375° F. Drizzle the inside of the squash with the olive oil and rub it down with 1/2 teaspoon of the salt, 1/4 teaspoon of the black pepper, and 1/4 teaspoon of the chipotle chili powder. Place it on a baking sheet with the insides facing up and roast for 40 minutes. Remove from the oven and allow to cool until safe to handle. While it's cooling, place the pecans on a baking sheet in an even layer and roast them in the oven (still at 375° F) for 10 minutes, then remove and allow to cool.
- Once the squash has cooled down a bit, scoop out the soft flesh with a large metal spoon and place it in a blender or food processor. Add the pecans, honey, broth, and the remaining spices. Blend at high speed until a smooth purée forms, about 1 minute.
- Pour the mixture into a medium-sized pot and warm over medium heat. Add the cream and Parmesan and stir until combined. Continue heating the soup for 15 minutes, stirring every few minutes, until nice and hot. Taste and add more salt, pepper, or chipotle if desired. Scoop out into individual bowls for serving and garnish with a teaspoon of cream, a pecan, and a sprinkle of black pepper and ground chipotle chili.

---

253. Roasted Squash Soup With Apples And Soju

Serving: Serves 6 | Prep: | Cook: |Ready in:

Ingredients

- 2 butternut squash
- 6 tablespoons olive oil
- to taste   salt
- to taste   pepper
- 1 large onion
- 2 large sweet apples (like Fuji)
- 2 teaspoons paprika
- 4 cups chicken or vegetable broth

- 1/4 cup Soju
- 1 handful sage leaves, for garnish

Direction

- Preheat oven to 400F. Cut open the squash lengthwise and remove the guts. Brush the insides with two tablespoons of olive oil and sprinkle with salt and pepper. Place in the oven to roast for an hour, or until the insides are soft.
- While the squash roasts, chop the onion and apples into half inch pieces. Set the apples aside. Place the onions in a large pot with the remaining four tablespoons of olive oil and cook over medium heat until the onions are soft, about 15 minutes. Stir in the paprika and cook for another two minutes.
- Add the apples and two cups of the broth to pot. Once the broth boils, reduce the heat and let it simmer for 20 minutes, or until the apples are soft.
- When the squash is cooked through, remove it from the oven and carefully scoop out the insides. Puree them in a blender or food processor with the apple mixture.
- Transfer the puree back to the pot and stir in the remaining two cups of broth, the 1/4 cup of Soju, and a few good pinches of salt and pepper. Bring the soup back to a boil for five minutes.
- To serve, garnish with a few chopped fresh sage leaves. Enjoy with a glass of Soju.

---

254.   Roasted Summer Vegetable Soup

Serving: Serves 6 | Prep: | Cook: |Ready in:

Ingredients

- 1 pound Beefsteak tomatoes, halved and cored
- 3 Yellow, orange, or red bell peppers, or any combination of the three, halved and cored

- 2 Zucchini or summer squash
- 1 Small eggplant, halved
- 3 Garlic scapes, or garlic cloves
- 2 Onions, peeled and halved
- Olive oil
- Kosher salt
- 1 tablespoon Fresh thyme
- 3 cups Vegetable broth
- 1/2 cup Coconut milk (optional)
- Basil leaves as garnish

Direction

- Preheat oven to 375F.
- Arrange tomatoes, bell peppers, zucchini, summer squash, eggplant, garlic, and onions on a baking sheet, cut side down, in a single layer. Drizzle generously with olive oil and salt. Bake for 35-40 minutes, until eggplant, and bell peppers, have a slight char on their skins. Check at 25 minutes, as garlic (cloves or scapes) may need to come out earlier so they don't burn.
- Working in batches, pulse vegetables in a food processor until they break down but there are still large chunks (do not puree). Transfer vegetables to a large pot and add vegetable broth and thyme. Cook for 15 minutes over medium heat, stirring occasionally.
- If you'd like to add a little creaminess to the soup, you can add coconut milk, but I think the soup is delicious without it as well. If you do add coconut milk, cook for 2-3 minutes more. Adjust salt and pepper to taste.
- Serve with basil leaves as garnish.

---

255.   Roasted Tomato Soup

Serving: Makes a lot of soup! | Prep: | Cook: |Ready in:

Ingredients

- 4 pounds mixed tomatoes, like cherry, plum, and heirloom
- 2 large onions, sliced into 1/2 inch rings

- 1 head of garlic, cloves peeled
- 20 sprigs fresh thyme
- 1 quart chicken stock
- 3 tablespoons butter
- 1 pinch red pepper flake
- salt
- pepper
- olive oil
- Dash liquid smoke
- 1/4 cup basil, chiffonade

Direction

- Preheat oven to 450 degrees.
- Mix tomatoes, onions, garlic, thyme, salt, pepper, and red pepper flakes together with some olive oil and spread out on a cookie sheet. Roast for 30 minutes. Tomatoes should be blistered and juicy. Onions should be brown. If garlic is burned, discard burned cloves.

---

256. Roasted Tomato And Garlic Soup

Serving: Makes 8-10 servings | Prep: | Cook: | Ready in:

Ingredients

- 2 1/2 pounds vine ripened tomates (or any nice looking variety)
- 1 28 oz. can San Marzano whole tomatoes
- 2 tablespoons tomato paste
- 1/2 pound carrots (leaves removed)
- 1 garlic head (1/4 inch of the head removed and excess paper removed)
- 1 shallots (diced)
- 1 medium yellow onion (diced)
- 1 quart Homemade chicken broth
- 1/2 cup cream
- 2 tablespoons basil (rough chop)
- 1/2 teaspoon crushed red pepper flakes
- 4 tablespoons unsalted butter
- 2 tablespoons olive oil

- salt and pepper

Direction

- Preheat the oven to 400 degrees. Toss carrots, tomatoes and garlic head in olive oil, salt and pepper. Transfer to foil lined baking sheets and pop in the oven. Remove the carrots after 20 minutes. Let the tomatoes and garlic cook for 35-40 minutes. Don't let them burn though! Cool and remove skins from both the tomatoes and garlic. Give the carrots a rough chop.
- In a large soup pot, heat 2 tbsp. unsalted butter and olive oil over medium heat. Add onion, shallot, salt and pepper and cook for about 10 minutes. Add tomato paste, crushed red pepper flakes and carrots and cook for another 7 minutes. Add a bit more salt.
- Pour all the chicken broth to the pan and raise heat to medium high. Add both the canned and roasted tomatoes. Put the whole roasted garlic cloves (already peeled out of the skin) in to the pan. Add some salt and pepper and bring to a boil. Lower to a simmer and let cook for 35-40 minutes.
- Turn off heat. Add basil to the soup. Puree mixture with an immersion blender or run through a food processor. Stir in the cream. Taste, and adjust salt and pepper.

---

257. Roasted Zucchini Soup

Serving: Serves 4 | Prep: | Cook: | Ready in:

Ingredients

- extra virgin olive oil
- 2 medium yellow onions
- 1 clove garlic, skin still on
- 1 1/2 pounds small or medium zucchini
- 1 quart vegetable stock, divided
- 1 1/2 tablespoons white wine vinegar
- Salt and white pepper to taste
- 2 slices crusty bread

Direction

- Heat oven to 425. Peel onions, cut into wedges with stem end trimmed but still intact; toss onion and garlic clove with 2 teaspoons of olive oil and spread out on a rimmed baking sheet. Season with salt, place in oven.
- Cut zucchini into 1/2 inch medallions, toss with 2 teaspoons olive oil and season with salt. After the onions have roasted 30 minutes, flip the onions a bit and add zucchini, making sure it's spread out and in one layer. Roast for 30-40 minutes more, until onion is soft and golden and edges of zucchini are browned and interiors are soft.
- Meanwhile, in a deep pot, heat all but 1/2 cup (reserve to the side) vegetable stock over medium high heat and bring to a simmer. Remove vegetables from oven, squeeze roasted garlic out of skin, and add all veggies to stock. Reduce heat but keep warm.
- Place roasting sheet over a burner (or two, depending on size), and heat on medium high. Use reserved stock to deglaze the baking sheet, using a wooden spoon to scrape up as much as you can. Pour deglazed drippings and stock into soup. You can skip this step and just add the reserved stock to the soup if there aren't enough good brown bits on your pan to warrant it. Wipe down your baking sheet for making your croutons.
- Add in the vinegar. Using an immersion blender puree until smooth. Taste soup for seasoning; add salt and white pepper to taste. Keep soup warm while you make your croutons.
- Set oven to high broil. Cut bread into 1/2 inch cubes and toss with 1 tablespoon olive oil. Spread out on baking sheet, sprinkle with salt and pepper; broil for just a minute or two, until crispy (keep close watch, this goes fast).
- Serve soup drizzled with a little extra olive oil and scattered with croutons.

---

258. Roasted, Moroccan Spiced, Sweet Potato Soup With Rum Cream

Serving: Serves 8 | Prep: | Cook: | Ready in:

Ingredients

- 4 large sweet potatoes, peeled and cut into 1 inch chunks
- 4 tablespoons butter
- 4 tablespoons dark brown sugar
- 6 tablespoons dark rum
- 1 medium onion, coarsely diced
- 3 bay leaves
- 1/4 teaspoon dried thyme leaves
- 2 quarts chicken stock
- 2 cups cream
- pinch fresh grated nutmeg
- pinch sugar
- pinch lemon zest
- 2 teaspoons Ras El Hanouf (or moroccan curry powder)

Direction

- Combine 2 T melted butter, brown sugar, 1 t Ras El Hanout, and 3 T rum. Toss potatoes with this and place on cookie sheet in 400 degree oven. Roast until potatoes are tender, about 20 minutes. If they start to burn lower level of cookie sheet
- In soup pot melt 2 T butter and add onion. Cook until soft. Add remaining Moroccan spice, bay leaves and thyme. Add stock and simmer.
- Add potatoes to stock and simmer 5 minutes. Puree with immersion or regular blender (after removing bay leaves). Add one cup of cream and simmer. Add fresh grated nutmeg just before pouring into bowls
- For rum cream whip 1 cup cream with 3 T rum and pinch of sugar and zest. Whip until just stiff and refrigerate. Top soup with cream

259. Romaine, Pea And Mint Soup With Sorrel Mint Pesto (Take 2)

Serving: Serves 4-6 (depending on the size of the bowl) | Prep: | Cook: | Ready in:

Ingredients

- Romaine, Pea and Mint Soup
- 2 pounds romaine lettuce (or mix of spring lettuces)
- 1 cup frozen peas
- 2 tablespoons unsalted butter
- 2 tablespoons olive oil
- 3/4 cup spring onions, white and green parts (green onions can be substituted here)
- 1/4 cup fresh mint, finely chopped
- 1 teaspoon lemon juice
- 2 teaspoons kosher salt
- 1 teaspoon ground black pepper
- 4 tablespoons flour
- 1 quart chicken stock, water or vegetable broth
- 2 tablespoons creme fraiche or greek yogurt
- 2 splashes of Worcestershire sauce
- Sorrel - Mint Pesto
- 1 bunch of sorrel leaves, stems removed (about 15 leaves)
- 10-15 mint leaves, stems removed
- 3 cloves of garlic, coarsely chopped
- 2 tablespoons pine nuts tossed in olive oil, Worcestershire sauce, salt and pepper, and toasted in a dry pan over medium heat
- 1/4 cup parmesan cheese, grated
- 1/4 teaspoon salt, to taste
- 1 teaspoon lemon juice
- 1/4 cup olive oil, or enough to make it slightly liquid

Direction

- Romaine, Pea and Mint Soup
- Bring a large pot of well salted water to a boil. Wash the lettuces and slice into 2" pieces. Blanch the lettuce in the boiling water for 5 minutes. Add the peas and cook another 5 minutes. Drain and set aside until cool enough to handle. (Note: if working with tender young spring lettuces, blanch only for 2-3 minutes before adding the peas.)
- In a large pot, melt the butter and oil together over medium heat. Sauté the onions, mint, lemon juice, salt and pepper until the onions are very soft.
- Sprinkle the flour over the onion - mint mixture and whisk to mix the flour in. Cook for 3-4 minutes to toast the flour. Gradually whisk in 1/4 of the broth until smooth and starts to thicken into a paste; then add the rest while whisking over medium-high heat for 2-3 minutes until smooth.
- Chop the blanched lettuce - pea mixture and add to the soup base. Bring to a simmer and cook for 5 minutes to mingle flavors.
- Puree the soup in a blender or food processor until very smooth. Reheat, add the crème fraiche (or yogurt, if you're using that instead) and adjust for seasoning. At the end add a couple splashes of Worcestershire sauce to round out the flavors.
- Serve with the pesto - the recipe follows below.
- Sorrel - Mint Pesto
- Put all ingredients except the olive oil in a food processor or blender and pulse 10-12 times. Then process fine while slowly pouring in the olive oil.
- Serve with a dollop in the soup.

260. Root Vegetable Miso Stew

Serving: Serves about 6 | Prep: | Cook: | Ready in:

Ingredients

- 2 tablespoons extra-virgin olive oil
- 2 tablespoons unsalted butter or coconut oil
- 4 large leeks (white part only) or 1 medium yellow onion, coarsely chopped

- 4 garlic cloves, minced
- 2 tablespoons fresh ginger root, peeled and finely chopped
- 1 fennel bulb, cored and coarsely chopped
- 1/4 teaspoon red pepper flakes (optional)
- sea salt
- 2 pounds (about 8 cups) assorted root vegetables, (such as winter squash, rutabaga, carrots, sweet potato, celery root, parsnips, turnips) peeled and coarsely chopped
- 2 teaspoons fresh thyme or 1 tsp dried thyme
- 1 piece of kombu seaweed
- 1 bay leaf
- 6 cups filtered water
- 4 tablespoons (heaping) of mellow miso paste

Direction

- In a large pot, heat oil and butter over medium heat. Add leeks or onion, garlic, ginger, fennel, 1/2 tsp sea salt, red pepper flakes if using and stir well. Reduce flame a bit and sauté for about 5 minutes or until the leeks or onion soften. Cover, reduce the heat to low, and slowly cook until the mixture is soft and juicy, about 15 to 20 minutes. Check a few times and stir.
- Add the root vegetables, thyme, bay leaf and kombu - raise heat to high and cook, stirring, for a few minutes. Pour in the filtered water and bring to a boil. Reduce the heat to low and simmer, about 30 minutes, or until the vegetables are tender.
- In a small bowl mix the miso paste with some of the hot broth to make a slurry. Mix the miso slurry into the soup pot, stirring to combine. Taste, adding a TB more miso or a dash of sea salt to taste. Serve hot with a sprinkle of fresh thyme or parsley leaves on top

261.   STILTON SOUP

Serving: Serves 6 | Prep: | Cook: | Ready in:

Ingredients

- 4 tablespoons butter
- 4 tablespoons flour
- 3 to 3 1/2 ounces yellow onions, minced
- 3 to 4 ounces fennel bulb, minced
- 2 cups milk
- 8 ounces Stilton cheese, shredded or cubed

Direction

- In a large pot melt the butter and add the minced fennel and onion and sauté until just translucent in color.
- Add the flour and stir for a couple of minutes until the flour and butter are incorporated.
- Add the milk and whisk until the mixture thickens. If it becomes too thick, add more milk.
- When the mixture is the desired thickness, pour it all into a blender and whirl away until it becomes very smooth. Then pour it back into the pot.
- Add the cheese and stir until the soup is very smooth.
- Ladle into soup bowls and garnish with grapes, chives, grated pepper and a little more cheese or all of these if you wish.

262.   Salmorejo Cordobes Spanish Cold Tomato Soup

Serving: Serves 4-6 | Prep: | Cook: | Ready in:

Ingredients

- 2 pounds heirloom tomatoes
- 8 ounces stale bread
- 1 large clove garlic
- 2/3 cup extra virgin olive oil
- 3 tablespoons apple cider vinegar
- sea salt to taste
- 2 hard boil eggs
- serrano ham or prosciutto slices, fried

Direction

- Cut off the crust from the bread, break bread into the pieces and soak in cold water for 10 minutes, squeeze excess water and keep on the side.
- Put tomatoes, vinegar, sea salt and garlic into the blender and puree, put true fine strainer. (If you have high power blender you are set)
- Back in the blender and add bread and slowly pour oil while processing.
- Keep in the fridge.
- Serve with diced boil egg serrano ham or prosciutto sliced and fried.

263.   Sausage Kale Soup With White Beans

Serving: Serves 8 | Prep: | Cook: | Ready in:

Ingredients

- 2 pounds bulk Italian sausage, local or small-batch if you can find it
- 1/2 onion, diced
- 1 bunch kale, sliced, about 4 cups total when cut up
- 4 cloves garlic, minced
- 28 ounces canned whole tomatoes in their juices
- 3 cups chicken, plus a bit more if needed
- 15 ounces canned white beans, don't drain
- salt, as needed
- for serving: bread, crushed red pepper, fresh parsley, grated parmesan

Direction

- In a large soup pot, add the sausage over medium-high heat. Cook the sausage for about 10 minutes, breaking it up with a spoon as you go, until crumbly, browned, and cooked through.
- Add the onion and stir it into the sausage for two minutes to soften slightly. Add the kale and garlic and cook, stirring occasionally, for 5 minutes or so to wilt the kale.

- Add the tomatoes with juices, beans with juices, and stock to the pot. Stir to combine and taste; add salt to your preference.
- Bring the soup to a bubble then reduce the heat to medium-low. Simmer the soup for 10-15 minutes or let sit turned off on the stove until you'd like to eat. If the soup reduces by a lot or gets too thick, add more stock to thin it about 1/2 cup at a time. Serve with bread for dunking, and crushed red pepper, fresh parsley, and grated parmesan cheese for sprinkling. Enjoy!

264.   Savory Wild Mushroom Soup

Serving: Serves 6 to 8 | Prep: | Cook: | Ready in:

Ingredients

- 3 tablespoons olive oil
- 3 tablespoons butter
- 1 large carrot, finely chopped
- 1 stalk celery, finely chopped
- 3 large shallots, thinly sliced
- 3 cloves minced garlic
- Kosher or sea salt, freshly ground black pepper, and crushed red pepper to taste
- 1 bay leaf
- 1 Parmesan rind, preferably Parmigiano-Reggiano
- 1 pound assorted chopped wild mushrooms, such as shiitake, crimini, chanterelle, or oyster
- 1 tablespoon fresh rosemary, minced
- 1 tablespoon fresh sage, minced
- 1 tablespoon fresh thyme, minced
- 15 ounces drained and rinsed canned or dried cannellini beans
- 1/2 cup good quality dry white wine
- 4 cups chicken stock, preferably homemade
- 1/4 cup heavy cream

Direction

- In a large Dutch oven or soup pot, add the olive oil and butter over medium heat. When the butter melts, add carrot and celery and sauté for about 15 minutes, stirring often.
- Add the shallots and continue to cook for about 5 minutes. Stir in the garlic and cook for another 5 to 10 minutes, until the shallots are browned and all vegetables are soft.
- Sprinkle in kosher or sea salt, freshly ground black pepper, and crushed red pepper, to taste. Toss in the bay leaf and Parmesan rind.
- Add mushrooms, stirring well to incorporate. Cook down for about 5 minutes and add the rosemary, sage, and thyme.
- Continue to stir the mixture until mushrooms have reduced, about 5 minutes, and add cannellini beans, stirring them in until warmed.
- Deglaze pot with white wine, removing any browned bits with a wooden spoon, and allow to reduce for a couple of minutes.
- Pour in chicken stock, and simmer for 10 to 15 minutes, allowing flavors to mingle. Remove bay leaf and Parmesan rind.
- Purée soup with a stick blender until very smooth. Stir in cream and serve with desired toppings. Enjoy!

265. Scandinavian Autumn Fruit Soup

Serving: Serves 6 | Prep: | Cook: |Ready in:

Ingredients

- 2 apples, peeled, cored and cut into eighths
- 2 pears, peel, cored, and quartered
- 1 cup frozen dark sweet cherries, pitted
- 1/3 cup prunes
- 1/3 cup dried apricots
- 1 tablespoon raisins
- 1 tablespoon dried currants
- 1 3-inch cinnamon stick
- 4 cups water

Direction

- Combine all ingredients in a pot; bring to a boil. Lower heat and simmer for 20 minutes. Remove from heat and discard cinnamon stick.
- Let cool slightly and then scoop out the apples and pears, puree them in a food processor, and return to soup.
- Serve warm for dessert.

266. Scandinavian Cold Fruit Soup

Serving: Serves 8+ | Prep: | Cook: |Ready in:

Ingredients

- ¾ c dried apricots
- ½ c dried cranberries
- ½ c currants
- ½ c raisins
- ½ c golden raisins
- ½ c dried cherries or 1 can unsweetened sour red cherries
- 1 cinnamon stick
- 2 T orange zest, minced
- 3 apples (a crisp and firm variety such as gala, pink lady, or honey crisp)
- 2 fresh and firm pears (such as a bosc or an Asian pear)
- 1 package unflavored gelatin
- 1 c cranraspberry, cranapple, or cranberry juice
- ¼ c sugar
- lemon slices

Direction

- In a large pot, soak dried fruit in 6 c cold water for 1 hour. Add cinnamon stick and orange zest. Peel and cut into chunks apples and pears and add to pot with other fruit. Simmer, covered, for 15 minutes, or until fruit is tender. If using canned cherries, add them, with juice from can (if using dried cherries, add another 1/2 c water to fruit). Bring to a boil.

- Heat cranraspberry juice to a boil, and in it dissolve the gelatin. Stir gently into fruit.
- Taste for sweetness, and if it's not sweet enough for you, add ¼ c sugar to taste.
- Chill overnight
- Serve with lemon slices.

267. Shrimp Tamarind Soup

Serving: Serves 4 - 6 people | Prep: | Cook: | Ready in:

Ingredients

- 10 cups water (preserved from washing rice)
- 1   onion sliced
- 3   tomatoes in quarters
- 1   peeled radish (350g)
- 18   Chinese string beans (260g)
- 15   okras
- 1   eggplant
- 2   long green peppers
- 2 1/2 tablespoons fish sauce
- 1   chicken bouillon cube
- 350 milliliters tamarind paste
- 1 teaspoon salt
- 1/2   bag of spinach (160g)
- 16   shrimps
- 1   lemon

Direction

- Rinse 2 cups of jasmine rice and preserve the water until you have a total of 10 cups. Proceed cooking the rice in a rice cooker (1:1 ratio) or any other method of your choice.
- In a large pot, combine the water, onion, and tomatoes. Season with salt. Cover and bring to a simmer for 10 minutes.
- Rinse vegetables and cut the radish, eggplant and string beans into three-inch sticks. Cut the top part of the okras only.
- Once the water is simmering, press the tomatoes using the sides of the pot.

- Add the radish and the string beans. Cover and bring to a boil for 5 minutes or until almost tender.
- Add the okras, eggplant and peppers.
- Season the soup with fish sauce, tamarind paste and bouillon cube. Stir and cover.
- With a pair of scissors, cut the rostrum from the head of the shrimps.
- Finally, add the shrimps and spinach and stir.
- The soup is ready once it starts to boil.
- Adjust the seasoning by adding fish sauce.
- Serve with a bowl of rice and squeeze a wedge of lemon to your soup.

268. Slightly Sour Chicken And Kale Soup

Serving: Makes one large pot | Prep: 0hours30mins | Cook: 1hours0mins | Ready in:

Ingredients

- 1   yellow onion (diced)
- 4   celery stalks (diced)
- 4   cloves garlic (minced)
- 1/2 teaspoon red pepper flakes
- 1 teaspoon turmeric
- 1/2 cup apple cider vinegar
- 1 tablespoon Worcestershire
- 8 cups homemade chicken stock (can be subbed with low sodium store bought)
- 6 cups water
- 1 pound chicken breast (about 2 breasts)
- 1   lemon (juice only)
- 1 bunch kale (stems removed, rough chop)
- salt and pepper

Direction

- Start by heating olive oil in a Dutch oven over medium heat. Add onions, celery, red pepper flakes, turmeric, salt and pepper. Let cook until soft, about 5 minutes. Add garlic and let cook for one minute.

- Add Worcestershire and apple cider vinegar, and let reduce for 3-4 minutes. Add the chicken stock and water, lots of salt and a pinch of pepper. Bring to a boil. Once at a boil, reduce to a simmer.
- Salt and pepper the chicken breasts, and drop into the simmering broth. Squeeze the lemon in, cover, and let simmer for 45 minutes - 1 hour.
- Turn off heat. Shred the chicken back into the soup. Serve hot, and optionally with parmesan shaved on top.

269.   Slow Cooker Lentil & Sausage Stew

Serving: Serves 4 | Prep: | Cook: |Ready in:

Ingredients

- 1 pound brown lentils, picked, rinsed, and drained
- 1 pound your favorite smoked sausage, sliced (I like beef smoked sausage)
- 5 cups your favorite stock (or water, but it won't be as tasty)
- 1 onion, diced
- 2 cloves of garlic, minced
- 1.5 cups bias-sliced carrots
- 1 teaspoon dried thyme
- 1 teaspoon dried sage
- salt & pepper to taste
- 2-4 cups chopped kale (to be added at the end)

Direction

- Mix all ingredients except kale in a medium-sized slow cooker.
- Cook on low for the better part of a day (7-10 hours). I have never tried cooking on high, but I assume it would take 3.5-5 hours. If someone is willing to try it, let me know how it turns out!

- Once stew is completely cooked, turn heat to high (if you were cooking on low) and add as much kale as you would like, stirring to mix. Cook 10-20 minutes more or until kale has begun to soften. Kale will greatly reduce in volume, so add as much or as little as you like. Enjoy!

270.   Slow Cooker Ramen

Serving: Serves 6-8 | Prep: | Cook: |Ready in:

Ingredients

- 3 pounds Boneless pork shoulder
- 2 tablespoons Neutral oil
- 1 Yellow onion, chopped
- 6 Garlic cloves, crushed
- 1 2-in piece ginger, peeled and chopped
- 8 cups Chicken broth (low-sodium preferred)
- 1 Leek, halved lengthwise, and chopped
- 1/4 pound Mushrooms, chopped
- 1 1/2 pounds Fresh ramen noodles
- 8 Eggs, soft boiled
- Soy sauce, sesame oil to taste for serving
- Green onions, to serve
- 2 cups Steamed veggies, like Bok Choy/ Mushrooms

Direction

- Season pork with salt and sear in a hot pan with oil, about 3-4 minutes each side. Put in to slow cooker.
- Add leeks, mushrooms, onion, ginger, garlic, and broth to the slow cooker. Cover and cook on the low setting for 8 hours, or until the pork shoulder is tender and broth is fragrant.
- In the last few minutes of cooking, boil noodles according to the package and boil eggs. Set both aside.
- Once pork is cooked, transfer to cutting board. Using 2 forks, shred the pork and discard any large pieces of fat.

- Strain broth through fine-mesh sieve and return to slow cooker.
- To serve:-Divide broth and noodles among 8 bowls.-Place soft-boiled egg in each.-Top with steamed vegetables and green onions.-Use soy sauce and sesame oil to season

- Remove the rosemary, Parmesan rind and bay leaf. Serve the soup topped with grated cheese and garnished with pancetta, if desired.

---

271. Slow Cooker Lentil & Root Veggie Soup

Serving: Serves 8 | Prep: 0hours0mins | Cook: 8hours0mins | Ready in:

Ingredients

- 3 cups chopped, peeled celeriac (celery root)
- 2 cups chopped parsnips
- 1 cup chopped carrot
- 1 cup frozen pearl onions
- 1 stalk celery, chopped
- 2 plum tomatoes, seeded and chopped
- 3 cloves garlic, minced
- 2 teaspoons herbes de Provence
- 8 cups vegetable broth
- 1 cup French green lentils or black lentils, rinsed
- 1 sprig fresh rosemary
- 1 (3-inch) Parmesan cheese rind
- 1/2 cup grated Parmesan, divided
- 1 bay leaf
- 1 teaspoon salt
- 1/2 teaspoon ground pepper
- 4 ounces pancetta, crisp-cooked and crumbled (optional)

Direction

- Combine celeriac, parsnips, carrot, pearl onions, celery, tomatoes, garlic and herbes de Provence in a 5- to 6-quart slow cooker. Add broth, lentils, rosemary, Parmesan rind, bay leaf, salt and pepper. Cover and cook on High for 4½ hours or on Low for 8 hours.

---

272. Slow Cooker Moroccan Spiced Lentil Soup

Serving: Serves 8 | Prep: 0hours0mins | Cook: 8hours30mins | Ready in:

Ingredients

- 2 cups chopped onions
- 2 cups chopped carrots
- 4 cloves garlic, minced
- 2 teaspoons extra-virgin olive oil
- 1 teaspoon ground cumin
- 1 teaspoon ground coriander
- 1 teaspoon ground turmeric
- 1/4 teaspoon ground cinnamon
- 1/4 teaspoon ground pepper
- 6 cups vegetable broth
- 2 cups water
- 3 cups chopped cauliflower
- 1 3/4 cups French green lentils or brown lentils
- 1 (28-ounce) can diced tomatoes
- 2 tablespoons tomato paste
- 4 cups chopped fresh spinach or 10 ounces frozen chopped spinach, thawed
- 1/2 cup chopped fresh cilantro
- 2 tablespoons lemon juice

Direction

- Combine onions, carrots, garlic, oil, cumin, coriander, turmeric, cinnamon and pepper in a 5- to 6-quart slow cooker. Add broth, water, cauliflower, lentils, tomatoes and tomato paste and stir until well combined.
- Cover and cook until the lentils are tender, 4 to 5 hours on High or 8 to 10 hours on Low.
- Add spinach to the slow cooker. Stir, cover and cook on High for 30 minutes.

- Just before serving, stir in cilantro and lemon juice.

---

273. Slow Cooker Pasta E Fagioli

Serving: Serves 6 to 8 | Prep: 0hours25mins | Cook: 5hours30mins | Ready in:

Ingredients

- 1/4 cup olive oil, plus more for serving
- 1 large white onion, finely chopped
- 1 large carrot, finely chopped
- 4 garlic cloves, thinly sliced
- 2 tablespoons fresh thyme, finely chopped
- 1 tablespoon fresh rosemary, finely chopped
- 1/2 teaspoon crushed red pepper flakes, plus more for serving
- Kosher salt
- Freshly ground black pepper
- 1 (28-ounce) can whole peeled tomatoes
- 2 (15 1/2–ounce) cans white beans, such as cannellini or navy, drained and rinsed
- 4 cups low-sodium vegetable or chicken stock
- 1 dried or fresh bay leaf
- 1 Parmesan rind
- 8 ounce small pasta, such as ditalini, shells, or elbow macaroni
- Chopped fresh parsley, for serving
- Grated Parmesan, for serving
- Good Italian bread, for serving (optional)

Direction

- Heat olive oil in a large skillet over medium heat. Add onion, carrot, and garlic, and sauté until aromatic and translucent, about 5 minutes. Add thyme, rosemary, and red pepper flakes. Season with salt and pepper. Sauté for an additional 3 minutes. Scrape mixture into slow-cooker insert. Alternatively, you can skip this step and add all ingredients (including the oil) into the slow cooker—you

won't get as much depth of flavor, but ultimately it will all be fine and taste great.
- Dump tomatoes into a medium bowl, then use your hands to break them into uneven pieces. Add to the slow cooker. Stir beans, stock, bay leaf, and Parmesan rind into the slow cooker. Season with more salt and pepper. Place lid on slow cooker and cook on high for 3 hours, or on low for 5 hours.
- Remove Parm rind and season with more salt and pepper. If you're not planning to finish all the soup tonight, cook the pasta separately in a medium pot of salted water according to the package directions until just al dente, even a little under. Scoop 1/4 to 1/2 cup cooked pasta into each serving bowl, then ladle the soup over. (Store leftover pasta separately from leftover soup—this prevents the pasta from turning into mush as you eat leftovers.) If planning to finish all the soup tonight, stir dry pasta directly into the soup, then cook for another 15 minutes.
- Serve with parsley, grated Parm, and bread.

---

274. Slow Cooker Shiitake Noodle Hot & Sour Soup

Serving: Serves 8 | Prep: 0hours0mins | Cook: 7hours30mins | Ready in:

Ingredients

- 24 dried shiitake or black Chinese mushrooms (2 to 3 ounces)
- 2 carrots, cut into ½-by-2-inch sticks
- 2 (8-ounce) cans bamboo shoots, rinsed
- 2 (14-ounce) packages extra-firm water-packed tofu, drained and cut into ½-inch pieces
- 1 teaspoon ground white pepper
- 4 cups thinly sliced green cabbage
- 4 1/3 cups water, divided
- 4 cups mushroom or vegetable broth
- 1/4 cup white vinegar or rice vinegar

- 1/4 cup red-wine vinegar
- 1/4 cup reduced-sodium soy sauce, plus more to taste
- 1 tablespoon chile-garlic sauce, plus more to taste
- 1 tablespoon minced fresh ginger
- 3 tablespoons cornstarch
- 1 tablespoon toasted sesame oil
- 3 cups cooked lo mein noodles (about 6 ounces dry)
- 1 cup sliced scallions

Direction

- Discard mushroom stems and cut the caps into ½-inch pieces. Spread the mushroom pieces in a 6-quart (or larger) slow cooker. Add carrots, bamboo shoots and tofu to slow cooker; sprinkle with white pepper. Top with cabbage.
- Combine 4 cups water, broth, white (or rice) vinegar, red-wine vinegar, soy sauce, chile-garlic sauce and ginger in a bowl; add to the slow cooker.
- Cover and cook for 4 hours on High or 7 to 8 hours on Low.
- Whisk the remaining ⅓ cup water, cornstarch and sesame oil in a bowl. Stir into the soup. If using the Low setting, turn to High. Cover and cook for 20 minutes. Stir in noodles, cover and cook for 10 minutes more. Serve topped with scallions and with more soy sauce and chile-garlic sauce, if desired.

275.   Smoky Leek And Potato Soup

Serving: Serves 4 | Prep: | Cook: |Ready in:

Ingredients

- 1 onion, chopped
- 2 leeks, cut in half, then sliced
- 2 garlic cloves, minced
- 1 teaspoon mustard powder
- 2 tablespoons flour

- 4 cups vegetable stock
- 2-3 yukon gold potatoes, peeled and chopped
- 2 tablespoons cream
- 2 teaspoons smoked paprika
- pickled peppers (optional)

Direction

- Warmed about a teaspoon of olive oil in a 3-quart pot. Add the onion, leeks and a sprinkle of salt and cook until they are softened and translucent. Add the garlic and cook for about 30 seconds longer.
- Sprinkle on the mustard powder and flour. Stir for a minute or two to make a roux.
- Whisk in the broth, then add the potatoes and smoked paprika. Bring to a boil, then reduce heat and simmer until the potatoes are cooked through.
- Stir in the cream and check for seasoning. Enjoy as is, or top with a few pickled peppers.

276.   Soba Noodle Soup With Miso And Veggies

Serving: Serves 2 hungry people | Prep: | Cook: |Ready in:

Ingredients

- 1 bunch Scallion, white and light green parts thinly sliced, green stalks reserved
- 1 bunch Baby bok choy, thinly sliced (or any desired green such as spinach, chard or cabbage)
- 2 Cloves Garlic, smashed
- 2 Inches Ginger, peeled and sliced in 1/4 inch rounds
- 6 Inch piece of Lemongrass, cut vertically and sliced
- 2-3 Carrots, thinly sliced
- 1 Package Enoki mushrooms, roots removed and chopped in half
- 1/2 teaspoon Instant Dashi (such as HON Dashi) (optional)

- 1/4 cup Shiro (white) miso paste
- 1 tablespoon Soy sauce
- 8 ounces Tofu, extra-firm, cubed
- 1 Bundle dried Soba Noodles (approx 3.25 ounces)

Direction

- Bring 4 cups of water to a simmer along with scallion tops (green), 2 smashed garlic cloves, ginger, sliced lemongrass and instant dashi (if using). Cover and let simmer for 30 minutes.
- Meanwhile, cook soba noodles according to package directions or until al dente (approximately 6 minutes), drain and set aside.
- Drain broth base through a fine sieve and return to pot. Bring back up to a low simmer and add carrots, half of sliced scallions and bok choy. Simmer for 10 minutes, add mushrooms and cook additional 5 minutes.
- Add soy sauce.
- Turn off heat and stir in miso paste until fully combined.
- Place soba noodles in large bowls along with cubed tofu and a large pinch of scallions. Ladle soup on top of the noodles, tofu and scallions. Enjoy.

277.   Soba With Crispy Shallots, Bonito & Cilantro

Serving: Serves 4 as the start of a meal | Prep: | Cook: | Ready in:

Ingredients

- For Crispy Shallots
- 2 ounces shallots (2 medium), trimmed, peeled, halved and thinly sliced
- 1 cup canola oil
- kosher salt
- For Soba and Dashi
- 1 3/4 cups chicken stock (homemade or store bought)

- 1 2" x 2" piece of dried kombu, wiped clean with a damp towel
- 1 1/2 inch piece of fresh ginger, peeled, sliced into 6 thick coins, smashed with the back of a knife
- 2 tablespoons sake
- 1 1/2-2 1/2 tablespoons soy sauce or Tamari
- 2 tablespoons rice vinegar
- 1 tablespoon shallot oil
- 7 ounces or 2 bundles dried soba noodles
- 1-2 teaspoons dried, shaved bonito flakes, also called katsuobushi
- crispy shallots
- 3-4 sprigs cilantro, washed, dried and leaves separated

Direction

- For Crispy Shallots
- Set a sieve over a medium heatproof bowl.
- Heat oil in a small saucepan over medium high to 275° F (use a deep-fry thermometer). Add shallots and cook until just turning golden, about 7-8 minutes. Remove shallots from hot oil with a fork or slotted spoon and drain on a paper towel lined plate. Turn heat up to high until thermometer registers 350° F. Add shallots (they will sizzle) and cook until crisp and golden brown, about 10 seconds. Carefully pour oil through sieve to stop cooking. Transfer shallots to paper towel lined plate and sprinkle with kosher salt. When cool, transfer oil to a glass jar with a lid. Shallot oil will keep for up to 2 weeks in the refrigerator. Leftover crispy shallots will keep for a day or two in an airtight container.
- For Soba and Dashi
- In a saucepan, combine chicken stock, Kombu, ginger and sake. Heat over medium-low, with lid slightly ajar. Allow mixture to slowly come to a bubble for 25 minutes. Remove Kombu (can reserve for a second use if desired) and add 1 ½ T soy sauce or Tamari, rice vinegar and shallot oil, whisking to combine. Taste for salt and add more soy sauce or Tamari if necessary (up to 1 T more). Reduce heat to low. Cover to keep warm.

- Meanwhile, cook soba noodles in a pot of boiling water according to directions on package. Drain in a colander, rinsing noodles under running cold water, using both hands to fluff noodles and remove excess starch. Drain again, gently shaking colander to remove water. Evenly distribute noodles into four individual bowls, using a large fork or small tongs to twirl into a mound. Top noodles with about a teaspoon of crispy shallots, ½-1 t of bonito and 3-4 cilantro leaves. Fill four ramekins with 1/3 cup hot dashi each. Serve noodles with ramekin of dashi on the side. Pour dashi over noodles just before eating. Enjoy.

278. Sorrel & Spinach Soup

Serving: Serves 2 | Prep: | Cook: | Ready in:

Ingredients

- 1 tablespoon olive oil
- 1 medium sweet spring onion, diced
- 2 ounces fresh sorrel, chopped
- 3 ounces fresh baby spinach, chopped
- 3 cups chicken or pork broth (I used homemade pork bone broth and it's partly why I think this soup turned out to be so great – so make it at home if possible!)
- 1 medium sized red potato – diced
- 1 clove garlic, smashed
- Kosher salt, freshly ground black pepper to taste
- Crushed red pepper flakes (for garnish)
- Drizzle of heavy cream or half & half (for garnish)

Direction

- Heat the olive oil in a saucepan over medium. Throw in the onions with a bit of salt and pepper and cook until translucent. Then, add in the garlic and cook until fragrant, about one minute. Next add in the sorrel and spinach.

The sorrel will turn brown almost immediately. Have no fear; it's just its nature. The spinach will help green things up a bit.
- Let the greens wilt and then pour in the stock, followed by the diced potato. Bring everything to a boil, then reduce the heat and simmer for about 25 minutes or so. After, remove the soup from the heat and use an immersion blender to puree the mixture. When smooth, put the soup back over the heat on low until ready to serve. Salt and pepper the soup to taste.
- When serving, drizzle each bowl with a small amount of heavy cream or half & half and sprinkle with crushed red pepper flakes.

279. Soupe Au Pistou From Jody Williams

Serving: Serves 6 to 8 | Prep: 0hours15mins | Cook: 1hours30mins | Ready in:

Ingredients

- 2 cups dried cranberry or cannellini beans (or a mix), soaked overnight and drained
- 2 celery stalks, diced
- 2 large carrots, peeled and diced
- 1 medium yellow onion, peeled and diced
- 1 fennel bulb, including the light green stems, diced
- one 15-ounce can whole peeled tomatoes, seeded if you like and chopped
- 6 large outer escarole leaves, torn into pieces (or another hardy green, like kale)
- 1 large handful green beans, trimmed and cut in half crosswise
- 1 leek, white and light green parts only, thinly sliced
- 2 small zucchini, diced
- Pinch red chili flakes, plus more as needed
- Coarse salt
- 2 cups fresh basil leaves, washed and dried
- 1/2 cup extra-virgin olive oil, plus more for serving

- 1/2 cup grated Parmigiano-Reggiano cheese, plus more for serving

Direction

- Place the soaked beans, all of the vegetables, the chili flakes, and 2 teaspoons of salt into a large soup pot. Cover with cold water, then add 2 additional cups of water.
- Bring the mixture to a boil, lower the heat, and allow it to simmer until the beans are tender, about 1 hour, adding more water as the soup cooks if it gets too dry or too thick at any point. Season the soup to taste with additional salt and chili flakes, if necessary.
- Meanwhile, place the basil leaves in a mortar and use a pestle to crush them with 2 teaspoons of salt. Work in the Parmigiano-Reggiano and the olive oil to make a coarse paste. Alternatively, you can pulse the basil, salt, and Parmigiano-Reggiano together in a food processor and stream in the olive oil to make the paste. Either way, season the pistou with additional salt, if necessary, and set it aside. A thin layer of olive oil poured on top will prevent the pistou from browning.
- Serve the soup hot, topped with a generous drizzle of olive oil, a big spoonful of the pistou, and a handful of grated Parmigiano-Reggiano.

---

280. Speedy, Spicy Corn & Black Bean Soup

Serving: Serves 4 | Prep: | Cook: | Ready in:

Ingredients

- FOR THE CORN STOCK
- Husks and cobs from 4 ears of corn
- 3 quarts warm water
- 5 tepin chiles or 3 japones chiles
- FOR THE SOUP
- 1 quart corn stock (cool and freeze the remainder)

- All of the corn kernels
- 1 yellow onion, peeled and sliced 1/4" thick
- 2 Anaheim chiles
- 1 can black beans, rinsed and drained
- 1 teaspoon cumin seeds
- 1 teaspoon coriander seeds
- 4 ounces sour cream
- Juice of 1 lime
- Fresh cilantro (optional)
- Lime wedges

Direction

- So. First make the corn stock. It is going to sweeten your soup immeasurably in ways that vegetable or chicken stock can only dream of, and you're going to need that sweetness to balance the peppers' notes. Tiny Tepin chiles have an intense heat, but it is short-lived. Japones chiles pack more of a punch, so use fewer if that is what you have. The chiles are going to deepen the flavor of your stock with a warmth that will be very different from layering them in on the soup end of things. I stripped the husks (keeping only the clean ones) and removed the kernels the night before, then refrigerated everything. An easy way to remove the kernels without them flying all over the kitchen is to lay the ear flat on its side on a cutting board. Use a knife to slice off a facet of kernels. Turn the ear, repeat until all kernels have been sliced off. That done, in the morning, all I needed to do was toss everything in the slow cooker and be on my way. Transfer the husks and cobs to the slow cooker, and add the warm (not hot) water so that it heats up faster (well, as fast as a slow cooker can heat anything up), and set the temperature to High while you get ready to leave. Before you go, reduce heat to low.
- When you're ready to make your soup, set a large soup pot in the sink and set a strainer, not a colander in it. Use tongs to lift the cobs and husks out of your stock. Throw them away. Pour the stock through the strainer to remove the fine particulates and chiles, then discard them.

- Set the pot over medium heat. Stir in the kernels of corn and the black beans.
- Once the onion has been peeled and sliced, arrange the slices on a plate or a baking sheet. Salt both sides and set them aside for about 15 minutes. You want its flavor to be fresh, but not harsh. The salt is going to break down the onion and take the edge off its "bite". By the way, this is a little transformative trick I learned from Chef Andrea Reusig in a conversation with Lynne Rosetto Kasper on The Splendid Table. Take a look at her Tomato Salad. You'll never see tomatoes, cucumbers, or onions the same again.
- While the onions are resting, roast the peppers. Anaheim peppers are quite mild, and when roasted, develop a wonderful, deep fragrance and flavor. Besides, you have to get the skin off, and honestly, it's the best way. Trim the ends off and split them in half the long way. Remove the seeds and white membranes (they're bitter). There are many ways to roast them, with these being the most common. Lay them skin-side-up on a baking sheet and run them under the broiler until they blister and char. Or hold them over the flame of a gas stove with a pair of tongs (hold the tongs with a hot pad!) until the same effect is achieved. In the end, put the slices into a plastic bag and seal it shut. Within just a few minutes, the steam generated will let you slip the skin off easily.
- Set a dry skillet over medium-high heat. Once it is hot, add the cumin and coriander seeds. Shake the skillet back and forth to toast the seeds. Once they are fragrant, they're done. If you over-toast cumin, it becomes extremely bitter and will overpower the flavor of whatever you put it in. Remove the skillet from the heat and immediately pour the seeds out into a mortar and pestle to grind them. Add them to the soup pot.
- By now, your peppers should be skinless and the onions ready to move on. Chop them both into a 1/4" dice and add them to the soup.
- Bring the soup just to a simmer. You want the corn and onions to retain some of their crunch,

so taste the soup periodically and remove it from the heat when all the ingredients are just heated through. Just before you remove it from the heat, season the soup to taste with salt and pepper.
- Stir the smoked paprika (add more, if you wish) into the sour cream along with the lime juice. Chop up a handful of cilantro.
- Ladle the soup into bowls. Garnish with a slop of the sour cream mixture and some cilantro (or not). Serve with wedges of lime.

281. Spicy Black Bean Soup With Andouille Sausage

Serving: Serves 6 | Prep: | Cook: |Ready in:

Ingredients

- 12 ounces Cajun style andouille sausage, sliced
- 1 large onion, finely chopped
- 1 large red bell pepper, chopped
- 3 cloves garlic, minced
- 2 chipotles in adobo, finely chopped
- 1 tablespoon Cajun seasoning (see note)
- 2 15.5 oz cans black beans, drained and rinsed
- 1 quart chicken stock

Direction

- Heat a large Dutch oven over medium-high heat and cook the sausage in a bit of olive oil until lightly browned. Remove to a plate and set aside.
- Add the onion, season with salt, and cook until translucent and slightly softened, adding more olive oil as necessary. Add red pepper and celery and cook until they being to soften.
- Add garlic, chipotle, and Cajun seasoning and cook, stirring, for about a minute. Add the beans and give everything a good stir, then add the stock. Bring the soup back to a simmer and return the sausage to the pot.

- Simmer for 30-40 minutes until the stock has reduced somewhat and the flavors have melded. Taste and adjust seasoning if necessary. Serve with a dollop of sour cream.

282. Spicy Cheese Pumpkin & Sweet Dumpling Squash Soup

Serving: Serves four | Prep: | Cook: | Ready in:

Ingredients

- 1 jalapeño pepper finely minced
- 1 tablespoon extra virgin olive oil
- 4 cups chicken or vegetable broth
- 15 ounces can of solid pack pumpkin or 2 cups fresh roasted pumpkin & squash puree
- 2 tablespoons freshly squeezed lime juice
- 2 tablespoons fresh cilantro finely chopped
- 1 tablespoon maple syrup or honey
- Toasted pumpkin seeds for garnish

Direction

- In large saucepan over medium high heat, sauté jalapeño in hot olive oil until just tender (about one minute). Gently stir in broth, pumpkin and lime juice. Bring to a boil and reduce heat. Add cilantro and simmer for five minutes. Stir in maple syrup or honey and garnish with toasted pumpkin seeds and a sprig of cilantro.
- *Note: I roasted a cheese pumpkin to use in the puree and to serve as the soup bowl. Then roasted two miniature pumpkins and two sugar dumpling squash to add to the puree. The two small pumpkins served as the soup cups.

283. Spicy Chicken Fiesta Soup

Serving: Serves 3-4 | Prep: | Cook: | Ready in:

Ingredients

- 4-5 cups chicken stock
- 1 jalapeño, halfway seeded and minced
- 2 garlic cloves, minced
- 2 roma tomatoes, seeded and diced
- small handful of cilantro, chopped
- 2 chicken breasts, cooked and shredded (I seasoned mine with cumin, chili powder, and chipotle pepper)
- juice from 1 lime
- avocado, shredded sharp cheddar cheese, and sour cream, for topping

Direction

- In a Dutch oven under medium high heat, add all ingredients except topping and heat for about 15 minutes. You can go longer to develop the flavor.
- Ladle into bowls and top with whatever you desire!

284. Spicy Chicken And Sausage Chili With White Beans And Peppers

Serving: Serves 8 | Prep: | Cook: | Ready in:

Ingredients

- 2 tablespoons Extra Virgin Olive Oil
- 5 Slices thick cut, smoked bacon, chopped
- 1 pound Boneless, skinless chicken breast, diced
- 2/3 pound Ground, sweet Italian sausage
- 2 Yellow onions, diced
- 1 Green bell pepper, diced
- 1 Red bell pepper, diced

- 1 Fresh jalapeno, seeds and veins removed, minced
- 2 4oz cans roasted, diced green chiles
- 3 Cloves fresh garlic minced
- 1 teaspoon Coarse ground black pepper
- 1 teaspoon Ground coriandar
- 3 tablespoons Roasted ground cumin
- 1 1/2 tablespoons Chili powder
- 3 tablespoons Dried oregano
- 1/2 teaspoon Chipotle chili powder
- 3 tablespoons All-purpose flour
- 6 cups Chicken stock
- 1 15.5 oz can cannelinni beans, partially drained
- 1 15.5 oz can great northern beans, partially drained
- 2 cups vegetable oil for frying
- 6 white corn tortillas, sliced into thin strips
- 1 cup shredded sharp, white cheddar cheese
- 1 lime, cut into 8 wedges
- 1/3 cup sour cream, for garnish
- 1/4 cup chopped, fresh cilantro, for garnish
- 1 avocado, diced, for garnish

Direction

- Heat the olive oil in a large stock pot over medium-high heat.
- Add the bacon, cooking until just turning brown, about 5 minutes.
- Add the chicken and sausage, stirring and cooking until the chicken is cooked through, about 12 minutes.
- Crumble the sausage with a spoon or end of whisk while cooking.
- Add the onion, peppers, jalapeno, green chilies and garlic, stirring and cooking until the onions are just tender, about 5 minutes.
- Add the black pepper, coriander, cumin, chili powder, oregano and chipotle chili powder, stirring and cooking for 3 minutes.
- Add the flour, stirring to combine and cook for 3 minutes.
- Add the chicken stock one cup at a time, stirring to thicken while scraping up bits on the bottom of the pot.
- Bring chili to boil, stirring.

- Add beans, stir to combine. Reduce heat to low, simmering for 20 minutes, stirring periodically.
- Meanwhile, heat about 2-inches of vegetable oil in a medium sauce pan until 350 degrees F.
- Add the corn tortilla strips, stir to separate and fry until golden, only about 1 minute or less. Transfer to a paper towel to drain, set aside.
- Serve chili in crocks, top each with cheddar cheese, a dollop of sour cream, chopped avocado, chopped cilantro and fried tortilla strips. Serve with wedge of lime for squeezing on top.

---

285. Spicy Italian White Bean & Sausage Soup

Serving: Serves 8 | Prep: | Cook: | Ready in:

Ingredients

- 2 tablespoons olive oil
- 1 large onion, diced
- 4 cloves garlic, minced
- 2 large peppers (red, orange, or yellow), chopped
- 2-3 carrots, chopped
- 1 pound hot turkey sausage, bulk or if using links, remove casings
- 2 tablespoons fresh sage, minced
- 2 tablespoons fresh rosemary, minced
- 1/4 teaspoon red pepper flakes
- 1/2 teaspoon salt
- 1/2 teaspoon black pepper
- 4 cups chicken stock (or broth)
- 1/2 cup almond milk (or fat-free half & half)
- 1 14oz can of petite-diced tomatoes in their juice
- 3 15 oz cans of Cannellini beans drained & rinsed (set aside beans from one can)
- 1 ~5oz container baby spinach
- 1/4 cup freshly grated Parmesan cheese, for garnish

Direction

- In a stockpot heat the olive oil over medium heat. Add onions, garlic, red pepper, and carrots and sauté until onions are tender.
- Stir in the sausage and cook until it is no longer pink. Add the sage, rosemary, red pepper flakes, salt, and black pepper.
- Stir in the chicken stock and tomatoes. Bring the mixture to a boil, and reduce the heat and simmer for 10-15 minutes.
- With a fork, coarsely mash the beans from one can in a small bowl (use a potato masher if necessary). Add them to the soup mixture. Stir in the remaining two cans of beans, and the milk. Allow the soup to simmer for 10 minutes.
- Put fresh spinach into each bowl just before serving, then ladle soup over it. Sprinkle the soup with some freshly grated Parmesan cheese.

---

286. Spicy Shrimp Bisque

Serving: Serves 6-8 | Prep: | Cook: | Ready in:

Ingredients

- 3 tablespoons unsalted butter
- 1 yellow onion, thinly sliced
- 1 medium carrot, thinly sliced
- 2 large cloves garlic, peeled and thinly sliced
- 2 pounds raw shrimp, shelled and deveined,reserve shells
- 3 plum tomatoes, coarsely chopped
- 3 tomatillos, coarsely chopped
- 1-2 chipotles en adobo, with added sauce, minced
- 4 cups fish stock, prepared clam broth or chicken broth
- 1/2 cup fine fresh bread crumbs
- 1/2 cup heavy cream
- 2 tablespoons dry sherry, optional
- Salt and pepper, to taste
- 1 pinch cayenne pepper

Direction

- In a heavy saucepan, melt the butter. Add the onion, carrot and garlic. Sauté, stirring until slightly softened, about 2 minutes. Add the shrimp shells and sauté until pink and vegetables are softened, about 5 minutes. Add the plum tomatoes, tomatillos, and minced chipotles en adobo along with the desired stock. Cook until tomatoes and tomatillos have softened, about 10 minutes. Will a slotted spoon, remove shrimp shells and discard.
- Process the mixture in a food processor until finely chopped. Remove to a fine-mesh strainer set over a soup pot. Press down on the solids with the back of a spoon to completely extract the liquid. Discard the solids.
- Reserve about 24 shrimp or roughly half the shrimp. Add remaining shrimp and bread crumbs to the pot. Cook over medium heat until the shrimp turn pink and are opaque and the bread crumbs have softened, about 3 minutes. Using a food processor, puree the soup in batches until smooth. An electric hand blend makes this an easy task.
- Still on medium heat, add the cream, optional sherry, salt and cayenne pepper. Cook another 2 minutes to blend the flavors. Taste and adjust seasonings. Chop the reserved shrimp in 1/2-1-inch pieces. Just before serving, add the shrimp pieces to the soup and cook until pink and opaque, 1-2 minutes longer. In warmed bowls, ladle the soup and sprinkle with cayenne pepper, if desired

---

287. Spicy Shrimp Pozole With Avocado & Bacon

Serving: Serves 4 | Prep: | Cook: | Ready in:

Ingredients

- 1 pound dried hominy (soaked overnight or simmered for 3 hours)

- 1 ounce dried red chile peppers, seeds removed
- 1 tablespoon olive oil
- 6 slices bacon, chopped
- 1 large onion, minced
- 2 jalapeños, minced
- 6 cloves of garlic, minced
- 1 pound shrimp, cleaned and sliced in half
- 1 large bunch cilantro leaves, plus more for serving
- salt, to taste
- 1 avocado, cubed, for serving
- sliced scallions, for serving

Direction

- First, you need to soak your hominy. You can either place it in a bowl of water, covered, for 12 hours, or you can place it in a pot, cover with water, and simmer gently for 3 hours. I went the simmering route because I did not think ahead, as usual. Simmer the hominy, covered, until it is tender, stirring every so often.
- Once the hominy is ready, set it aside. Now you need to rehydrate your chiles. Cut off the tops of the dried chiles and shake out any seeds (a few seeds remaining is fine). Place them in a bowl and cover with boiling hot water (I just used the microwave to heat up the water). Cover with a paper towel or plastic wrap and allow to sit for 30 minutes or so. Once the chiles are rehydrated, reserve 3-4 cups of the chile water, then drain the rest and puree the chiles in a food processor or blender until smooth, adding in a bit of water as needed. Set aside. As a side note, you will have a lot of chile puree and probably won't use all of it. I divided mine up into smaller portions and froze it to use at later dates in other recipes.
- In a large, heavy bottomed pot, heat your olive oil over high heat. Add in your bacon and cook until crisp, about 5-7 minutes. Remove the bacon with a slotted spoon and set aside. Add your onion and jalapeños to the bacon fat, and cook until the onions have become

translucent, about 5-7 minutes, stirring often. Add in the garlic and stir for 1 minute. Add in 2 tablespoons of the chile puree, stir, then add in 3-4 cups of the chile water (if you'd like it to be less spicy, you can just use regular water or use half chile water and half regular water) and the hominy.
- Taste and add another tablespoon of chile puree if you would like more heat (I did). Stir to combine and add some plain water to cover the hominy if it isn't completely covered. Simmer for 10 minutes or so, then add in the bacon, a big handful of cilantro leaves, and the cleaned and sliced shrimp. Simmer for an additional 10 minutes over medium heat. Taste and add salt as desired. Serve with cilantro leaves, avocado and scallions.

288.　　　Spicy Tofu Coconut Noodle Soup

Serving: Serves two | Prep: | Cook: | Ready in:

Ingredients

- fresh lemongrass, fresh ginger, coconut oil, Laksa paste (can be found in Asian grocery stores), tofu, fresh or dried rice noodles, coconut milk, chicken or vegetable broth
- 1 tablespoon minced lemongrass center
- 1 tablespoon grated ginger
- 1 tablespoon coconut oil or cooking oil
- 2 tablespoons laksa paste
- 1/2 cup cubed firm tofu
- 1 cup broth, chicken or vegetable
- 1/2 cup coconut milk
- 1 packet dried or fresh rice noodles
- Garnishes: bean sprouts, cilantro, green onion, mint, basil,thai chili, lime
- 1/2 cup blanched bean sprouts
- 1 handful combined herbs such as basil, cilantro, mint, stemmed and chopped
- 2 green onions, sliced thinly on diagonal
- 1 thai chili, thinly sliced

- 2 lime wedges

Direction

- Prepare rice noodles according to package directions. While noodles are being prepared, heat pan and add coconut oil. Add lemongrass and ginger until fragrant but not browned. Next, add Laksa paste and cook on medium heat for about 2 minutes. Add tofu and very gently stir until tofu is covered with paste and browning slightly. Add coconut milk and chicken broth and simmer for about 5 minutes. Season to taste with salt.
- Meanwhile prepare garnishes and divide rice noodles into 2 large bowls (sometimes it helps to rinse the noodles if they are sticking together); cover noodles with steaming soup. Garnish as desired.

289.   Spicy Chicken & Vegetable Rice Noodle Soup For One

Serving: Serves 1 | Prep: | Cook: | Ready in:

Ingredients

- 2 cups hot chicken stock, home-made and rich in flavor
- 1/2 cup chicken, diced (cooked leftovers or raw)
- 3 tablespoons peanut oil
- 1/2 cup red onion, diced finely
- 1 garlic clove, diced finely
- 1 small chili, diced finely
- 1 teaspoon ginger, grated
- 1/2 cup red bell pepper, chopped
- 2 scallions, chopped
- 1 cup baby spinach
- 1/2 cup coriander, chopped
- 6 drops sesame oil
- 1 handful rice noodles

Direction

- Soak the rice noodles in boiling water in a bowl while preparing the rest of the meal.
- Add peanut oil to a hot wok and stir fry briskly the following ingredients: onion, garlic, chili and ginger. Then add the chicken pieces and stir. Add the chopped Bell pepper and stir again.
- Pour in the hot chicken broth and gentle slide in the drained noodles to the wok and incorporate all the ingredients.
- Stir in the baby spinach leaves and chopped scallions. Sprinkle the sesame oil drops over the surface and do the same with coriander leaves. Viola! Healthy dinner for one. Living alone has its challenges ... but last night all was good.

290.   Spinach And Lentil Soup

Serving: Serves 6 | Prep: 0hours15mins | Cook: 0hours45mins | Ready in:

Ingredients

- 1 1/4 cups brown lentils (dry)
- 6 cups fresh spinach (chopped)
- 1 piece carrot (diced)
- 1 piece celery (diced)
- 1 onion (diced)
- 3 pieces garlic (minced)
- 3 sprigs thyme
- 4 bay leaves
- 1 teaspoon cumin
- 1 teaspoon turmeric
- 1 teaspoon black pepper
- 1 teaspoon paprika
- salt (optional)
- 900 milliliters vegetable broth
- 5 cups water

Direction

- Place the lentils in a large pot and pour the water over the lentils. Cover the pot and bring the water to a boil over medium heat. Lower the heat to low-medium and cook for 15 minutes or until it's al dente.

- Add the carrots, celery, thyme, bay leaves, cumin, paprika, turmeric, black pepper, and vegetable broth to the pot and mix everything together. Cover the pot and cook for 10 minutes.
- Add the spinach and diced tomatoes to the soup and cook for 20 minutes or until everything is cooked through and you're satisfied with the thickness of the soup.

291. Spinach And Mint Soup (Tribute To Evan Kleiman)

Serving: Serves 4 | Prep: | Cook: |Ready in:

Ingredients

- ½ cup extra virgin olive oil (and if you ever refer to it as EVOO I'm going to come down there and smack you with Maxwell's silver hammer and it will leave a mark).
- 1/2 cup chopped sweet onion
- 1 or 2 large new, white potatoes.
- 1 green garlic head including tender green parts (if you can't find garlic and you probably won't, substitute 2 scallions and 2 garlic cloves)
- 2 bunches fresh spinach*
- 3 cups chicken stock preferably homemade. You can use boxed but I won't respect you in the morning.
- A big bunch of fresh mint, chopped
- A bunch of cilantro, chopped. Sorry you cilantro sissies, but it's essential to the flavor. Don't leave it out.
- 2 tsp pimenton de la vera or piment d'esplette.
- 1 tbs crushed and lightly toasted pistachio nuts

Direction

- Begin with ¼ olive oil in a large pan. Sweat down the chopped onion until translucent but not brown. Add the potatoes and garlic clove and continue to sauté. After about 5 minutes of cooking time add your chicken stock and the green garlic (or scallion garlic mix). After fifteen minutes add your washed spinach, followed by the mint and the cilantro. Cover and simmer again. When your soup is cooked through and soupy, season it with salt and pepper.
- Now, welcome to the devil's workshop. Get out your big ass blender, not the wimpy one you use for making Jägermeister margaritas. It should be sturdy. In batches puree the soup mixture. Never fill the blender up to more than half way when using hot liquids. And unless you want to decorate your kitchen in Jackson Pollack green, keep the lid on and hold it down with a towel and your hand while it's running. Repeat as needed.
- In a small pan heat up the remaining olive oil. Don't let it reach the smoke point. To this add your pimenton. Meanwhile in a dry skillet lightly toast the pistachios.
- Serve the soup into individual bowls and drizzle with the pepper oil. If you are using the pistachios sprinkle those on top.
- *Evan used frozen spinach which is perfectly fine especially since you might be whipping this up when you are tired from work. So feel free to substitute.
- **The name "Paprika" covers a multitude of sins. Most of the stuff out there is only good for adding color to deviled eggs. Such as your basic supermarket variety. You can find good Spanish pimentons (and there are many) through specialty markets. My preference here is for the piment d'espelette, because I think it suits the dish better.

292. Spinach, Tomato, Lamb And Rice Broth

Serving: Serves 4 | Prep: | Cook: |Ready in:

Ingredients

- 1 tablespoon light olive oil
- 1 large onion, peeled and chopped/sliced
- 2 cloves garlic, peeled and crushed
- 1 teaspoon sea salt crystals
- 500 grams lamb mince
- 750 milliliters lamb or vegetable stock
- 1 400g tin chopped tomatoes
- 150 grams pre-cooked brown rice
- 1 tablespoon Worcestershire sauce
- 1 200g bag fresh spinach leaves
- Freshly ground black pepper

Direction

- Warm the oil in a soup pot, add the onion, garlic and salt, stir well, cover and sauté over a very low heat until the onion is pale and soft - around 15 minutes.
- Meanwhile, in a hot pan, brown the minced lamb, stirring constantly until the pink color disappears and each mince morsel is slightly crisped around the edges. Remove from the heat, cover and set aside.
- Add the stock and tomatoes to the soup pot, bring just to the boil, lower the heat and simmer for 5 minutes before adding the lamb (with juices) and simmering for a further 5 minutes.
- Add the rice, Worcestershire sauce and a few good grindings of black pepper and simmer for a further 10 minutes then add the spinach and continue simmering until it has just wilted but is still bright green.
- If the soup is a little thick for your liking, add more stock or water then check the seasoning, adding more salt, pepper and/or Worcestershire sauce to taste.
- If you make the soup ahead of time and either refrigerate or freeze it you will likely have to add more stock or water as the rice will swell and absorb quite a bit of the liquid.
- NB: instead of lamb mince and lamb stock you can use beef mince and beef stock, chicken/turkey mince with chicken stock or use vegetable stock with whichever mince you choose.

293.   Split Corn Soup

Serving: Serves 4 | Prep: | Cook: |Ready in:

Ingredients

- 3 tablespoons olive oil
- 1 onion, sliced
- 2 carrots, sliced thick
- 1 leek, sliced thin
- 2 garlic cloves, minced
- 1 tablespoon fresh thyme
- 1 bay leaf
- 2 tablespoons chickpea miso
- 1/2 cup yellow split peas
- 1 yukon gold potato, peeled and diced
- 3 ears corn, kernels cut from the cob
- 2 tablespoons Dijon mustard
- 1/2 teaspoon pepper
- 1 lemon, juiced
- 1/4 cup flat-leaf parsley, chopped

Direction

- In a heavy-bottomed pot, heat the olive oil over low heat. Add the onion, carrot, leek and garlic. Cook the veggies until they turn soft, about 10 minutes.
- Add the thyme, bay leaf, miso and 6 cups of water. Bring to a boil and then let simmer, uncover, stirring occasionally for about 1 hour.
- Add the split peas, potato, and another cup of water. Turn the heat up to medium and continue to cook, stirring occasionally, for another hour.
- Remove the bay leaf. Transfer half the soup to a blender and blend until smooth. If you like your soup smooth, blend the entire batch.
- Add the corn, Dijon, pepper, lemon juice, and parsley. Simmer for another 5 minutes, so everything is warmed through. Serve immediately.

294.   Split Pea Soup

Serving: Makes 2 quarts | Prep: | Cook: | Ready in:

Ingredients

- 1 pound green split peas
- 1 proscuitto head, ham hock, smoked poultry or similar ingredient
- 1 onion
- 2-3 carrots
- 2-3 celery stocks or one fennel bulb (save the leaves and/or fronds)
- 1 quart chicken or vegetable stock
- 4-6 small waxy potatoes, chopped (optional)
- 2-3 cups water
- - salt
- 1 teaspoon dried thyme
- 6-8 peppercorns
- 2 bay leaves
- 4-6 whole cloves
- olive oil

Direction

- Rinse dried green split peas; check for stones and/or pebbles. Slice onion and chop carrots and celery (if using fennel, slice fennel). Prepare aromatics by placing whole cloves, peppercorns, bay leaves, and celery leaves or fennel fronds in tea bag (paper tea bags are available at reputable tea shops in your area); set aside.
- Heat olive oil on medium heat in stock pot, to cover bottom of stock pot. When warm, add vegetables and sauté for 10-12 minutes on medium-low to medium heat. Don't brown the vegetables. When soft, add pinch of salt and the dried thyme; sauté for 30-45 seconds, when the ingredients become aromatic.
- To the sautéed vegetables, add split peas, waxy potatoes (if using), tea bag with aromatics, chicken stock, 2 cups water, and prosciutto head (or smoked meat/poultry).

Bring to a boil, remove scum that has accumulated, & reduce to a simmer. Cover partially and cook for 60-75 minutes. If liquid doesn't cover prosciutto, turn every 20 minutes. After 30 minutes, begin checking liquid; add up to 1 cup of water if soup seems "dry." Be sure to bring soup back to a boil if adding additional liquid, then reduce to simmer.

- When soup is finished cooking, remove prosciutto and bag of aromatics. Allow soup to cool for 10-15 minutes then blend in stock pot, using an immersion blender. You may chop up the meat and add to soup when serving. Serve and enjoy!
- Adding the meat to the cooking process is optional. For meat eaters, it does add to the flavor.

295.   Split Pea Soup With Ham

Serving: Serves 4-6 | Prep: | Cook: | Ready in:

Ingredients

- 2 cups slit peas
- 1 small ham hock
- 150 g thick slices of smoked ham
- 4 leeks
- 4 onions
- 1 tablespoon butter
- 1 celery stalk, diced
- 3 sprigs Thyme
- Bay leave
- 2,5l water
- Pepper
- 4 slices of thick bread

Direction

- Cut the onion and cook it in butter in a pot. Add the celery, lard, leek, ham hock and slices of smoked ham

- Add the 2,5L of water, thyme, bay leave and add pepper to taste. Do not add salt because there is enough salt in the meat already.
- Bring to a boil and let simmer for 1 1/2hr.
- In the meantime, cut the bread into dices and fry the in olive oil. Dry with a towel and set aside
- Take the ham and smoked ham, ham hock, thyme and bay leave out of the soup. Blend the soup in a blender
- Cut some smoked ham and ham hock into bite size pieces, put back in soup. When you serve the soup, top with bread croutons.

---

296. Spring Asparagus Soup With Warm Herbed Chevre Crouton

Serving: Serves 4-6 (depending on the size of the bowl) | Prep: | Cook: | Ready in:

Ingredients

- Spring Asparagus Soup
- 2 bunches of asparagus (about 4 cups when ends are trimmed off)
- 6 cups water
- 1/2 onion, cut into 1" wedges
- 2 cloves of garlic, peeled and crushed
- 1 tablespoon lemon juice
- 6-7 sprigs of fresh thyme
- 3-4 sprigs of parsley
- 10 whole peppercorns
- 3 tablespoons butter
- 2 tablespoons olive oil
- 1 cup spring onions, white and light green parts, sliced (about 4 large onions)
- 1 cup yellow onion, sliced (about 1/2 onion)
- 1 cup sliced leeks
- 3 cloves of garlic, peeled and crushed
- 3/4 teaspoon fresh thyme leaves
- 2 tablespoons fresh parsley leaves, coarsely chopped
- 2 teaspoons yellow mustard seeds
- 2 teaspoons kosher salt, to taste
- 1/4 teaspoon black pepper
- 1/2 cup white wine
- 1 quart asparagus stock
- 2 teaspoons freshly squeezed lime juice
- splash of soy sauce or sriracha hot sauce
- Herbed Chevre Crouton
- 4 ounces chevre
- 2 tablespoons creme fraiche
- 1 garlic clove, minced
- 1/4 teaspoon salt
- 1 1/2 teaspoons mixed herbs, minced (chives, thyme, basil, tarragon)
- 2 tablespoons olive oil
- 1/4 cup bread crumbs

Direction

- Spring Asparagus Soup
- Make the asparagus stock by bringing the water to a boil in a large pot. Break or cut off the bottom 3" of each asparagus stalk. Reserve the top half of the stalk for the soup. Put the bottom half of the stalk in the boiling water and add the next 6 ingredients. Simmer covered for 1 hour. Strain and set aside the stock.
- Melt the butter and oil together in a Dutch oven or large pot over medium-low heat. Slice the asparagus into 2" pieces, which should amount to about 4 cups. Throw them into the Dutch oven along with the leeks, spring onions, yellow onion, garlic, herbs and spices. Cover with a lid, reduce the heat to low and sweat at a very low simmer for about 30 minutes or until the asparagus is very soft.
- Remove the lid, increase the heat to medium-low and add half the wine. Reduce until the wine is completely gone. Add the rest of the wine and reduce again.
- Add the asparagus stock and bring to a simmer for 10 minutes. Puree in a blender or food processor and reheat over medium heat.
- Add the lime juice, a splash of soy or sriracha sauce, correct for seasoning.
- Serve hot with a warm goat cheese crouton in the middle. Since the crouton is already warm

and the soup is hot, it can easily be stirred into the soup when it's eaten. The crouton will dissolve and flavor the soup with herbs and goat cheese.

- Herbed Chevre Crouton
- Heat your oven to 350F. In a small bowl, mix the chevre, crème fraiche, garlic, salt and herbs together until smooth.
- Take a teaspoon of the cheese and form a small patty with your fingers about 1" in diameter. Dip it quickly in olive oil to coat both sides and then into the bread crumbs.
- Bake until soft, about 4-5 minutes. With a spatula, place a crouton in the middle of the bowl of soup and serve.

297. Spring Onion Soup En Croute

Serving: Serves 4-6 servings | Prep: | Cook: | Ready in:

Ingredients

- 4   bunches spring onions or scallions (about 28)
- 1 tablespoon Olive Oil
- 3   cloves Garlic
- 1/2 cup White Wine
- 6 cups Vegetable Broth
- 1 cup Buttermilk
- 2 ounces Goat Cheese
- 2 tablespoons Flour
- 1/2 cup Sour Cream (light)
- 1 teaspoon Horseradish
- 1/4 teaspoon Salt
- 1/4 teaspoon Pepper

Direction

- (NOTE: Follow the instructions for the puff pastry, and thaw overnight in the refrigerator.) Rough chop 2/3 of the onions into 1 inch pieces. Separate the white parts from the green parts. Dice 3 cloves of Garlic.

- Heat up 1 TBLS Olive Oil in a soup pot. Sauté the chopped onion whites for about 4 minutes. Add the Garlic, and sauté for another minute.
- Pour in the Vegetable Broth, and add in the Green Onion tops. Bring to a simmer for about 3 minutes, then turn off the heat.
- Working in batches, ladle about 1 1/2 - 2 cups of the onions and broth at a time into a blender. Hold a towel over the lid, and start on a slow speed, then work up to a faster speed to puree. Pour into a separate bowl until all the soup is blended.
- Pour the blended soup back into the soup pot. Turn heat on to medium. Next, add the Buttermilk, Goat Cheese, Flour, Horseradish and Sour Cream into the blender, and blend until smooth.
- Temper the buttermilk mixture by adding a ladle of the broth mixture and stirring. Slowly stir the buttermilk mixture into the soup pot until mixed.
- Chop the last bunch of Spring Onions, and add to the soup. Bring to a low simmer over medium heat, and simmer for 3 minutes, then turn off the heat.
- Preheat oven to 400 degrees. Roll out the thawed Puff Pastry according to the package, and cut to size for your serving container. Ladle the soup into the serving bowl/cup, and then cover with the puff pastry. Brush the top with an egg wash, and bake for 12 minutes.

298. Spring Pea Soup, Garlic Croutons, Lemongrass Cream

Serving: Serves 6 | Prep: | Cook: | Ready in:

Ingredients

- For the Garlic Croutons
- ciabatta bread, crust removed, cut into 1 inch cubes, to make about 2 cups of cubes
- sea salt and pepper
- olive oil

- unsalted butter
- 2 garlic cloves, sliced
- For the Soup
- 4 tablespoons lemongrass, fat bulb end sliced thin like scallion rounds
- 1 1/2 cups heavy cream
- 4 fluffy tablespoons grated Parmigiano Reggiano (grated with a microplane grater)
- 3 tablespoons unsalted butter
- 2 large garlic cloves, crushed
- sea salt
- 5 cups water
- 2 sprigs parsley
- 2 sprigs mint
- 2 pounds fresh or frozen spring sweet peas (I used mostly frozen and a cup of fresh)

Direction

- For the Garlic Croutons
- Toss bread cubes with salt and pepper. Drizzle lightly with olive oil and toss again.
- In a cast iron pan, melt a hunk of unsalted butter over medium-low heat. Add garlic. When pan is hot, add bread cubes. Cook slowly, turning the cubes as each side browns, or by giving the pan a good shake every now and then (with a dish towel covering the handle, of course.) When nice and golden, remove croutons, and set aside.
- For the Soup
- In a small pot, heat the cream and lemongrass. Let it gently simmer and infuse while you make the soup.
- In a medium soup pot, melt the butter over medium-low heat. Add the garlic and salt, and cook until fragrant and soft, but not browned.
- Add the water. Bring to a boil, then add the herbs and peas. Turn down to a simmer and cook for 5 minutes, or until the peas are tender. Reserve a few spoonful of peas for dressing up your soup, if desired.
- In a blender, puree the peas, herbs and water in batches to minimize hot splashes when you turn the blender on. Make sure your top is on! Place each pureed batch in a large bowl. When done pureeing all the soup, return it to the soup pot, taste for salt, and keep warm over low heat.
- Strain the lemongrass from the cream into a warm-ish bowl. Discard lemongrass. Stir in Parmigiano, and whisk until lightly frothy. I tried using my milk frother, without success. I wonder if it would froth better with half and half? Will try that next time.
- If using, place a spoonful of reserved peas into warmed soup bowls. Ladle soup into bowls. Drop 5 croutons into each bowl. Spoon lemongrass cream over soup, and pull a knife through it to make a decorative pattern, that is, if you're good at that sort of thing (clearly, I am not). Or, much easier, place cream in a small pitcher and let your guests help themselves.
- If serving cold, chill soup and sauce separately in refrigerator for a few hours.

| 299. | **Spring Pea Soup With Rhubarb** |

Serving: Serves 4-6 | Prep: | Cook: | Ready in:

Ingredients

- Pea soup with coconut
- 2 tablespoons olive oil
- 1 small yellow onion, peeled and chopped
- 1 spring leek, washed and sliced, just the white and light green portion
- 1 teaspoon minced fresh ginger
- 2 cups good chicken or vegetable stock
- 2 cups fresh English peas (you could use frozen defrosted peas in a pinch, I think)
- 1 cup coconut milk
- salt and pepper
- rhubarb sauce (see below) and chopped fresh mint for serving
- Rhubarb sauce
- 2 cups chopped rhubarb
- 1/4 cup sugar
- 1 tablespoon water

- salt and pepper

Direction

- Pea soup with coconut
- Heat the olive oil over medium-high heat in a medium soup pot. Add the onion, leek, and ginger stir to coat with oil, then cover and cook over medium for about 5 minutes until soft. You want them to "sweat" but you don't want them to get brown.
- Add in the stock and bring to a simmer (if you like a thicker soup, you could also throw in a chopped potato at this point and simmer it until tender. Once the potato is ready you would add the peas). Then, stir in the peas and cook until the peas are just tender. This goes quickly, just a couple minutes. Then take off the heat.
- Puree the soup in a couple of batches in a blender until quite smooth (and quite green!). Return the soup to the pot and stir in the coconut milk. Season to taste with salt and pepper.
- Spoon the soup into bowls, swirl in a dollop of rhubarb compote and sprinkle generously with chopped fresh mint. I served this soup warm, but I should think it could also be quite good chilled though if you go for chilled you may need to re-blend it to keep the coconut emulsified.
- Rhubarb sauce
- Combine the rhubarb, water and sugar in a small saucepan. Cover and cook over low heat until the rhubarb is falling apart and cooked down into a sauce, this takes around 15 minutes.
- Taste and season with salt and pepper as desired. You could also try stirring in a pinch of coriander. Serve dolloped atop the pea soup.

300. Squid Curry Soup

Serving: Serves 4 | Prep: | Cook: | Ready in:

Ingredients

- 4 ounces thin rice noodles
- 1 bunch scallions
- 2 teaspoons peanut oil
- 2 tablespoons red Thai curry paste
- 14 ounces can reduced fat coconut milk
- 1 1/2 cups low sodium chicken broth
- 1 pound squid tubes and tentacles
- 2 cups bean sprouts
- 1 tablespoon nam pla (Thai fish sauce)
- 1 lime, juiced
- 1 handful fresh cilantro or parsley

Direction

- Prepare the rice noodles. Place noodles in a bowl and pour boiling water over them to cover. Let them soak as you prepare the rest of the soup, but stir them a few times so they don't stick together.
- Heat oil in a medium or large saucepan. Add the curry paste to the oil and cook for 3 minutes, stirring often, until fragrant. Stir in the coconut milk and the chicken broth, then simmer for 2 minutes. Add the squid to the pan, then simmer for 2-4 minutes, until the tubes and tentacles have become opaque.
- Stir in the bean sprouts and the greens of the scallions. Season the soup with nam pla, lime juice, and a pinch or two of sugar if you want to add a little sweetness, then remove it from the heat.
- Drain the noodles and divide them among 4 serving bowls. Ladle the soup over the noodles, then garnish with cilantro or parsley.

301. Strawberry & Tomato Gazpacho

Serving: Serves 4 | Prep: | Cook: | Ready in:

Ingredients

- 250 grams strawberries

- 250 grams tomato
- 3-4 tablespoons aged balsamic vinegar
- fleur de sel to season
- Bunch of basil leaves

Direction

- Finely chop strawberries, add balsamic vinegar, fleur de sel and half of the finely chopped basil leaves.
- Chill and let marinate for at least 5 hours.
- Finely chop tomatoes and add them to the strawberry mixture. Then add the other half of chopped basil.
- If needed, finish with some additional salt and balsamic.

302.   Strawberry Gazpacho

Serving: Serves 5 | Prep: | Cook: | Ready in:

Ingredients

- 1 cup tomato juice
- 1 1/2 cups strawberries
- 2 shallots, minced
- 1 english cucumber, seeded removed and chopped
- 1 red pepper, chopped
- salt and pepper
- 2 tablespoons olive oil
- Toppings: feta, chopped jalapeno, mint, chopped strawberries

Direction

- Put everything in the blender, until nice and smooth. Refrigerate for 1 hour, serve and add any toppings you want. I added feta, mint and jalapeño and the mix of flavors was just divine. (Goat cheese would be nice as well)
- Et Voila, Bon Appetit!

303.   Stuffed Mussels In Tomato Sauce (Cozze Ripiene)

Serving: Serves 4 | Prep: 0hours0mins | Cook: 1hours0mins | Ready in:

Ingredients

- 2 pounds (1 kilogram) live mussels in their shells, cleaned of their beards and any grit
- 3 tablespoons olive oil
- 2 cloves garlic
- 1 14-ounce (400 grams) can of tomatoes (chopped or peeled)
- 1 bunch parsley
- 2 cups (200 grams) dried breadcrumbs
- 3 1/2 ounces (100 grams) stale bread, soaked in a little milk until soft
- 3 1/2 ounces (100 grams) Pecorino cheese, grated
- 2 eggs
- 1 dash Salt and pepper

Direction

- Open the cleaned mussels by steaming them in a large, covered pot. Set aside the liquid for use in the tomato sauce.
- In a large pot, prepare the tomato sauce by gently sauteing one of the garlic cloves, smashed or sliced, in some olive oil until aromatic and soft. Add the can of tomato plus a splash of water and the liquid from the mussels. Turn up the heat until it comes to a boil. Simmer for a few minutes or until reduced slightly then take off the heat, add the parsley and set aside.
- Prepare the stuffing mixture by combining the other garlic clove, chopped finely, the breadcrumbs, the stale bread (squeezed of excess liquid and crumbled into the bowl), the pecorino and eggs. It shouldn't be too solid, but rather a wet mixture. You can add a bit of water to loosen if necessary. Season with salt and pepper.
- Fill the opened mussel shells with a spoonful of mixture, then close them, wrapping some

kitchen string around them to keep them shut. Once they are all filled, add them to the tomato sauce and bring to a simmer. Make sure you are using a pot large enough to fit the mussels and deep enough to that the mussels are all submerged in the sauce (if needed, top up with water). Cook the mussels again for about 15 minutes.

- Serve as is, with a sharp knife to cut the strings, or remove the mussels from the sauce and serve the sauce with pasta and the mussels separately.

304.	Summer Corn And Fish Chowder

Serving: Serves 4 | Prep: | Cook: | Ready in:

Ingredients

- 3 ears of corn, unshucked
- 1 large onion, cut into ½ inch dice
- 1 tablespoon olive oil
- 1 tablespoon unsalted butter
- ½ cup of finely chopped celery and leaves (I use Chinese celery, but conventional will do)
- ½ cup carrots, cut into ½ inch dice
- ½ cup dry white wine
- 1 tablespoon of fresh thyme leaves, coarsely chopped, unless they're small
- 4 cups chicken stock (preferably homemade)
- 1 teaspoon finely chopped fresh marjoram, or more or less to taste
- 3 slices of natural bacon, cooked and drained, and cut into ½ inch dice
- ½ cup half-and-half (See note below.)
- 1 ½ cups whole or 2% milk
- 1 to 1 ½ pound firm white fish (we generally use cod), cut into bite-sized pieces
- 3 or 4 tablespoons parsley, finely chopped
- Salt
- Freshly ground pepper, to taste

Direction

- PREPARE THE CORN STOCK: Shuck the corn, reserving about a half a dozen of the greenest inner husks. Rinse and cut crosswise into 2" strips. Remove the kernels from the corn, using a sharp knife or whatever other method you prefer. Put the cobs and the sliced corn husks in a wide pot with a lid; cover with 3 cups of cold water and turn the heat on high. If you have trimmings from your celery and some extra parsley stems, they can go in the stock, too. When the stock starts to boil, turn it down and simmer for at least 20 minutes. Remove the cobs to a plate to cool, while continuing to simmer the stock.
- When the cobs are cool enough to handle, squeeze all of the milky stuff off of the cob and into the stock, stir well and simmer for a few more minutes. You should have about 2 cups of stock.
- MAKE THE SOUP: In a heavy soup pot, soften the diced onion in the oil and butter with a small pinch of salt over medium heat.
- Add the celery and carrots and cook for a few minutes over medium heat, stirring occasionally. Then add the garlic and cook it for about a minute, stirring frequently to prevent the garlic from burning.
- Add the white wine and give it a good stir, scraping the bottom of the pan to get off any stuck bits.
- Add the thyme leaves, the chicken stock and the corn stock (no more than 2 cups) and bring the soup to a boil. Immediately turn it down and let it simmer, covered, for about five minutes. The carrots should be tender but still firm.
- Turn the heat off, and add the corn and the marjoram. Cover the pot, and let it sit for another ten or fifteen minutes, or more if you have the time.
- A few minutes before you are ready to serve the soup, bring the soup back to a low simmer, and add the fish. Bring it back to a simmer, and add the milk and the half and half. Cook over medium heat just long enough to cook the fish. Depending on the size of the pieces and the type of fish, this should not take more

than a few minutes. Do not under any circumstances allow the soup to boil.

- Test for salt and add some, if necessary. Add freshly ground pepper, to taste.
- Stir in the fresh parsley and serve topped with the chopped bacon pieces.
- N.B. For a lighter soup, use just 2% milk (2 cups) and no half-and-half. You can also leave out the fish, if you like.
- Enjoy!! ;o)

305.   Summer Crab Soup

Serving: Serves 3 | Prep: | Cook: | Ready in:

Ingredients

- 1/2   pound sushi crab, cut into pieces OR 1/2 lb. shrimp, raw OR 1/2 pound oysters, raw
- 1/2   can yellow sweet corn
- 1 bunch   cilantro, chopped
- 1   cup sliced white mushrooms OR black tree-ear mushrooms
- 1   large chicken bouillon cube, crumbled
- 1 teaspoon   dried chopped garlic
- 1/2   bunch green onions, chopped (green only)
- 1/2 teaspoon   powdered ginger
- 1/2 cup   ShaoXing wine
- 1/2 tablespoon   cornstarch

Direction

- Put 2 quarts water on to boil and add the ginger, garlic and bouillon. When the broth begins to boil, add the crab/shrimp/oysters (whichever you prefer) and mushrooms (black or white). Let simmer on low heat for 10 minutes
- Add the corn, cilantro, cornstarch and Shaoxing wine last, and simmer for another 5 minutes, stirring well. Pour into soup bowls and garnish with fresh green onion. Let it sit to cool a moment before serving (this helps it thicken a bit).

306.   Summer Fruit Gazpacho

Serving: Serves 4 | Prep: | Cook: | Ready in:

Ingredients

- 2/3 pound watermelon, peeled and chopped
- 7 ounces cantaloupe, peeled and chopped
- 4 ounces frozen mixed berries (strawberries, blackberries, raspberries, blueberries)
- juice of 1 lime
- 1 tablespoon sugar
- 1/4 teaspoon salt
- 4 tablespoons fat-free yogurt

Direction

- Put the berries in a blender and blend until smooth. Strain through a fine mesh colander to remove the seeds and put the puree back into the blender. Add the rest of the ingredients, except the yogurt, and blend until smooth.
- Serve in a bowl with a tablespoon of yogurt on top.

307.   Sunchoke Lemongrass And Leek Soup

Serving: Serves 6 first courses or 4 lunch entrees | Prep: | Cook: | Ready in:

Ingredients

- 3 tablespoons unsalted butter
- 1   large leek, divided, sliced across the width in thin strips, white and light green parts only
- 4   shallots, peeled and thinly sliced
- 2   garlic cloves, peeled, smashed, and minced
- 2   stalks lemongrass, smashed and cut in two to fit in the pot (they need to be easy to retrieve before pureeing the soup)

- 1 pound sunchokes, well-scrubbed to remove most of the skin and sliced 1/8" thick
- 4 cups vegetable or chicken broth
- 1/3 cup heavy cream
- 1/8 teaspoon ground nutmeg
- 1/2 teaspoon kosher salt, or to taste
- 1/2 teaspoon freshly ground black pepper
- lemon zest to taste
- 1/2 teaspoon chives, minced

Direction

- Important: See the notes above in the summary for prepping tips for the sunchokes. This can take 20-30 minutes to do for 1 lb. of sunchokes, so this should be done first. Slice fairly thinly and soak in lemon water to keep them from turning color.
- Melt the butter in a soup pot and sauté one-half of the leeks and all of the shallots, garlic, and lemongrass until the leeks and shallots are soft and the mixture is very aromatic (about 10-15 minutes).
- Add the sunchokes and mix to thoroughly cover the sunchokes with the leeks lemongrass mixture. Cook for another 5 minutes.
- Add the broth and bring to a simmer until the sunchokes are tender (about 40 minutes). If you don't have any broth, you can use water. Remove the lemongrass stalks and puree the soup in a blender until very smooth. Pour back into the soup pot and reheat. Add the cream, nutmeg, salt and pepper. Add lemon zest to taste.
- For a garnish, I fried the other half of the leek strips in olive oil and a squeeze of lemon juice until they were fairly crispy. I topped the soup with a pinch of them and a few minced chives.

308.   Susan Miglore's One Pot Chicken Chile Soup

Serving: Serves 6 | Prep: 0hours15mins | Cook: 1hours15mins | Ready in:

Ingredients

- 1 whole chicken (or 4 boneless, skinless chicken breasts)
- 3 cups water
- Salt and pepper
- 1 onion, chopped
- 1/2 teaspoon ground cumin
- 1/2 cup rice, uncooked
- 5 ounces frozen corn
- 1 to 2 4-ounce cans chopped green chiles
- 4 to 5 fresh or canned tomatoes, chopped
- Chopped green onion (for garnish)
- Tortilla chips (for garnish)
- Grated cheddar cheese (for garnish)

Direction

- Place chicken, water, salt and pepper to taste, onion, and cumin in a 4-quart pot and simmer for one hour.
- Remove chicken from pot, saving broth.
- If using a whole chicken, debone and remove skin.
- Chop or dice chicken in bite-size pieces.
- Return chicken to pot and add rice, corn, green chiles and tomatoes.
- Let simmer until heated through and rice is cooked.
- Serve in soup bowls over tortilla chips and topped with grated cheddar cheese and chopped green onions.

309.   Sweet Potato & Leek Soup

Serving: Makes 2.5 quarts. | Prep: | Cook: | Ready in:

Ingredients

- 3 large leeks, cleaned and trimmed, halved, and sliced into 1/2" pieces.
- 3 sweet potatoes. peeled, cut into approx. 1/2" cubes
- 8 cups vegetable broth (chicken broth okay)

- 1 teaspoon dried basil
- 4 cloves of garlic, coarse chop.
- 1 dried bay leaf
- 1.5 tablespoons butter
- 1.5 tablespoons olive oil
- .5 teaspoons kosher salt
- 1/3 cup coconut milk

Direction

- In a heavy pot (I used a cast iron Dutch oven), heat the butter over medium high heat until it melts and then bubbles. Add the olive oil and allow it to heat for approximately 10-15 seconds.
- Once the oil has heated, add the leeks and stir to coat with the butter/oil mixture. Stir in the salt. Sauté the leeks, stirring occasionally until they're soft but not browning, approx. 10 minutes.
- Add the potatoes, the stock, the coconut milk, the basil and the bay leaf, stir, and bring to a boil. Once boiling, reduce heat and allow to simmer until the potatoes are cooked through, about 15 minutes.
- Remove the bay leaf. (It's much harder to do this step after you've blended the soup.)
- Once potatoes are cooked through, reduce heat to low, and, using an immersion blender, puree the soup until it's mostly smooth but with a slightly chunky texture.
- Continue simmering over medium heat until the soup thickens to your liking, at least 10 minutes is recommended (mine took about 30).
- Season with salt and fresh ground pepper to taste.
- Serve at your leisure. It goes well underneath a dollop of Greek yogurt and finely chopped green onions.

310. Sweet Potato And Celery Cream Soup

Serving: Serves 4 | Prep: | Cook: | Ready in:

Ingredients

- 1 Sweet Potato (about 0.25lb)
- 1/2 Small Onion
- 1 Garlic Clove, minced
- 1/2 cup Chopped Celery
- 1 tablespoon Butter
- 2 cups Water
- 1 Vegetable Bouillon (1 cube)

Direction

- Peel and cut sweet potatoes into small cubes.
- In a sauce pan, heat butter and cook garlic, onion and celery until tender. Add sweet potatoes. Sauté for a couple of minutes.
- Add water and vegetable bouillon and bring to boil. Cook over medium heat until sweet potatoes are tender.
- Transfer to the blender. Puree all vegetables. Then transfer to the sauce pan again and heat over low heat, season with salt and pepper and simmer for about 5 minutes. Add sour cream and stir well. Turn off the heat. When ready to serve, sprinkle minced parsley.

311. Sweet Potato, Orange And Ginger Cream Soup With Crispy Sweet Potatoes And Chilli Flakes

Serving: Serves 6 | Prep: | Cook: | Ready in:

Ingredients

- 1 pound white sweet potato
- 1 pound orange sweet potato
- 2 medium red onions
- 1 big leek, only white part

- 2 garlics, green part removed
- 2 cups milk
- 2 bay leaves
- 3 cups vegetable stock
- 1/2 cup orange juice freshly squeezed (choose sweet oranges)
- 2 ounces butter
- 2 inches fresh ginger
- salt
- 1 dash freshly ground nutmeg
- pepper freshly ground
- 2 pinches chilli flakes for garnish
- 1 tablespoon fresh cilantro chopped for garnish
- 1 tablespoon Extra Virgin Olive Oil for garnish
- 1/2 cup canola oil for frying the sweet potatoes
- 2 pinches Maldon salt for garnish

Direction

- In a pan over medium heat, put the milk and bay leaf and let simmer for 5 minutes. Set aside and let infuse. Wash and dry the cilantro leaves, chop and set aside.
- Warm up your vegetable stock and keep it on a low simmer.
- Peel and wash the sweet potatoes. If you prefer you can use only orange or only white sweet potatoes, you choose. From the orange sweet potato cut 3/4 cup of straw thin potatoes with a lemon zester. Put them in a bowl with cold water and set aside. Cut the remaining potatoes in small cubes, wash and put in a bowl with cold water.
- Chop the onions and crush the garlics removing the green part from the inside. Cut the bottom of the leek with the roots, remove the outer leaf plus the dark green part of the top. On a chopping board, slice the leek down the middle and then slice in 1/2 inch pieces. Put in a bowl under running cold water and wash thoroughly to remove any sand attached. Drain and set aside. Peel the ginger and cut it up in pieces.

- In a large enough pot, over medium heat, melt the butter cut up in pieces. As soon as it starts to sizzle add the onions, leeks and garlic, and stir until the onion is translucent. Watch the heat so it doesn't burn any of the vegetables as it will make the soup taste bitter. Add the drained potatoes cut up in cubes, stir all the vegetables together for 2 minutes. Add the milk infused with the bay leaf and enough vegetable stock to cover the vegetables. Keep the remaining vegetable stock warm.
- Cover the pot and simmer over low heat about 25 minutes until the potatoes are cooked. Add salt, freshly ground black pepper and the nutmeg.
- Discard the bay leaves and put the soup in a food processor or use a hand held immersion blender and blend very well until creamy. Add the orange juice and blend again. If the soup is too thick add some more vegetable stock. If it's too thin let it simmer over low heat, without lid, until you obtain the right consistency.
- Strain the soup over a clean pot, through a medium mesh sieve, pressing with the back of a ladle. Discard all the fibrous parts that remain mainly from the ginger and the leek.
- Check the seasoning. Set aside and keep warm.
- In a medium pan bring the canola oil to a boil. Pat dry the finely shredded orange sweet potato in a clean tea towel and fry until just barely golden. Drain on kitchen paper towel. Keep warm.
- Heat up the soup, pour in plates, sprinkle some cilantro, add in the middle of the plate the fried sweet potatoes, sprinkle with Maldon salt and chilli flakes, add a drizzle of Extra Virgin Olive Oil and serve immediately.
- Enjoy as much as we do!

312.   TLCs Chili

Serving: Makes 8 qt | Prep: | Cook: | Ready in:

Ingredients

- 1 medium yellow onion, chopped
- 1 medium sweet yellow pepper, chopped
- 1 medium sweet red pepper, chopped
- 3 small chili peppers, seeded and chopped
- 2 Jalapeño peppers, seeded and chopped
- 3 garlic cloves, minced
- 2 tablespoons extra virgin olive oil
- 15 ounces chicken broth
- 30 ounces regular canned black beans, rinsed and drained
- 1.5 lbs. ground chicken
- 15 ounces can, solid pack pumkin
- 14.5 ounces can, diced tomatoes with chiles
- 2 teaspoons dried parsley
- 12 ounces bottle of chili sauce
- 1.5 teaspoons dried oregano

Direction

- In a stainless 12-Quart Stockpot, you will want to sauté' the onions, garlic, and peppers in olive oil until the onions just start to soften. Add the ground chicken to the pot, breaking it up and then the wine. Simmer until the chicken is just cooked through. Add the remainder of the ingredients to the pot and bring to a boil. Turn down the heat to a simmer for 30 minutes, stirring as needed to prevent sticking or burning. Welcome to Chili Heaven... Enjoy...

---

313. Tabbouleh Soup

Serving: Serves 4-6 | Prep: | Cook: | Ready in:

Ingredients

- 1 cup bulgur
- 1 tablespoon olive oil
- 1/2 purple onion
- 1 garlic cloves
- 4 cups quality vegetable stock
- 1 bunch fresh parsley, chopped

- 1 bunch fresh mint, chopped
- 1-2 lemons
- 1 cup cucumber, chopped
- 200 grams cherry tomatoes

Direction

- Bring water to a boil and pour over the bulgur, covering with a few inches. Allow to sit aside until the water has been absorbed and the bulgur is tender. Strain away remaining liquid.
- Heat up olive oil in a stockpot and sauté garlic and onions for a few minutes. Add vegetable stock and bring to a simmer.
- Add the mint, half of the chopped parsley, and lemon juice gradually to taste (this will vary depending on how much soup stock you want to use). Simmer for 15 minutes and adjust the seasonings to taste, especially if you've used homemade stock.
- Stir in the tomatoes and cucumbers, allowing to cook gently for another few minutes.
- To serve, ladle warm broth over bowls of bulgur and sprinkle with the remaining half of chopped parsley. Drizzle with extra virgin olive oil and a sprinkle of freshly cracked black pepper. Lovely with some toasted pita to dip and scoop.

---

314. Taco Soup

Serving: Serves 6 people | Prep: | Cook: | Ready in:

Ingredients

- 1 onion, chopped
- 1 red pepper, chopped
- 1 green pepper, chopped
- 1 packet Taco Seasoning mix
- 1 packet Dry Ranch Dressing Mix
- 1 can chili beans
- 1 can black beans
- 1 can kidney beans
- 1 can diced tomatoes

- 2 cans Rotel tomatoes
- 1 can corn

Direction

- Throw everything into crockpot without draining any of the cans.
- Stir together and cook on low for 6-8 hours
- Serve with corn chips, shredded cheese and sour cream. If you want it spicer, serve with diced jalapenos also.

---

315.   Thai Red Curry Chicken Soup

Serving: Serves 4 | Prep: | Cook: | Ready in:

Ingredients

- 5 cups chicken stock, homemade or purchased
- 1   package, rice noodles, preferably medium thickness
- 2 tablespoons Thai red curry paste
- 3 tablespoons fish sauce
- 1/2 can, coconut milk
- 2 tablespoons sugar
- 2   limes, zested and juiced
- 3 tablespoons Cilantro, minced
- 2 tablespoons mint, minced
- 1-2 cups shredded rotisserie chicken or roasted chicken
- 1 tablespoon sesame oil

Direction

- Sauté the curry paste in the oil for a few seconds to infuse the oil. Add the stock, fish sauce, coconut milk, sugar, lime zest and half the juice, and let it come to a boil.
- Add the rice noodles and cook for a few minutes until softened. Add the chicken and allow to warm through.
- Off the heat, add the herbs and the remaining lime juice and serve.

---

316.   Thai Red Curry Soup With Prawns And Glass Noodles

Serving: Serves 2 | Prep: | Cook: | Ready in:

Ingredients

- 1 large can coconut milk
- 2 stalks lemongrass
- 2 cloves garlic, finely diced
- 1 thumb sized piece of ginger, finely diced
- 1 onion, finely diced
- 1 lime
- 2 handfuls mushrooms
- 1 red bell pepper
- 2 handfuls morning glory
- 3 tablespoons red curry paste, maybe more depending on the paste
- 1 teaspoon sugar
- cilantro (optional)
- 1 ounce glass noodles
- 7 ounces prawns, peeled and cleaned
- coconut oil
- salt and pepper

Direction

- Soak the noodles in cold water (according to packaging). Slice the mushrooms, the red pepper and cut the leaves from the morning glory. Set aside.
- Cut a cross into the lemongrass stems and smash them with the back of the knife. Cut the lime in quarts. In a large pot heat 2 tablespoons of oil over medium high heat. Once hot, add ginger, garlic and onion. After 2 minutes add the curry paste and fry for two more minutes, stirring occasionally. If you like it spicy, add some more. Reduce heat to medium.
- Add the lemongrass, coconut milk, the juice of a quart of the lime, sugar and a cup of water (250 ml). Add the mushrooms, pepper, prawns and stems of the morning glory. Season with salt and pepper and cook for about 3 minutes.

Strain the glass noodles and add them to the soup. Cook for about two minutes (or what it says on the package, if they need to cook longer, add earlier). Just before they are done, add the leaves of the morning glory.

- Serve with the remaining lime wedges.

Serving: Serves 2 | Prep: | Cook: | Ready in:

Ingredients

- For the marinade
- 1 Lime, zested and 1/2 juiced
- 1 Red chili pepper, grated (The pepper's skin will be left over, which should be diced and saved for later)
- 1 teaspoon Ginger, grated
- 2 -3 Cloves garlic, grated
- 1 tablespoon Vegetable or coconut oil
- 1 teaspoon Honey
- 1 bunch Basil leaves, chopped (chopped Reserve half to use in the soup later)
- 1 pinch Salt
- For the soup
- 2 Chicken thighs with legs attached OR 2 diced chicken breasts
- 1/2 Onion, diced
- 1 tablespoon Ginger, diced
- 2 Cloves garlic, diced
- 1 teaspoon Fish sauce
- 1 teaspoon Tamarind paste
- 12 ounces Coconut milk, fresh or canned
- 1/4 Lemon, juiced
- Salt, to taste
- Dried chili flakes, to taste

Direction

- Combine all the ingredients of the marinade together in a small bowl and whisk with a fork to combine. Place the chicken in a plastic bag and pour over the chicken. Let stand for 20-30

minutes at room temperature or up to 2 hours in the fridge. (Be sure to remove 15-20 minutes before cooking to bring the chicken to room temperature)

- Heat a soup pot over medium-high heat and add vegetable oil. Add the chicken and sear until golden brown on the outside, then remove.
- Add some more oil, then add the onions and a pinch of dried chili flakes, then fry until translucent (about 5 minutes).
- Add the ginger, garlic, and red pepper skins (left over from the marinade) and fry for 1-2 minutes until the garlic is fragrant. Then add the fish sauce and tamarind paste, then give everything a good stir to combine the flavors. (Don't forget to scrape the bottom of the pot to remove all the charred bits of pure flavor left over from the chicken ☐)
- Re-add the chicken to the pot, followed by the coconut milk. Let simmer over medium-low heat for 10-20 minutes, or until the chicken is cooked and beginning to flake apart. (Check back relatively frequently since coconut milk has the tendency to boil over!)
- Add a pinch of healthy salt, red chili flakes, remaining lime juice, a dash of lemon juice, and some more chopped basil. Taste and adjust accordingly. Plate, garnish with some chopped fresh cilantro, and enjoy out in the sun with a side of freshly-made rice ☐ ☐

Serving: Serves 4 | Prep: | Cook: | Ready in:

Ingredients

- Rich Chicken Broth , Noodles,Fennel and Salmon
- 5 cups rich chicken broth(10 cups canned or fresh mild stock)
- 2 teaspoons toasted fennel seed

- 2 cups of fennel bulb, cut into 1/4 inch dice
- olive oil
- 4-8 ounces ramen or whole wheat dry spaghetti-thin noodles , broken into 2 inch pieces
- 8 ounces skinless boneless salmon filet, cut into 4 pieces
- Finishing the soup base; Assembly
- 5 cups rich chicken broth
- 8 large eggs
- 1/3 - 1/2 cup fresh lemon juice
- 2-3 teaspoons tamari to deepen flavor
- freshly ground black pepper
- optional fennel fronds for garnish
- optional garnish of shredded nori (kizumi nori)

Direction

- Reduce chicken stock with the fennel seed by 1/2 till you have a rich tasting stock. About halfway through reducing, taste the stock. If there is not a subtle fennel flavor, add more seeds. When you have a rich stock, strain out and discard the fennel seeds. Set aside broth over low heat. (A flame tamer is perfect for this.)
- Cook noodles in boiling salted water till al dente. Drain in a colander under cold water, set aside. Pour out half the pasta water and keep the remainder on medium heat with a lid (you will use it to reheat the pasta before serving.).
- Dice fennel and sauté in hot olive oil till tender, 5-8 minutes, over medium high heat
- Preheat broiler.
- In a bowl, whisk together the eggs and lemon juice. Briskly whisk in 1 cup of hot chicken stock and then whisk this back into the pot, whisking continually and stirring the pot bottom with a flat edged wooden paddle or a heat -proof spatula to keep the avgolemono from overcooking and curdling in the bottom corners of the pot. Stir often with whisk for about 10 minutes till mixture thickens slightly and will coat the back of the spatula. Do not allow it to get bubbles around the edge or the

soup will curdle. Season with tamari, pepper and salt.
- When the soup has thickened slightly, return the pasta to the hot water fora few minutes before draining. Set the salmon, oiled, on a pan very close to the broiler flame. Broil it for just a few minutes, until browned and rare to medium rare inside.
- Add the hot drained pasta and the sautéed fennel to the thickened soup and stir well till hot. Taste and add lemon juice, tamari or S&P as needed. Portion into bowls, topping each with one piece of salmon. Garnish with a fennel frond, pepper, optional kizumi nori; serve.

319. The Best Vegetable Broth Ever

Serving: Makes about 2 quarts | Prep: 0hours0mins | Cook: 0hours0mins | Ready in:

Ingredients

- 1 large carrot
- 5 celery stalks (with leaves)
- 1 large yellow onion, cut in half but not peeled
- 1 medium parsnip
- 1 small fennel bulb, cut in half, with fronds
- 1/2 pound fresh shelled English peas OR 1 (12 oz) bag frozen peas
- 1 bunch fresh parsley
- 1 small golden beet, stemmed and halved
- 1/4 head cabbage, roughly chopped
- 6 whole cloves
- 12 whole black peppercorns
- Pinch of crushed red chile flakes
- 3 quarts water

Direction

- Rinse any lingering dirt from the vegetables. Combine all ingredients in your largest stockpot–if you need to, cut the veggies into chunks to fit in the pot. Cover, bring to a boil, and then reduce heat to keep at a bare simmer. Simmer for 2-3 hours, or until the broth is richly flavored. Strain out the solids.

- Use the broth immediately, or freeze for 4-6 months.

320.   The Zuppa

Serving: Makes 1 large stockpot of soup | Prep: | Cook: | Ready in:

Ingredients

- 1 small yellow onion
- 1 1/2 pounds pork sausage
- 6-8 russet potatoes
- 32 ounces chicken broth
- 4 cups water
- 10.5 ounces cream of chicken soup (1 can)
- 1 1/2 tablespoons Italian seasoning
- 1/2 teaspoon crushed red pepper flakes
- 1 1/2 tablespoons minced garlic (jar)
- 2 bay leaves
- Salt and pepper to taste
- 1/2 pint heavy whipping cream
- 3 cups fresh kale
- crumbled bacon
- shaved parmesan

Direction

- Slice onion into smaller pieces and place in skillet on stove with two tablespoons of salted butter. Cook on medium until onions start to soften. Set aside.
- Brown the sausage. We sprinkle some crushed red pepper flakes in with the sausage!
- Slice the potatoes with the skin on. Do not cut into too small slices because as they cook down they shrink!
- Place sliced onions, sausage, sliced potatoes, chicken broth, water, cream of chicken, Italian seasoning, minced garlic, bay leaves, and salt and pepper in a stock pot. Cook on medium to

high until potatoes are soft. After potatoes are soft taste the base of your soup and add more salt and pepper to your liking!

- Time for garnishes! Frozen bacon is so much easier to work with. It slices pretty nice when it's froze! Slice bacon with kitchen scissors into 1 inch pieces and cook until crispy!
- Add the heavy whipping cream and chopped kale into the soup and heat until heated through. Serve immediately.
- Garnish soup with crumbled bacon, shaved parmesan cheese and crushed red pepper flakes!

321.   Three Day Ribollita (From Soup To Fritters)

Serving: Serves 6 | Prep: | Cook: | Ready in:

Ingredients

- Day 1
- 3 tablespoons olive oil
- 1 large onion, chopped
- 2 carrots, chopped
- 2 celery stalks, chopped
- 2 garlic cloves, thinly sliced
- 1 tablespoon chopped fresh thyme
- 28 ounces can of whole, peeled tomatoes
- 1 pound cavolo nero, or a combination of kale, Savoy cabbage, collard greens, Swiss chard, and/or spinach, de-ribbed and sliced
- 16 ounces can of cannellini beans, drained
- 3 cups water
- Kosher salt and freshly ground black pepper, to taste
- Day 2 and 3
- 8 slices day old Tuscan or country bread, crusts removed
- Good quality extra virgin olive oil, to finish
- 2 tablespoons Olive oil, for pan-frying
- Grated Parmigiano-Reggiano, for garnishing

Direction

- Day 1
- Day 1: In a large Dutch oven or saucepan, heat the olive oil over medium heat. Add the chopped onion, carrots, celery, and a pinch of salt and cook until the onion is soft and translucent, about 10-15 minutes. If the vegetables start to brown, lower the heat. Add the garlic, thyme, and another pinch of salt and cook for another minute or two, until fragrant.
- Add the tomatoes and their juices and the sliced greens. Bring to a boil and keep stirring until the greens are wilted and cooked down. Add the beans and enough water to just cover all the vegetables, about 3 cups. Bring to a boil and then lower the heat and simmer until all the vegetables are tender. Salt and pepper to taste. You can serve the soup at this point with some fresh Tuscan bread. Refrigerate the remaining soup.
- Day 2 and 3
- Day 2: Tear the bread into small pieces and add to the soup. Bring to a boil again, and then simmer for 30 minutes, stirring to dissolve the bread into the soup. It should be thick enough that you can stand a wooden spoon in the soup. Ladle the soup into bowls and drizzle with a generous amount of your favorite finishing olive oil.
- If there are still any leftovers, continue to simmer the soup until most of the liquid has evaporated and then refrigerate.
- Day 3: Make handful size patties from the leftover soup and then refrigerate the patties for at least 30 minutes.
- Heat 2 tablespoons of olive oil in a frying pan over medium-high heat. Pan fry the patties, flipping once after the bottom is brown and crispy, about 5 minutes. Fry on the second side until the patties are heated through. Serve immediately, finished with additional olive oil drizzled on top and some grated Parmigiano-Reggiano.

322.   Tomato & Basil Soup

Serving: Serves 4 | Prep: | Cook: |Ready in:

Ingredients

- 4   Tomatoes
- 2   Garlic Cloves
- 1 tablespoon Balsamic Vinegar
- 1   tin of Chopped Tomatoes
- 200 milliliters Chicken/Vegetable Stock
- 1 handful Basil

Direction

- Pre-heat your oven to 200C/400F/Gas Mark 5.
- Slice the tomatoes and add them to a baking dish.
- Cover with the balsamic vinegar, and add salt and pepper to taste.
- Roast in the oven for 30mins.
- After 20mins of the roasting time has elapsed, chop and onion and put it into a saucepan, on a medium heat.
- Fry for 5mins, adding the chopped garlic. Fry for a further 5mins.
- Take the tomatoes out of the oven, and add to the onion and garlic. Fry for 5mins further.
- Add in the tin of chopped tomatoes. Fill the tin with chicken stock, and add to the soup base.
- Bring to the boil, and then simmer for 45mins with the lid on the saucepan.
- Take the soup off the heat, and add in the basil. Stir through, and cover with the lid. Leave for 10mins.
- Blitz the soup in a liquidizer, and then pour back into the saucepan.
- Either serve now, or reheat later!

323.   Tomato Basil Soup

Serving: Serves 6-8 or more | Prep: | Cook: |Ready in:

Ingredients

- 9-10 large tomatoes, peeled and chopped
- 1/4 cup olive oil
- 1 tablespoon kosher salt
- 1 1/2 teaspoons freshly ground black pepper
- 2 cups Vidalia onions, chopped
- 6 cloves of garlic, minced
- 2 tablespoons butter
- 1/4 teaspoon crushed red pepper flakes
- 1 28 oz can chopped tomatoes, with juice
- 4 cups packed with shredded fresh basil
- 1 quart chicken stock

Direction

- In a large stockpot over medium heat, sauté the onions and garlic with some of the olive oil, the butter, and red pepper flakes until the onions start to brown.
- Add all of the tomatoes, basil, and chicken stock.
- Bring to a boil and simmer uncovered for 40 minutes.
- Use an immersion blender to puree everything in the pot. The basil will still be in strips and pieces, but everything else will be blended.
- Season to taste with the salt and pepper. If the tomatoes are very acidic, you may want to add a little sugar.
- Optional: 1 cup of cream or half and half may be added at this time. It is very good without it. This soup is also very good cold.

324.   Tomato Soup From Fresh Tomatoes

Serving: Serves 4 | Prep: | Cook: | Ready in:

Ingredients

- 1000 grams ripe tomatoes
- 1 onion
- 3 cloves of garlic
- 1 small carrot
- 2 bayleaves
- salt, pepper to taste

- fresh basil
- 1 dash balsamic vinegar
- olive oil
- 1 tablespoon sourcream

Direction

- Wash and dry the tomatoes, then chop them roughly. Try to squeeze out excess water and seeds. Peel onion, garlic and carrot. Finely slice onion and garlic cloves and grate the carrot.
- In a soup pot, heat olive oil, then add onions and lightly fry them until translucent. Add grated carrots and garlic, stir-fry for about a minute or two, until the carrots tenderize. Then, add in chopped tomatoes and a dash of balsamic vinegar, stir well and let it cook down for a few minutes, stirring regularly.
- Add vegetable stock, bay leaves and season to taste with salt & pepper. Bring to a boil, then lower the heat and cook for about 15 minutes.
- When the tomatoes are cooked, remove the pot from heat, then remove the bay leaves and blend into a smooth soup with a stick blender.
- Roughly chop basil leaves and add to the soup for taste and garnish, add a teaspoon of sour cream and serve.

325.   Tomato And Egg Soup

Serving: Serves 2 | Prep: | Cook: | Ready in:

Ingredients

- 4 cups chicken broth
- 2 tomatoes, chopped
- 1 egg
- a pinches of salt
- 1 scallion, sliced into thin rounds

Direction

- Chop the tomatoes into small chunks.
- Heat a little oil in a soup pan, add tomatoes and cook for a couple minutes.

- Add the chicken broth to the pan and cook until it starts to boil. Let it simmer for a couple minutes.
- Beat the eggs in a bowl. Slowly drop the beaten egg into the soup and stir gently until egg is set. Add salt and scallions, and serve.

326.   Totally Inauthentic Tortilla Soup

Serving: Serves a crowd | Prep: | Cook: | Ready in:

Ingredients

- Soup
- 1 large onion, diced
- 1 red or yellow pepper, diced
- 1 jalapeño, minced
- 1 tablespoon Cumin, divided
- 8 ounces cream cheese (low fat is fine)
- 1 10 oz can rotel (or other brand diced tomatoes with chilis) - your choice of heat
- 1.5 quarts chicken broth
- 1 14 oz can black or pinto beans, rinsed and drained
- 1 14 oz can corn, rinsed and drained (or fresh, if available)
- 1 Rotisserie Chicken, skin discarded (or nibbled on by the chef) and meat shredded
- 2 limes, zest and juice
- 1 bunch cilantro, leaves and stems finely minced
- salt & pepper
- olive oil
- Toppings
- grated cheddar or jack cheese
- sliced avocado
- quartered limes
- tortilla chips
- sliced scallions

Direction

- Sauté the onion, jalapeño, and pepper in a couple tablespoons of olive oil over medium high heat until soft, 4-5 minutes
- Add 2 tsp. of cumin and stir for 45 seconds.
- Add the cream cheese and stir until melted and completely incorporated with the onions and peppers. This step is important - if the cream cheese is not completely incorporated, it will clump when you add the broth.
- Stir in the rotel and stir until incorporated.
- Add the broth and stir. Bring to a boil and then lower heat. Let simmer for 5-8 minutes.
- Add the corn, beans, lime zest, remaining 1 tsp of cumin and chicken. Simmer for five more minutes.
- Remove from the heat and stir in the lime juice and cilantro
- Place the toppings in individual bowls.
- Serve the soup, allowing each guest to add the toppings of his or her choice.

327.   Touchstone Sweet & Sour Cabbage Soup

Serving: Serves 8? | Prep: | Cook: | Ready in:

Ingredients

- 2 1/2 pounds Beef short ribs or shanks (or any flavorful bone-in cut)
- 4 cups Low sodium beef broth (or homemade beef stock)
- 5 cups Water
- 1 28 oz. can crushed tomatoes (or canned whole tomatoes, broken up into small pieces, with their juices)
- 1 Head (2 – 2 ½ pounds) cabbage, roughly chopped in bite size pieces/strips
- 3 Medium onions, quartered and sliced
- 4 Good sized carrots, sliced
- 1-2 teaspoons Kosher salt, or to taste, depending on saltiness of broth
- Freshly ground black pepper, to taste (about 1/2 tsp)

- 5 tablespoons Light brown sugar
- 1 Lemon, juiced
- 1 Bay leaf
- 2 tablespoons good Hungarian sweet paprika (not Spanish smoked)
- 5 tablespoons Dried currants
- Sour cream (optional)

Direction

- In a large soup pot, bring broth, water and beef to a boil. Lower heat and simmer about 10 minutes, skimming any residue that rises to the surface.
- Add all the remaining soup ingredients, except the currants. (It will seem like a lot of cabbage at first, but will cook down substantially.)
- Bring back to a boil, then lower the heat, cover and simmer for around 2 hours, stirring occasionally. Then add the currants and cook another 30 minutes, or until the meat is falling off the bone tender.
- Taste and adjust flavor, if needed, by adding more salt, or pepper, lemon juice and/or brown sugar. It should be sweet and sour, but not cloyingly sweet or mouth-puckeringly sour.
- Discard the bay leaf and fish out the bones and any large chunks of meat that have fallen away. When cool enough to handle, discard the bones, shred the meat into bite-size pieces and put it back into the soup.
- You can eat the soup right away, but the flavor improves after a night or two in the refrigerator, which also allows you to easily discard the solidified fat from the surface. Reheat gently, stirring occasionally.
- Serve hot, topping each bowl with a dollop of sour cream.

328.   Turkish Farmers Soup

Serving: Serves 4 | Prep: | Cook: | Ready in:

Ingredients

- 1/3 cup Bulgur wheat or Pearled barley (or ~1.5 cup cooked)
- 1 cup Plain Greek style or full fat yogurt
- 2 cups Stock or water
- 2 tablespoons Lemon juice, or to taste
- 1/4 cup Fresh dill, finely diced
- Salt, to taste

Direction

- Cook the Bulgur or Barley in lots of salted water until tender (~30 minutes for cracked bulgur, ~1 hour for pearled barley).
- Bring the stock or water to a boil.
- Turn the heat down to low-medium and whisk in the yogurt until it's smooth and well-blended.
- Slowly whisk in the lemon juice - that is, whisk quickly and add the lemon slowly. I don't like it too lemony, but if you like a lemony taste, you could probably use as much as 1/4 cup.
- Add the bulgur or barley to the soup and simmer lightly (without boiling!) for 5 - 10 minutes. Salt to taste.
- When the soup is hot, but not boiling, turn off the heat and whisk in the dill (if you're using dry, use ~1.5 tablespoons). Serve!

329.   Turmeric & Coconut Cream Add A New Dimension To The Classic Leek & Potato Soup

Serving: Serves six 8 oz. portions | Prep: | Cook: | Ready in:

Ingredients

- 1 pound Fresh Leeks
- 2 Medium Russet Potatoes
- 3 Large shallots
- 5 Cloves of garlic
- 4 cups Water

- 3 tablespoons Olive oil
- 1/3 teaspoon Black ground pepper
- 1 teaspoon Salt
- 1.5 teaspoons Turmeric powder
- 1 tablespoon Unsalted butter
- 2 tablespoons Low fat plain Greek yogurt
- .5 cups Coconut cream
- 2 tablespoons Fresh chopped parsley

Direction

- Prepare ingredients and gather cooking pots and utensils. Peel and cut the potatoes into 1 inch squares, slice the leeks into 1/4 to 1/2 inch slices and soak in cold water for 10 minutes, then remove into a dry bowl with your hands, chop shallots, crush garlic with a knife and then chop finely.
- In an 8 to 10 inch diameter pot, heat the olive oil over medium high heat. When oil is hot, saute the shallots until translucent, then add the garlic. Continue to saute for another minute.
- Begin to add the leeks a handful at a time, saute for about a minute between handfuls. Once all leeks are cooking, stir and continue to saute for another few minutes reducing heat to medium.
- Next, add the 4 cups of water and bring to a boil. Once water is boiling, add the potatoes, salt, and pepper and lower heat to low, cover, and continue to cook for about 20 minutes.
- After 20 minutes, using a fork, check to make sure the potatoes are tender and cooked. Using a ladle, transfer approximately 4 scoops into a prepared food processor.
- To the food processor, now add the coconut cream, butter, and Turmeric powder. Process until everything is well blended and the mixture is silky smooth. Once accomplished, return the mixture to the pot with the remainder of the soup, stir until well blended.
- Lower heat to simmer and allow to finish on simmer for another 5 minutes. Serve hot, with a sprinkle of chopped fresh parsley or cilantro. Perform a final taste to adjust your salt and pepper to your desired level. Enjoy.

- This preparation should serve 8 ounce portions for a party of six. Tips: When preparing the leeks, cut the top 2 inches of the stalks and discard; however, please use the rest of the green as well as the white parts. The green part is where most of the nutrients are and it enhances the flavor of your soup.

330.　Tuscan Bean Soup With Pumpkin And Kale (Zuppa Frantoiana)

Serving: Serves 4-6 | Prep: | Cook: | Ready in:

Ingredients

- 1 small carrot, finely chopped
- 1 stick celery, finely chopped
- 1 small onion, finely chopped
- 1 14 ounce tin (400 grams) of cooked Borlotti (cranberry) beans (cannellini beans or chickpeas also work well here)
- 1 wedge of pumpkin (about 7 ounces/200 grams), peeled and diced
- 1-2 small-medium potatoes, peeled and diced
- 1 small bunch of cavolo nero (you could use silverbeet or spinach instead)
- 4 cups (1 litre) of water or vegetable stock
- salt and pepper to taste
- Extra virgin olive oil, for drizzling
- Toasted bread rubbed with garlic, optional for serving

Direction

- Gently cook the carrot, celery and onion in a few tablespoons of olive oil and a good pinch of salt in a heavy-bottomed saucepan or stovetop casserole on low heat. Let the vegetables sweat, not color, for about 10 minutes or until softened. Add the borlotti beans with about a cup of water (enough to cover) and bring to a simmer. Cook 15 minutes. Blend about half of the mixture to a smooth paste and return to the pot.

- In the meantime, prepare the cavolo nero by slicing out the long, central stalk of the leaves and discarding—this is very tough—and chop just the leaves roughly.
- Add the pumpkin, potatoes and cavolo nero (if using silverbeet or spinach hold onto it until a few minutes towards the end of cooking) and top with enough water or stock to cover (up to 4 cups or 1 liter) and cook for 30 minutes, uncovered, over an active simmer so that the liquid reduces slightly and the vegetables are tender. Adjust seasoning.
- Serve with a good grinding of black pepper, a drizzle of olive oil, and toasted bread rubbed with garlic and drizzled with olive oil.

331.   Ukrainian Borscht Served With Garlicky "Pampushki"

Serving: Serves a crowd | Prep: | Cook: |Ready in:

Ingredients

- For the Borscht
- 4 Duck leg quarters and the carcasses of two young birds washed, excess fat removed and reserved
- 3 to 3 1/2 quarts cold water
- 1 large onion, peeled, make a deep X-shape cut not all the way through
- 1 head of garlic, washed and cut in half crosswise
- 2 medium carrots, peeled and cut in half lengthwise
- 2 celery stacks, (preferably with leaves) each cut in two or three pieces
- 1 large or 2 medium parsley roots, peeled and cut in half lengthwise
- 1 medium fresh beet, peeled and cut in half
- 1 red bell pepper, seeds and membranes removed and cut in half
- 4 teaspoons coarse salt
- 2 bay leaves

- A bunch of fresh thyme, parsley and dill, tied together
- 3 medium russet potatoes, cut in about 1/2-inch chunks
- 1/2 head of a medium cabbage, or more for a thicker consistency, shredded a little wider then for a coleslaw
- 2 cups homemade or prepared tomato sauce (I like 100% natural Hunt's no salt added)
- Sour cream, lemon juice, additional chopped parsley, dill and garlic for serving
- For the Pampushki: Makes 16
- 1 1/2 cups warm water
- 1 tablespoon active dry yeast
- 2 tablespoons sugar
- 2 tablespoons olive oil
- 1 teaspoon salt
- 4 cups bread flour

Direction

- For the Borscht
- Place the meat into an about 5-5 1/2 quarts large stock pot. Cover with cold water, transfer to stove and bring to boil on medium heat. Skim off any foam that rises to the top a few times, put in all the vegetables (reserve potatoes and cabbage) bay leaves, herbs and salt.
- Cover and simmer on low heat for 2 hours. (If I use beef I cook it for a long time to make sure the meat is extremely soft and practically melts in your mouth.)
- When the meat is tender, using a slotted spoon, transfer it and all the cooked vegetables and herbs to a colander placed over a bowl, strain the stock and return to the pot.
- Cook potatoes in the stock, then add tomato sauce and cabbage. I add the cabbage after the tomato sauce to prevent it of getting too soft, I like it still a little crunchy. Cut the cooked beet into matchsticks and add to the borscht, the acid in tomato sauce keeps the bright color of the beet.
- Take of the meat from the bones, discard the skin and pull the meat apart in bite-size pieces,

return the meat to the pot or keep it separately and add to each bowl of borscht when serving.

- When serving, you can also add some additional flavors to compliment borscht, so here are some traditional variants. Add a tablespoon of sour cream in your soup bowl or some lemon juice, sprinkle with a mix of chopped parsley, dill and very fine minced garlic or put a pinch or more of dried red pepper flakes in each bowl. Be careful because it is pretty spicy!

- If you are expecting some dear or important guests, you can amaze them with Pampushki. Pampushki are small dinner rolls, baked and while still hot, spread with a mix of: For the 16 Pampushkis you will need: freshly ground black pepper to taste, 4 cloves of minced garlic, 1 teaspoon of vinegar, 1 1/2 teaspoons of sunflower (or vegetable) oil, and a few drops of water. Since I had the reserved duck fat, I rendered it and used instead of oil.

- For the Pampushki: Makes 16

- Mix together warm water, yeast and sugar and let stand for about 10 minutes. In large bowl, combine yeast mixture with oil, salt and 2 cups of the flour. Stir well to combine.

- Stir in remaining flour 1/2 cup at a time, kneading well after each addition. Turn out onto a lightly floured surface and knead until smooth and elastic.

- Lightly oil a large bowl and place dough in and turn to coat with oil. Cover with cloth and let rise in warm place until doubled, about 1 hour.

- Deflate the dough and turn out onto floured surface. Divide dough into 16 equal pieces and form into rounds. Place rolls onto lightly greased baking sheet at least 2-inches apart. Cover rolls with cloth and let rise until doubled, about 40 minutes.

- Preheat oven to 400 degrees and bake rolls for 20 minutes or until golden brown. Spread with the garlicky mix and serve with a hot bowl of Ukrainian Borscht.

- You can also fill the Pampushkis with deferent fillings and serve as a snack or as a part of a buffet table.

Serving: Serves 4-6 | Prep: | Cook: |Ready in:

Ingredients

- 2/3 cup sausage meat
- 1   medium onion chopped
- 1/2 cup green pepper chopped
- 1/2 cup red pepper chopped
- 1/4 cup celery chopped
- 1 handful mushrooms chopped
- 6.5 ounces chopped clams (opt.)
- 14.75 ounces can cream corn
- 3 pieces of bacon cut or chopped
- 1/4 teaspoon garlic salt flakes
- 1/2 teaspoon steak seasoning
- 1/2 cup heavy cream
- 2 tablespoons cream chesse (opt.)
- 2/3 cup milk
- 4 tablespoons butter
- 1/2 cup grated sharp cheddar cheese
- 1 dash salt
- 1 dash pepper

Direction

- In skillet brown up sausage meat, separate it into small pieces. Then add 2 tbsp. butter, garlic salt flakes.
- Sauté onions, peppers, celery, mushrooms, bacon pieces, clams (opt.). When cooked down, remove from heat.
- Add steak seasoning, stir in let set for 3 mins.
- In medium saucepan combine cream corn, all sautéed ingredients.
- Over medium heat add the heavy cream, cream cheese (opt.), milk, remaining butter.
- Cook for 2-3 mins. Then add grated sharp cheddar cheese.
- Stir occasionally to incorporate all the ingredients.

- Then add the dash of pepper, dash of salt to taste.

---

333. Unambigously Baked Baked Potato Soup

Serving: Serves 6 | Prep: | Cook: | Ready in:

Ingredients

- 4 pounds potatoes (about 10 medium), washed and dried
- 2 tablespoons olive oil (divided)
- 1 and 1/2 teaspoons coarse sea salt (divided)
- 3/4 teaspoon coarse black pepper (divided)
- 6 slices uncooked bacon (about 6 ounces total)
- 2 tablespoons white all-purpose flour
- 3 cups chicken stock
- 1/2 teaspoon fine kosher or table salt (and maybe more to taste)
- 1/4 teaspoon dried ground sage (and maybe more to taste)
- 3 cups coarsely grated cheddar cheese
- 6 tablespoons sour cream
- 6 tablespoons chopped green onions

Direction

- Preheat oven to 450°F.
- Place the potatoes on a large baking sheet. Drizzle with 1 tbsp. olive oil and sprinkle with 1 tsp coarse sea salt and ½ tsp black pepper. Rub each potato to coat with the oil and to spread the seasoning around. Put the pan of potatoes into the oven and bake until they yield easily to a fork prick, about 45 minutes.
- Meanwhile, cook the bacon according to package directions. Reserve 2 tbsp. of the bacon fat. Coarsely chop the cooked bacon.
- In a large pot, warm the reserved bacon fat over medium-low heat. Whisk in the flour, reduce heat to low and cook while stirring for one minute. Slowly whisk in 1/2 cup of the chicken broth making sure the mixture is smooth. Gradually whisk in the remaining chicken broth and 2 cups of water.
- Chop half of the potatoes into 1 inch chunks and add these pieces to the pot along with the chopped bacon. Slice the remaining potatoes in half and scoop the fluffy white insides into the pot. Slice the hollowed out potato skins into 2-inch pieces. Put the sliced potato skins back onto the baking sheet. Drizzle them with 1 tbsp. of the olive oil and sprinkle with 1/2 tsp coarse sea salt. Toss to coat and spread them in a single layer. Put the pan back into the oven for 20-25 minutes or until skins are well-browned and crispy.
- While the potato skins are browning add the table salt, 1/4 tsp coarse pepper and the sage to the soup pot. Bring the pot of soup to a simmer over medium-high heat, stirring occasionally. Taste the soup and add more salt, pepper and sage if needed. Reduce heat to low and cover the pot to keep the soup warm until the skins are ready. Stir the soup occasionally.
- Place six oven-safe soup bowls onto a large jelly roll pan (this makes it easier to get them in and out of the oven). Fill each bowl 2/3 full of the soup. Sprinkle each with 1/2 cup cheese. Now the pan of potato skins and the pan of bowls swap places (skins onto counter, bowls into oven). Bake the soup until the cheese is melted (5-ish minutes).
- Top each bowl of carb-y cheesiness with some crispy potato skins, a tbsp. of sour cream and a tbsp. of green onions. Slurp! Crunch! Crunch! Slurp! Slurp!

---

334. Unbelievably Quick Black Bean Soup

Serving: Serves 6 | Prep: | Cook: | Ready in:

Ingredients

- 2 cups low-sodium salsa

- 2 15-ounce cans low sodium black beans, rinsed and drained
- 1 15-ounce can white hominy
- 2 cups vegetable stock
- 1 lime, juiced
- low-fat shredded cheddar cheese
- sliced jalapeños
- baked tortilla chips

Direction

- Place salsa in a large saucepan over medium-high heat and bring to a boil.
- Reduce heat and simmer 5 minutes, or until most of the excess liquid has been reduced.
- Add hominy, stock, and lime juice. Cook 15 to 20 minutes, or until heated through. If you prefer a thicker soup, you can remove and puree 1 cup of bean mixture and stir it back into soup.
- Serve with garnishes: cheddar cheese, jalapeños, and tortilla chips.

---

335.   Vadouvan N.28 Butternut Soup

Serving: Serves 10 | Prep: | Cook: |Ready in:

Ingredients

- 1/2 cup olive oil
- 3 cups thinly sliced onion
- 2 cups thinly sliced celery
- 2 cups thinly sliced leeks, thoroughly washed
- 3 tablespoons chopped garlic
- 1/2 cup peeled and thinly sliced carrots
- 1 Granny smith apple, peeled, cored, and thinly sliced
- 2 tablespoons Vadouvan N.28 spice blend
- 1 tablespoon freshly grated ginger
- 2 tablespoons light brown sugar
- 5 pounds butternut squash, peeled, seeded, and cut into ½-inch dice
- 2 1/2 quarts water or low sodium chicken stock

- 1/2 cup heavy cream (optional)
- Salt and pepper

Direction

- In a large heavy bottomed stockpot heat the olive oil. Add the onions, celery, leeks, garlic, apple, and carrots. Cook over medium heat for about 15 minutes until tender, stirring every few minutes. Add the Vadouvan spice, ginger, and brown sugar and cook for 5 more minutes. Add the butternut squash and water. Season with salt and pepper, and bring to boil over high heat. Reduce the heat, and simmer for 1 hour, or until the squash is very soft. Add the heavy cream, if using, bring to boil, and simmer for 10 more minutes. Blend until smooth using a blender or an immersion blender. Season to taste before serving.
- Serving ideas:
- • Add the juice of one lemon to the soup just before serving.
- • Drizzle a spoonful of yogurt on top of each soup bowl before serving.
- • Use this soup recipe as a sauce for your favorite pasta, adding a few toasted pumpkin seeds as garnish.

---

336.   Vegan & Gluten Free Pot Stickers

Serving: Makes 16 dumplings | Prep: | Cook: |Ready in:

Ingredients

- Filling
- 250 grams spinach, wilted, drained and chopped
- 100 grams mung bean sprout, wilted, drained and chopped
- 2 dried shiikate, hidrated, drained and chopped
- 1 carrot, chopped
- 100 grams chopped mushrooms (I used cremini)

- 1/2 courgetted, chopped
- 1 tablespoon tamari soy sauce
- 1 teaspoon sesame oil
- 1/2 teaspoon salt
- cracked pepper to taste
- 1 tablespoon corn starch
- 1 teaspoon vegetable oil
- Dumpling wrappers
- 160 grams Gluten free flour (I used Schär bread mix)
- 125 grams boiling water
- 1 pinch salt

Direction

- For the filling, fry the finely chopped carrots, courgettes and shiitake with a bit of oil until slightly cooked. Take off the heat
- Combine the pan mix with all the other ingredients. Reserve
- Make the dough: in a bowl, combine flour, salt and boiling water with a fork. Once cold enough to touch roll the dough into a ball.
- Pinch small portions of the dough, about the size of a big grape (roughly 15g) and open into a circle with a rolling pin. Add flour if it starts sticking.
- Add about a tablespoon of filling for each wrapper. Damp the edges of the wrapper with water. Lift opposite sides of the circular wrapper and pinch them together. Make 3 folds on each side of this pinch and close the dumpling. Repeat until the dough is finished.
- To cook them, add enough oil to cover the bottom of a nonstick frying pan. Once warm, add the dumplings being careful with the hot oil. They will become golden at the bottom. At this point add water to cover the bottom of the pan (about 1/3 cup). Place a lid and cook on medium low heat until all the water is evaporated. Serve.
- Tips: Be careful not to overcrowd the pan. It's ok for the dumplings to touch each other. I cook them in a 20in pan, 6 at a time.

337.   Vegan Roasted Vegetable Everyman Ramen

Serving: Serves 4 | Prep: | Cook: | Ready in:

Ingredients

- Roasted Vegetable Ramen Broth
- 2 medium yellow onions (about 1 ½ pounds), peeled and roughly chopped
- 6 heads garlic , tough stem removed, then halved
- 4 medium Asian pears (about 2 pounds), cut into eighths and deseeded
- 4 large carrots (about 1 pound), roughly chopped
- 1/2 cup olive oil
- 12 cups filtered water
- 1 cup low sodium soy sauce
- 4 inch knob fresh ginger (about ¼ pound), diced
- 6 dried shiitake mushrooms
- 1 piece dried kombu
- Vegan Roasted Vegetable Everyman Ramen
- 4 cups cooked ramen noodles
- 6 cups roasted vegetable ramen broth (recipe above)
- 1 cup red kale, tough stems removed and roughly chopped
- 4 ounces mushrooms of choice, thinly sliced and sautéed
- 1/4 cup cilantro, roughly chopped
- 1/4 cup green onions, sliced into thin rings
- sriracha and togarashi (optional)

Direction

- Roasted Vegetable Ramen Broth
- Preheat oven to 425 degrees F, rack in the middle.
- On a rimmed baking sheet lined with parchment paper, toss onions, garlic, pears, carrots and olive oil until well combined. Place in oven and roast for 60 minutes, tossing every 15 minutes for even cooking, or until vegetables are fork tender and slightly charred.

- Transfer roasted vegetables to large pot. Add filtered water, soy sauce, ginger, mushrooms, and Kombu, and bring to a boil over high heat. Reduce heat to medium-low and simmer until stock is reduced by half (about 2 hours). Thoroughly strain solids from broth. Set broth aside.
- Vegan Roasted Vegetable Everyman Ramen
- Disperse ramen noodles evenly amongst four large bowls.
- In a large pot return broth to a boil. Add kale and mushrooms and simmer for 1 minute, or until kale has just wilted. Pour broth and vegetables evenly over each of the ramen bowls. Top with cilantro, green onions, sriracha, and togarashi. Serve and enjoy!

338. Vegetable Soup With Roasted Tomato Pistou

Serving: Serves 6 to 8 | Prep: 0hours45mins | Cook: 1hours0mins | Ready in:

Ingredients

- Roasted Cherry Tomato Pistou
- 1 pint cherry tomatoes, halved
- 6 tablespoons extra-virgin olive oil, divided
- Kosher salt, to taste
- Freshly ground black pepper, to taste
- 2 sprigs fresh thyme (or ¾ teaspoon dried thyme)
- 1 pinch red pepper flakes (optional)
- 6 garlic cloves, left whole with skin on
- 1/2 cup reserved fennel fronds (see Vegetable Soup below)
- 1/2 cup fresh basil leaves, roughly chopped
- Vegetable Soup
- 2 tablespoons extra-virgin olive oil
- 9 ounces baby potatoes, scrubbed and halved (for larger potatoes, do a 1/2-inch dice)
- 2 medium carrots, scrubbed and chopped in to 1/2-inch coins (2 cups chopped)
- 1 medium bulb fennel, roughly chopped in 1/4- to 1/2-inch pieces (2 cups)
- 1 leek, cleaned and sliced 1/4-inch inch thick (or 1 small yellow onion, peeled and cut into 1/4-inch dice)
- Kosher salt and freshly ground black pepper
- 1 tablespoon chopped fresh rosemary, thyme, or another hearty herb such as marjoram or savory
- 3 quarts vegetable stock
- 1 (15-ounce) can white beans, drained and rinsed (or whatever beans you have on hand)
- 6 ounces green beans or wax beans, tips removed and cut into 1 1/2–inch pieces
- 1 medium bunch of greens (such as kale, collards, escarole, or chard), washed, stemmed and sliced crosswise into 1/2-inch ribbons.

Direction

- Heat the oven to 400°F. Dump the cherry tomatoes onto a parchment-lined sheet pan and toss with 1 tablespoon of olive oil, the salt, pepper, thyme, and red pepper flakes if using. Combine the garlic cloves and 1 tablespoon of olive oil in a small piece of foil (about 12x7-inch). Fold the foil over the cloves and crimp to make a packet; nestle next to the tomatoes on the sheet pan.
- Roast for 25 to 30 minutes on the top rack of the oven, rotating the tray and stirring the tomatoes halfway through. When they are done, the tomatoes should be soft, wrinkled, and beginning to caramelize in spots. The garlic cloves should give instantly when pierced with a toothpick or paring knife. Remove from the oven.
- While the tomatoes and garlic are roasting, begin the soup: Warm the olive oil over medium-high heat in a large pot. Add the potatoes, carrots, fennel, and leek, with a generous pinch of salt. Sauté over medium heat, stirring occasionally, for about 7 minutes, until the fennel and leek have begun to caramelize, and the potatoes and carrots vegetables have begun to soften. Add 1 tablespoon of chopped fresh rosemary or

thyme (or a combo of both) and continue to stir, adding olive oil along the way if the pot seems dry.

- Slowly add the stock, stirring and scraping up the bits stuck to the bottom of the pot. Add the white beans and bring to a low boil. Continue to cook for 10 to 15 minutes at a simmer, adjusting the heat as needed until the potatoes are soft (check around 8 minutes) and the beans have absorbed some brothy flavor.
- Add the green beans and greens to the pot and let these simmer for 5 to 7 minutes, until the green beans are bright and tender. Taste the broth for seasoning and adjust with salt and pepper. Cut the heat and let the soup mingle while you finish the pistou.
- Transfer the roasted tomatoes (including all their oils and juices) to a food processor or clean cutting board. Push the soft garlic cloves from their skins and add to the tomato mixture.
- If you're using a food processor, pulse a few times to roughly chop. Add the fennel fronds and basil and pulse to combine. With the food processor running, stream in the remaining 1/4 cup of olive oil until the pistou is nearly smooth but a few chunks of tomato remain. If you're using a knife and board, chop until the pieces are about 1/8-inch in size and scrape the mixture into a medium bowl. Now finely chop the herbs and add to the bowl with the tomatoes. Drizzle in the olive oil and stir to combine well. Regardless of method, taste for seasoning here, adding more chile flakes, salt, and/or pepper to taste.
- To serve: Ladle your soup into serving bowls. Top with a generous spoonful of the tomato pistou. Optional but highly recommended — serve with grated cheese, toasted bread, or lemon wedges to squeeze on top.

339.   Vegetarian Borsch

Serving: Serves 4-6 | Prep: | Cook: | Ready in:

Ingredients

- 2 tablespoons olive oil
- 1   onion
- 2   cloves of garlic, minced
- 0.5 teaspoons caraway seeds, ground
- 1 pound beets, peeled and diced
- 2 cups cabbage, shredded
- 1   potato, peeled and diced
- 2   sticks of celery, diced
- 0.5 fennel bulb, thinly sliced
- 2 tablespoons tomato paste
- 0.25 cups brown sugar
- 2 liters good quality vegetable stock
- 3 tablespoons apple cider vinegar
- sour cream, chopped dill, drizzle of gin, black bread to garnish (optional)

Direction

- In a large pot, heat olive oil.
- Add onion, garlic, caraway seeds and cook for 2 minutes.
- Toss in vegetables and continue cooking until tender.
- Add stock, tomato paste and sugar and simmer for 30 minutes, uncovered.
- Remove from heat and add the vinegar.
- Season to taste.
- Garnish with a dollop of sour cream, chopped dill and a drizzle of gin and serve with black bread on the side.

340.   Vegetarian Pho Broth

Serving: Makes about 3 quarts (enough for two 4-serving batches of pho) | Prep: | Cook: | Ready in:

Ingredients

- 1   large or 2 small onions, peeled and quartered lengthwise
- 2 ounces fresh ginger (a 3- to 4-inch piece, depending on thickness)
- 2 tablespoons peanut oil

- 2 medium leeks, white and green parts, coarsely chopped into 1-inch pieces
- 2 large carrots, coarsely chopped into 1-inch pieces
- 1 medium daikon radish (12 ounces), peeled and coarsely chopped into 1-inch pieces
- 10 garlic cloves, peeled
- 1 stalk fresh lemongrass, smashed and coarsely chopped
- 3 whole star anise
- 3 whole cloves
- 2 cinnamon sticks
- 1/2 teaspoon fennel seeds
- 5 dried shiitake mushrooms
- 1 handful fresh cilantro stems

Direction

- Preheat the broiler. Arrange the onions and ginger on a foil-lined baking sheet. Once the broiler is hot, broil the vegetables close to the heat source until charred all over, flipping them with tongs as needed. Remove the onions if they cook more quickly than the ginger, or vice versa.
- Alternatively, char the onions and ginger over the open flame of a gas burner, turning them periodically, until blackened all over. This will need to be done in a few batches.
- Heat the oil in a stockpot over medium-high heat. Once hot, add the leeks, carrots, daikon, garlic, lemongrass, star anise, cloves, cinnamon, and fennel seeds. Stir to coat in the oil, then cover and cook for 5 minutes, until fragrant and the colors of the vegetables are vibrant. Coarsely chop the charred ginger, then add it, along with the onions and the mushrooms, to the pot and cover with cold water; you'll need about 4 quarts. Bring to a boil, then reduce to a gentle simmer and cook for 1 hour, at which point the broth should be strongly flavored. Add the cilantro stems and cook for another 5 minutes.
- Strain the broth through a cheesecloth-lined sieve, in batches as necessary, gathering up the ends of the cheesecloth so as to squeeze out as much liquid as possible. Once completely

cooled, pack in containers and store in the refrigerator for up to 1 day, or in the freezer for up to 2 months.

---

341. Vegetarian Split Pea Soup

Serving: Serves 6 | Prep: 0hours10mins | Cook: 0hours40mins | Ready in:

Ingredients

- 1 carrot, diced
- 2 onions, diced
- 1 teaspoon salt
- 1 tablespoon olive oil
- 1/2 pound mixed mushrooms, chopped
- 16 ounces Split Peas
- 1 cup white wine (optional - could replace with 1-2 tbsp vinegar or lemon juice)
- 5 cups vegetable stock or water
- 2 - 3 handfuls spinach
- Hot smoked paprika, for serving (optional)
- 1.5 cups croutons, for serving (optional)

Direction

- Prepare carrots, onion, and mushrooms. Heat olive oil in stock pot over medium heat. Add carrot and onion, cook until onion is translucent (5 min). Add the mushrooms and brown lightly. Deglaze pan with white wine scraping up bits at the bottom of the pot.
- Add split peas stirring in with vegetables. Then add stock or water and bring to boil. Reduce heat to simmer and cook for 35 minutes. Add a few handfuls of spinach and continue to simmer until spinach is wilted.
- When spinach has wilted, using either an immersion blender or regular blender, puree half of the soup until smooth. Return to pot. Season with additional salt and pepper to taste. Serve with smoked paprika and croutons.

342.   Vegetarian Taco Chili

Serving: Serves 8 | Prep: | Cook: | Ready in:

Ingredients

- 2 tablespoons oil
- 1 jalapeno, seeded and diced
- 1 onion, diced
- 2 cloves garlic, minced
- 3/4 cup brown rice, uncooked
- 1 package taco seasoning (or 1 tablespoon)
- 1 (15 oz) can diced tomatoes
- 1/2 cup salsa
- 1 (15 oz) can black beans, rinsed and drained
- 1 (15 oz) can kidney beans, rinsed and drained
- 1 (11 oz) can corn, drained
- 1 quart vegetable broth or water

Direction

- Sauté jalapeño, onion, and garlic in a large pot over medium heat. Cook until soft, about 5 minutes. Add seasoning and rice. Stir together. Add canned ingredients, broth and salsa. Bring to a boil and simmer, covered, for 45 -60 minutes. Serve with avocado, green onion, cilantro, and corn chips. Serves 4-6.
- This stores well in the fridge for 2-3 days or freeze in individual portions for up to 3 months.

343.   Viet Hapa Pho

Serving: Serves 6 | Prep: | Cook: | Ready in:

Ingredients

- For the soup
- 2 medium yellow onions, halved
- 1 4-inch piece of ginger, quartered
- 6 pounds beef bones
- 1 pound oxtail
- 5 quarts water
- 1/2 cup fish sauce
- 2 bay leaves
- 1 cinnamon stick
- 1 tablespoon black peppercorns
- 3 pieces star anise
- 6 cloves, whole
- 2 tablespoons brown sugar
- Salt and pepper, to taste
- 1 packet rice sticks (pho noodles)
- 1/2 pound beef tenderloin, thinly sliced
- Garnishes
- Bean sprouts
- Cilantro
- Lime wedges
- Thai basil

Direction

- Over the open flame of a burner, char onion and ginger halves until fragrant and blackened.
- In a 10 to 12-quart stockpot, place beef bones, onion, ginger and oxtail. Cover with 5 quarts of cold water (bones should be completely covered. If not, add more water).
- Bring beef bones and water to a boil over high heat, then reduce heat to medium-low and simmer for 1-1/2 hours, skimming all impurities from bones that float to the surface.
- Add cinnamon stick, star anise, bay leaf, cloves, peppercorns, fish sauce and sugar to broth. Continue to simmer for another 1-1/2 to 2 hours, skimming surface of broth as needed.
- Taste broth. Depending on how much marrow is in the bones you use, you may need to simmer for longer and reduce the liquid to get that full-bodied beef taste. Remove bones and spices from broth. Season with salt and pepper.
- (This is an optional step.) When broth is to your liking, cool broth and place in refrigerator overnight. In the morning, take pot out of fridge and skim fat off of surface of broth.

- To assemble: Reheat broth to a boil. Soak pho noodles in a bowl of water until soft. Drain.
- Heat water in a 4- to 5-quart pot. When water comes to a boil, add soaked noodles. Cook for 3 to 5 minutes, or until noodles are soft. Drain, and portion noodles into bowls.
- Place thinly sliced raw tenderloin on top of noodles. Ladle broth over meat and noodles. Top with garnishes and serve hot.

---

344. Vietnamese Chicken Noodle Soup (Pho Ga)

Serving: Serves 4 | Prep: | Cook: | Ready in:

Ingredients

- 3 chicken breast, shredded
- 8 cups homemade chicken stock
- 1 medium yellow onion, cut in half and unpeeled
- 1 small piece of fresh ginger, unpeeled
- 1 teaspoon coriander seed
- 2 whole star anise
- 1 cinnamon stick
- 2 garlic cloves
- 1 teaspoon sugar
- 2 tablespoons cooking fish sauce
- rice noodles
- lime wedges
- fresh cilantro leaves

Direction

- Char the ginger and onion by placing them over an open flame, hot griddle, or under the broiler (~8 minutes).
- In a pan, dry roast the spices (~2 minutes) and stir to prevent burning. This will bring out the flavor!
- Peel and scrape away the charred skin of the onion and ginger.
- In a large pot, add 8 cups of homemade chicken stock. Place spices in a spice bag. Add the spices, ginger, onion, sugar, and cooking

fish sauce into the pot. Cover and bring to a boil and then reduce heat to medium low (~30 minutes). Remove spice bag. Add your shredded chicken pieces.
- Add cooked rice noodles to the soup bowls. Ladle chicken broth over the noodles. Serve with lime wedges and cilantro.

---

345. Warm Up White Chili

Serving: Serves 5-6 | Prep: | Cook: | Ready in:

Ingredients

- 2 tablespoons olive oil
- 1 onion, chopped
- 3 garlic cloves, minced
- 15 ounces can of diced tomatoes w/ green chilies
- 6 tomatillos, chopped
- 1 jalapeño, halfway deseeded
- 2 cups chicken stock
- 7 ounces can of green chilies, chopped
- 3 chicken breasts, cooked and shredded
- 1/4 teaspoon oregano
- 1/4 teaspoon cumin
- 2 15 ounce cans of Great Northern beans, undrained
- juice from 1 lime
- salt and pepper to taste
- crushed tortilla chips and shredded cheddar cheese to garnish

Direction

- In a Dutch oven, under medium high heat, heat up the oil and sauté the onions until soft, about 5 minutes. Then add in garlic and stir until fragrant, a minute or two.
- Stir in tomatillos, tomatoes, and jalapeño. Cook for another 5 minutes so tomatillos can soften.
- Add chicken stock, green chilies, chicken, oregano, cumin, beans, and lime juice. Season with salt and pepper to taste. Cover and

simmer until ready to serve, stirring occasionally. I let mine sit for about 30-45 minutes to let the flavors really meld together.

- Ladle into soup bowls and garnish the tortilla chips and cheddar cheese.

346.   Watercress Soup

Serving: Serves 4 | Prep: | Cook: |Ready in:

Ingredients

- 3/4 liter Chicken Stock
- 1 tablespoon Butter
- 2 tablespoons rapeseed/canola oil
- 1/2 small onion, finely chopped
- 300 grams watercress blanched
- 1/2 stalk of leek chopped in strips
- 1/2 cup heavy cream
- Amaranth pops and some fresh leaves of watercress for decoration

Direction

- Prepare your chicken stock, or use store bought chicken stock, blanch your watercress: by cooking for 2 min in boiling water then transferring to ice water - this helps keep the color bright green.
- The onions and the leeks are sautéed in butter, the warm soup added, simmer on medium heat until all the leeks are tender, 12 min approx. Take the soup off the heat. Blend on high speed, leave no clumps!
- The blanched Watercress goes into the blender and with the help of the rapeseed oil mixed into a bright green paste!
- This paste is added to the creamy soup (NO more cooking from now on, only gently heating) and once again blended, add the cream, mix again, salt and chili and garnish shortly before eating with the Amaranth Pops and the fresh sprig of watercress.

347.   West African Chicken Peanut Stew

Serving: Serves 4 | Prep: | Cook: |Ready in:

Ingredients

- 8 chicken thighs
- 1 teaspoon ground coriander (cilantro)
- salt to taste
- ground black pepper to taste
- 2 red bell peppers
- 1/4 scotch bonnet chillies
- 2 1/2 tablespoons vegetable oil
- 2 bay leaves
- 1 jumbo cube (optional, see notes)
- 8 tablespoons smooth peanut butter
- 3 tablespoons tomato puree
- 4 1/4 cups water (1 litre)

Direction

- Season the chicken pieces with coriander, salt and pepper and set aside.
- Peel and slice the onions and garlic.
- Deseed and chop peppers and scotch bonnet chilies.
- Heat 1.5 tbsp. of oil in a nonstick frying pot and quickly brown chicken pieces. You might have to do this in two or more batches as you don't want to crowd the pieces in the pot. Remove pieces from the pan and set aside on a plate.
- Heat the remaining oil in the pot and throw in the onions, garlic, scotch bonnet, bay leaves and 6 tbsp. of water and stir very well. Fry for about 5 minutes until the mixture very fragrant. (Take note of this fragrance as this is what I call the real salone food smell).
- Throw in the red pepper, stir it and fry the mixture covered for another 5 minutes. Then add in the peanut butter, tomato puree, jumbo cube and stir fry quickly for 30 seconds until these are both mixed in.

- Add in the browned chicken pieces and the water, bring to the boil, reduce and simmer for about 50 minutes. Stir the mix a couple of times during the 50 minutes as the peanut butter could settle at the bottom of the pot.
- Taste stew and adjust salt and pepper and then turn off.
- Serve with rice (plantains or bread) and garnish with nuts, herbs and spring onions.
- Notes -The peanut stew foams up during boiling, so you need to reduce it to a simmer as soon as it starts to boils. Jumbo cube (or maggi cube) is a stock cube used to flavor food in Sierra Leone. It can be bought in a lot of shops selling ethnic food. If you don't want to use a jumbo cube then omit it and replace the water with some stock.

---

348. White Bean Soup

Serving: Serves 6-8 | Prep: | Cook: | Ready in:

Ingredients

- 1/4 cup extra virgin olive oil, plus additional for drizzling
- 1/2 cup celery, diced (about 2 stalks)
- 2 cups carrots, diced (about 3 whole)
- 1 tablespoon fresh garlic, minced (about 3 cloves)
- 1/4 teaspoon crushed red pepper, more if you want a kick
- 1 teaspoon dried oregano
- 1/2 teaspoon whole fennel seed, lightly crushed with the back of a knife
- 2 tablespoons tomato paste
- 6 broth or bean soaking water
- 7 white beans, soaked and cooked
- 1/2 teaspoon salt, more to taste (depends upon the saltiness of your broth)

Direction

- Heat olive oil in a large soup pot. Add celery, carrot, garlic, crushed red pepper, oregano,

and fennel. Cook, stirring until vegetables begin to soften and everything is fragrant.
- Add salt and tomato paste, continue to cook for a few more minutes, stirring to coat the vegetables in tomato paste.
- Add broth and cooked beans. Bring to a boil, then turn heat down to a simmer. Use a potato masher to mash the beans right in the pot. You don't need to mash up every bean, just break them down to add thickness to the soup. Let simmer partially covered for about 20 minutes until soup is thick and bubbly, stirring occasionally. Taste, and add additional salt if needed.
- Serve with an additional drizzle of olive oil.

---

349. White Bean Soup With Garlic And Sausage

Serving: Serves 4 | Prep: | Cook: | Ready in:

Ingredients

- At home:
- 1/4 cup plus 1 tablespoon olive oil
- 2 mild Italian sausages sliced into 1-inch rounds
- 2 cloves garlic, finely chopped
- 2 cups dried cannellini beans, cooked and drained
- Salt
- Freshly ground black pepper
- 1 cup warm chicken stock
- 1/2 cup fresh flat-leaf parsley leaves, chopped
- Pizza (optional, see headnote)
- At work:
- 2 tablespoons olive oil

Direction

- Heat a small sauté pan over medium heat for a moment. Add 1 tablespoon of the oil, and heat for 1 minute. Add the sausage to the pan. The heat must be lively enough that they sizzle but not so intense that they burn—adjust it accordingly. Cook the sausages for 6 to 8 minutes, turning them several times while they brown and cook through. (Alternatively, heat the oven to 375° F. Coat the sausages lightly in oil, place them on a rimmed baking sheet or roasting pan, and bake for 25 minutes. Do not prick the sausage — you want them to cook from within. Let them cool before slicing them into rounds). Remove them from the pan with a slotted spoon, and set them aside on paper towels to drain.

- In a soup pot, heat the remaining 1/4 cup of the oil and the garlic over medium heat. Cook, stirring occasionally and keeping careful watch, until it is aromatic, 2 to 3 minutes. (If you brown the garlic, start over; the heat was too high, and the burnt taste will ruin the delicate soup.)

- Add the beans, stirring them into the oil and garlic. Season with some salt and pepper, and cover the pan. You want to aromas to infuse the beans. Cook the beans, covered, for 3 minutes, and then stir in 1/2 cup of the stock.

- Using a slotted spoon, remove about one-third of the beans and process them through a ricer back into the pan. This will thicken the soup. Gradually add the remaining stock to the mix, stirring and keeping the mixture at a simmer. The warm stock will loosen the soup, so add more or less to suit the consistency you desire. You will find the balance of the whole beans and the mashed beans and the liquid — that is your soup. Taste and season with salt and pepper, add the sausage and the parsley, and stir to combine.

- The soup will keep in an airtight container in the refrigerator for 3 to 5 days.

- When you reheat the soup at work, add 2 tablespoons of water to loosen its surface, then stir the top to combine everything evenly. Drizzle the top with a thin line of the oil just before serving.

- Serve the soup with slices of soft white bread to sop it up, or serve it at room temperature as a side dish to a salad. Or, follow the directions in the headnote to make pizza soup.

Serving: Serves 8-10 | Prep: | Cook: |Ready in:

Ingredients

- 2 cups cannellini beans, soaked
- 2 bay leaves
- 1/2 white onion, stuck with 2 cloves
- 1/4 cup chopped parsley
- 1 teaspoon sea salt
- 1 tablespoon olive oil
- 1/2 white onion, chopped
- 4 cloves garlic, minced
- 3 ribs celery, chopped
- 2 carrots, chopped
- 1 bunch kale or other dark leafy green, tough stems removed, chopped
- 2 cups sugar pumpkin or winter squash, chopped
- 6 cups water or vegetable stock
- 2 tablespoons butter
- 1 shallot, minced
- 1 cup dry red wine
- sea salt and black pepper to taste
- a little crème fraîche for garnish-optional
- minced fresh herbs such as parsley, dill, and thyme for garnish-optional

Direction

- Start by placing 2 cups of dried white cannellini beans in a large bowl. Cover with water and soak overnight or for at least 4 hours. Pick out any beans that have floated to the surface and then drain.

- Put the beans in a large soup pot with water to cover by 2 inches. Bring to a boil and cook for 10 minutes, skimming off and discarding any foam that rises to the surface. Lower the heat and add the bay leaves, 1/2 onion with cloves, and parsley. Lower the heat and simmer for 1 1/2 hours.

- While the beans are simmering, heat the olive oil in a cast iron skillet and add the chopped onion and garlic. Cook for about 1 minute over medium heat and then add the chopped celery, carrot and kale. Add a little water to the pan and then cook for about 5 minutes, until the vegetables are soft.
- Back to the beans: remove the onion, cloves, and bay leaves. Pour off the cooking water and mix 1 tsp. salt into the cooked beans. Add the cooked vegetables and the chopped pumpkin, along with 6 cups of water or vegetable stock (chicken stock could also be used). Cook over low-medium heat for another 1/2-1 hour, until the beans are quite tender (the veggies will be very soft at this point). Add a little more stock or water as needed.
- In your skillet, melt the butter with the shallots. Cook for several minutes over medium heat, and then add the wine. Simmer until the wine is reduced by 1/2-3/4 and then add what remains to the beans. Season with salt and pepper and simmer for another 5 minutes.
- Garnish with a dollop of crème fraîche and minced herbs, if desired, and serve alone or with a big thick slice of your favorite bread.

351. White Bean And Kale Soup With Sausage

Serving: Serves 5 | Prep: 0hours15mins | Cook: 0hours40mins | Ready in:

Ingredients

- Olive oil
- 2 shallots, small diced
- 2 cloves of garlic, finely chopped
- 2 medium carrots, diced
- 4 ounces cremini mushrooms, roughly chopped
- 1/2 cup white wine
- 3 cups vegetable stock
- 1 15-ounce can white beans (like Great Northern), drained and rinsed
- 2 tablespoons chopped rosemary
- 1/4 bunch kale, stems removed and leaves torn or roughly chopped (should yield about 2 packed cups)
- 1 pound sausage (like kielbasa or chorizo)
- Kosher salt and freshly ground black pepper
- Crushed red pepper flakes
- Parmesan cheese

Direction

- Heat a few tablespoons of olive oil in a heavy bottomed pot over medium heat. Add the shallots and season with salt and pepper; cook down until almost transparent, about 5 minutes. Add the garlic, carrots, mushrooms, and a pinch of the red pepper flakes. Season and cook, stirring occasionally, until slightly softened.
- Add the wine and use it to loosen and scrape up all the awesome brown bits from the bottom of the pot. Cook until the liquid is reduced slightly.
- Add the stock, beans, and rosemary. Bring to a boil, and then add the kale. Reduce to a simmer and cook for 15 to 20 minutes.
- While the soup is cooking, brown the sausage in a medium pan. If crumbled, add directly to the soup. If linked, transfer to a cutting board. Thinly slice crosswise, stir into the soup.
- Serve with a sprinkling Parmesan cheese. Plus bread — you're no fool.

352. White Bean And Quinoa Chili

Serving: Makes about 6 to 8 servings | Prep: | Cook: | Ready in:

Ingredients

- 1 1/2 cups diced onion
- 2 tablespoons olive oil

212

- 1 cup diced green bell pepper
- 5 cloves minced garlic
- 2 tablespoons ground cumin
- 3 tablespoons ancho chili powder
- 2 teaspoons salt
- 1 teaspoon black pepper
- 1/4 teaspoon crushed red pepper flakes
- 2 14 to 15 ounce cans tomatoes, chopped
- 1 to 2 12 ounce cans V8 or tomato juice
- 12 ounces beer, preferably a brown ale
- 1 to 2 teaspoons brown sugar
- 3 cups cooked white beans (or two 14 to 15 ounce cans drained and rinsed)
- 3/4 cup quinoa simmered in 1 1/2 cups water for 10 to 15 minutes

Direction

- In a soup pot or Dutch oven saute the onions and bell pepper in the olive oil until the onions begin to soften. Add the garlic and saute another minute or two.
- Stir in the cumin, chili powder, crushed red pepper flakes, salt and pepper and saute another minute or two.
- Add the tomatoes, beer and one can of the tomato juice, bring up to the boil and gently simmer for about 15 minutes. Taste at this point and if the mixture seems to acidic, stir in some of the brown sugar.
- Stir in the cooked beans and cooked quinoa and if the chili seems too thick, add some or all of that second can of tomato juice. Bring up to the boil and serve. You can certainly garnish with your favorite toppings - green onion, avocado, grated cheese, sour cream, etc.
- Note: Make this early in the day or the day before serving for better flavor.

353.   White Asparagus Soup

Serving: Serves 6 | Prep: | Cook: | Ready in:

Ingredients

- 2 tablespoons olive oil
- 2 large onions, chopped
- 1 large potato, chopped
- 2 pounds white asparagus, chopped
- 1 liter chicken stock
- 200 milliliters cream
- Salt and freshly ground black pepper
- Fresh thyme and edible flowers to serve (optional)

Direction

- In a medium-sized sauce pan, heat the olive oil. Add the onions and sauté until they become tender and almost translucent, without colouring. Add the potato and asparagus and stir well. Add the stock and bring to a simmer. Cook for 20 minutes over medium to medium-low heat, until the asparagus are tender.
- Puree the soup with a hand blender until completely smooth. Bring the soup back to a simmer and add the cream. Season to taste with salt and pepper and cook for 5 minutes.
- Ladle the hot soup into serving bowls and garnish with fresh thyme and edible flowers.

354.   White Chili

Serving: Serves 8 | Prep: | Cook: | Ready in:

Ingredients

- 1 Rotisserie chicken shredded
- 2 Poblano peppers
- 1-2 Jalapeno peppers
- 1 large white onion
- 5 Large cloves of garlic
- 1 tablespoon Chili powder
- 1 teaspoon Ground Cumin
- 6.5 cups Chiken brooth
- 1 teaspoon Anise seed
- 2 Cans of Great Northern beans
- 0.5 teaspoons Cayenne pepper
- 2 Limes, juiced

- 1/4 Cilantro
- Greek yogurt
- Avacodos
- Fried corn tortilla strips

Direction

- Blacken the peppers over a grill or in a broiler, once blackened place in a boil and cover with plastic wrap to allow to steam.
- Dice the onion and garlic, peel the burnt skins from chilies and then dice.
- Heat a heavy bottom pot with a tablespoon or two of oil (any oil will do, I use canola for the stability under higher heat) and when hot add the onions, garlic, and chillies. Cook until soft.
- When the onions are starting to get a little color add the spices and saute another minute. Add the chicken broth and beans with the can fluid and bring to a low boil.
- After 20 mins reduce the heat, add the chicken, any accumulated juices, the lime juice, and cilantro. Simmer another twenty minutes or so.
- Serve hot, with cheese, tortilla strips, avocados, and a dollop of Greek yogurt (or sour cream). Sprinkle with fresh cilantro.

355. Whole Slow Cooker Poached Chicken

Serving: Serves 4 | Prep: 0hours15mins | Cook: 4hours0mins | Ready in:

Ingredients

- 3 bunches scallions
- 1 bunch cilantro, stems and leaves
- 1 whole chicken (about 4 pounds)
- 2 celery stalks, chopped into 2-inch pieces
- 12 shiitake mushrooms, stemmed
- 6 thin slices of ginger
- 6 star anise
- 1 teaspoon peppercorns (white, if possible)
- 1 tablespoon plus two teaspoons coarse salt

- 8 cups water

Direction

- In a 5- to 6-quart slow cooker—a smaller slow cooker will be too small—place two bunches of scallions and half the cilantro on the bottom. Then place the chicken on top, breast up. Add the celery, mushrooms, ginger, star anise, peppercorns, and salt. Then add the water, adding more if the chicken isn't covered (or almost covered). Cook on high for 2 to 3 hours (or on low for 4 or more hours), or until the chicken reaches 165 degrees.
- When the chicken is cooked, carve it into portions and divide it among the bowls. Divide the mushrooms among the bowls, too. Strain the broth and ladle it over the chicken and the mushrooms. Coarsely chop the remaining cilantro and scallions and sprinkle them over each bowl. Serve.

356. Zucchini Soup With Avocado And Basil

Serving: Serves 3-4 | Prep: | Cook: | Ready in:

Ingredients

- 3 pounds zucchini (about 5 medium)
- 1 shallot
- 2-3 cups vegetable broth
- 2 garlic cloves or 1 teaspoon roasted garlic
- 1 avocado
- 1/4 cup nutritional yeast
- 1/4 cup basil leaves
- salt and pepper to taste

Direction

- Wash the zucchini and cut into chunks, excluding the stem and the bottom nubby (is there a true word for this?). I also seed the zucchini before cutting into chunks, but that's a personal preference. Do whatever's best for you.

- Put the first 5 ingredients in a small pot or wide pan over medium heat. Cover, bring to a simmer and cook for about 5 minutes or until the zucchini are tender.
- Scoop out the meat of the avocado and place it into a blender with the nutritional yeast. When zucchini is done, cool slightly before transferring the mixture to the blender with the avocado. Add the basil leaves to the top before blending until smooth. Adjust the consistency adding more vegetable broth if you like thinner soups. Add salt and pepper to taste.

Serving: Serves 6 | Prep: | Cook: | Ready in:

Ingredients

- 2 tablespoons olive oil
- 1/2 a red onion, finely sliced
- 3 salted anchovy fillets
- 1 tablespoon pine nuts, lightly toasted
- 1 tablespoon sultanas, soaked in hot water
- 2 garlic cloves: 1 whole, 1 finely chopped
- 1 tablespoon fennel seeds
- 12 whole sardines, filleted
- Sea salt and freshly ground black pepper
- 11 ounces borlotti beans, cooked
- 6 ciabatta bread
- 2 tablespoons chopped flat-leaf parsley
- extra virgin olive oil

Direction

- Heat 2 tablespoons of olive oil in a heavy saucepan. Add the onion and gently cook until soft and translucent but not brown. Add the anchovies and crush into the onion, then add the pine nuts, sultanas, sliced garlic, and fennel seeds and stir to combine.

- Lay the sardines in the pan and season. Pour over just enough boiling water to cover the sardines, then cover and cook over a low heat for 5 minutes, or until the sardines are cooked. Add the borlotti beans and stir, crushing and breaking up the sardines.
- Toast the bread and rub lightly with garlic on one side. Place each of these crostini in a bowl and ladle over the soup. Sprinkle with parsley and drizzle with extra virgin olive oil to serve.

Serving: Makes a family size pot | Prep: | Cook: | Ready in:

Ingredients

- soup
- 1 big fist size celariac peeled and sliced 1/4 in
- 3 cups thinly sliced leek (white and pale green only)
- 1 pound thick asparagus, bottoms trimmed, cut in 1 in. pieces
- 1 clove a garlic sliced
- 2 sprigs tarragon
- homemade chicken stock to cover veg by an inch
- salt and finely ground white pepper
- 1 tablespoon butter
- 1 tablespoon olive oil
- tarragon creme fraiche
- 1 cup creme fraich
- 1 tablespoon finely minced trarragon
- 1/2 teaspoon lemon juice (mayer if possible)
- 1/4 teaspoon microplaned lemon zest

Direction

- Soup
- Sweat leek and garlic in oil/butter for fine minutes on low heat

215

- Add remaining ingredients, bring to boil, cover and simmer on low 15 to 20
- Run through food processor or puree with immersion blender till very smooth
- Tarragon crème fraiche
- Stir well and serve one dollop with each bowl of soup

---

359. Cabbage & White Bean Soup

Serving: Serves 8-10 | Prep: | Cook: |Ready in:

Ingredients

- 2 tablespoons grapeseed oil
- 1 medium cooking onion, diced
- 1 medium carrot, diced
- 2 celery stalks, diced
- 1 leek, white + light green parts only, diced
- 1 teaspoon dried oregano
- 1 sprig rosemary, leaves minced
- 3 cloves of garlic, minced
- 1 tablespoon tomato paste
- 1 28 oz can crushed tomatoes
- 1 liter vegetable stock
- 1/2 head green cabbage, shredded
- 2 cups cooked white beans
- 1 handful flat leaf parsley, chopped
- salt
- pepper

Direction

- Heat the grape seed oil in a large soup pot over medium heat. Add the onions, carrots, celery, and leeks to the pot and stir. Sauté until the onions are soft and quite translucent, about 5 minutes. Lower the heat if necessary to avoid browning.
- To the pot, add the tomato paste, dried oregano, rosemary, and garlic. Stir until oregano and garlic is fragrant and tomato paste is incorporated into the vegetables,

about 1 minute. Season the vegetables with salt and pepper.
- Add the crushed tomatoes and vegetable stock, and stir. Bring the soup to a boil and add the cabbage shreds. Simmer the soup for 15-20 minutes, or until the cabbage is mostly tender.
- Add the white beans and bring the soup to a boil one more time. Add the chopped parsley and stir to incorporate. Check the soup for seasoning and serve hot.

---

360. Celeriac Soup + Thyme Oil And Horseradish Croutons

Serving: Serves 4 | Prep: | Cook: |Ready in:

Ingredients

- 1 tablespoon olive oil
- 1 medium leek, white and green parts chopped
- 3 garlic cloves, minced
- 3 sprigs thyme, leaves removed
- 1/2 teaspoon smoked paprika
- 1 pound celeriac, peeled and chopped
- 1 pound new potatoes, cubed
- 4 cups vegetable stock
- 1 cup water
- 1 lemon's juice
- 1/2 loaf crusty bread, cubed
- 1 tablespoon oil
- 1 1/2 tablespoons horseradish

Direction

- Heat oil in large Dutch oven or soup pot and add leek. Sauté until softened and fragrant, 7-10 minutes. Add garlic, thyme, and paprika and cook 2 minutes to release flavors. Add celeriac, potatoes, stock, and water. Bring to a boil and reduce, simmer 30-40 minutes half-covered, or until vegetables are tender.
- Stir in lemon juice and, working in batches if needed, blend soup on high to a smooth

consistency. Thin with stock or water if too thick.

- To make croutons preheat oven to 400 degrees. In a small bowl whisk together oil and horseradish. Dress bread cubes with oil and roast on a sheet pan for 20 minutes.
- Serve soup with thyme oil, celery leaves, and horseradish croutons.

361.   Chilled Cucumber Soup

Serving: Serves 8 | Prep: | Cook: |Ready in:

Ingredients

- 35 ounces Fage or similar Greek yoghurt
- 1 extra large seedless (or persian) cucumber, unpeeled and chopped
- 1/2 cup 2% milk
- 1/2 cup whole milk
- 5 scallions, white and green parts, chopped
- 1/2 cup red onion, chopped
- 1 tablespoon 1 tsp kosher salt
- 1/2 tablespoon freshly ground pepper
- 1 tablespoon dry dill
- 2 tablespoons freshly chopped dill
- 1/2 lemon, juice of
- 16 large shrimp (or 2 per bowl)
- lemon wedges and fresh chopped dill for garnish

Direction

- In a large bowl, combine yogurt, both milks, cucumbers, red onion, scallions, salt and pepper. Using a hand held blender, process until the cucumbers have broken up into a grainy mixture.
- Add the chopped dill, lemon juice, and more salt if needed. Cover and place in the refrigerator to chill for at least 1/2 hour.
- Before serving, drizzle more fresh lemon juice, place 2 large shrimp and dress with fresh dill.

362.   Creamy Cauliflower Soup With Cucumber Raita

Serving: Serves 6 | Prep: | Cook: |Ready in:

Ingredients

- Pureed Cauliflower Soup
- 6-8 cups chicken or vegetable stock
- 2 tablespoons EV olive oil
- 2 tablespoons butter
- 1 head cauliflower separated into florets
- 2 small leeks, white and light green part, thinly sliced
- 1 small red pepper, diced
- 1/4 head savoy cabbage, chopped
- 3-4 slices of fresh ginger root
- 1 cup leftover mashed potatoes, optional
- sea salt and ground white pepper to taste
- 1/4 cup fresh cilantro leaves
- cucumber raita
- 2 medium persian cucumbers, chopped
- 1 cup greek yogurt
- 1/2 lemon (meyer lemon, if possible)
- 2 tablespoons chopped cilantro
- sea salt; black, white or cayenne pepper to taste
- 2 cups wild arugula

Direction

- Pureed Cauliflower Soup
- Sauté vegetables in olive oil and butter, until softened and translucent. Add stock and simmer until soft. Add mashed potatoes if using.
- Puree with hand blender or blender, season to taste with salt and white pepper.
- Serve with dollop of cucumber raita, recipe below, and added cilantro, if desired.
- Cucumber raita
- Mix cucumbers, yogurt, lemon juice and seasoning, serve over arugula or add as a dollop to soup, to taste

363.   Dadi's Methi Daal

Serving: Serves 4 | Prep: | Cook: |Ready in:

Ingredients

- 1 cup toor dal (in english, split pigeon pea lentil) or another dal lentil, washed and picked through
- 2 medium onions, chopped
- 1 1/2 stick cinnamon
- 2-3 cloves
- 2 cloves garlic, chopped
- 1 inch pieces ginger, chopped
- 2 tablespoons chopped cilantro
- 2 tablespoons dried coconut
- 4 tablespoons ghee (clarified butter) or oil
- 3-4 teaspoons curry powder
- 1 bunch (medium) methi (fresh fenugreek), chopped fine
- 1/2-1 teaspoons turmeric
- 1 teaspoon sugar
- 3-4 whole kashmiri chilis, deseeded
- cilantro, chopped, for garnish
- juice from 2 limes

Direction

- Cook the toor dal (or other lentil of your choice) with a little water until the lentils are soft and tender but not too mushy.
- In a mixer/blender, make a paste of chopped onion, 1/2 cinnamon stick, cloves, garlic, ginger, cilantro, coconut, and red chiles.
- Heat 4 tbsp. ghee or oil in a 4 quart saucepan. Fry the blended mixture for 3-4 minutes, then add the curry powder and fresh chopped fenugreek and cook for a few minutes more.
- Add the turmeric into the mixture, cook for 30 seconds, then add the cooked daal and as much water as you would like, depending on how thick you like your daal. Add salt to taste, and then add the sugar and lime juice.
- Garnish with more cilantro and serve hot, with some brown rice.

364.   Loaded Potato Soup

Serving: Serves 6 | Prep: | Cook: |Ready in:

Ingredients

- main ingredients
- 6 pounds fresh mashed potates
- 1/2 cup unsalted butter
- 4 pieces celery (chopped)
- 1 onion (chopped)
- 8 ounces cream cheese (cubed)
- 32 ounces chicken broth
- 32 ounces half & half
- 1 pound polish kielbasa (minced)
- 8 ounces sour cream
- 1 teaspoon dill weed
- 2 tablespoons accent
- salt & pepper to taste
- instant potatoes
- toppings
- 6 tablespoons cooked bacon (chopped)
- 6 tablespoons green onion (green end only, minced)
- 6 tablespoons sour cream
- 1/2 cup chedder cheese (shredded)

Direction

- In large pot cook onion, celery in butter till soft, add potatoes, chicken broth stir until mixed well, add half & half, cream cheese, sour cream, kielbasa and seasonings mix well, cook for 20-30 min./ If not thick enough add instant potatoes to thicken it
- When soup is done put in bowl top with cheese, sour cream, green onion, bacon ENJOY

365. "Why Am I Not In Gascony The Week After Labor Day?" Carrot And Red Pepper Soup

Serving: Serves 4 as a first course | Prep: | Cook: | Ready in:

Ingredients

- 4 tablespoons salted butter
- 1 large shallot, diced
- 2 large carrots, peeled and sliced into 1/4" thick discs
- 1 small, sweet red pepper, seeded and diced
- 1 small, ripe tomato peeled, seeded and diced
- 1 tablespoon chopped fresh sages leaves
- 1 bouillon cube - chicken or vegetable - preferably a Maggi cube
- 2 cups warm water
- 1/2 cup heavy cream
- 2 slices of good, leftover country bread cut into small cubes for croutons

Direction

- Melt 2 T of the butter in a 2 qt. saucepan. Add the shallots and the carrots. Give them a stir in the warm butter. Cover them with a round of buttered wax paper, put the lid on the pot and sweat them, over medium heat, until they're all nicely relaxed and exuding their sweet juices. This should take about ten minutes.
- Lift the wax paper and add the pepper, the tomato and the sage. Give it all another stir, replace the wax paper and let the pepper, tomato and sage add their perfumes to the mix. Replace the wax paper, cover the pot again, turn the heat to low and allow the mix of vegetables and herbs to sweat for another ten minutes.
- After ten minutes, the vegetables and sage should all be happily bubbling in some very aromatic juices. Add the bouillon cube and the water. Turn up the heat, bring the soup to a simmer and allow it to cook until the carrots are soft.
- When the carrots are soft. Remove the pot from a heat and, using a hand-held immersion blender, puree the soup. Return the pot to the heat and add the cream, stirring to incorporate. Keep the soup warm over a very low flame, but do not bring it to a boil.
- In a small skillet, melt the remaining butter and add the cubes of bread. Fry them until they are hot and crisp all over.
- Serve the soup garnished with the hot, buttery croutons.
- Raise a nice glass of red to Lulu Peyraud, Richard Olney and the intelligence of cooks who can teach us that simple cooking is, sometimes, the best cooking.

Index

Conclusion

Thank you again for downloading this book!

I hope you enjoyed reading about my book!

If you enjoyed this book, please take the time to share your thoughts and post a review on Amazon. It'd be greatly appreciated!

Write me an honest review about the book – I truly value your opinion and thoughts and I will incorporate them into my next book, which is already underway.

Thank you!

If you have any questions, **feel free to contact at:** *author@syruprecipes.com*

Karen Hurd

syruprecipes.com

Manufactured by Amazon.ca
Acheson, AB